PSYCHOLOGY IN TWENTIETH-CENTURY
THOUGHT AND SOCIETY

PSYCHOLOGY IN TWENTIETH-CENTURY THOUGHT AND SOCIETY

Edited by
MITCHELL G. ASH
University of Iowa

WILLIAM R. WOODWARD
University of New Hampshire

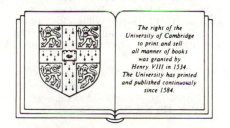

The right of the
University of Cambridge
to print and sell
all manner of books
was granted by
Henry VIII in 1534.
The University has printed
and published continuously
since 1584.

CAMBRIDGE UNIVERSITY PRESS

Cambridge

New York   Port Chester

Melbourne   Sydney

Published by the Press Syndicate of the University of Cambridge
The Pitt Building, Trumpington Street, Cambridge CB2 1RP
40 West 20th Street, New York, NY 10011, USA
10 Stamford Road, Oakleigh, Melbourne 3166, Australia

First published 1987
First paperback edition 1989

Printed in the United States of America

Library of Congress Cataloging-in-Publication Data

Psychology in twentieth-century thought and society.
Includes bibliographies and index.
1. Psychology – History – 20th century.   I. Ash,
Mitchell G.   II. Woodward, William Ray, 1944–
[DNLM: 1. Psychology – history.   BF 105 P974]
BF105.P79   1987   150′.9   87-22405

British Library Cataloguing in Publication Data

Psychology in twentieth-century thought and society.
1. Psychology – History – 20th century
I. Ash, Mitchell G.   II. Woodward,
William R.
150′.9′04   BF105

ISBN 0-521-32523-4 hard covers
ISBN 0-521-38920-8 paperback

CONTENTS

ABOUT THE AUTHORS

Erika Apfelbaum is Directeur de Recherche at the Centre National de la Recherche Scientifique (C.N.R.S.) and is associated with the Laboratoire de Psychologie Sociale, University of Paris VII. She studied in Paris with P. Fraisse, D. Lagache, and J. Piaget, receiving her Doctorat d'Etat at the Sorbonne in 1969. She is the author of book chapters and journal articles on conflict, interpersonal relations, social identity, women's leadership, and the development of social science and French social psychology.

Mitchell G. Ash earned the PhD in history at Harvard University (1982) and is now Assistant Professor of History at The University of Iowa. He has published essays on the history and historiography of German and American psychology, and co-edited two books: *The Problematic Science: Psychology in Nineteenth-Century Thought* (New York: Praeger, 1982), with W. R. Woodward; and *Geschichte der deutschen Psychologie im 20. Jahrhundert: Ein Überblick* (Opladen: Westdeutscher Verlag, 1985), with U. Geuter. He is presently writing a book on the history of Gestalt psychology.

Kurt Danziger, Professor of Psychology at York University, Toronto, Canada, obtained the D. Phil. degree at the University of Oxford, England, in 1952. He has authored books on socialization and interpersonal communication and is currently working on a book on the history of investigative practices in psychology.

Laurel Furumoto earned a PhD in experimental psychology from Harvard University in 1967, then joined the faculty of Wellesley College, where she is now Professor of Psychology. Her recently completed book, co-authored with Elizabeth Scarborough, is *Untold Lives: The First Gen-*

eration of American Women Psychologists (New York: Columbia University Press, 1987).

Ulfried Geuter received his PhD in psychology from the Free University of Berlin in 1982. He is currently a journalist specializing in science and is associated with the Psychological Institute of the Free University. His work in the history of psychology includes: *Die Professionalisierung der deutschen Psychologie im Nationalsozialismus* (Frankfurt a.M.: Suhrkamp, 1984); *Geschichte der deutschen Psychologie im 20. Jahrhundert: Ein Überblick* (Opladen: Westdeutscher Verlag, 1985), co-edited with M. G. Ash; and *Daten zur Geschichte der deutschen Psychologie*, 2 vols. (Göttingen: Hogrefe, 1986, 1987).

Christiane Hartnack received a Diploma in psychology from the University of Bonn and studied at the University of Delhi with a stipend from the German Academic Exchange Service (DAAD). She has taught at the Psychological Institute of the Free University of Berlin and worked in the Psychological Department of the German Agency for Technical Cooperation (GTZ), a West German developmental aid organization. She is now writing a book on the history of psychoanalysis in British India.

Louise E. Hoffman is Associate Professor of Humanities and History and Director of Graduate Studies in Humanities at the Pennsylvania State University at Harrisburg. She received her Ph.D. in history from Bryn Mawr College in 1975. She has published numerous essays on the history of psychoanalysis and its influence on historical writing, and is presently investigating the uses of other psychological systems in interpreting history and biography.

David Joravsky holds a PhD in history from Harvard University, and is Professor of History at Northwestern University. He is the author of *Soviet Marxism and Natural Science, 1917–1931* (New York: Columbia University Press, 1961) and *The Lysenko Affair* (Cambridge, MA: Harvard University Press, 1970). He is now writing a book entitled ''Soviet Psychology – And Our Own.''

David E. Leary holds a PhD in history of science from the University of Chicago (1977). He is Professor of Psychology and the Humanities and Chair of Psychology at the University of New Hampshire, and is co-editor, with Sigmund Kock, of *A Century of Psychology as Science* (New York: McGraw-Hill, 1985). His current research interests include the role of metaphor and rhetoric in the history of psychology.

Ian Lubek is Associate Professor of Psychology at the University of Guelph, Ontario, Canada, and a frequent Visiting Researcher at the Laboratoire de Psychologie Sociale, University of Paris VII. He holds a PhD in social psychology from the State University of New York at Stony Brook (1971), and has written journal articles and book chapters on violence, the political roots of social psychology, and the power structure in science.

Matthias Petzold received his PhD in psychology from the University of Düsseldorf in 1983, and is now Lecturer in developmental and educational psychology there. Publications include *Entwicklungspsychologie in der VR China* (Saarbrücken and Fort Lauderdale: Breitenbach, 1983) and *Indische Psychologie* (Munich: Psychologie Verlags-Union, 1986). He continues research on the history of psychology in Asia.

Ryan D. Tweney holds a PhD in experimental psychology from Wayne State University (1970). He is co-editor, with W. G. Bringmann, of *Wundt Studies* (Toronto: Hogrefe, 1980) and, with M. E. Doherty and C. R. Mynatt, of *On Scientific Thinking* (New York: Columbia University Press, 1981). He is currently working on a cognitive biography of Michael Faraday.

Fernando Vidal earned degrees in psychology at Harvard University and the University of Geneva, and in the history and philosophy of science at the Sorbonne. He is currently a doctoral candidate at the University of Geneva, and is writing a historical biography of Jean Piaget to 1932.

William R. Woodward earned his PhD in history of science and medicine at Yale University (1975), and is now Associate Professor of Psychology at the University of New Hampshire. He has published widely on the history and historiography of modern psychology, and is co-editor, with M. G. Ash, of *The Problematic Science: Psychology in Nineteenth-Century Thought* (New York: Praeger, 1982). He is now writing an intellectual biography of Rudolf Hermann Lotze and is preparing, with Reinhardt Pester, an edition of Lotze's works.

INTRODUCTION

MITCHELL G. ASH

Psychology has been central to the thought and society of our day. In the explorations of experimental novelists and psychotherapists, the psyche has been a primary focal point for attempts to describe, understand, and deal with massive alienation and rapid social change. At the same time, society has increasingly been viewed as a laboratory, and the laboratory as a metaphor for society, as psychologists joined widespread efforts to achieve rational control of modern hearts and minds, allying themselves in the process with various political regimes. These struggles to realize hopes – or to come to terms with despair – have inevitably left their mark on the history of the discipline called psychology. Indeed, perhaps the most prominent feature of psychological thought and practice in this century has been the relatively successful institutionalization of some of it. Both the intellectual and the institutional development of that discipline in their constant and complex interactions with one another and society are topics in this volume.

The essays collected here contribute to four interrelated trends in recent history and philosophy of science. First, the recent "social turn" in the history of science has encouraged a general shift to the discipline as a unit of analysis, in addition to individual scientists, theories, or problem areas. Guiding this shift are an interest in the institutionalization of science under different social and political conditions, and the realization that the history of disciplines is a productive way of subjecting both this question and the notorious issue of the role of "internal" and "external" factors in science to empirical scrutiny.[1] Recent research along these lines has led to a useful distinction among three levels of social-historical analysis: the history of individual scientific institutions, and their roles in generating and controlling the direction of research programs; the history of scientific disciplines and communities as social groups bound by intellec-

1

tual interests; and the historical relations of both scientific institutions and scientific communities with politics, society, and culture. The availability of all these levels of analysis to historians of both so-called hard and soft sciences implies that the history of psychology can and should be written in the same way as that of any other department of knowledge, for the kinds of issues involved are broadly similar across disciplines.[2]

Another trend to which these essays speak, albeit implicity, is the "pragmatic turn" in philosophy and philosophy of science, evident in the writings of Richard Rorty and others.[3] This suggests that some philosophers are prepared to recognize and deal with the embeddedness of thought and behavior, including science, in belief systems. Both the concomitant challenge to an exclusive preoccupation with science as a rational reconstruction of reality and the attempts by others to save rationalist models from the allegedly relativist consequences of pragmatism, with the help of evolutionary theory or by other means, also tend to break down the supposed barriers between hard and soft sciences.[4] Such shifts have also contributed to increasing interest in the philosophy and history of the social sciences, especially psychology. Behaviorism, psychoanalysis, Piagetian thinking, and Gestalt psychology have been beneficiaries of philosophical-historical scholarship.[5] An important part of this trend is the discovery that some leading philosophers of science, most notably Karl Popper, have been strongly influenced by psychology, despite their rejection of epistemological psychologism.[6]

Intellectual history has traditionally been open to and aware of connections of twentieth-century psychology, especially psychoanalysis, with politics and ideology. Recently, however, intellectual history, too, has taken a "social turn"; the revival of social history of ideas intersects with a growing interest among social historians in the history of education and the professions.[7] Science and science policy have obvious places here; and here, too, apparently clear-cut distinctions between hard and soft sciences tend to loosen, as academic and scientific disciplines turn out to behave in many respects like other interest groups with which historians are familiar. However, the fact that specifically intellectual interests are also involved, which can be pursued for their own sake, raises intriguing issues that require differentiated analysis.

Finally, there is the historiography of psychology itself. Scholarship in this field has evolved far beyond the situation deplored over twenty years ago by Robert Young.[8] Criticizing Whig interpretations of psychology's history incorporated in texts written by amateur scholars, Young called for more concentrated, monographic research by specialists. Since then, textbook histories have proliferated because there is a large and growing demand for them in undergraduate and graduate psychology curricula. Concurrently, however, serious scholarship has also expanded rapidly, and has modified or rendered untenable many textbook generalizations.[9]

Recent research has undermined traditional conceptions of psychology's history in two important ways. Where standard textbooks often told the story of a continuous upward climb from the depths of philosophical speculation to the heights of cumulative experimentation, newer work shows that psychology's intellectual development in this century was based in part on a *rapprochement* with certain kinds of philosophy, in the United States with logical positivism and operationism.[10] On the other hand, perhaps for pedagogical reasons, standard texts have treated psychology's development largely as a history of ideas, isolated from the discipline's social and cultural contexts. Recent work has brought to light new material about the impact of social and cultural change on psychological thought and practice. In the process it has shown that psychology, like other disciplines, is not only a set of ideas and methods, but also a set of institutions having definable connections with the societies in which they are located – a point of particular significance in the age of "big science."

In a previous volume, we attempted to point up some implications of this scholarship for the emergence of psychology as a science in the nineteenth century.[11] In the twentieth century, that gradual, problematic emergence became an explosion of both research and applications. In addition, a discipline largely limited to Western and Central Europe, especially Germany, and the United States spread throughout the world. No single volume can do justice to all these developments in the depth that serious scholarship requires. Moreover, that scholarship is still evolving, and much remains to be explored. It would be at best inappropriate to force a systematic presentation now. Instead, we offer a selection of representative recent work in the field, focusing on connecting the history of psychology with the history and philosophy of science and general intellectual history. The lines of research described above serve as analytical foci for the volume as a whole, while the book's organization is topical.

The first portion contains chapters about the disciplinary development of psychology in the United States and the German-speaking lands. The section begins with Kurt Danziger's analysis of the emergence of statistical methods in psychology, with special attention to their social roots in the practical needs of American education administrators. These needs, Danziger maintains, made educators more receptive to the group data generated by Galtonian styles of research than in data about individual minds, even when these came in statistical form. In addition, Danziger compares this development with the role of group data in Germany, the other major center of psychological research early in the century. He finds that, although the amount and the proportion of such research increased there in the 1920s and early 1930s, it was never as much in demand as in America. This was so in part because the German education system was differently structured, placing less of a premium on organizing masses of pupils and more on the selection of elites, but partly also because the intellectual interests of German psychologists, philosophers as they remained, continued far longer than in America to dictate concentration on cognitive processes and individual minds.

The second chapter is Ryan Tweney's discussion of the dominant research program in American psychology at the turn of the century, that of Edward Bradford Titchener. The relationship of Titchener's methods and system to that of his erstwhile mentor, Wilhelm Wundt, has recently been the subject of intense debate. Clear enough, however, is that Titchener wished to establish experimental psychology as, in his words, an experiential science of consciousness. Thus his creation of a vastly ambitious research program with the aim of subjecting all aspects of conscious experience to introspective scrutiny. Both the program and Titchener's methods owe much to the epistemology and philosophy of science of Ernst Mach and Richard Avenarius. Tweney's account explores these dependencies, but focuses explicitly on Titchener as a director of progammatic research, rather than on Titchener the system builder. In the process, Tweney brings to bear important insights from the philosophy of science on the construction of scientific research programs, suggesting, among other things, that such programs need not be limited to the verification of propositions derived from a previously constructed theory.

Titchener's program was gradually superseded, but not by the behaviorism of John B. Watson alone, as often implied in standard accounts. Methodologically, Titchener's program of controlled introspection was overtaken by the increasing use of statistics, which, as Danziger shows, was by no means limited to intelligence testing. On the theoretical side, the dominant role of Titchener's school was assumed less by Watsonian radicals than by various proponents of so-called neo-behaviorism, most prominently by Clark Hull, Kenneth Spence, Edward Tolman, and their students. Recent research, cited above, has illuminated the intricate connections of neo-behaviorism with American philosophy in the 1920s and 1930s, most notably with the neo-realism of E. B. Holt, F. O. Lovejoy, and R. B. Perry, and with logical empiricism.

Ian Lubek and Erika Apfelbaum show in their essay that neo-behaviorism did not establish and maintain its dominance by sheer power of ideas alone, but also by taking control of important journals in the field and founding new ones. Applying what they call a social psychology of science to this phenomenon, Lubek and Apfelbaum describe the emergence of the neo-behaviorist schools in the 1930s, the operation of the journal network from then onward, and the way in which established behaviorists dealt with differing modes of thinking, exemplified by the anomalous Garcia effect. As they maintain, journal referees vehemently objected to and excluded the work of Garcia and his students less because of methodological flaws – though they claimed these existed to shield their real motives – than because Garcia openly and aggressively insisted that it undermined reinforcement theory, which was central to behaviorism. Only after ways of reintegrating these findings with established thinking seemed to have been found was Garcia granted the Distinguished Scientific Contribution Award of the American Psychological Association. But the conflict about his work, and his battles with editors, continue.

In the following chapter, Laurel Furumoto shows how, as the discipline of psychology developed, women were excluded from all but the more marginal positions in the growing academic network. Although some achieved a certain amount of respect, they were unable to train further researchers in the same numbers as their male counterparts. Building on her research on the first generation of women psychologists, Furumoto then moves forward in time, to 1940, exploring the role of women in the increasing differentiation of the discipline into academic and applied fields. Not surprisingly, she shows that women were more numerous in the lower-status areas within applied psychology, and that they were fully aware of and sometimes protested their situation. As in other professions, Furumoto suggests, women were relegated to those fields where personal contact was most immediate and the social problems most difficult. Indeed, she maintains, the case of psychology illuminates the process most clearly, since it became in this period both a pure and applied science.

The next chapter illuminates the intellectual development of the new discipline in the United States by analyzing the career of the Viennese psychologist Egon Brunswik, who entered it as an immigrant in the 1930s. David Leary notes in his essay that experimental psychology's hybrid identity in German-speaking lands required a synthesis of explicitly philosophical goals and natural-scientific methods. One result was the different kind of functionalism Leary calls European, concerned as it was more with the mind's functioning per se than with its (or the subject's) adaptation to the environment. Yet Brunswik's version of European functionalism, derived from his teacher Karl Bühler, conflicted with the presuppositions of the Vienna logical positivists. Brunswik's creative resolution of this dilemma, which he called probabilistic functionalism, thus had European roots. Leary argues, however, that Brunswik learned to combine his probabilistic theory of cognition with statistical method in America, developing one of psychology's most important contributions to the probabilistic viewpoint in science. Brunswik's thinking was received ambivalently in America, if at all. Nonetheless, his work influenced the discipline indirectly, and his American sojourn affected his theorizing significantly as well. The fact that German-speaking scholars and scientists not only contributed to, but were also influenced by their new setting is sometimes mentioned in the literature on the so-called intellectual migration, but rarely analyzed in detail, as Leary has done.

The essays by Leary and Danziger raise the issue of national differences in psychological thought and research. This issue is pursued further throughout the book, but with emphasis on developments outside the United States. As in previous chapters, the studies offered focus on the interaction of intellectual and institutional dimensions of discipline development, but they indicate that the interactions took a variety of forms in different settings.

My own essay considers the issue of continuity and change in institutionalized psychology at the University of Vienna, where Egon Brunswik began his career. Viennese philosophers such as Franz Brentano participated in the development of empirical psychology from the late nineteenth century; but institutionalized research there did not begin until the city's politics changed. The driving force was the school reform movement launched by the Austrian Social Democrats when they took over the city government after World War I. The reformers supported – in fact they made possible – the appointment of Karl and Charlotte Bühler in 1922. Here was a case in which the needs of a changing education administration created demand for psychological research, as Kurt Danziger describes in his chapter. However, both the intellectual and the political interests of the Bühlers and their students did not always match those of their patrons. The resulting system of tensions became exceedingly complex – a possibility allowed for in Danziger's analysis – as the institute's different departments developed a variety of research programs using different sources of funding. Much productive theory and research came out of this dynamic context, but it was not always clear who was using whom. This remained the case after the overthrow of the Social Democrats by the authoritarian regime of Dollfuss and Schussnigg in 1934. After the Nazi takeover in 1938, pro-Nazi academics were able to destroy what had been built and helped to drive Karl and Charlotte Bühler and many of their students into exile. But they were unable to replace the Vienna school with an institutionally stable, Nazified psychology.

The next chapter also raises the issue of continuity and change in German-speaking psychology. Ulfried Geuter, in a summary of his recent research on psychology under National Socialism, refutes a number of often-repeated myths on the basis of extensive primary research. Though it lost its internationally best-known thinkers, academic psychology in Germany was not destroyed, nor even actively discriminated against by the Nazis. Instead, it established itself as a fully recognized discipline separate from philosophy for the first time. This occurred not primarily as a result of ideological concessions to Nazism, though these were made, but because psychological techniques proved useful in the selection of officers for the German military. Geuter's essay, like other chapters, shows that the cultural and social contexts were formative influences on psychological thought and practice. In this case, the need to select elite commanders supported a shift already underway in German psychology since the 1920s, from experimental psychology to "characterology." Much of this was quite compatible with American personality theory; indeed, American researchers showed interest in the Germans' work even during World War II. The implications of Geuter's research for commonly accepted notions of professionalism in science are profound. Professionalism here was no shield. Instead, the triumph of disciplinary legitimacy was purchased by willing participation in aggressive war, which, after all, was the aim of the state being so professionally served.

David Joravsky's chapter deals with psychology in a different, but also dictatorial political context. Lev S. Vygotskii, he writes, was able to take advantage of the relative leeway offered by Soviet cultural policy in the 1920s to develop an original, Marxist approach to psychology. In the short run, Vygotskii was successful, and was elevated quickly to intellectual leadership in the discipline. In his analysis of the "crisis" of psychology – only recently published – and in other works, he attempted to critically assimilate contemporary European and American ideas into his and his countrymen's thinking. However, both the academic and the general cultural politics of Vygotskii's attempt were fraught with risk from the start. In particular, his reinterpretation of consciousness as action implied a possible reworking of Marxism-Leninism that left him open to attack by party ideologues. Further, his recognition of the universality of aesthetic experience, though firmly supported in Marx's writings, seemed equally threatening to advocates of narrow economic determinism and socialist realism. In the end, Stalinism swept both Vygotskii's thought and his discipline into a memory hole. Even now, Joravsky maintains, a complete description and assessment of Vygotskii's life and work remains impossible in the Soviet Union.

The next two chapters confront yet another aspect of psychology's history in this century. European expansionism and colonialism were reflected at first only indirectly in the psychological literature, through colonial officials', missionaries', travelers', and anthropologists' accounts of so-called primitive behavior and thinking. Despite the frequent amateurism of these accounts, they were enough to raise the issue of the universality of knowledge about mind and behavior derived from the study of Europeans. In the twentieth century, the situation changed, as institutionalized psychology joined the other sciences' push into colonized lands.[12] Though the methods and ideas involved were often in profound conflict with traditional ideas and practices in the colonized regions, the Europeans were not always entirely unwelcome. Some members of the "native" elites seem to have seen in European thinking, including psychology, a way of enhancing their standing in colonial society, or of resolving conflicts of allegiance between cultures. Thus, Western psychology entered a complex, dialectical interaction with traditional thought and society. In the process, the psychologists living in colonial countries became caught up in rapid social and political changes both before and after independence. Much data about these developments has accumulated in a large and growing literature.[13] But this work has not always been guided by the kind of analysis already applied to the history of European and North American psychology. The two essays by German scholars printed in this volume take first, exploratory steps in this direction.

Matthias Petzold, after briefly sketching core doctrines of traditional Chinese psychological thinking, the first contacts with Western psychology and the beginnings of institutionalization, focuses in his essay on the roller-coaster history of the discipline under the Communist regime. Here the dependence of science on politics, especially ideology, is clear. As in the Soviet Union, the proximity of psychology's subject matter to that of Marxism-Leninism or Maoism made tension between academics and party ideologues inevitable. However, as Petzold shows, the psychology that required, and still requires, official support, or at least tolerance, to survive in China is not in all respects the same as Euro-American psychology. Many traditional categories, for example, the notion of the psyche as a unity of head and heart, have survived, and the people brought up according to them do not always conform to Western developmental norms.

In her chapter, Christiane Hartnack, like Petzold, addresses the issue of the relationship of psychological thinking to political contexts, but concentrates specifically on the colonial period. She describes and analyzes the work and influence of Owen Berkeley-Hill and Claud Dangar Daly, the only foreigners living in India who published psychoanalytic papers. As she shows, the needs of the colonial administration made it possible for Berkeley-Hill to create relatively liberal conditions for mentally disturbed Europeans under his care at the European Asylum in Ranchi, north of Calcutta. In addition, he and Daly were both able to serve as links between the group of psychoanalysts in Bengal and the international psychoanalytic community. However, such connections were no guarantee that either man truly understood or sympathized with the alien culture in which they found themselves. Rather, both used, or misused, psychoanalytic concepts as labels to reinforce British feelings of self-satisfied superiority over their colonial wards, and offered their supposed expertise to the colonial administration as an aid in its fight against the rising independence movement in the 1920s. Berkeley-Hill, however, was described by his friend Ernest Jones, later Freud's biographer, as wanting to improve understanding between the races—an indication, perhaps, of the ignorance behind the enlightened pose of much psychoanalytic thought at the time.

The last two essays explore more fully the relationship of psychological thinking in some of its most influential incarnations with main currents of twentieth-century political thought. In her chapter, Louise Hoffman provides a synthesis and interpretation of the ideological significance of Sigmund Freud's social thought. She reminds us of the historical setting in which Freud's ideas about society and culture emerged and analyzes the effects of specific life experiences, especially of World War I and after, on the development of his ideas. In doing so she detects elements of continuity, such as Freud's patriarchal attitudes toward women. But she also reveals dimensions of change, such as Freud's shift from the metaphor of the crowd as irrational mob to the notion of a group ego derived from his revised individual psychology. As the explicitly anti-Communist position taken in *Civilization and its Discontents* shows, Freud must, in Hoffman's analysis, be considered a Burkean conservative, who advocated reforms but nonetheless held onto fundamental assumptions of Central European bourgeois society.

In the final chapter, Fernando Vidal confronts us with a linkage between psychology and politics that may be surprising even to specialists. Jean Piaget is usually described as a biologist of the mind or as an experimenting philosopher; the relations of his thought to evolutionary theory, Bergsonism, and twentieth-century philosophy of mind are frequent topics. But the possibility that Piaget's goals might also have been religious and political seems not to have been considered. Vidal provides the context of, and considerable evidence about, Piaget's membership in the liberal Protestant youth movement in Switzerland, and for his continuing allegiance to its ideals while he conducted the research that eventually made him famous. The fundamental conflict in this milieu was between immanentism – the view that God's law is not at variance with the law of nature, indeed that the law of nature reveals the presence of God – and transcendentalism, the insistence of Karl Barth and others on God's otherness and power. Before World War I, Vidal shows, liberal Protestants could comfortably maintain a distinction between the realms of science and belief. Piaget's answer to the widely perceived crisis that followed the war was a reassertion of immanentism on new grounds. Because individual mental and moral development and the history of human thought are all subject to the same universal law, he proclaimed, reason is inherent to God's order. Vidal concludes that such thinking may have been comforting to some liberal Protestants, but it ignored or explained away the obvious irrationality of much of twentieth-century politics.

As stated above, this book is not intended to be a complete account of twentieth-century psychology. Developments in some countries, such as Great Britain, France, and Italy, and in some professional fields could not be included for technical reasons. However, the chapters presented here are representative of the direction scholarship is taking – toward more thorough, historically informed reflection on psychological thought and practice in their relations with politics and society. We hope this work will encourage others to take up related issues in further research. William Woodward's concluding essay initiates such further exploration by drawing together findings from the book's chapters and bringing out some of their implications for the study of science in culture.

NOTES

1 For an early summary and assessment of these developments, see R. Mac-Leod, "Changing Perspectives in the Social History of Science," in I. Spiegel-Rösing and D. de S. Price (eds.), *Science, Technology and Society* (London and Beverley Hills: Sage Publications, 1977), 149–195.

2 See, e.g., S. Shapin, "History of Science and its Sociological Reconstructions," *History of Science* 20 (1982):157–211; cf. W. R. Woodward, "Committed History and Philosophy of the Social Sciences in the Two Germanies," *History of Science* 23 (1985):25–72.

3 R. Rorty, *Philosophy and the Mirror of Nature* (Princeton: Princeton University Press, 1979) and *Consequences of Pragmatism: Essays 1972–1980* (Minneapolis: University of Minnesota Press, 1982); see also R. Rorty, J. B. Schneewind, and Q. Skinner (eds.), *Philosophy in History: Essays on the History of Philosophy* (New York: Cambridge University Press, 1984).

4 For a survey and critical discussion of some of these developments, see R. Richards, "Natural Selection and Other Models in the Historiography of Science," in M. B. Brewer and B. E. Collins (eds.), ·*Scientific Inquiry and the Social Sciences* (San Francisco: Jossey-Bass, 1981), 37–76.

5 B. D. Mackenzie, *Behaviorism and the Limits of Scientific Method* (Atlantic Highlands, N.J.: Humanities Press, 1977); A. Grünbaum, *The Foundations of Psychoanalysis: A Philosophical Critique* (Berkeley: University of California Press, 1985); M. Boden, *Jean Piaget* (New York: Viking, 1980); B. Smith (ed.), *On Gestalt Theory* (Munich: Philosophia Verlag, in press).

6 W. Berkson and R. Wettersten, *Learning from Error: Karl Popper's Psychology of Learning* (LaSalle, IL: Open Court, 1984).

7 Some recent examples from an abundant literature: F. K. Ringer, *Education and Society in Modern Europe* (Bloomington: Indiana University Press, 1979); J. Goldstein, "The Hysteria Diagnosis and the Politics of Anticlericalism in Late Nineteenth-Century France," *Journal of Modern History* 54 (1982):209–239; Konrad Jarausch, "The Crisis of the German Professions, 1918–1933," *Journal of Contemporary History* 20 (1985):379–398; M. Kater, "Professionalization and Socialization of Physicians in Wilhelmian and Weimar Germany," ibid., 677–702; W. Conze and J. Kocka (eds.), *Bildungsbürgertum im 19. Jahrhundert, I. Bildungssystem und Professionalisierung in internationalen Vergleichen* (Stuttgart: Klett-Cotta, 1985). For additional references, see W. R. Woodward, "Con-

clusion: Professionalization, Rationality and Political Linkages in Twentieth-Century Psychology," this volume.

8 R. M. Young, "Scholarship and the History of the Behavioral Sciences," *History of Science* 5 (1966):1–51.

9 An early review of this trend is W. R. Woodward, "Toward a Critical History of Psychology," in J. Brozek and L. Pongratz (eds.), *Historiography of Modern Psychology* (Toronto: Hogrefe, 1980), 29–67; more recent literature on the United States is discussed in H. Cravens, "History of the Social Sciences," *Osiris,* 2nd Series, Vol. 1 (ed. S. G. Kohlstedt and M. W. Rossiter), 183–207. See also Woodward, "Conclusion," note 2.

10 S. Toulmin and D. E. Leary, "The Cult of Empiricism in Psychology, and Beyond," in D. E. Leary and S. Koch (eds.), *A Century of Psychology as Science* (New York: McGraw-Hill, 1985), 594–617; L. D. Smith, *Behaviorism and Logical Positivism: A Reassessment of the Alliance* (Stanford: Stanford University Press, 1986).

11 W. R. Woodward and M. G. Ash (eds.), *The Problematic Science: Psychology in Nineteenth-Century Thought* (New York: Praeger, 1982).

12 Cf. L. R. Pyenson, *Cultural Imperialism and Exact Sciences: German Expansion Overseas, 1900–1930* (New York, Berne, Frankfurt: Peter Lang, 1985).

13 E.g., D. Sinha, *Psychology in a Third-World Country: The Indian Experience* (New Delhi, London, Beverley Hills: Sage Publications, 1986); G. H. Blowers and A. M. Turtle (eds.), *Psychology Moving East: The Status of Western Psychology in Asia and Oceania* (Boulder and London: Westview Press, 1987).

1

SOCIAL CONTEXT AND INVESTIGATIVE PRACTICE IN EARLY TWENTIETH-CENTURY PSYCHOLOGY*

KURT DANZIGER

INTRODUCTION

The historiography of psychology has gained immeasurably by recent tendencies to investigate the specific social and institutional contexts within which psychologists had to operate. The emergence of modern psychology in different countries took place against a varying background of existing social arrangements within which psychology had to find a niche and with whose responses and expectations the new discipline had to come to terms. Inevitably, the studies that have attempted to explore these relationships have done so on the basis of specific case studies that did not go beyond a particular national context. Sound historical scholarship demanded as much. However, if one aims at an analytical, rather than an essentially narrative, account of these historical relationships, a comparative perspective must eventually be adopted. The analysis of particular national developments has to be supplemented by comparative studies, if only because there may be fundamental aspects of historical situations that are seen to be problematic only when one examines them in the light of comparable situations elsewhere. It is a major purpose of this chapter to place such a comparative perspective on the historical agenda.

Just as it is necessary to consider social context in terms of specific institutional patterns and real social interest, it is necessary to see the content of the discipline in terms of characteristic practices. What actually constitutes the discipline whose historical development is to be investigated must not be thought of as bodies of crystallized doctrine or accumulated information. Both of these levels are the products of under-

* The content analysis of the psychological journal literature referred to in this chapter was supported by a grant from the Social Sciences and Humanities Research Council of Canada. I wish to thank Peter Shermer and Renate Schober for their assistance with this analysis.

lying practices that generate the surface appearance of the discipline. It is the structure of these generative practices that imposes a characteristic form on the theoretical formulations and the empirical content of the discipline. Because they are necessarily embedded in a social framework, these generative practices also mediate between the social context and the cognitive content of the discipline.

One level of generative practices is purely discursive in nature and involves the production of specific kinds of discourse through the activation of characteristic cognitive schemas, root metaphors, and so on. Another level involves practices that manipulate parts of the world in a more direct manner. These latter are the practices that began to contribute to the constitution of the subject matter of psychology when it became an empirical science and a technology for social control. This chapter is concerned only with this second level of generative practices. Among these one can distinguish between practices primarily engaged in for the purpose of producing some specific social intervention, such as routine mental testing, and practices primarily engaged in for the purposes of generating products that count as scientific psychological knowledge. These latter constitute *investigative practices,* and their structure is of decisive importance in determining the actual content of scientific psychology. Whereas investigative practices involve specific cognitive operations that can often be described in rational-logical terms, they are also inescapably social in character. Historically, they are of special interest because they constitute a nodal point at which social contextual factors external to the discipline are transmuted into logical tasks that appear to be of purely cognitive significance.

Oddly enough, the history of investigative practices has been a rather neglected field. Two areas of existing research are relevant to it. On the one hand, there are studies of the practical uses of psychological techniques, notably mental testing, often in terms of their social functions, both for the wider society and for the profession.[1] Such studies have usually stopped at the doors of the psychological laboratory. On the other hand, there have been studies of research practice that have generally taken the form of accounts of the progress of technique.[2] Unlike the first type of study, this second approach tends to accept the self-understanding of practitioners at face value.

To understand psychological practice it is necessary to study research practice as well as so-called applied practice. But this study of research practice will have to go beyond an essentially justificationist account of technical progress in two ways. First, it cannot exempt research practice from the general requirement that professional practice must be seen for what it is, namely, as a form of *social* practice. Second, it has to extend its analysis beyond the technical concerns of the practitioners to focus on the fundamental presuppositions and implications of their practical research activity.

ORIGINAL PATTERNS OF INVESTIGATIVE PRACTICE

The investigative practices of modern psychology that emerged toward the end of the nineteenth century exhibited three clearly distinguishable patterns as far as their social arrangements were concerned.[3] Each pattern grew out of a distinct institutional context and bore the marks of its origin.

The first social pattern of investigative practice was associated with the group of investigators gathered around Wilhelm Wundt at Leipzig. In this case, psychological research took the form of a collaborative activity in which the participants frequently exchanged experimenter and subject roles. This fluidity in the allocation of the social tasks involved in psychological experimentation had its logical counterpart in a certain conception of psychological knowledge. For Wundt and his students such knowledge pertained to universal features of adult human mental life. What the psychologist was trying to get at were processes going on within individual minds that were however replicated in all (normal, adult) minds. Thus, the psychological experiment was designed to provide evidence of these universal intraindividual processes and their special form of determination known as psychic causality. Because psychic causality had volitional (i.e., agentic) qualities, and because its operations were replicated in each human individual, experimenters and subjects could change places.[4] Insofar as there was any asymmetry between these roles, the subject role was of higher status.

A very different pattern of investigative practice appeared simultaneously with the Wundtian experiment. It emerged in the context of experimental hypnosis, and its earliest systematic use occurred among a group of investigators located in Paris. Contrary to the Leipzig model of psychological experimentation, experimenters and subjects were not interchangeable in this case, and there was a clear status difference in favor of the experimenter. The latter was clearly in control of the experimental situation, while the subject role in the experiment was merely an extension of the role of a medical patient which the individual already occupied. Unlike the Leipzig experiment, which was essentially a research seminar using special means, these Paris experiments emerged in a prestructured medical context whose arrangements were part of the quest for knowledge about abnormal mental states. The processes that were of interest were not universal and depended on an abdication of normal conscious control. Hence experimenters had to operate *on* subjects and could not change places with them. However, the two forms of early investigative practice did share one crucial feature. They were both quite definitely concerned with determinate processes located in individual minds. Therefore, they both involved a sequence of quite intense and fairly prolonged interaction among experimenters and subjects. Only in this way could such intraindividual processes be brought under effective psychological scrutiny.

Precisely this feature becomes transformed in the third distinguishable pattern of early investigative practice. The recently expanded and bureaucratized educational systems of the economically advanced countries had produced large captive groups of young people who were not only a source of new psychological problems but who could also be seen as a potential fund of psychological knowledge. Although there were some tentative European moves in this direction, the systematic use of mass methods of psychological investigation flourished particularly in the United States, with major early centers for this type of work developing first at Clark University and subsequently at Columbia. This style of investigation was not limited to questionnaire studies and early forms of mental testing but spread to experimentation as such. The crucial shift of interest involved here is from the *analysis* of psychological processes manifested in individual minds to the *distribution* of psychological characteristics in populations. Age and sex differences, as well as differences among various educationally or clinically defined populations, were at the very core of psychological knowledge for this type of research practice. This meant that the individual subjects became totally anonymous, their specific contributions to the research enterprise remaining unidentified and unreported. Research contacts between investigator and subjects necessarily became much less intense and extended over much briefer periods of time. Paper and pencil instruments became the favored medium for this impoverished exchange.

It must be emphasized that this last investigative pattern does not depend on any special preference for quantitative data. The use of quantification as such does not make the difference but the context in which quantification occurs. The Leipzig model of psychological experimentation frequently involved the use of quantitative data (such areas as psychophysics and reaction time studies provide abundant examples), but these data were typically presented as the product of personally identified individual subjects. The crucial change in the knowledge base occurs when the data presented in the public report of the investigation are no longer attributed to specific individuals but to groups or populations.

There is clearly an intimate relationship between the form taken by psychological knowledge and the structure of the relationship between those who function as investigators and those who function as the source of data. To obtain information that characterizes populations it is generally not necessary to have more than a relatively brief encounter with each member of that population, nor is it economically feasible. The contact between investigator and subject does not of course have to take place in a group situation for it to be brief, superficial, and impersonal. Group administration of psychological tasks is merely an extreme form of this kind of investigative practice. The essential features of this practice depend on the kind of knowledge it is designed to produce. Thus, the form of this knowledge provides an index of the essential structure of the investigative practice.

THE ROLE OF EDUCATIONAL PSYCHOLOGY

The issue to which I now wish to turn – and which represents the main concern of this chapter – involves the question of how these patterns of investigative practice fared within the discipline during the earlier part of the twentieth century, up to the time of World War II. In tracing these developments, I will pay special attention to the third of these patterns, for it comes as no surprise to find that this pattern, rather than the other two, comes to play a predominant role in twentieth-century psychology. I will suggest specific reasons for this predominance and examine the explanation offered in the light of comparative data on relevant developments within American and German psychology.

The relative incidence of different forms of investigative practice within the discipline may be established by a systematic analysis of research reports published in its major scientific journals. For the early years of American psychology this includes the *American Journal of Psychology,* the *Psychological Review* and its *Psychological Monographs,* the *Pedagogical Seminary,* and later the *Archives of Psychology.* Up to the period of World War I the predominant investigative style undoubtedly follows the Leipzig model, with interest focused on the response patterns of individual subjects under various experimental conditions. The use of average data to characterize the pattern of responses in relatively large groups of subjects is not frequent in terms of the discipline as a whole, though it is prominent in studies involving school children, mainly reported in the pages of the *Pedagogical Seminary.* It is clear that a good deal of resistance exists among experimental psychologists to the widespread adoption of group methods of experimentation. A psychological experiment is still felt to be a direct exploration of processes located in individual minds, and so-called statistical studies do not enjoy a high status within the discipline.

This situation begins to change during the second decade of the twentieth century. The beginning of the change is signalled by a significant addition to the journal literature that occurs in 1910. In that year the *Journal of Educational Psychology* began publication, and, from the beginning, it featured a high proportion of psychological investigations whose data were purely statistical in nature. For the period 1914–1916 three-quarters of all the empirical studies published in this journal reported virtually no data on individual subjects at all, while only 12% of these reports limited themselves to individual data. During this same period over two-thirds of the studies reported in the *American Journal of Psychology* were of the latter type. The second volume of the *Journal of Educational Psychology* (1911) carried a statement of editorial policy which makes it clear that the selective attention to group data was a matter of conscious commitment. The editors state: "It may be confidently asserted, however, that the measurement of a large group of individuals is, on the whole, more satisfactory than the attempt to measure a single individual." It becomes apparent that this new journal is to serve as the vehicle for the propagation of a pattern of investigative practice that was at variance with the then predominant style of psychological research. In subsequent years the *Journal of Educational Psychology* continued to promote an essentially statistical conception of psychological knowledge; the proportion of its studies mainly devoted to the reporting of group data exceeded 90% in the decades after World War I.

Not only did the research practices so prominently featured in the pages of the *Journal of Educational Psychology* represent a departure from the relative value accorded to these practices in the more traditional sections of the discipline, they also involved a significant development of these practices in two major directions. In the first place, the distribution of psychological characteristics in populations is no longer crudely described by means of averages and percentages but is subjected to an application of a calculus of probabilities. These procedures, inspired by Galton's anthropometry and the work of British biometricians like Pearson, allow group data to be used for something that is called psychological measurement. This involves the comparison of the results of any individual's psychological activity with the aggregate results of the activity of some population of individuals. Basically, this was a refinement of practices long established in educational systems that sought to foster interindividual competition.

The second major development that emerges in the context of a statistically oriented educational psychology at this time involves the introduction of comparative experimentation. For many years there had been a separation between systematic experimentation and the gathering of data on the psychological characteristics of school populations. In the latter case the investigative intervention would generally take the form of a single probe without any attempt at studying the effect of a variation of conditions. These methods had more in common with census taking than with experimentation. This was to change when comparative experiments with groups began to find favor among educational psychologists.

One now sees classroom experiments that are concerned with such topics as the effects of mental fatigue on performance, the relative effectiveness of different training methods, and the possible existence of specific transfer effects in learning.[5] There had been a certain amount of earlier laboratory work on these topics, but it was in a more traditional mold that focused on changes in the behavior of individual subjects. The novel feature of the new type of study was that it was not interested in the specific effects of variations of conditions on individual behavior, but only in aggregate or statistical effects that could be demonstrated in groups of individuals.

Thus, the greatly enhanced scope of group methods of psychological investigation in the field of education depended on the extension of these methods to encompass comparative experimentation as well as the measurement of the products of psychological activity. Now, it is remarkable that these extensions fitted quite precisely into the programmatic requirements that were then being laid down by the main architects of a rationalized educational system, namely, the new breed of professional educational administrators. This was a group that had itself been formed in the course of the rapid adaptation of American education to the changed social order of corporate industrialism.[6] Emphasizing the role of research in making American education more efficient, they provided the first large-scale external market for the products of psychological investigation.

But to these major potential clients of the academic psychologists research meant something that was rather different from the latter's traditional laboratory practice. Research, to the administrators, was an activity whose results had to be relevant to managerial concerns. It had to provide data that were useful in making immediate decisions in restricted administrative contexts. This meant research that produced essentially statistical data on relatively large numbers of individuals. It was, in other words, technological research that would help in dealing with the practical tasks of sorting individuals and selecting programs.

Within this context, the framework for research was established by an extension of the principles of scientific management from industry to education. In the considerable literature devoted to this topic[7] the most succinct formulation of these principles, as they were understood by the educational administrators, appears to have been given by Frank Spaulding in 1913:[8]

1. The measurement and comparison of comparable results.
2. The analysis and comparison of the conditions under which given results were secured especially of the means and time employed in securing those results.

3. The consistent adoption and use of means that justify themselves most fully by their results, abandoning those that fail so to justify themselves.

Such a scheme assigned an important and clearly defined role to research. It had to provide the information necessary for steps one and two, so that the administrator could take the appropriate action specified by step three. Two kinds of research data were required: first, comparable measurements of results, defined as performance, and, second, a comparison of the relative efficiency of various conditions in producing these results.[9] What was needed were scales that measured performance and experiments that assessed the relative effectiveness of such conditions as were potentially under the control of the administrators who had to choose between them.[10]

For American education the early years of the twentieth century were a period of extraordinarily rapid expansion and of greatly increased financial resources. But the channelling of these resources was governed by an ideology of rationalized efficiency for which analogies between the education of children and the manufacture of steel rails were a source of inspiration.[11] A significant group of American psychologists was able to exploit this situation for the benefit of their own discipline by joining forces with the educational administrators who set the tone for the ongoing process of rationalization. Prominent in this group were men like E. L. Thorndike, who occupied a strategic position at Columbia Teacher's College, and Carl Seashore, one of the founding editors of the *Journal of Educational Psychology,* whose unerring sense of professional opportunities enabled him to convert his Iowa Department into one of the top three in the 1920s.[12] What is most significant in the present context, however, is that this professional adaptation was necessarily accompanied by changes in investigative practice and changes in the relative importance of different practices within the discipline. In many respects the new practices reflected in the pages of the *Journal of Educational Psychology* represented a break with the procedures pioneered by G. Stanley Hall and his *Pedagogical Seminary.* These latter had proved to be unsuitable for enhancing the professional image of psychologists because they were technically crude and could be freely employed without special training. However, even though the techniques of the new educational psychology required a certain level of technical sophistication, this does not negate a basic continuity between them and the population studies of an earlier generation of American psychologists. There is also a certain irony in the fact that the professional enhancement of the new educational psychologists involved a severe constriction of disciplinary aims.[13] The developmental psychology of men like Baldwin and Hall, which could have a prescriptive significance for education, was now replaced by practices that limited themselves to the sorting of individuals and of instrumental means within an administratively pre-established framework.

AMERICAN PSYCHOLOGY ADAPTS

The establishment of a vigorous educational psychology, whose investigative practices were firmly anchored in administrative requirements, was only the first step in the transformation of American psychology. The experience gained in research for educational administration made it possible for psychologists to exploit the professional opportunities presented by certain requirements of military administration in World War I. These requirements called for the rapid gathering of statistical information on very large numbers of individuals for what was essentially a process of administrative streaming of human material. The task was quite analogous to the institutional requirements to which educational psychologists had been adapting their practices for some years, and it is not surprising that they were in a position to offer techniques that had an appearance of usefulness in this kind of context. From the point of view of the advancement of the profession it was irrelevant that the real usefulness of these techniques lay in the rationalization of administrative decisions rather than in any increase of psychological knowledge.

In the years immediately following the war applied psychology really began to blossom. It spread to new areas while consolidating its position in the educational system which had always remained the bedrock of its influence. The rising volume of applied psychological research found a publication outlet in the *Journal of Applied Psychology* launched in 1917. The research style, and the type of knowledge sought after, was virtually the same as in the *Journal of Educational Psychology*. In over three-quarters (77%) of the empirical studies published in the first three volumes of *JAP* the reporting of statistical data on groups of subjects represented the essential empirical content. By the mid-1920s the percentage of such studies had risen to 83% of all the empirical studies appearing in the pages of this journal, and by the mid-1930s the figure was 93%. This suggests that the promotion of a statistical style of psychological research practice did not arise out of any highly specific requirements of educational psychology, but was a function of general features of the kinds of rationalized bureaucratic contexts for which applied psychological knowledge had relevance. What was required in such contexts was primarily information that could be used to rationalize administrative decisions. That entailed the compilation of aggregate data that made possible the comparison of individuals to group norms and the comparison of groups exposed to different conditions. By the 1920s American psychology included a large and rapidly growing body of research based on investigative practices that had adapted themselves to these requirements.

The most interesting issue, however, involves the question of whether this vigorous development of an applied psychology with characteristic research goals and practices had any influence on the rest of the discipline. One line of evidence relevant to this issue is derived from an extension of the analysis of investigative practices to psychological journals serving the more purely academic parts of the field. The two most prominent journals in this category were the *American Journal of Psychology* and the *Journal of Experimental Psychology*. Does the research reported in these journals rely as heavily on the use of group data as the research reported in the applied literature, or is there more interest in exploring psychological regularities in individual subjects?

The answer is that there is a clear difference between the "pure" and the applied literature in this respect. The research reported in the more academic journals shows an unmistakable preference for individual data, at least at the beginning of the period we are interested in. For the years 1914–1916 only a quarter (26%) of the empirical studies appearing in the *American Journal of Psychology* relied mainly on group data, while over two-thirds (69%) essentially focused on individual data.[14] However, this trend is somewhat less marked in the *Journal of Experimental Psychology,* where the incidence of the two kinds of study already approaches equality in the first three volumes (38% relying on group data, 43% on individual data, the rest on both).[15] Nevertheless, even this represents a clear difference from the overwhelming reliance on group data characterizing the applied literature. Thus, up to the end of World War I the traditional focus of psychological experimentation on the analysis of individual behavior remains strong.

However, further analysis of the experimental literature provides evidence for the occurrence of a crucial shift in investigative practices during the 1920s and 1930s. When we examine these practices as reported in the two key journals, the *American Journal of Psychology* and the *Journal of Experimental Psychology,* we find signs of a change that is still quite tentative during the 1920s, but has become pronounced by the time we get to the sample years 1934–1936.[16] For the *Journal of Experimental Psychology,* 60% of the studies have now adopted the reporting of group data as their main focus, while 29% remain devoted to an analysis of individual data. For the *American Journal of Psychology* during this period the corresponding figures are 54% and 30%.

During the second decade of the century, studies that reported mainly data representing the response patterns of individuals still predominated over those reporting mostly aggregate group data. But that relationship was reversed by the fourth decade. The change is more dramatic for *AJP* than for *JEP,* because the base line is somewhat different, but by the mid-1930s the distribution is practically the same for the two journals. Thus, the academic literature changes during this period toward a distribution of investigative practices that approximates more closely to a pattern that had always been characteristic of the applied literature. It should be noted that what emerges is a trend, and some distinction between the two categories of research literature always remains.

Nevertheless, the trend appears to be very clear and calls for an explanation. One possibility is that the use of statistical data pertaining to groups arises out of the strong and growing interest of American psychologists in the study of individual differences. With the spread of Galtonian techniques, group data became relevant to the measurement of individual differences and therefore would appear with increasing frequency in the literature. However, such an explanation would at best account for only part of the observed effect. Many of the studies that rely solely on group data have no concern whatever with individual differences; investigations of learning using aggregate data from many subjects provide numerous instances of this state of affairs.

But beyond this it is also necessary to ask precisely what the investigation of individual differences involves when it is conducted in a statistical framework. An interest in the empirical study of individual differences antedated the widespread application of Galtonian techniques to this area.[17] What was involved in this application was not the question of individual differences as such but rather a particular way of posing the question. An older tradition had defined the issue of individual differences in terms of questions of individuality and unique qualitative configurations, in other words, in terms of the characteristics of individuals *qua* individuals. What happens in early twentieth-century American psychology is that the characterization of individuals becomes limited to the specification of their position in an aggregate. The basis for such a specification is of course provided by certain properties of the aggregate and not by the individuality of its members. What is involved in the shift to the Galtonian study of individuals, therefore, is not simply an unqualified interest in individual differences, but a specific interest in the placing of individuals with respect to norms that characterize the performance of groups. This specific interest quite clearly arises in practical contexts, especially in the context of educational administration. If it spreads to areas of research that do not have a direct and immediate link to practical concerns, this seems to suggest that the investigative practices of applied psychology have to some extent become the model for other parts of the discipline.

Another possibility that must be considered is that the trend toward a heavier reliance on aggregate group data is the result of the increasing theoretical appeal of behaviorism during this period. The evaluation of such an explanation would depend on what is meant by behaviorism. If one means the specific set of doctrines propagated by men like Watson and Skinner, then the explanation clearly does not work because in their investigative practices some of the arch-behaviorists were always to be found on the other side of the fence, preferring and even explicitly advocating the analysis of data from individual organisms.[18] There was certainly nothing in the core doctrines of behaviorism that would necessarily lead one to prefer group data.

If, on the other hand, one means by behaviorism a commitment to the general idea of psychology as a practically useful science of human performance, then one would be closer to a plausible explanation. In fact, the burgeoning sympathy for behaviorist perspectives during the period in question does seem to have had more to do with notions about what kind of psychology would be practically useful than with any great respect for the special theories of classical behaviorism. Insofar as behaviorism became what O'Donnell has so aptly termed "the insignia of the practicalist," it may indeed have had some connection with the gradual shift in research practices toward a norm first established by applied psychology.[19] But, in that case, the general ideological preference for behaviorist perspectives must be regarded as an expression of an underlying orientation rather than as a causal influence in its own right. This orientation seems to involve a recognition that the future of psychology as a discipline depended on its ability to find a large-scale external market for its products. The only such market that had materialized was provided by the demands of educational administration, and to a lesser extent by other institutional contexts. But the kind of knowledge product that was relevant for this market was based on the distribution of psychological characteristics in populations rather than on the analysis of psychological processes in individuals.

Thus, the early success of a certain kind of applied psychology enhanced its role in the advancement of the discipline as a whole. The knowledge this kind of applied psychology dealt in, and the investigative practices it used to produce such knowledge, became canonical for other parts of the discipline and gradually displaced other practices. The effect of the successful marketing of psychological products like mental tests on the content of psychological research is clear enough. In the long run, however, the more profound effect may have been the one that involved not just content areas, but the fundamental investigative practices considered generally appropriate for the discipline as a whole.

A COMPARATIVE PERSPECTIVE: THE GERMAN CASE

The scope of our historical interpretation must remain limited as long as we confine ourselves to data derived from a single social context, that is, the American one. Therefore, it now becomes appropriate to examine analogous aspects of the investigative practices of psychology in a different social context. This is quite possible, because during the relevant time period a considerable amount of psychological research took place in Europe as well as in the United States. However, only in Germany was the sheer volume of work large enough to allow us to perform a meaningful statistical analysis that would be comparable to the analysis we have made of the American research literature. German psychology will therefore provide our comparison case.

As in the American case, the German journal literature of the early twentieth century comprises both publications with an applied orientation and those that are devoted to pure research. In the applied category we will look at the *Zeitschrift für pädagogische Psychologie und experimentelle Pädagogik* and the *Zeitschrift für angewandte Psychologie;* in the pure category we will examine the *Archiv für die gesamte Psychologie,* the *Zeitschrift für Psychologie,* and also *Psychologische Forschung.*[20]

The first question that must be asked is whether the German applied psychological literature shows any preference for investigative practices that yield purely statistical data on groups of individuals. It will be recalled that such a preference was clearly at work in the American applied literature. Analyzing the empirical studies published in three volumes of the *Zeitschrift für pädagogische Psychologie* over the period 1911–1913, we find some evidence of such a preference. Fifty-four percent of these studies report mainly group data, while 40% report mainly data pertaining to individuals. Similarly, for three volumes of the *Zeitschrift für angewandte Psychologie* published during 1915–1916, the proportion of studies essentially limiting themselves to group data is 56% while 41% are studies of individual subjects. This certainly differs from the pattern in the German journals devoted to pure research, where there are virutally no studies reporting only group data during this period. However, it also seems that the predominance of this kind of study is not as great in the German as in the American applied literature.

This pattern is confirmed when we extend the analysis into the next decade, the 1920s. For the period 1924–1926, the proportion of studies producing only group data is 60% for the *Zeitschrift für pädagogische Psychologie* and 53% for the *Zeitschrift für angewandte Psychologie.* By this time well over 80% of the studies reported in the two American applied journals fell into the group data category. Thus, the German applied literature shows some of the same general tendency to emphasize information pertaining to groups of individuals as found in the American applied literature, but it also lags behind the latter in the predominance achieved by this feature of investigative practice.

What kinds of factors might be at work here? One possibility that must be considered is that the appropriate statistical techniques for the analysis of psychological group data were more readily available to American investigators, because the primary source of these techniques was in Great Britain. Such techniques would enhance both the utility and the apparent scientific status of group data, and so might well encourage their use. Now, it is true that by and large the level of statistical sophistication tends to be higher in the American than in the German applied literature of this period. However, this seems to be less a question of the availability of the relevant information than of its reception. The relevant technical information was widely disseminated through such vehicles as well-known textbooks and publications in the specialist journal literature.[21] The influence of Galtonian conceptions of human variability is by no means absent in the German research literature of the period, but it never remotely approaches the overwhelming impact it had on the parallel American literature.

In speculating about the source of this divergence, it is impossible to overlook certain differences in the market for the products of applied psychological research. An expanding system of universal education that was adapting itself to the requirements of industrial capitalism certainly provided the major market for these products in both countries.[22] In both cases the effects of this market can be detected not only on the level of psychological content, but also on the level of investigative practices. These frequently become geared to the production of a kind of psychological knowledge that is relevant to administrative decisions concerning the selection of persons and of programs in terms of the criterion of performance efficiency.

However, the social situation in Germany appears to have imposed far greater limitations on this process than in the American context. In the latter case education had never been an important source of social status as it had been in nineteenth-century Germany, where rigid segmentation among different types of schools was intimately tied to rigid social class distinctions.[23] Thus, in Germany there were powerful and well-established social mechanisms in place that traditionally governed the selection, both of individuals and of programs, within the educational system. Education officials had a vested interest in the maintenance of these traditional mechanisms and seldom saw any need to replace or even supplement them with the new mechanisms that applied psychology could provide. The situation did not change substantially during the Weimar period, because of the political weakness of the forces of educational reform.[24] A limited market for the products of applied psychology did exist, yet it bore no comparison to the vast education industry that was the powerhouse of the rapid growth of American applied psychology.[25] Instead of functioning as a repository of preindustrial patterns, as it did in Germany, American education quickly adapted itself to provide an almost perfect reflection of the requirements of the new industrial order.[26] The chief agents of this process were the new educational administrators who provided applied psychology with its most important and most reliable market.

By contrast, the main consumers of educational psychological research in Germany appear to have been classroom teachers. The teachers' associations *(Lehrervereine)* of some of the larger cities played an extremely active role in promoting the dissemination of the products of this research. In a few key instances they established research laboratories and subsidized psychological research from their own funds. The first of these was the Institute for Experimental Pedagogy and Psychology of the Leipzig teachers' association, founded in 1906; this was quickly followed by similar initiatives in Berlin and in Munich; other important centers were Breslau and Hamburg.[27] Here there was a direct collaboration of teachers and academics guided by a common interest in classroom teaching and by the goal of persuading the authorities of the need for educational reform. Unlike administrators, classroom teachers were directly concerned with psychological processes in the minds of individual children and therefore had an interest in psychological research conducted on this basis. This is not to say that group data were irrelevant to their practice, but merely to indicate that these interests were tempered by other concerns. Thus, one reason for the difference between German and American educational psychology in the overall pattern of investigative practices may have to be looked for in the different professional alliances that were feasible and advantageous in these two cases.

However, one must be careful to avoid the kind of oversimplification that would result from considering the educational system as a purely external market for the discipline of psychology. The key figures in the adaptation of psychological investigative practices to the requirements of this market were after all themselves products and functioning parts of the educational system, by virtue of their academic qualifications and appointments. Thus, certain characteristics of the system were not experienced by these individuals as external demands but as internalized values. This often expressed itself in a characteristic duality of goals among those German academics who took the lead in advancing the cause of applied psychology. The same men who pioneered the advancement of psychological techniques as instruments of social control, and of quantitative methods for providing administratively useful knowledge, often devoted a large part of their energies to the pursuit of philosophical goals that had been sanctified by the humanistic traditions of German higher education.[28] Such split loyalties contrast rather sharply with the single-minded devotion to the ideal of calculated efficiency and rationalized performance that was the common characteristic of their American counterparts. The juxtaposition of the intellectual goals of the two leaders in the field of "mental measurement," Edward Lee Thorndike and William Stern, provides a perfect illustration of this contrast.[29]

We are therefore led back from a consideration of market conditions, external to the discipline, to the question of intellectual interests operating within the discipline. These become particularly important when we enlarge the scope of our inquiry to consider the influence of the investigative practices of applied psychology on the discipline as a whole. It was shown earlier that in American psychology the fundamental shift from the analysis of psychological processes in individuals to the analysis of the distribution of psychological characteristics in populations had significantly affected investigative practices in the area of pure research by the 1930s. Can an analogous effect be demonstrated in the German literature of the time? The answer is yes – in a very limited way. During the years 1934–1935 the proportion of empirical studies relying entirely on group data reached a mere 13% in *Psychologische Forschung,* 20% in the *Zeitschrift für Psychologie,* and 23% in the *Archiv für die gesamte Psychologie.* While these figures are far below the corresponding American figures, where this approach already accounted for more than half the published studies, they do represent a small but consistent increase over the German figures a decade earlier. For the period 1924–1926 the proportion of studies relying solely on group data varies from zero in *Psychologische Forschung* to 13% in the *Archiv für die gesamte Psychologie.* This approach to psychological research was always less heavily represented in the German than in the American research literature. However, a slight tendency to follow the lead of applied psychology in adopting this approach does eventually become noticeable.

The difference in the historical development of investigative practices in the American and the German case is not an absolute one. Analogous forces seem to be at work, but their relative weight is very different. In both cases the research literature shows a mixture of fundamentally different research practices geared to the production of different kinds of psychological knowledge. In what I have previously called the Wundtian model, psychological research aims to analyze processes located in individuals, whereas in the Galtonian model the concern is with the distribution of psychological characteristics in populations and the placing of individuals with respect to such group characteristics.[30] Both in American and in German psychology the Galtonian approach is strongly favored by the emergence of an important market for the products of psychological research in the field of education. Also, in both cases there is a detectable shift in the general research literature toward the Galtonian model.

However, these effects appear to be much stronger in the American than in the German case. Two kinds of factors are likely to account for this difference. In the first place, certain differences in the social role and structure of the educational system had the effect of turning American education into a far more powerful market for psychological products and services than was the case for German education, at least during the first half of the century. But this does not account for the curiously ambivalent response on the part of German academics interested in applied psychology, nor for the extremely weak effect that the Galtonian model of psychological research had on the discipline as a whole. For an explanation of these phenomena we have to consider the way in which members of the discipline defined their intellectual interests. Among American psychologists there was an early recognition that the progress of their discipline depended on its ability to supply knowledge that would be useful for the practical management of human affairs. This was very clear to William James when he put the goal of "prediction and control" on the agenda of the new science, meaning by control not experimental, but social control.[31] Such early pioneers as G. Stanley Hall and James McKeen Cattell already grasped that the pursuit of this goal would require a switch to research practices that yielded statistical information about defined groups of individuals. Thus, the response to the requirements of the educational market was rapid and unambiguous. This did not mean that there was unanimity within the discipline, but simply that a convergence of external and internal factors existed that proved decisive for the overall development of the discipline in the long run.

By contrast, German academic psychologists found themselves in a situation where their enterprise was obliged to legitimate itself in terms of the values represented by a well-entrenched traditional intellectual elite, if it was to prosper.[32] On the level of research practices there was no chance of accomplishing this by means of methods that were seen as a kind of superficial census taking that negated human individuality as well as the traditionally recognized mandate of psychology to explore the individual mind and personality. In any case, these judgments were characteristic not merely of groups completely outside the discipline, but of academic psychologists who had complex external and internal ties to these groups. Again, it must be emphasized that this did not necessarily preclude the existence of a spectrum of opinions within the discipline. However, in terms of the overall development of research practices this factor undoubtedly acted as a powerful brake on the widespread adoption of Galtonian methods in psychology.

Although it is convenient, for the sake of conceptual clarity, to make analytic distinctions between factors external and factors internal to the discipline, the limitations of such distinctions must be clearly recognized. Internal definitions of disciplinary goals are themselves adaptations to external conditions and, conversely, disciplinary projects contribute to the formation of external markets for their products.[33] The constellation of intellectual interests that constitutes such disciplinary projects faces both outward and inward. These interests mediate between the possibilities and demands that confront the community of practitioners and the range of investigative practices accepted as legitimate within the community. These practices in turn circumscribe the kind of knowledge that the discipline is able to produce and define the limits of that knowledge.[34]

Technical rationality has a great deal of scope for producing a wide variety of effects, but only insofar as it accepts the limitations of the framework within which it operates.

NOTES

1 E. G. R. Marks, *The Idea of IQ* (Washington D.C.: University Press of America, 1981).

2 An example of this approach to history is provided by E. G. Boring, "The Nature and History of Experimental Control," *American Journal of Psychology* 67 (1954):573–589.

3 K. Danziger, "The Origins of the Psychological Experiment as a Social Institution," *American Psychologist* 40 (1985):133–140.

4 K. Danziger, "Wundt's Psychological Experiment in the Light of His Philosophy of Science," *Psychological Research* 42 (1980):109–122.

5 Typical examples are: W. H. Winch, "Mental Adaptation During the School Day as Measured by Arithmetical Reasoning," *Journal of Educational Psychology* 4 (1913):71–84; M. E. Lakeman, "The Whole and Part Methods of Memorizing Poetry and Prose," *Journal of Educational Psychology* 4 (1913):189–198; W. H. Winch, "Accuracy in School Children. Does Improvement in Numerical Accuracy 'Transfer'?," *Journal of Educational Psychology* 1 (1910):557–589.

6 R. E. Callahan and H. W. Button, "Historical Change and the Role of the Man in the Organization: 1865–1950," in D. E. Griffiths (ed.), Behavioral Science and Educational Administration, *Yearbook of the National Society for the Study of Education* 63 (1964):73–92.

7 See R. E. Callahan, *Education and the Cult of Efficiency* (Chicago: University of Chicago Press, 1962); and D. Tyack and E. Hansot, *Managers of Virtue: Public School Leadership in America, 1820–1980* (New York: Basic Books, 1982).

8 F. E. Spaulding, "The Application of Principles of Scientific Management," *National Education Association, Journal of Proceedings and Addresses of the 51st Annual Meeting* (1913), 260.

9 Cf. E. P. Cubberley, *Public School Administration* (Boston: Houghton Mifflin, 1916), 336.

10 See, e.g., G. Melcher, "Suggestions for Experimental Work," *Yearbook of the National Society for the Study of Education* 17 (1918), part 2, 134–151.

11 See F. Bobbitt, "Some General Principles of Management Applied to the Management of City-school Systems," *Yearbook of the National Society for the Study of Education* 12 (1913):7–96.

12 For Carl E. Seashore's view of the world, see, e.g., his editorial, "The Educational Efficiency Engineer," *Journal of Educational Psychology* 4 (1913):244, and his retrospective *Pioneering in Psychology* (Iowa City: University of Iowa, 1942).

13 R. L. Church, "Educational Psychology and Social Reform in the Progressive Era," *History of Education Quarterly* 11 (1971):390–405.

14 All the percentages referred to in this chapter are derived from the results of a coding process based on a five-point scale that ranged from "studies that contained no group data whatever" to "studies that contained no individual data whatever." In the middle were studies in which the reporting of individual and group data was given more or less equal weight. Two further categories were separately identified, but have here been combined with the extreme categories because they did not affect the nature and direction of the differences that are of interest. These categories comprise studies that mainly focus on individual data but also add averages for several individuals, and studies that mainly report group data but make some reference to individuals by way of illustration.

15 The dates of these volumes are 1916, 1919, and 1920.

16 Here, as previously, the results for three successive volume years are combined to correct for random minor fluctuations from year to year and to arrive at a better estimate of the overall trend.

17 W. Stern, *Über Psychologie der individuellen Differenzen (Ideen zu einer differentiellen Psychologie)* (Leipzig: Barth, 1900). This work and its greatly revised later version (1911) contain numerous references to this extensive literature. See also A. Binet, *L'étude expèrimentale de l'intelligence* (Paris: Schleicher, 1903).

18 Although he was not a behaviorist, Pavlov and his methods were greatly respected by most behaviorists during this period, and Pavlov's investigative practices surely represented a veritable triumph of the individual approach to data collection and analysis.

19 J. M. O'Donnell, *The Origins of Behaviorism: American Psychology, 1870–1920* (New York: New York University Press, 1985). This work is indispensable for a critical understanding of the historical foundations of American psychology. On the problematic reception of radical behaviorism see F. Samelson, "Struggle for Scientific Authority: The Reception of Watson's Behaviorism, 1913–1920," *Journal of the History of the Behavioral Sciences* 17 (1981):399–425.

20 As in the case of the American literature, our aim is not to cover every single psychological research report published during the period in question, but merely to examine those major channels of publication that will permit a broad characterization of disciplinary practices.

21 W. Stern, *Die differentielle Psychologie in ihren methodischen Grundlagen* (Leipzig: Barth, 1911); W. Stern, *Die psychologischen Methoden der Intelligenzprüfung und deren Anwendung an Schulkindern* (Leipzig: Barth, 1912); W. Betz, "Über Korrelation: Methoden der Korrelationsberechnung und kritischer Bericht über Korrelationsuntersuchungen aus dem Gebiete der Intelligenz, der Anlagen und ihrer Beeinflussung durch äussere Umstände," *Zeitschrift für angewandte Psychologie und psychologische Sammelforschung,* Beiheft 3 (1911):1–80; G. Deuchler, "Über die Methoden der Korrelationsrechnung in der Pädagogik und Psychologie," *Zeitschrift für pädagogische Psychologie und experimentelle Pädagogik* 15 (1914):114–131, 145–159, 229–242. Spearman's statistical approach was well known in Germany some years before these publications.

22 It should be noted that the content of the great majority of the empirical contributions published in the pages of the *Zeitschrift für angewandte Psychologie* directly reflects educational interests.

23 P. Lundgreen, *Sozialgeschichte der deutschen Schule im Überblick,* Teil I (Gottingen: Vandenhoeck & Ruprecht, 1980).

24 P. Lundgreen, op. cit., Teil II, 1981.

25 For reasons of space I omit separate consideration of industry as a market for the products of psychological research. In terms of any influence on the discipline as a whole this market was much less important, both in Germany and in America, than the market provided by the educational system. This does not exclude

important specific effects, such as the influence of personnel selection on methods of personality research and the influence of advertising on the investigation of judgment. Although the effect of the industrial system was ultimately decisive, it was an effect primarily mediated by the educational system. On the role of industrial psychology in Germany, see S. Jaeger and I. Staeuble, "Die Psychotechnik und ihre gesellschaftlichen Entwicklungsbedingungen," in F. Stoll (ed.), *Die Psychologie des 20. Jahrhunderts,* vol. 13 (Zurich: Kindler, 1980).

26 For the specific considerations that underlie this highly synoptic statement, see F. K. Ringer, *Education and Society in Modern Europe* (Bloomington: Indiana University Press, 1979), chap. 5.

27 On the foundation of the Leipzig and Berlin research institutes, see *Zeitschrift für experimentelle Pädagogik* 7 (1908):218–223 and 10 (1910):133–139, respectively. Subsequent volumes of the *Zeitschrift für pädagogische Psychologie and experimentelle Pädagogik* contain regular reports on the activities of these and other similar institutes, including their budgets. Ernst Meumann, the leading figure in the empirical educational psychology of the time, regarded his experimental work as "the scientific parallel movement to our current efforts at school reform," *Z.f. Pädag. Psychol. u. exper. Pädagogik* 12 (1911):1. See also K. Ingenkamp, "Das Institut des Leipziger Lehrervereins 1906–1933 und seine Bedeutung für die empirische Pädagogik," *Empirische Pädagogik* 2 (1987), in press.

28 Prominent examples of this pattern are Karl Marbe and William Stern. See their autobiographical statements in Carl Murchison (ed.), *A History of Psychology in Autobiography,* Vols. 1 and 3 (Worcester, MA: Clark University Press, 1930 and 1936). Although most of his influence was exerted in the United States, Hugo Münsterberg's background resulted in his following the same pattern. See M. Hale, Jr., *Human Science and the Social Order: Hugo Münsterberg and the Origins of Applied Psychology* (Philadelphia: Temple University Press, 1980).

29 For an analysis of Thorndike's beliefs and values, see G. Joncich, *The Sane Positivist* (Middletown, CT: Wesleyan University Press, 1968). The ambiguity of Stern's position when faced with practical questions emerges rather clearly in W. Stern, "Der personale Faktor in Psychotechnik und praktischer Psychologie,"*Zeitschrift für angewandte Psychologie* 44 (1933):52–63; for an overview in English there is his *General Psychology from the Personalistic Standpoint* (New York: Macmillan, 1938). See also the works referred to in notes 17, 21, and 27 and I. Staeuble, "William Stern's Research Program of Differential Psychology: Why Did Psychotechnics Outstrip Psychognostics?" Paper read at the 15th annual meeting of the Cheiron Society, Toronto, June 1983.

30 K. Danziger, "Statistical Method and the Historical Development of Research Practice in American Psychology," in G. Gigerenzer, L. Krüger, and M. Morgan (eds.), *The Probabilistic Revolution: Ideas in Modern Science,* vol. 2 (Cambridge: MIT Press, 1987).

31 W. James, "A Plea for Psychology as a Natural Science," *Philosophical Review* 1 (1892):146–153.

32 See M. G. Ash, "Academic Politics in the History of Science: Experimental Psychology in Germany, 1879–1941," *Central European History* 13 (1980):255–286. For suggestions about the social factors involved in the different distribution of intellectual interests in the earliest stages of modern American and German psychology see K. Danziger, "The Social Origins of Modern Psychology," in A. R. Buss (ed.), *Psychology in Social Context* (New York: Irvington, 1979).

33 These issues are obviously closely related to the question of professionalization, but a consideration of this relationship goes beyond the scope of the present chapter. From the point of view of the process of professionalization, cognitive schemas and technical practices can be treated as a resource, whereas in the present analysis it is precisely these resources that are regarded as problematic. Nevertheless, I consider the present analysis to be broadly compatible with M. S. Larson, *The Rise of Professionalism: A Sociological Analysis* (Berkeley: University of California Press, 1977). For a clear statement of the issues in comparative perspective, see D. Ruschemeyer, "Professionalisierung: Theoretische Probleme für die vergleichende Geschichtsforschung," *Geschichte und Gesellschaft* 6 (1980):311–325. U. Geuter, *Die Professionalisierung der deutschen Psychologen im Nationalsozialismus* (Frankfurt: Suhrkamp, 1984) has an excellent comprehensive account of the problems of professionalization in the case of German psychology.

34 I have explored this issue in K. Danziger, "The Methodological Imperative in Psychology," *Philosophy of the Social Sciences* 16 (1985):1–13.

By Gilman & Co., Oxford, England

EDWARD BRADFORD TITCHENER

Photograph taken just before Titchener left England to study at Leipzig. Reproduced by permission from the collection of Rand Evans.

2

PROGRAMMATIC RESEARCH IN EXPERIMENTAL PSYCHOLOGY: E. B. TITCHENER'S LABORATORY INVESTIGATIONS, 1891–1927*

RYAN D. TWENEY

THE PROGRAMMATIC CONTEXT OF EXPERIMENTAL PSYCHOLOGY

Recent history of science has concentrated increasingly on the cognitive aspects of scientific inquiry. Successively detailed accounts of the microstructure of science have resulted, with some of the accounts relying on concepts derived from contemporary cognitive science. For example, Gruber's well-known account of Darwin's creativity relies on a genetic epistemology derived from Piaget's theory of cognition, while A. I. Miller's account of the emergence of quantum physics is based on Piagetian, Gestalt, and information-processing theory.[1] Even where explicit use of cognitive science is not made, for example, in Holmes' studies of Claude Bernard's notebooks or Rudwick's work in the history of geology, there is nevertheless a focus on the detailed day-to-day activities of scientists.[2]

As part of this effort, historians of science have shifted from an earlier preoccupation with issues of theory development and theory change to more balanced approaches that emphasize the role of laboratory activity as well as theoretical activity. This chapter is conceived in a similar spirit. By concentrating on the laboratory experimentation of a famous psychologist, I hope to supplement existing studies that have considered his theoretical views.

The chapter will focus on one aspect of the experimental method that is especially important in the discovery process, namely, the power of

* The author is indebted to the Faculty Research Committee of Bowling Green State University, which provided partial support for the research reported in this chapter. Specific thanks are due to the library staffs of Cornell University, Bowling Green State University, and the University of Michigan for much help. The comments of Mitchell Ash, Wolfgang Bringmann, Michael Doherty, Rand Evans, and William Woodward on earlier drafts of this paper resulted in substantial changes and are gratefully acknowledged.

35

experiment to serve as a self-regulating process for generating, as well as evaluating, hypotheses. Experimentation is a method for putting questions to nature, and for getting answers. It is most effective when a series of experiments is carried out, each building on or clarifying the results of preceding studies. Research that uses the outcome of one study to modify subsequent inquiry, and which conceives of the research enterprise as an ongoing, necessarily unfinished, process, I shall refer to as *programmatic*. Programmatic experimentation should be distinguished from isolated experiments, on the one hand, and experimental attempts to confirm theories, on the other. The latter need not qualify as programmatic in the intended sense, since there is no necessity that the experiments constitute a self-regulating system of inquiry in their own right. Note also that programmatic experimentation is possible whether or not the experiments have a particular relationship to theory development.[3] Thus, while Michael Faraday discovered electromagnetic induction using a series of programmatic experiments closely related to his developing conception of field, he discovered the liquefaction of gases in a relatively atheoretic context, but, again, using programmatic experiments.[4]

The present level of analysis complements recent work on the role of theory in science, work that has emphasized the "theory-ladenness" of even the most elementary facts.[5] This is certainly a valid and important point, but it is often overlooked that, while all science begins and ends in theory (whether formally developed or informally held in the guise of assumptions about reality), all science *also* holds itself to empirical criteria that may undercut hypotheses derived from theory, or even the guiding assumptions themselves.[6] Such criteria constitute the underpinnings of the uncontrivability of research.

TITCHENER AS A CASE STUDY

According to the standard account, Edward Bradford Titchener (1867–1927) was "an Englishman who represented the German psychological tradition in America" and "a most zealous disciple of Wundt's, with all the ardor and narrowness of view that characterize a new convert to any faith."[7] For many, Titchener was merely the American agent for "Wundt's Structuralism," overthrown in the populist revolution that produced American behaviorism. Antiquarians might find his ways curious or quaint, or give him a nod as a worthy opponent of true progress in American psychology, but serious scholars were advised to look elsewhere for psychology's heroic past, or for relevance to current psychology. As we shall see, a focus on Titchener's experimental activity, rather than on his personal career or his theoretical system, reveals a very different Titchener than the one presented in most textbook accounts.

The standard account is based on misconceptions of both Titchener and of Wundt. In recent years, many have sought to clarify the point that while Titchener was a structuralist, Wundt was not; that Wundt's *voluntaristic* psychology was very different from Titchener's *structuralistic* psychology.[8] Further, the breadth of Wundt's psychology, ranging from physiological processes, through cognition, to social and cultural issues, was not shared by his American followers, who focused primarily on his experimental work. Some have blamed Titchener for distorting Wundt's work. Wundt, it is said, would never have been overlooked in America except for Titchener's misrepresentations. From the quaint and curious, then, Titchener was changed into something mildly (or not so mildly) demonic. Although a reassessment of Titchener now seems overdue, one point requires emphasis: Titchener was not a *follower* of Wundt.[9]

Titchener's life[10]

Titchener was born in 1867 and raised in Chichester, near the southern coast of England. He attended public school on a scholarship, and went to Oxford University where he studied classics, philosophy, and physiology, receiving his AB in 1889. Under John Scott Burdon-Sanderson (1828–1905) he carried out research in physiology that led to 10 minor articles, all published in *Nature* between 1889 and 1891, on coloration of bird's eggs and on feeding behavior in birds. Titchener apparently first acquired an appreciation of the role of experimentation in science from Burdon-Sanderson who, along with Michael Foster, was one of the first to introduce the pioneering experimental physiology of Claude Bernard to England.[11] Burdon-Sanderson's writings reflected a preoccupation with methodological issues, and it is significant that he edited and co-authored an important *Handbook for the Physiological Laboratory,* a positivist work that avoided theoretical speculation. Further, his concern with appropriately distinguishing structure and function may also have influenced the young Titchener.[12]

Burdon-Sanderson's *Syllabus of Lectures on Physiology* suggests what Titchener was exposed to as a student.[13] The syllabus included a description of the measurement of "'personal time,' which is made up of the time required for recognizing the sensation (perception) and the time required for transforming it into muscular action (intention)" estimating this to be about one-sixth of a second in simple cases. Neither Wundt nor Donders was acknowledged, though both presented essentially the same facts. An appendix described the apparatus needed to carry out such measurements. Burdon-Sanderson also described Weber's psychophysical law and some rudimentary introspective experiments on sensation using controlled presentation of stimuli. Titchener was thus first exposed to experimental psychology before going to Leipzig in 1890 to work on his PhD in Wundt's laboratory. Titchener's assertion that he had completed a translation of the third (1887) edition of Wundt's 1874 *Gründzuge* while at Oxford makes the same point.[14]

From Oxford, Titchener went to Leipzig, where he received his PhD in 1892. He participated as a subject in some of Wundt's experiments and carried out his dissertation research on the problem of binocular vision.[15] Among his close associates at Leipzig was Oswald Külpe (1862–1915), a strong influence on the young Titchener, stronger than Wundt himself. Külpe's use of experimental methods to approach problems like attention and imagery and his positivism differed radically from Wundt's views, but were embraced by Titchener. Nonetheless, Titchener's first psychological paper, "Dr. Münsterberg and Experimental Psychology," published in 1891, was a defense of Wundt's concept of apperception, and was soon followed by an account of the research being conducted in Wundt's laboratory.[16]

In 1890, when Titchener arrived in Leipzig, the magnetic attraction of Wundt's laboratory for foreign students was at its peak. Titchener was one of only a few Englishmen to be attracted; most of Wundt's impact was on German and North American psychology. Following a brief stint lecturing in biology at Oxford, Titchener went to Ithaca, New York, in 1892 as assistant professor of psychology at Cornell University, where he remained until his death in 1927.

Titchener's career

At Cornell, Titchener developed the psychology laboratory into a thriving concern, somewhat along the lines of Wundt's Leipzig laboratory. Like Wundt, Titchener worked tirelessly to expand his laboratory, to enlist support from the university, and to recruit graduate students. Titchener was filled with missionary zeal and possessed boundless energy.[17] Like Wundt in the 1870s and 1880s, Titchener worked to establish experimental psychology on a secure institutional footing, and to present it to a wider public. Between 1894 and 1927, 56 persons received their PhDs in his laboratory, fewer than the 186 graduated by Wundt from 1876 to 1920 but an enviable list even so.[18]

Wundt's role as the head of Germany's first laboratory of psychology was self-consciously modelled by Titchener. Like Wundt, Titchener trained psychologists who then established their own laboratories, for example, Margaret Floy Washburn at Vassar. As with Wundt's students, Titchener's students played an important role in administering the newly emerging departments of psychology that sprang up everywhere, for example, Walter B. Pillsbury at the University of Michigan and Edwin G. Boring at Harvard. Like Wundt, Titchener guided (though he did not establish) an important periodical, the *American Journal of Psychology,* which he co-edited with G. Stanley Hall and E. C. Sanford from 1895 to

1921, and edited alone from 1921 to 1925. Like Wundt, Titchener provided the new field with textbooks, first by translating German texts, later by writing his own.[19]

For Titchener, a psychological system was useful primarily as a framework on which experimental research could be mounted. He was a structuralist because he felt that the first goal of psychology was the analysis of mind into elementary units of sensations (or attributes of sensations), the structural arrangement of which could then be used to account for higher-order processes such as emotion, will, and attention. This goal in turn heavily influenced Titchener's choice of methodology, in particular the use of controlled introspection in which trained observers reported the elements of their conscious awareness in response to controlled stimuli. All other methods, especially those derived from psychophysics and physiology, were at best subsidiary ones; Titchener was data-oriented rather than theory-oriented. Even so, as will be shown later, his pursuit of data was always carried out in the context of highly systematized efforts and driven by a strong urge toward consistency. Finally, Titchener was a positivist; he distrusted theoretical entities, such as Wundt's apperception, which could not be firmly anchored in observables, and he constantly sought to unify and simplify the framework of his experimentation.

The results of Titchener's laboratory work and his theoretical views were presented in seven books and 216 articles. Between 1889 and 1917, he published nearly 7,000 printed pages, not including revisions of his textbooks, and not counting his numerous articles in Baldwin's 1901/1902 *Dictionary of Philosophy and Psychology*. His publication lagged after 1917. In the next ten years, until his death in August 1927, he published only 244 pages and no new books, except the posthumously published *Systematic Psychology: Prolegomena*.[20] The sudden decline in publishing was not, however, accompanied by lesser activity in the laboratory; between 1917 and 1927, he supervised 25 PhD dissertations, and it is clear from his correspondence that he was actively involved in his students' research. During the decade, Titchener labored on a systematic treatise, but, at the time of his death, had not yet begun the central part of the work.

Titchener was closely involved with graduate student projects in his laboratory; Evans has compared him to a military commander, in which these projects were the weapons deployed against the issues.[21] Such "campaigns" are evident in Titchener's earliest contribution to the experimental literature. His first research paper from the Cornell lab was a brief apparatus note, but this was preceded by two student contributions.[22] In all, there were 19 such "Minor Studies" in the *American Journal of Psychology* between 1893 and 1899, after which many further papers by students bore the footnote "From the Psychological Laboratory of Cornell

University." The topics investigated ranged from cutaneous sensation to habit formation. There was a strong emphasis on emotion and attention, areas in which Titchener had disagreed with Wundt, and for which the student projects represented the empirical front line. There is no doubt that Titchener controlled, or even commanded, the choice of topic in all of these studies.

During his entire career Titchener remained a laboratory scientist. In a letter to Harvard's President Lowell, Titchener declined an offer of a position at Harvard, saying that, "for me, however, the laboratory is all-important, the vital centre of the whole department, the source of inspiration, instruction, training and scientific advance for undergraduates, graduates and instructing staff. I gave up Oxford for Cornell solely because Cornell offered me a laboratory."[23] This is not the attitude that Wundt held, nor, for that matter, the attitude of very many other Americans during the early years. For Wundt, the laboratory was a necessary part of psychology, but not the only part. For men like James Mark Baldwin and William James, the laboratory was less interesting than philosophy. For Titchener, "the laboratory was all-important," and it is in the laboratory that we must seek the significance of his achievement.

Titchener's laboratory activity can be divided into four main phases, as shown in Table 2-1. Athough the exact dates of each phase could be subject to argument, the four phases each reveal a somewhat different pattern of activity, with different consequences for the way Titchener incorporated laboratory work into his overall goals.

The table is based on a quantitative analysis of the publications of Titchener and his students. Given the normal publication lag, it is safe to assume that the major divisions between the phases of Titchener's career would be located one to two years earlier, if we were to base them on Titchener's actual thinking, rather than his publications. For the present purpose, the error is unimportant; what is important is that the quantitative distinctions reflected in Table 2-1 are correlated with substantial qualitative differences in the nature of his work.

Two characteristics are common to all four phases. First, Titchener published very little experimental work under his own name. Instead, he himself focused on the writing of books, theoretical articles, reviews, and critiques of the work of others, while his students published experimental studies. Like Wundt, he placed himself at the head of his research enterprise, defending it, relating it to other enterprises, promulgating it to students, professionals, and laypersons. Unlike Wundt, Titchener exerted direct control over the experimental work of his students. Thus, Titchener's social role, the way he defined and directed the activity of his co-workers, gave him the possibility of a coherent, multifaceted research program.

The second thing to notice is that all of Titchener's programmatic work

Table 2-1. *Phases in Titchener's career*

Phase	Dates	Major publications	Titchener's article publication rate	Students' publication rate	PhD's granted
I. Establishing the approach	1891–1899 (8 years)	*Outlines* (1896) "Postulates of a Structural Psychology" (1898) "Structural and Functional Psychology" (1899)	Rising, then high and steady $\overline{X} = 6.8$/yr	Erratic $\overline{X} = 3.5$/yr	6 (0.75/yr)
II. Methodological	1899–1907 (8 years)	*Experimental Psychology* (1901, 1905)	Declining $\overline{X} = 4.1$/yr	Declining $\overline{X} = 3.4$/yr	7 (0.88/yr)
III. Programmatic, defensive	1907–1915 (8 yrs)	*Feeling and Attention* (1908) *Thought Processes* (1909) *Textbook* (1909/1910) "Description vs. statement of meaning" (1912) "Prolegomena to a study of introspection" (1912) "Sensation and system" (1915)	Rising $\overline{X} = 6.9$/yr	Steady $\overline{X} = 3.25$/yr	17 (2.12/yr)
V. Programmatic, aggressive	1915–1927 (12 yrs)	"Brentano and Wundt" (1921) "Functional psychology and the psychology of act" (1921, 1922)	Abrupt decline, then rising, then declining $\overline{X} = 4.5$/yr	Abrupt rise, then high and steady, then declining $\overline{X} = 7.6$/yr	26 (2.17/yr)

was "Leipzig Model" experimentation, in Danziger's terms.[24] In general, Titchener's experimenters were Titchener's subjects – there was no social division of labor, making Titchener's research increasingly different from that of other American researchers during his lifetime. This point supports the claim that Titchener derived from Wundt his conception of the social structure of psychological science, rather than his theoretical presuppositions.

THE FOUR PHASES IN DETAIL

The remainder of this chapter will examine each of the four phases in turn and will show, rather surprisingly, that true programmatic research emerged only in the third phase, achieving its full power only in the fourth and final phase. The first three phases were, in effect, preparation for the fourth.

Establishing the approach, 1891–1899

Titchener first set himself the task of locating his efforts within the larger movements of psychology. His lifelong pattern of publishing reviews, critiques, and summaries of the works of others was begun, while his students published laboratory results. Each student was given a fairly large topic to investigate, and there was minimal overlap between topics. For example, Washburn worked on space perception, Hamlin on attention, Irons on emotion, and Pillsbury on apperception. The topics of his students' research correspond closely to those Titchener described in an 1894 article as especially in need of attention from experimental psychology.[25] These investigations were programmatic in spirit, but were less empirically consequential than some of his later efforts. In fact, they strike the modern reader as overambitious, as if Titchener set out to do too many things simultaneously.

The goal of the program was spelled out clearly in 1898.[26] Titchener set up a correspondence between the divisions of psychology and the division of biology into morphology, physiology, and ontogeny. The counterpart of morphology, namely, the experimental determination of the structural basis of mind, was for Titchener the most promising domain for experimental investigation, rather than the counterpart of physiology, that is, the functional basis of mind. The paper further reveals that Titchener had no fixed system. Rather, his "system" was a set of assumptions about the most likely place to find useful observations. He employed laboratory studies to raise and answer questions that led him to other questions. In exactly this sense, Titchener's research was intended to be programmatic.

Methodological development, 1899–1907

Titchener refined his approach during this period. His publication rate, and that of his students, declined. His production of PhDs slowed as well. Titchener's most enduring contribution during this period was the profusely illustrated four-volume *Experimental Psychology* of 1901–1905– two thin volumes for students, two thick ones for instructors.[27] This work is divided into two parts, qualitative experiments and quantitative experiments. The student manual for the former included basic experiments and demonstrations in sensation (20 experiments), affective qualities (4 experiments), attention and reaction time (2 experiments), perception (9 experiments), and association (2 experiments). The student manual for quantitative experiments focused on psychophysics (23 experiments), but also included reaction time methods (3 experiments) and time estimation (one experiment). The quantitative volume is more advanced, and seems to have been used far less often as a text.[32] The level of both student volumes is very high – knowledge of French and German is assumed, and mathematics up to calculus is freely used in the quantitative volume. The basic physics of electric currents is explained in the quantitative volume, but there is no physiology in either.

The instructor's manuals constitute true handbooks of research methods and research literature, and are remarkable for their thoroughness. They were written to insure that techniques were correctly applied, and that the laboratory experiments described in the student manuals were correctly related to larger, systematic issues in psychology. The instructor's manuals cover everything needed to run a lab course, and remain a rich source for the historian of psychology. Titchener left nothing to chance: There are surveys of relevant literature, detailed descriptions of apparatus, hints on procedures and cost cutting, review questions, test questions, general background, and even a list of books and periodicals that should be on hand. The quantitative volume contains an introduction, over 150 pages long, entitled "The Rise and Progress of Quantitative Psychology," which is as complete a review of psychophysics up to 1900 as has ever been written. Titchener overlooked nothing in his zeal to be thorough, to produce an encyclopedic handbook for the laboratory instructor. Thus, the instructor's qualitative volume gives *twelve* alternative explanations for the Müller-Lyer illusion. The evidence for each explanation is summarized (though no position is taken on which is to be preferred), and full citations are made to journal literature. Seven student experiments are devoted to the Müller-Lyer and related illusions of extent, and instructors are cautioned against either oversimplification, which can result if only one explanation is preferred, or fragmentation, which can occur if the student concludes from the variety of explanations that "anything goes." Here, too, we see Titchener advocating a programmatic approach.

The *Experimental Psychology* was not a Wundtian text, though it showed a clear influence from Leipzig:

> My greatest debt, here as elsewhere, is to Wundt. I was impelled toward experimental psychology by dissatisfaction with the logical constructions of the English school; and it was Wundt who taught me the essential lesson of systematic introspection.[29]

Perhaps because of the deviations from Wundt, at least one other Leipzig-trained American, Charles H. Judd, then at Yale University, felt impelled to prepare his own text and lab manuals, along lines more like those Wundt would have approved.[30] Judd's student laboratory manual is very brief, but the selection of topics is revealing: 10 experiments (40% of the total) on sensation and perception against 52 (84%) for Titchener, 10 experiments (40%) on movement against four (6%) for Titchener, five experiments (20%) on memory, attention, and the higher mental processes against six (10%) for Titchener. Voluntary processes are emphasized throughout, in keeping with Wundt's voluntarism. The instructor's manual deals with equipment alone. Instead of Titchener's encyclopedic coverage, only selected tried-and-true devices are described. The available evidence suggests that Judd's manuals enjoyed nowhere near the success of Titchener's, even though very few people used all of Titchener's material at any level, and Judd's text was far more carefully adjusted to the capacities of American undergraduate students.[31]

The impact of Titchener's manuals was foreseen by James R. Angell, who claimed that they would lead to "a radical alteration of the status of this branch of science," and predicted that they would become the classical reference on the topic.[32] Admiration of Titchener's manuals was expressed by John B. Watson in a letter: "I did not know a great deal of experimental psychology until your Instructor's Manual (qualitative) fell into my hands. I went to work on that and then I began to see the amount of work you must have done in order to have written that."[33]

Defensive programmatic, 1907–1915.

In spite of Titchener's advocacy of programmatic research up to 1907, we cannot see Titchener's early work as programmatic, in and of itself. The groundwork was being laid, but he had yet to deliver fully on the promise.

First, however, Titchener needed to defend the territory he had so painstakingly defined prior to 1907. We see this initially in his 1908 lectures at Columbia University, published the same year as *Lectures on the Elementary Psychology of Feeling and Attention*.[34] Titchener set out his anticipated program, and contrasted it with those of Wundt, Münsterberg, and Ebbinghaus. It is a revealing book, because it makes clear that Titchener was not yet fully launched on his program. References to empirical studies in his own laboratory derive primarily from the first phase (prior to 1899), and do not definitively establish his claims. Instead, Titchener makes clear that he is setting out to discover and to define problems he intends to address in the laboratory: "We set out from uncertainty and chaos; and we have at least achieved a fairly definite point of view, and have laid out a programme of experimental work for the future."[35] In 1909, invited lectures at the University of Illinois formed the basis of his *Experimental Psychology of the Thought Processes.*[36] Here, the defensiveness of his position is even more apparent. He was no longer able, as he was in 1908, to easily discredit the methodology of the opposition, for he was now forced to deal with a major empirical assault on his approach from the "imageless thought" school of Külpe and his followers.

The imageless thought controversy centered around reports that no imagery or sensory content could be introspectively detected in certain task situations.[37] For example, if one is asked to introspect on the meaning of a proverb, the meaning often makes a sudden appearance in consciousness, without prior warning and without imagery or sensory content. Such occurrences led Karl Bühler to argue for the existence of thought elements, which A. Mayer and Johannes Orth called *Bewusstseinslagen* (roughly, states of consciousness), or *Bsl.* for short. These *Bsl.* posed a great threat to Titchener's introspective approach, because they implied that "the process of thinking was directed, controlled, 'determined' by machinery of the working of which we are largely unconscious." If the existence of *Bsl.* were accepted, a new thought element would need to be added to the structuralist claim that mind was composed of sensations, feelings, and images.[38]

Titchener approached the challenge by arguing that, while meaning, as the context of a sensation, could be unconscious, the *Bsl.*, the directing tendencies of thought, were themselves kinesthetic sensations rather than thought elements as such.[39] What the Würzburg school had presented as elements of thought could be reduced, so he believed, to sensations that accompanied thought or the preparation for thought. Titchener was, of course, developing an argument that fit nicely with attempts to develop a motor theory of thought.[40] More to the point, however, is that Titchener conceived the problem as an empirical one, and initiated a program of research: "The unanalysable and irreducible *Bewusstseinslagen* of other investigators may, I conceive, prove to be analysable when they are scrutinised directly and under favourable experimental conditions."[41]

"Direct scrutiny" was applied in a series of six interrelated studies carried out by Titchener and his graduate students between 1909 and 1912.[42] The series was described and defended in an article in which Titchener responded to a variety of criticisms leveled at the work by Koffka. Titchener felt that Koffka had failed to "recognise the serial nature of our work; he does not see that we have been feeling our way to clearness, step by step and problem by problem."[43]

Okabe presented subjects with statements that aroused either belief or disbelief, and asked for introspective reports.[44] He found marked individual differences, and correlates of belief (or disbelief) that included visual images, verbal images, and kinesthetic sensations, though not necessarily together in the same subject. Pyle found similar results when subjects were asked to introspect on their feelings of expectation prior to a stimulus presentation. Clarke asked for introspections of a slowly developing verbal stimulus in an attempt to detect the *Bsl.* directly. She found sensory aspects in a continuous series from clear images to "imageless thoughts." The latter were often very vague – for example, reports of "bodily attitudes," "organic sensations," "dull pressures," – but there was always a sensory basis. Jacobson found similar results. Titchener reported kinesthetic sensations accompanying the feeling of self-consciousness, though the experience was intermittent and was not subjected to experimental analysis. Finally, in the capstone of the series, Titchener required subjects to consciously separate their descriptions of the contents of consciousness from statements of the meaning of the stimuli, as had Jacobson. He found distinctly different attitudes characterizing the two kinds of report – one based on logical or everyday meanings, the other based on analytic descriptions. The latter, essentially the attitude of the "trained introspector," was the only attitude appropriate for the kind of analysis Titchener had in mind; the former was merely "stimulus error," that is, an unwarranted intrusion of the meaning of a stimulus into an observer's report.

Titchener argued that the studies constituted a series of progressive improvements in method that improved the analyzability of the *Bsl.* In effect, he claimed to have shown that reports of *Bsl.* could be reduced, under appropriate experimental conditions, to reports of imagery or sensory experiences. The work led Titchener to conclude that the "method of questions" central to the Würzburg approach was of primary value only in exploratory studies of complex processes. It could not, however, finally resolve the issue of the existence of imageless thought, "for the reason that there was no hope of gaining sufficient experimental control over the conditions of the introspective reports."[45] In particular, while one could find sensations in all introspective reports, how could one prove the *absence* of thought elements?

In fact, however, the series was of greater consequence than this primarily negative conclusion suggests. To see this, consider the shift after 1915 in Titchener's account of sensation.[46] Whereas "sensations" had been unitary elements in Titchener's earlier writings, in 1915 he speaks of them as inferred constructs abstracted from the results of experiment and observation. This change in the systematic status of sensations was based in part on theoretical considerations, but was also related to the outcome of the imageless thought series. In all the studies cited above, the results of the introspective analyses could not be reconstituted into the original meanings of the stimulus. When presented with a factual statement, it is possible to go from, say, an experience of doubt (the everyday awareness of the event) to a report of "a feeling of strain in the neck" (the introspective analysis of the event). It is not possible to go the other way, *from* a feeling of strain *to* an experience of doubt, as Titchener apparently first realized in the imageless thought series.[47]

Did the series have empirical consequences for further experimental research, aside from its theoretical consequences? Woodworth argued that the imageless thought controversy as a whole led to the incorporation of the concept of set in the psychology of thinking.[48] Even more to the point, Titchener's series had a direct influence on the later work by Jacobson on the progressive relaxation technique. After some initial experiments at Harvard, Jacobson came to Cornell as a student and conducted several studies of the inhibition of conscious activity in one sensory mode by activity in another.[49] The progressive relaxation technique itself was later developed by Jacobson at Chicago under Harvey Carr. Jacobson felt that the work of the Würzburg school, of Titchener, and of proponents of motor theories of thought, like Woodworth, together suggested that a decrease in physiological activity might be incompatible with thought. Jacobson made use of Titchener's work in several ways, for example, in his careful training of subjects on the proper mode of introspection. In particular, they were to avoid stimulus error! Jacobson's results were perfectly consistent with Titchener's series on imageless thought, with the addition of a physiological relationship not described by Titchener: "All the *S*s and patients who attained high skill in progressive relaxation spontaneously arrived at, and agreed in, their conclusions regarding psychological activities. With visual imagery there is a sense as from tenseness in the muscles of the ocular region. Without such faint tenseness, the image fails to appear."[50] Since progressive relaxation is still considered a useful therapeutic device, it is clear that Titchener's programmatic series on imageless thought had tangible empirical outcomes.

Aggressive programmatic, 1915–1927.

It is only in this final phase that Titchener's work became fully programmatic. Only here do the students outpublish the master himself. Further, the publications of his students during this period were far more tightly focused than during the earlier phases. Most deal with very basic issues in sensation and perception; here, as never before, Titchener was the general and his students the troops.

The flavor of Titchener's workaday use of introspection in this period is captured in the following letter, written to Samuel Fernberger in 1922:[51]

> I am taking up this year a study of lifted weights by the constant method, and a study of arm movements by the method of equivalents combined with the constant method, both under varied instructions more or less like your own, with a view partly to clearing up certain points about the methods themselves and partly also of confirming or extending the results already obtained that bear upon the effect of attitude. . . . I am . . . not instructing our observers, in the alternate experiments, to attend to sensations in the wrist or fingers or wherever–I have long been of the opinion that one cannot attend to sensation at all–but rather to the pressure pattern localised in the fingers, the pressure pattern localised in the wrist, and so on.

Notice that Titchener is speaking the language of independent variables (instruction and place of localization), studied under controlled conditions, with standard procedures. The orientation of Titchener's thought is modern in its reliance on design and on the search for operationally tractable variables. Note also the important shift away from sensations as elemental units, and toward *attributes* of sensation.

For Titchener, psychology would progress only by directing experiments against the problems of mind. If the experiments were well controlled, the observers properly trained, and the pitfalls of armchair introspection and stimulus error avoided, then psychological science could generate reliable knowledge just as the natural sciences had. But the field needed guardians, and the right problems. If one aimed too high – as Külpe did – the result might be nothing. If one aimed too low, then cumulative progress could not be expected. The following letter to a former student captures Titchener's vision of where psychology stood as of 1922 and where it needed to go in the future:[52]

> You understand that I gave up sensations altogether and have long done so. What I am concerned with in my own mind is the number and nature of the dimensions of the psychological world, just precisely as the physicist is concerned with mass and time and space as the dimensions of his physical world. The immediate difference between the two worlds is that psychology has a dimension of quality. Our first step in grappling with this dimension is, of course, to secure the intramodal arrangements, such as we already have in the colour pyramid, the taste and smell figures, and possibly in my own

touch pyramid. . . . When we have all these intramodal groups of qualitative series properly worked out and arranged, then we can go on to two further questions: first, to your question of the intermodal relationships, and secondly to the more general question of integration.

The letter reveals a closeness to models of laboratory data that tells us a good deal about how Titchener pursued psychology. He was, above all, a data-driven psychologist for whom "the laboratory is all-important," and he conceived of the laboratory as an ongoing source of new knowledge, rather than as the source of applied technologies, or of demonstrations of principles derived elsewhere.

Most important, the letter reveals what Titchener regarded as the programmatic goals of his laboratory – first to map the intramodal arrangements, then to establish the intermodal arrangements. The publication of his students during the fourth period reveal just how systematically this goal was pursued. Of 91 published experimental studies, 67 (74%) deal with sensory issues, and most of these fit within the context described in his 1922 letter to Ruckmick. Boring's 1933 book, *The Physical Dimensions of Consciousness,* provides the best summary of the outcome of the program – a view of mind as composed of interlocking dimensions of consciousness, with each sensory attribute varying along a continuum.[53] As Boring points out, we do not know if Titchener would have agreed with all aspects of his construal of the data, even though the 91 papers mentioned earlier form the basis of the book. But Titchener had clearly provided a large share of the laboratory underpinnings for such a view, and his own views were changing as a result.

In the standard account, Titchener's laboratory is said to be modeled after Wundt's in its use of the method of introspection. This view is false, first because Wundt's lab placed more emphasis on the programmatic use of reaction time methods than on introspection as such, and second because Titchener placed prime emphasis on the careful control of conditions leading up to the introspection.[54] Titchener's was an *experimentally* based introspection, in which the observer's judgments occurred only under strictly controlled conditions of stimulus presentation and manipulation. The emphasis on introspection as the major dependent variable distinguished his procedure from that of Wundt, with whom Titchener differed publically on this issue in 1899.[55] Further, for Wundt, experimental methods were only useful for the analysis of low-level physiological processes, whereas for Titchener they could be applied to higher processes, provided that the proper techniques were used.

Finally, we are in a position to re-evaluate two earlier claims about the shift in Titchener's system after 1915. As noted previously, both Boring and Evans have described such a shift, but both, it seems to me, place it in the wrong context. The first stirrings of systematic change occurred during the imageless thought series, beginning in 1907. After 1915 the change accelerated; it was only during this phase that large numbers of coordinated experiments were directed against the fundamental tenets of the system, sensations and the attributes of sensations. The laboratory results came quickly and so did the theoretical shifts. One part of the great tragedy of Titchener's early death is the interruption of his laboratory program.

TITCHENER AND POSITIVISM

Positivism in the broadest sense, the view that only scientific method can lead to knowledge and that science must be based on facts, has been an underlying theme in English philosophical thought at least since Hume. Later positivists argued that a science of mind could be based on experimental methods, a view that was especially popular in Germany and in England, where experiment was seen as the foundation of a scientific psychology distinct from physiology. Titchener combined an English insistence on the primacy of sensations and sensory attributes as elements of mind with a Germanic emphasis on the importance of experiment. At Leipzig, Titchener became close friends with Külpe, whose *Outlines of Psychology* (1894) approached the topics of Wundtian psychology from a Machean positivist standpoint. Titchener, like Külpe but unlike Wundt, set no limits to the power of the experimental method in psychology. Furthermore, Titchener took a strong stand against excessive reliance on philosophy:[56]

> I think I must have told you, when you were here, that I thought it was impossible in our generation to write a system of psychology. That position I still adhere to. I have, however, never denied that we are now in a position to write at psychology systematically; and this is all that I myself have in mind to do. A system of psychology, fully rounded out and complete, could hardly nowadays be more than philosophical—at any rate that is my judgment still. But I think we have a large enough body of data to be able to present the subject in a systematic schema, so that future generations may see that we had not been altogether dependent upon philosophy for our conceptual scaffolding.

Titchener derived his positivism most clearly from Ernst Mach, whose view of the essential identity of all science was reflected in Titchener's lifelong attempt to argue that all science deals with experience considered from different points of view.[57] Titchener, like Mach, had no theory of the self. His was not a functionalist view, with an adapting organism at the center of its environment, but a structuralist view like Mach's or even

Hume's, rather than Darwin's. From this vantage point, we can see why Titchener wanted to avoid "stimulus error," which he considered to be a functionalist trap, and how very different his psychology was from that of Wundt or William James. In fact, Titchener represented a third pole. Both Wundt and James regarded Darwin's theory of evolution by natural selection as an important contribution to psychology, whereas Titchener paid relatively little attention to Darwinian notions in his work.[58]

For Wundt and James, purpose and will were important, if problematic, constructs. Wundt constructed a psychological system in which willed acts were at the center of psychological functioning. He used his system in the *Völkerpsychologie* to account for the historical development of consciousness. For James, the primacy of the willed act was expressed in the pragmatic solution to a psychological conundrum: The first act of will was to believe in free will, a formulation that led him to pragmatism.[59] For Titchener, the conundrum of will was eliminated. The goal of science was served only by eliminating constructs, like will, that could not be brought directly into observation. The radical extirpation of such concepts from psychology continued when behaviorism emerged, but traces of the same spirit can be clearly seen in Mach's and James' treatment of will as movement, and in the de-emphasis of such topics by Külpe and Titchener.[60] In his texts, Titchener provided only the most superficial account of will and volition. These were teleological concepts based only on common sense – the business of science was to get beyond such views. Insofar as Titchener dealt at all with will, it was to consider it as an aspect of sensation.[61] Similarly, attention was regarded as an attribute of sensation, a reductionist approach further developed by Titchener's student Dallenbach.[62]

Most radical, perhaps, was Titchener's attempt to remove meaning from the domain of phenomena to be explained by psychology: "I have no theory of meaning. It seems to me that the logic of science must assume both fact and meaning as given; the one is as ultimate as the other."[63] It is possible to see in this statement the close affinity of Titchener and the behaviorists. It explains in part his close personal relation with John Watson and the surprising similarity of Titchener's views to those of some later positivist psychologists.[64] In particular, B. F. Skinner based his psychological investigations of language on the premise that meaning could play no direct role in a psychology of language.[65] Skinner, like Titchener, eschewed formal sources of hypotheses in favor of those derived from experimentation. It is interesting that Skinner was a graduate student and fellow at Harvard during a period (1928 to 1936) when E. G. Boring ran the department and supervised a course taken by Skinner that used Titchener's quantitative manual – a book that repelled Skinner.[66] Yet both Titchener and Skinner are the intellectual descendents of Ernst Mach.[67] If the young behaviorist revolted against the older psychology, he did not revolt against its basic conception of how science ought to be conducted.[68]

TITCHENER'S ROLE IN HISTORY

If the above account is correct, then we must rethink Titchener's role in the development of American psychology. It is not his reliance on introspection that is the most important aspect of his thought, nor his structuralist theory of the analysis of mind. Instead, his reliance on experimental laboratory research and his espousal of a positivist view in psychology were the important influences emerging from Titchener's career. Titchener believed that psychology was a new endeavor, one that would necessarily change as it developed: "Generations will come and pass before the straight road of psychological endeavour lies, plain and unobstructed, before the eyes of the student."[69] That road could only be made clear by programmatic experimentation.

Conceived in this fashion, experimentation imposes a hard discipline. The uncontrivability of laboratory results sometimes demands that the investigator be willing to give up cherished views. This is psychologically difficult: Scientists, like anyone facing a difficult inference, are subject to confirmation bias, a tendency to seek and use only information that confirms their own views, and to ignore disconfirmatory information.[70] Yet disconfirmation does occur. Its importance is sometimes acknowledged, and it constitutes an essential heuristic in actual science.[71]

Titchener's experiments functioned, in this regard, in a normative fashion; they led him to change his theoretical views about the nature and role of sensations, and led him and his followers to new empirical findings. We tend to regard his system as a failed one; there are no Titchnerian structuralists today. But there are, and have been, other experimentalists of a Titchnerian stripe – programmatic, data-driven, and open to the consequences of disconfirmation. Historically, Titchener must then be credited with helping to collapse Wundt's distinction between the experimental study of basic mental processes and the comparative study of higher mental processes. Although Titchener's method of controlled introspection has no adherents today, his view of the broad power of the experimental method is, in some quarters, received doctrine. For better or worse, Titchener helped to create the doctrine, and it is this fact that, for the historian, requires close analysis of his work.

NOTES

1 H. Gruber, *Darwin on Man* (New York: Dutton, 1974); A. I. Miller, *Imagery in Scientific Thought* (New York: Birkhauser, 1985).

2 F. L. Holmes, *Claude Bernard and Animal Chemistry* (Cambridge: Harvard University Press, 1984); M. Rudwick, *The Great Devonian Controversy* (Chicago:

University of Chicago Press, 1985). A similar tendency can be seen among sociologists of science, e.g., in K. D. Knorr-Cetina, *The Manufacture of Knowledge* (Oxford: Pergamon Press, 1981), and among philosophers of science, e.g., T. Nickles (ed.), *Scientific Discovery, Logic, and Rationality* (Dordrecht: D. Reidel, 1980).

3 The present argument clearly owes much to the work of I. Lakatos, *Proofs and Refutations* (Cambridge: Cambridge University Press, 1973).

4 I have used a cognitive approach to analyze Faraday's diary records in "Faraday's Discovery of Induction: A Cognitive Approach," in D. Gooding and F. James (eds.), *Faraday Rediscovered* (London: Macmillan, 1985). See also the chapter introductions in R. D. Tweney, M. E. Doherty, and C. R. Mynatt (eds.), *On Scientific Thinking* (New York: Columbia University Press, 1981).

5 See, in particular, L. Fleck, *Genesis and Development of a Scientific Fact* (1935) (Chicago: University of Chicago Press, 1979).

6 C. Glymour, *Theory and Evidence* (Princeton: Princeton University Press, 1980).

7 E. G. Boring, *A History of Experimental Psychology* (1929), 2nd ed. (New York: Appleton-Century-Crofts, 1950); D. Schultz, *A History of Modern Psychology,* 2nd ed. (New York: Academic Press, 1975), 84.

8 A. L. Blumenthal, "A Reappraisal of Wilhelm Wundt," *American Psychologist,* 30 (1975):1081–1088; W. B. Bringmann and R. D. Tweney (eds.), *Wundt Studies: A Centennial Collection* (Toronto: C. J. Hogrefe, 1980); K. Danziger, "The Positivist Repudiation of Wundt," *Journal of the History of the Behavioral Sciences* 15 (1979):205–230.

9 R. D. Tweney and S. Yachanin, "Titchener's Wundt," in Bringmann and Tweney (eds.), *Wundt Studies.* See also T. H. Leahey, "The Mistaken Error: On Wundt's and Titchener's Psychologies," *Journal of the History of the Behavioral Sciences* 17 (1981):273–282; S. Toulmin and D. E. Leary, "The Cult of Empiricism in Psychology and Beyond," in S. Koch and D. E. Leary (eds.), *A Century of Psychology as Science* (New York: McGraw-Hill, 1985); R. Evans, "Introduction," in E. B. Titchener, *A Textbook of Psychology* (1910) (Delmar, NY: Scholar's Facsimiles and Reprints, 1980).

10 The account of Titchener's life given here is very brief. A longer account is given by E. G. Boring, "Edward Bradford Titchener, 1867–1927," *American Journal of Psychology* 38 (1927):489–506. Critical evaluations of Titchener's work are given by E. Heidbreder, *Seven Psychologies* (New York: Appleton-Century-Crofts, 1933) and M. Henle, "Did Titchener Commit the Stimulus Error? The Problem of Meaning in Structural Psychology," *Journal of the History of the Behavioral Sciences* 7 (1971):279–282. A good primary source introduction is E. B. Titchener, "The Schema of Introspection," *American Journal of Psychology* 23 (1912):485–508.

11 G. L. Geison, *Michael Foster and the Cambridge School of Physiology* (Princeton: Princeton University Press, 1978); J. T. Merz, *A History of European Thought in the Nineteenth Century (1896),* 3rd ed., Vol. 2 (Edinburgh: William Blackwood and Sons, 1903), 428–429.

12 J. Burdon-Sanderson (ed.), *Handbook for the Physiological Laboratory* (Philadelphia: Lindsay and Blakiston, 1873).

13 J. Burdon-Sanderson, *Syllabus of a Course of Lectures on Physiology,* 2nd ed. (Philadelphia: Lindsay & Blakiston, 1880).

14 Tweney & Yachanin, "Titchener's Wundt."

15 E. B. Titchener, "Über binoculare Wirkungen monocularer Reize," *Philosophische Studien* 8 (1892):231–310; E. B. Titchener, "On the Binocular Effects of Monocular Stimulation," *International Congress of Experimental Psychology* (London: 1892), 120–121.

16 E. B. Titchener, "Dr. Münsterberg and Experimental Psychology," *Mind* 16 (1891):621–634; E. B. Titchener, "The Leipsic School of Experimental Psychology," *Mind* N.S. 1 (1892):397–400.

17 G. Adams, "Titchener at Cornell," *American Mercury* 24 (1931):440–446; F. Angell, "Titchener at Leipzig," *Journal of General Psychology* 1 (1928):195–198.

18 E. G. Boring, "Edward Bradford Titchener, 1867–1927," *American Journal of Psychology* 38 (1927):489–406; cf. M. A. Tinker, "Wundt's Doctorate Students" (1932), in Bringmann and Tweney (eds.), *Wundt Studies.* Furthermore, the bulk of dissertations sponsored by Wundt were not based on experimental work, whereas nearly all of Titchener's were.

19 W. Wundt, *Principles of Physiological Psychology (1874),* Vol. 1, trans. E. B. Titchener from 5th German ed. (1902) (London: Swan Sonnenschein, 1904); O. Külpe, *Outlines of Psychology, Based Upon the Results of Experimental Investigation* (1893), trans. E. B. Titchener (London: Swan Sonnenschein & Co., 1895); E. B. Titchener, *A Text-book of Psychology* (New York: Macmillan, 1909/1910); E. B. Titchener, *An Outline of Psychology* (New York: Macmillan, 1896).

20 E. B. Titchener, *Systematic Psychology: Prolegomena,* ed. H. P. Weld (New York: Macmillan, 1929).

21 R. B. Evans, "E. B. Titchener and his Lost System," *Journal of the History of the Behavioral Sciences* 8 (1972):168–180.

22 E. B. Titchener & E. W. Scripture, "Some Apparatus for Cutaneous Stimulation," *American Journal of Psychology* 6 (1893):424–426; H. C. Howe, "Mediate Association," ibid., 239–241; A. R. Hill and R. Watanabe, "Sensorial and Muscular Reactions," ibid., 242–246.

23 Titchener to Lowell, 13 June 1917. This and all subsequent quoted letters (except as noted) are in the collection of the Department of Manuscripts and University Archives, John M. Olin Library, Cornell University.

24 K. Danziger, "The Origins of the Psychological Experiment as a Social Institution," *American Psychologist* 40 (1985):131–141.

25 E. B. Titchener, "Some Current Problems in Experimental Psychology," *Natural Science* 4 (1894):446–449.

26 E. B. Titchener, "The Postulates of a Structural Psychology," *Philosophical Review* 7 (1898):449–465.

27 E. B. Titchener, *Experimental Psychology, A Manual of Laboratory Practice. Vol. I, Qualitative Experiments; Vol. II, Quantitative Experiments,* Two volumes in four parts (New York: Macmillan, 1901/1905).

28 The evidence for this claim is my subjective sense of the comparative ease with which surviving copies of the qualitative student manual can be located in American libraries and in the antiquarian book market, compared to the quantitative student manual.

29 *Experimental Psychology,* Vol. I, vii–viii.

30 C. H. Judd, *Psychology: General Introduction* (New York: Scribner's, 1907); *Laboratory Manual of Psychology* (New York: Scribner's, 1907); *Laboratory Equipment for Psychological Experiments* (New York: Scribner's, 1907). Judd's revision of his text in 1917 diluted the voluntarism with heavy doses of functionalism. By 1917, Judd was engaged in research on educational psychology at the University of Chicago, and no longer appeared "Wundtian," as he had during his Yale days.

31 Comparative frequency of surviving copies is again the indicator I am using.

32 J. R. Angell, "Review of E. B. Titchener's *Experimental Psychology, Volume I, Qualitative Experiments, Parts I & II,*" *American Journal of Psychology* 12 (1901):596–600, here: 596, and J. R.Angell, "Review of E. B. Titchener's *Experimental Psychology, Volume II, Quantitative, Parts I & II,*" *American Journal of Psychology* 17 (1906):585–593, here: 585.

33 Watson to Titchener, 19 December 1908 (see note 23).

34 E. B. Titchener, *Lectures on the Elementary Psychology of Feeling and Attention* (New York: Macmillan, 1908).

35 Ibid., 316.

36 E. B. Titchener, *Lectures on the Experimental Psychology of the Thought Processes* (New York: Macmillan, 1909).

37 G. Humpherey, *Thinking: An Introduction to its Experimental Psychology* (London: Methuen and Co., 1951).

38 Ibid., 104. See also Titchener's letter to T. A. Hunter of 17 May 1908, in L. B. Brown and A. H. Fuchs, *The Letters Between Sir Thomas Hunter and E. B. Titchener* (Victoria University of Wellington Publication in Psychology, No. 23; Wellington, N.Z.: Department of Psychology, Victoria University of Wellington, 1969).

39 Titchener, *Thought Processes.*

40 M. F. Washburn, *Movement and Mental Imagery* (Boston: Houghton Mifflin, 1916); R. S. Woodworth, "A Revision of Imageless Thought," *Psychological Review,* 22 (1915):1–27.

41 Titchener, *Thought-processes,* 182.

42 W. H. Pyle, "An Experimental Study of Expectation," *American Journal of Psychology* 20 (1909):530–569; T. Okabe, "An Experimental Study of Belief," *American Journal of Psychology* 21 (1910):563–596; H. M. Clarke, "Conscious Attitudes," *American Journal of Psychology* 22 (1911):214–249; E. Jacobson, "On Meaning and Understanding," ibid., 553–577; E. B. Titchener, "A Note on the Consciousness of Self," ibid., 540–552; E. B. Titchener, "Description vs. Statement of Meaning," *American Journal of Psychology* 23 (1912):165–182.

43 E. B. Titchener, "The Method of Examination," *American Journal of Psychology* 24 (1913):429. For Koffka's critique, see M. G. Ash, *The Emergence of Gestalt Theory: Experimental Psychology in Germany 1890–1920* (Ph.D. Dissertation, Harvard University, 1982). Koffka disliked Titchener's use of concepts that were merely descriptive and not functional. Whereas the Gestalt psychologists regarded form as irreducible, Titchener's elementism could not accept this. In later years, he may have moderated this view; see Titchener to T. A. Hunter, 31 July 1924, cited in Brown and Fuchs, note 38.

44 See footnote 42 for references.

45 Titchener, "The Method of Examination," 436.

46 E. B. Titchener, "Sensation and System," *American Journal of Psychology* 26 (1915):258–267; Evans, "Titchener and his Lost System"; E. G. Boring, *The Physical Dimensions of Consciousness* (New York: The Century Co., 1933).

47 Many criticisms of Titchener have made the same point in recent years, without acknowledging the fact that Titchener himself raised the issue, and that it led to a revision of his views. See for example, Humphrey, *Thinking,* and Henle, "Did Titchener Commit the Stimulus Error?" An excellent recent analysis is K. A. Ericsson & H. A. Simon, *Protocol Analysis: Verbal Reports as Data* (Cambridge: MIT Press, 1984), 50–57. See also E. G. Boring, "Titchener and the Existential," *American Journal of Psychology* 50 (1937):470–483.

48 R. S. Woodworth, *Experimental Psychology* (New York: Holt, 1938), 790.

49 E. Jacobson, "Further Experiments on the Inhibition of Sensations," *American Journal of Psychology* 23 (1912):345–366.

50 E. Jacobson, "Progressive Relaxation," *American Journal of Psychology* 36 (1925), 86.

51 Titchener to Fernberger, 2 December 1922 (see note 23).

52 Titchener to C. A. Ruckmick, 26 October 1922.

53 Boring, *Physical Dimensions* (note 46).

54 On Wundt's methods, see Danziger, "Wundt's Psychological Experiment"; W. G. Bringmann, D. G. Balance and R. Evans, "Wilhelm Wundt 1832–1920: A Brief Biographical Sketch," *Journal of the History of the Behavioral Sciences* 11 (1975):287–297.

55 E. B. Titchener, "Zur Kritik der Wundt'schen Gefühlslehre," *Zeitschrift für Psychologie* 19 (1899):321–326; W. Wundt, "Bemerkungen zur Theorie der Gefühle," *Philosophische Studien* 15 (1900):149–182.

56 Titchener to G. Tschelpanow, 25 October 1924 (see note 23).

57 E. Mach, *Die Analyse der Empfindungen und das Verhlältnis des Physischen zum Psychischen* (1886) (Jena: Fischer, 1896); *The Analysis of the Sensations and the Relation of the Physical to the Psychical,* trans. from the 1st German Edition by C. M. Williams, revised and supplemented from the 5th German edition by S. Waterlow (Chicago: Open Court, 1911). Cf. Danziger, "The Positivist Repudiation of Wundt" (note 8).

58 R. J. Richards, "Wundt's Early Theories of Unconscious Inference and Cognitive Evolution in Their Relation to Darwinian Biopsychology," in Bringmann and Tweney (eds.), *Wundt Studies* (note 8).

59 H. James (ed.), *The Letters of William James,* Vol. 1 (Boston: Atlantic Monthly Press, 1920), 147.

60 Mach, *Analysis of Sensations,* 100; James, *Principles of Psychology* (New York: Holt, 1890), Vol. 2, 486–592; Külpe, *Outlines,* 214–215, 265–267; Titchener, *Outline,* 234–236.

61 Titchener, *Feelings and Attention.* Mary Henle has recently shown that Titchener similarly reduced emotion to sensory elements. See her *1879 and All That: Essays in the Theory and History of Psychology* (New York: Columbia University Press, 1986).

62 E. G. Boring, "Karl M. Dallenbach," *American Journal of Psychology* 71 (1958):1–49; K. M. Dallenbach, "The Measurement of Attention," *American Journal of Psychology* 24 (1913):465–507.

63 Titchener to Boring, 14 January 1927 (see note 23).

64 A. C. Catania, "The Psychologies of Structure, Function and Development," *American Psychologist* 28 (1973):434–443; C. Larsen and J. L. Sullivan, "Watson's Relation to Titchener," *Journal of the History of the Behavioral Sciences* 1

(1965):338–354. Evans has argued that Titchener's views on meaning were formed in the 1890s as an outgrowth of his dissatisfaction with Wundt's concept of apperception. See R. B. Evans, "The Origins of Titchener's Doctrine of Meaning," *Journal of the History of the Behavioral Sciences* 11 (1975):334–341.

65 See B. F. Skinner, *Verbal Behavior* (New York: Appleton-Century-Crofts, 1957) and *The Shaping of a Behaviorist* (New York: Alfred A. Knopf, 1979); cf. W. F. Day, "The Historical Antecedents of Behaviorism," in R. W. Rieber and K. Salzinger (eds.), *Psychology: Theoretical-Historical Perspectives* (New York: Academic Press, 1980).

66 Skinner, *Shaping of a Behaviorist,* 8–9, 47.

67 See also Boring's *Physical Dimensions of Consciousness,* which is physicalistic and Titchenerian.

68 In an attempt to gain further information on this point, I wrote to Skinner inquiring whether he had been influenced by any particular figure as a model of programmatic research as such. His reply does not directly settle the issue, but is of some interest as a confirmation of the point that his work was carried out in a programmatic fashion:

> You raise an interesting point which I hope to treat at the end of Volume IV [of his ongoing autobiography]. My work was certainly inner-directed in comparison, say, with Tolman, Hull, Harlow, Hilgard, and Hebb, who were . . . "eclectic." They did experiments on a great many topics.
>
> I am afraid the explanation is mainly my ignorance of the field of psychology. I never read widely, never had undergraduate instruction in the field, and only occasionally experimented on a topic out of curiosity. B. F. Skinner to R. D. Tweney, 27 June 1980, in the collection of the author.

In another context, Skinner added: "I am quite sure that Titchener had no programmatic effect on me through Boring or through his laboratory manual. . . . Bridgman, Mach, and Poincare did the job." B. F. Skinner to R. D. Tweney, 18 May 1981, in the collection of the author.

69 Titchener, *Systematic Psychology,* 270.

70 The literature on this topic up to 1980 is reviewed in Tweney, et al., *On Scientific Thinking,* note 4. See also R. D. Tweney and M. E. Doherty, "Rationality and the Psychology of Inference," *Synthese* 57 (1983):139–162; I. C. Mitroff, *The Subjective Side of Science* (Amsterdam: Elsevier, 1974); C. R. Mynatt, M. E. Doherty and R. D. Tweney, "Consequences of Confirmation and Disconfirmation in a Simulated Research Environment," *Quarterly Journal of Experimental Psychology* 30 (1978):395–406; R. Nisbett and L. Ross, *Human Inference: Strategies and Shortcomings of Social Judgment* (Englewood Cliffs, NJ: Prentice-Hall, 1980).

71 Tweney, "Faraday's Discovery of Induction" (note 4).

3

NEO-BEHAVIORISM AND THE GARCIA EFFECT: A SOCIAL PSYCHOLOGY OF SCIENCE APPROACH TO THE HISTORY OF A PARADIGM CLASH*

IAN LUBEK and ERIKA APFELBAUM

GARCIA AND SCIENTIFIC PROGRESS IN PSYCHOLOGY: SUCCESS OR BLOCKAGE?

Our discussion of the development of the experimental learning or learning theory subarea of psychology will focus on just one episode: the 30-year challenge that psychologist John Garcia's novel, anomalous research offered to a deeply established mainstream's neo-behavioristic version (or vision) of learning theory.[1] The paradigm clash began in 1955 with Garcia's first publication on learning, in which he demonstrated that thirsty rats would radically reverse their consummatory behavior, adamantly refusing to drink a previously preferred saccharine solution following exposure to an unusual stimulus – gamma or X rays.[2] This novel finding, since labeled the Garcia effect, gave rise to a program of research that has had both important *theoretical* ramifications for long-standing neo-behaviorist principles of learning and important *practical* implications for the understanding of radiation sickness, substance abuse treatment, control of predators by farmers and ranchers, and other problems.[3]

Suddenly, however, in 1965 Garcia found his articles no longer welcome in mainstream journals, at precisely the moment when his accumulating evidence insistently pointed to the need for a reformulation of

* Written while the first author was visiting the Laboratoire de Psychologie Sociale of the C.N.R.S. and Université de Paris VII. The authors wish to thank J. Garcia, S. Revusky, P. Swingle, E. Cahan, N. Innes, H. Hurwitz, and G. McGuire for their assistance at various stages of the research, and colleagues who provided feedback on earlier versions presented as colloquia and at the 1981 meeting of the Cheiron Society. We also thank J. Garcia and S. Revusky for permission to cite personal communications and documents from their files. We gratefully acknowledge the financial support of Canada Council, Social Sciences and Humanities Research Council (Leave Fellowship and Research Grants Programmes), Research Advisory Board of the University of Guelph, and the program of scientific exchanges between the C.N.R.S. of France and the SSHRC.

S-R learning theory. To shed light on the complex historical roots of this paradigm clash between Garcia effect research and the neo-behaviorist formulation, our account must consider seemingly contradictory indications about the reception of Garcia's ideas within the discipline of psychology. By the late 1970s, his manuscripts were still being rejected by mainstream journals, although at the same time his research was receiving professional recognition and prestigious awards. In 1978, he was elected to the Society of Experimental Psychologists and presented with the 44th H. C. Warren Medal for Outstanding Research in Psychology; in 1979, he joined 71 other psychologists awarded the Distinguished Scientific Contribution Award of the American Psychological Association (APA); and by 1983, he was among the less than 100 psychologists elected to the National Academy of Sciences since 1901. Everett Wyers, a consulting editor of the APA's *Journal of Comparative Psychology,* pointed out that this last award may signify Garcia's impact not just on comparative and learning psychology, but his "contributions to other sciences and their acceptance thereof: e.g., radiation research, toxicology, ethology, and biology in general."[4]

But if we probe beyond the surface of this seeming professional success, the contradictions and problems emerge. For example, when Garcia received the APA's Distinguished Scientific Contribution Award, his acceptance talk at the 1980 convention was published, as was the custom for all award winners, in the most widely distributed mainstream psychology journal, the *American Psychologist.*[5] In this article, entitled "Tilting at the Papermills of Academe," Garcia made allusion to, and drew illustrations from, the tale of Don Quixote, indicating that he had had difficulties with various journal editors and humorously attributing the rejection of his papers to the "neophobia of editorial consultants." Several of the nine illustrations accompanying the paper, which were satirically critical of learning theory, were removed from the published version by the *American Psychologist* editors. More important is that this article was only the *second* to appear in an APA journal authored or co-authored by Garcia during the previous *eighteen* years. Thus, a puzzling question remains: Why should the APA honor a psychologist whose work was conspicuously absent for almost two decades from its own mainstream journals?

We will treat the discovery and dissemination of the Garcia effect and related unusual findings as both an overall scientific success story and as a case study of a mainstream, "normal science" paradigm's supporters' attempts to block, marginalize, or reject a deviant set of scientific ideas anomalous enough to merit a paradigmatic shift.[6] From a social psychology of science perspective, we will look at the interactions between editors and authors in order to examine the roles of mainstream journals and their editorial decision makers in the control and dissemination of normal science and novel ideas. Sam Revusky used personal and archival data to create an intraparadigmatic or internalist account documenting, in almost Talmudic detail, the maltreatment of Garcia's work by the psychological establishment.[7] Using public domain materials as well, we have tried to adopt a broader approach. With the cooperation of Garcia and others involved, we were able to amass additional archival documentation, correspondence, and interviews.[8]

Because of the important practical implications of Garcia's work, research funding was always available, and he was therefore able to conduct research actively while struggling to find alternate channels for diffusion of his ideas. In this way, Garcia's ideas did not become completely invisible, as might happen to work of a researcher or apprentice deprived of both institutional support and publication outlets. Garcia's research and perspective thus persistently confronted, albeit frequently from nonmainstream publications, the dominant neo-behaviorist learning theory at a time when that paradigm, once the core element in the thinking, research, and training of psychologists, was already showing its age. In the long run, his findings may therefore have helped to speed up its decline.

S-R WARS: THE SAGA BEGINS

Learning theorists have generally shared the same superordinate goal of wishing to reveal scientifically the complex laws causally linking such concepts as reinforcement, stimulus (S), and response (R). During the 1930s and 1940s, the rival paradigmatic formulations offered by Edward Tolman, E. R. Guthrie, B. F. Skinner, the Gestalt psychologists and Kurt Lewin, and the neo-behaviorism of Clark Hull, Kenneth Spence, and their colleagues and students at Yale and Iowa, battled it out in the pages of the journals to see whether S-R, S-S, or R-R laws would triumph. Between the 1930s and the 1960s, all challenges, including that from Tolman's S-S cognitivist rebels, were outgunned by the legions of S-R warrior-researchers from the neo-behaviorist empire. Thus, Garcia's confrontation with neo-behaviorism must be seen against the backdrop of this wider struggle for theoretical, methodological, and institutional dominance, waged at a time when the area of experimental learning was considered central to all psychological theory and practice.

Paradigmatic development and rivalry

In the 1930s, Hull began a program of research to generate, via the hypothetico-deductive method, a systematic set of laws, principles, and mathematical formulas to describe "the fundamental, molar principles of behavior." Aided by a talented group of productive collaborators

(Spence, Neal E. Miller, O. Hobart Mowrer, Carl I. Hovland, Robert R. Sears, and numerous others), the Hull-Spence system was carried forth beyond Yale and Iowa, and to areas beyond experimental psychology – for example, to social, developmental, clinical, and physiological psychology – to the point where it had obtained an almost "prescriptive" hold on general psychology.[9] Hull was a tireless proselytizer with a wide network of researchers who shared his enthusiasm for creating a systematic learning theory.[10] According to data gathered for us by Emily Cahan at Yale University, Hull, during his tenure of about 23 years, directed the PhD theses of 21 students. In addition, a total of 18 other PhDs offer some acknowledgment of Hull's assistance. Among 22 pre-1955 Yale PhDs who provided comments, several suggested that until failing health intervened after World War II, Hull's influence through his teaching was quite strong.[11]

Other theses at Yale were probably also influenced to varying degrees by Hull's thought and its neo-behaviorist derivatives. Hovland and Miller, for example, each supervised 17 doctorates during the period 1939–1955. Spence, in conjunction with Miller's student, J. S. Brown, and his own student, I. Farber, helped spread S-R theory at Iowa, where he managed to train 73 PhD students between 1940 and 1964.[12] He then moved to the University of Texas and supervised two more PhDs before his untimely death in 1967. (Hull died in 1952.) In the decade 1941–1950, according to Spence, 70% of learning and motivation articles in the *Journal of Experimental Psychology (JEP)* and the *Journal of Comparative and Physiological Psychology (JCPP)* cited one or more of Hull's works, while Guttman found that the proportion of all *JEP* articles citing Hull or Spence had increased from 4% in 1940 and 39% in 1950, to 24% in 1960, but fell back to 4% in 1970.[13] Thus, the Hull-Spence formulation appeared to be dominant in the 1940s, 1950s, and into the 1960s, when it encountered a new set of strong paradigmatic challenges.

Space limitations preclude discussion of several competing formulations that were prominent in the journals and textbooks of the 1930s through the 1950s, for example, Guthrie's, or gestalt-field formulations such as Kurt Koffka's or Lewin's. The Skinnerian operant paradigm developed slowly after the publication of *The Behavior of Organisms.*[14] By the time the Skinnerian *Journal for the Experimental Analysis of Behavior (JEAB)* was founded in 1957, there were only about 24 active operant researchers.[15] Eventually that number grew and APA's Division 25, the Society for the Experimental Analysis of Behavior, came to represent the operant research community, with 1,530 members (or about 4% of total APA members) in 1975, and 1,465 members in 1983 (now only 2.6% of the total). Rather than appearing in the pages of, for example, the *Journal of Experimental Psychology,* operant ideas were disseminated in applied areas such as education and psychotherapy. By remaining in relative isolation and avoiding a direct confrontation with other learning theories, this formulation emerged relatively unscathed from the debates in the literature of the 1930s, 1940s, and 1950s, and slowly gestated and expanded during the 1960s and 1970s, while the S-R formulation was beginning to come under attack and wane.[16]

Edward Chace Tolman's formulation of purposive behavior, sign-gestalt or cognitive learning, added a phenomenological dimension to behaviorism – something vigorously opposed by the neo-behaviorists.[17] In addition, Tolman put forward an alternate methodological position to that of the hypothetico-deductive model preferred by neo-behaviorists, the ecological, probabilistic functionalism of Brunswik.[18] Disagreements about whether rats and other creatures learned neo-behaviorist S-R associations through incremental buildup of habit or whether they cognitively developed "hypotheses" or "insights" about problem solutions pitted the mushrooming Yale-Iowa, neo-behaviorist, S-R learning theorists against the University of California at Berkeley's small band of S-S learning, purposive behaviorists, which included Tolman, Isidor Krechevsky (later David Krech), B. F. Ritchie, and others.[19] Followers of the "cryptophenomenologist" Tolman, the "Tolmaniacs," described rats as "little furry people," while S-R theorists thought of them as "little furry machines."[20] Although Tolman "deeply influenced those who worked with him," many of his students and colleagues went their own way, and he "left no 'crown prince' to carry on his theorizing" following his death in 1959.[21] Thus, the Tolman formulation was not as strongly defended as that of the rival neo-behaviorists, and by the end of World War II the latter was ascendant.[22] We have seen how the neo-behaviorist formulation came to dominate, and we will shortly look into the specific problems Garcia had in finding publication outlets for his anomalous ideas. First, however, let us look at how the organization of mainstream journals may mediate theoretical, methodological, and paradigmatic disputes. In keeping with our social psychology of science analysis of factors affecting scientific progress and/or blockage – to be described in a later section – we place special emphasis on the interactions between editorial decision makers and authors.

Journal editors: Promoters of paradigm progress or professional gatekeepers?

Editors have variously been described as censors, producers of conformity, or gatekeepers in the diffusion of information or innovations.[23] In the publish or perish atmosphere of many academic institutions, editorial decisions perform a joint function of "knowledge filtration" and contributing to the "social stratification system in science."[24] They thus determine both the progress of ideas and the progress of careers. Although much of their work involves routine quality-control decisions about whether "normal science" research fits the prevailing scientific standards, their role becomes more visible and critical when fraudulent science appears, during inter- or intraparadigmatic conflicts, or when lines of innovative or anomalous research are blocked or marginalized.[25]

When Garcia's anomalous findings confronted the neo-behaviorist mainstream, the major problem he encountered was with editorial gatekeepers. Before looking specifically at Garcia's interactions with various editors, we should first recall the research context within which learning theorists were working at the time and the legacy of the interparadigmatic battles from about 1930 onward. We want to question the extent to which, by the 1960s, these conflicting groups of researchers were represented in mainstream journal pages and on the editorial boards of mainstream journals. And we will want to see if there is a positive correlation between representation among editorial decision makers and acceptance or rejection of research manuscripts.

We had previously collected data for the 31 editors and associate editors of four important APA outlets for learning theory and research during the period 1955–1975: *Journal of Comparative and Physiological Psychology (JCPP), Psychological Review (PR), Psychological Bulletin (PB)* and *Journal of Experimental Psychology (JEP),* which subdivided into four sections in 1975.[26] Now, with the aid of Gregory McGuire, we are compiling data, as part of a more detailed study, on the contributions to these four journals of four prominent learning researchers – Hull, Spence, Tolman, and Skinner – and the students whose PhD theses they personally supervised.[27] We follow standard textbook practice and consider Hull and Spence together, in order to compare the impact of their neo-behaviorism with that of purposive behaviorism and Skinner's operant or radical behaviorism. We recorded their contributions as editorial *decision makers* (as editors, associate editors, and consulting editors), but not the *advisory roles* (as issue consultants, referees, or editorial consultants) and then looked at their published articles during the period 1930–1970 in the four APA mainstream journals (*JEP, JCPP, PR, PB*).

A preliminary analysis of this data seems to show some differences. Tolman and students preferred *JCPP;* the Hull-Spence group chose *JEP* more frequently; while Skinnerians, largely absent from all four, showed a slight preference for *JEP.* In fact, in none of the four decades did the Skinnerians contribute more than 1% of the articles in any journal. Although Tolman and company dominated the 1930s, with almost 4.4% overall for the four journals (and 10% of *JCPP* articles), productivity of this group in these mainstream journals declined steadily in the next 3 decades. By contrast, the Hull-Spence group expanded steadily to a peak of 9.3% of the total articles in all four journals for the 1950s, before experiencing a downturn to 4.2% in the 1960s. At the height of their ascen-

neo-behaviorists, and Skinnerian radical behaviorists in four APA journals.[a]

	1930–1940			1941–1950			1951–1960			1961–1970		
	Tol[b]	H-S	Sk	Tol	H-S	Sk	Tol	H-S	Sk	Tol	H-S	Sk
JCPP articles[c]	45	24	1	27	21	4	13	65	8	21	63	0
% total	9.7	5.2	.22	6.1	4.7	.9	1.1	5.5	0.7	1.2	3.7	0
Ed. Pers./Yrs.	0	0	0	0	0	0	0	9	3	5	28	10
% total	0	0	0	0	0	0	0	10.6	3.5	1.7	9.5	3.4
JEP articles	9	28	0	14	81	6	7	178	13	3	114	4
% total	1.1	3.4	0	2.0	11.8	.9	0.5	13.9	1.0	0.1	4.9	0.2
Ed. Pers./Yrs.	0	0	0	0	0	0	0	32	2	8	58	4
% total	0	0	0	0	0	0	0	18.8	1.2	2.1	15.2	1.1
PR articles	25	20	0	9	26	4	10	35	4	0	15	2
% total	7.1	5.7	0	2.3	6.7	1.0	2.3	8.2	0.9	0	3.9	0.5
Ed. Pers./Yrs.	0	0	0	0	0	0	5	5	1	0	0	0
% total	0	0	0	0	0	0	3.2	3.2	0.6	0	0	0
PB articles	7	4	0	5	4	0	6	20	1	0	9	0
% total	2.2	1.3	0	1.4	1.1	0	2.0	6.6	.3	0	1.3	0
Ed. Pers./Yrs.	0	0	0	0	1	0	2	5	0	4	8	0
% total	0	0	0	0	1.09	0	2.4	6.1	0	2.5	5.0	0
Total Articles	86	76	1	55	132	14	36	298	26	24	199	6
% total	4.4	3.9	.05	2.9	7.0	0.8	1.13	9.3	0.8	0.5	4.2	0.1
Ed. Pers./Yrs.	0	0	0	0	1	0	7	51	6	17	94	14
% total	0	0	0	0	0.5	0	1.4	10.3	1.2	2.5	11.1	1.7

[a] *Journal of Comparative and Physiological Psychology (JCPP); Journal of Experimental Psychology (JEP); Psychological Review (PR);* and *Psychological Bulletin (PB);* 11 years were studied in the 1930s.

[b] Key: Tol = Tolman and first-generation PHDs; H-S = Hull, Spence, and PhDs; Sk = Skinner and PhDs.

[c] (Number of published) Articles; Articles as a percentage of total articles published by journal during the decade; Number of years of service by persons on editorial boards as decision makers (Editor, Associate or Consulting Editor, but not editorial consultant, referee, or advisory editors); percentage of total person/years devoted to editorial decision making that decade.

dancy, during the 1940s and 1950s, the first-generation neo-behaviorists alone accounted for 11.8% and 13.9% of *JEP* articles.

Editorial board presence among direct participants in the "S-R Wars" was surprisingly absent until the later years. With the exception of one year of service by a neo-behaviorist on the *PR* editorial board in the 1940s, there was no other presence of the Tolman, neo-behaviorist, or Skinnerian first generations on any editorial board during the 1930s or the 1940s. In the 1950s and the 1960s, as the three groups began to gain representation in editorial decision-making positions, there was a rough parallel between the number of editorial board person-years and the number of articles contributed by each group.[28] Further time-sequence analyses will be required to decide between two hypotheses commonly found in the sociology of science literature: (1) the favoritism, cronyism, or conspiratorial group hypothesis suggests that when one gets decision-making or gatekeeping powers, they can *then* be used to promote research by like-minded colleagues and students; (2) the eminence hypothesis suggests that hard-working researchers are rewarded with honorifics such as editorial gatekeeping tasks, *after* their ideas have saturated the journals.[29]

This is part of the context in which we must examine Garcia's efforts to seek outlets for his ideas in mainstream APA journals during the 1950s, 1960s, and 1970s. At this time, the neo-behaviorist ideas of Hull-Spence learning theory were dominant, and Garcia's ideas, based on the teachings of Tolman and Krech, represented a minority on marginalized position. Table 3-1 indicates that during the two decades 1950–1970, four major APA outlets for experimental learning researchers (*PR, PB, JEP,* and *JCPP*) were decreasingly publishing Tolmanian articles, were publishing almost eight times as many articles by first generation neo-behaviorists, and had between 5.5 and seven times as many first-generation neo-behaviorists in place on editorial decision-making boards.

THE CAREER AND IDEAS OF JOHN GARCIA

I aspire to the cosmos, to the throne of God, not to discovering the laws of the two-lever Skinner box.[30]

Psychology from the standpoint of a Berkeleyist

After working as an automobile mechanic and a farm laborer, John Garcia entered the University of California at Berkeley on the GI Bill, and by 1949 had completed his MA in psychology. After a brief flirtation with social psychology, Garcia's interest in learning came under the influence of Tolman and such cognitivist co-workers as Krech and Ritchie.[31] They left Garcia to his own initiatives, all the while being "*very* supportive but also rather puzzled."[32] The intellectual climate at Berkeley was a rather eclectic and unique mix of ecological and probabilistic cognitive learning concepts and psychoanalytic social psychology, with a variety of researchers asking questions about genetic, personality, developmental, physiological, and (social) perceptual issues. Within such an intellectual milieu, Garcia reports that: "Quite naturally, I came to be sceptical about traditional learning theory."[33] In rejecting the mechanistic, S-R hypothetico-deductive formulations of neo-behaviorism and adhering to a Tolman-Brunswik phenomenological, cognitive, probabilistic perspective colored by his own interest in biology, Garcia's apprenticeship became indelibly stamped, perhaps even imprinted, with a meta-language of hypotheses, hedonic shifts, thoughts and insights, all of which would later identify his research as coming from the wrong side of the theoretical tracks. These were also stimulating times politically. Garcia recalls the turmoil during the McCarthyesque loyalty oath dispute at Berkeley, which caused Tolman to leave between August 1950 and January 1953. In 1951, Garcia left the program to take a full-time job as research psychologist with an interdisciplinary team at the U.S. Naval Radiological Defense Laboratory in San Francisco, where he could expand on his own biologically based variant of the cognitivist perspective. When he later embarked upon a full-time academic career in 1959, his advisors Krech and Ritchie encouraged him to finish his PhD (1965) for purposes of professional advancement.[34]

His apprenticeship at Berkeley had brought Garcia into the Tolman camp at a time when the rival Hull-Spence formulation of neo-behaviorism dominated. However, as we will see, Garcia's exclusion from learning theory was not immediate: he was given a 10-year period of grace before the mainstream publication doors were slammed shut.

An untrumpeted anomaly: the Garcia effect

Hindsight suggests that the publication in *Science* of the anomalous results of the conditioned taste-aversion study that would become known as the Garcia effect should have been immediately unsettling for mainstream learning theory for a number of reasons.[35] As the conditioned stimulus in this study, Garcia chose not to use the narrow range of traditional stimuli (tone, light, air-puff, or electric shock) but instead employed long-duration ionizing radiation. Also, Garcia did not focus on the usual motor responses used by Pavlovian, Skinnerian, or neo-behaviorist conditioners (running, jumping, blinking, pressing, etc.) but on the organism's alimentary and olfactory response systems. The novel choice of stimulus combined with an unusual response system helped highlight behavioral anomalies not seen in other studies. In this first study, the relative radiosensitivity of the effect and the relation of dosage to both strength of learning and resistance to extinction were discussed, and the suggestion was made that this phenomenon might exist for other avoidance behaviors.

A follow-up study reported on the temporal sequence of stimuli in conditioning, and quietly pointed out that the stimulus duration was "measured in hours, rather than seconds, as is the case in most classical conditioning studies."[36] Another study eliminated the visual system as a factor in saccharine avoidance and pointed to further anomalies, while yet another discussed the long duration of the stimulus, spatial aversions, and differences between their findings and that "traditionally observed" in avoidance learning.[37] When Garcia replied to a review article by Furchtgott, he stressed the peculiarities of ionizing radiation as a stimulus with both arousal and cue properties.[38] The period 1955–1965 was rather productive for Garcia, and his publications were easily visible to psychologists in highly prestigious journals. Each of the above-mentioned articles had appeared in an APA journal or in *Science*. Each article contained novel, unusual findings; however, during this period, these were couched in somewhat neutral language that did not aggressively attack the dominant S-R formulation. All of this was to change drastically in 1965.

The epistemological breakaway

The year 1965 was a breakaway year for Garcia. With a position waiting at Harvard, Garcia submitted two papers on X-ray aversions, based on his PhD dissertation and follow-up work.[39] Compared with his 23 previous publications, the language now used to discuss his findings was suddenly much bolder. In fact, we suggest that it is at this very point in his intellectual career that Garcia made an *epistemological breakaway* and offered a clear and unambiguous challenge to the dominant S-R paradigm. Until now, the knowledge-generation system used by Garcia was considerably at variance with that of the mainstream, but for 10 years his research had "passed" because it was generally couched in the language of the dominant system. Now Garcia openly identified his research as the product of a viewpoint radically more biologically and cognitively oriented than that of the neo-behaviorists. "The stage was set for a crucial test between two views: From the evolutionary view, the rat is a biased learning machine designed by natural selection to form certain CS-US associations rapidly but not others. From a traditional learning viewpoint, the rat was an unbiased learner able to make any association in accordance with the general principles of contiguity, effect and similarity."[40]

Garcia's findings in these two papers indicated that not all neutral stimuli could be associated with learned aversive behavior, as was commonly assumed by most S-R theorists. He criticized traditional parameters used to investigate associations of cue and consequence (e.g., temporal relation, stimulus intensity, and frequency of trials) and the neglect of "organizational concepts based on the structural nature of the organism." Finally, by bringing into the discussion such concepts as "hypothesis" (borrowed from Tolman, Ritchie, and Krech) and "belongingness," and by invoking the name of Gestalt psychology, he gave clear verbal cues of this theoretical breakaway.[41]

By openly disputing the long-held notion of the equipotentiality of stimuli, by advocating different varieties of avoidance behavior, and by couching all this in language from outside the dominant S-R paradigm, Garcia had made a declaration of epistemological independence. Instead of continuing to describe his findings politely in neutral terms, Garcia took off the theoretical kid gloves and went on the offensive against certain ideas of mainstream learning theory. For the first time, he began specifically calling an anomaly an anomaly. At the same time as his research had gradually led him to make his epistemological breakaway, Garcia also chose to make a geographical and career breakaway, by accepting a position at Harvard. He had not planned on the subsequent publication breakaway, which would see his research rejected from mainstream journals for almost two decades.

SCIENTIFIC PROGRESS AND BLOCKAGE: A SOCIAL PSYCHOLOGY OF SCIENCE APPROACH

Garcia and others continued to produce additional anomalous research further questioning the adequacy of the theoretical status quo. His 1965 epistemological break had shown that he advocated a paradigm shift. Several learning theorists then concluded that the S-R paradigm could be patched up and reformed; a few thought a revolutionary shift was necessary; but for many, especially mainstream journal editors, these findings evoked considerable resistance. To understand more clearly the dynamics of such resistance, and in particular the problems Garcia encountered in publishing his research after 1965, we rely on a social psychology of science approach. This is based on a mapping of the interpersonal, group, and institutional contexts of science, the social interactions among scientists, and the evolving social rules governing their behaviors, their research consensuses and disputes.[42] As such, it goes beyond Thomas Kuhn's "paradigm" reformulation, which Imre Lakatos somewhat inaccurately labeled social psychological. Such an approach may be equally useful for accounts involving history or social studies of science.[43]

In our view, scientific research is a work situation filled with a variety of social interactions, so that the conventional scientific wisdom – the findings, truths, facts, or conclusions of scientific research – is, to a certain degree, the result of a social consensus negotiated before it reaches the stage of "public knowledge."[44] Such consensus may be relatively bound to a particular community or group in a particular historical-cultural setting.[45] This version of social psychology of science – neo-Kuhnian, social constructivist, and relativist – deviates from a Popperian position, where scientific data collection and theorizing are often perceived as being logical, rational, and objective activities.[46] For us, the *actual* creation, verification, and dissemination of scientific ideas, the conduct of research, and scientific career progress are highly *inter*personal activities, governed by situational and social rules and constraints.

An analysis based on this view focuses on interpersonal influence activities – those occurring between the *paradigm/community* and the *paradigm/exemplar*.[47] The paradigm/community represents an institutional grouping of members of the scientific community and their apprentices, who share a common research interest, broadly or narrowly defined, organized in structures such as "invisible colleges" or research networks, with channels of communication and shared notions of professional hierarchy.[48] The paradigm/exemplar refers to an agreed-on, specific way of asking scientific questions and as such represents both a research *model* and the *cumulative knowledge base* generated by the continued use of that model. Examples of paradigm/communities include Skinnerians, cognitive social psychologists, turn-of-the-century crowd theorists, and verbal learners. Examples of paradigm/exemplars would include the Stanford-Binet IQ test and all research conducted with it, aggression research using the Buss shock box, Prisoner's Dilemma game studies, and operant Skinner-box pigeon studies.

A paradigm/community will form around a paradigm/exemplar when there is sufficient interest, ideas, and resources. Much of normal science research involves productive paradigm/community members sharing the same paradigm/exemplar. Crises may occur when: (a) a community supports a paradigm/exemplar that is found to be faulty (e.g., IQ data that have been fabricated) or discovers a major methodological problem that has long gone undetected; (b) a community supports an exemplar that is no longer heuristic; (c) a generation gap splits a paradigm/community between advocates of the accepted exemplar and a proposed alternative; (d) a community is decimated through political exile, abrupt shifts of funding and curricula, or a national brain drain; or (e) a community stubbornly rejects evidence from a rival exemplar that informs their work.

Our approach focuses on what occurs at the social psychological level *between* the paradigm/community and the paradigm/exemplar, emphasizing those scientific role relations and social interactions that involve unequal or *asymmetric power relations*.[49] In these role-defined interactions involving authors and editors, grant applicants and funding panels, students and supervisors, researchers and administrators, one party, invested with power by the paradigm/community, affects the scientific outcomes of another. Such decisions, for the most part, are final, occur within one-way communications systems, and permit no appeal or negotiation. Scientists or apprentices wishing to contribute to a particular paradigm/exemplar make a *submission* – the term itself points to the asymmetric power relations involved. The (s)elected representatives of the paradigm/community (e.g., the editorial committee of a journal or publishing house, a funding agency panel, a hiring or tenure and promotion committee, a PhD thesis committee) make an eventual decision about the outcome (acceptance, modification, speed up or delay, rejection, etc.).

It is difficult, methodologically, to gauge the precise effect of such asymmetric social interactions on an individual scientist's research output. There are, of course, some global indicators: data are available for academic salaries, prestigious awards, the rejection rates of journals, the funding decisions of granting agencies, the number of graduate students passing or failing a program, or the number of positive and negative promotion and tenure decisions. But it is probably only at the individual case history level that an accurate assessment of the personal or motivational impact of asymmetric power relations can be made. Our study of Garcia only deals with professional, rather than personal effects of these interactions. Primary attention will be given to the *author-editor* relationship, as this was the major area of scientific blockage in this case history.[50]

S-R WARS, PART 2: THE EDITORS STRIKE BACK

If we look closely at Garcia's publication record and the pattern of citations of this work, nothing at first appears to be untoward. Table 3-2 indicates that during the period 1966–1985, Garcia's work was cited in journals covered by the *Social Science Citations Index (SSCI)* 95 times per year, with 19% of those citations found in APA journals; during the period 1961–1984, *Science Citation Index (SCI)* showed 86.8 citations annually, with 19.3% from APA sources. Garcia's work, as described in the articles of others, was *visible* in APA journals, in *Science* and *Nature,* as well as to readers of a variety of other psychology and nonpsychology journals and books.[51]

However, as Table 3-3 (pp. 74–75) indicates, Garcia's publications were no longer visible in APA's journals during the period 1965–1978 – he is junior author, with a student, of just one paper in *JCPP* – although these same journals had previously accepted his work. This pattern seems markedly different from that of a comparison group of other APA award winners; in this case the disappearance coincides exactly with the period between Garcia's epistemological breakaway and the first of his scientific awards.

To help explain this publication pattern, and the apparent shift in

Table 3-2. *Frequency of citation of John Garcia's research in the scientific literature, 1961–1985*

	JEP, JCPP, PR, PB[a]	Other APA Journals	Science & Nature	Other journals & chapters	Total
Citations in *Social Science Citation Index (SSCI)* 1966–1985[b]					
1966–1970	33	9	12	108	162
1971–1975	105	14	22	261	402
1976–1980	107	7	34	531	679
1981–1985	52	33	2	569	656
Total	297	63	70	1469	1899
Citations in *Science Citation Index (SCI)* 1961–1984[b]					
1961–1964	11	0	21	60	92
1965–1969	23	4	22	142	191
1970–1974	127	13	36	277	453
1975–1979	117	10	39	564	730
1980–1984	96	0	12	508	616
Total	374	27	130	1551	2082

[a]*Journal of Experimental Psychology (JEP,* includes all four continuators after 1975); *Journal of Comparative and Physiological Psychology (JCPP* separates into two journals after 1982); *Psychological Review (PR); Psychological Bulletin (PB).* [b]The Institute for Scientific Information publishes both *SCI* and *SSCI;* however, their five-year cumulations are not aligned.

mainstream journal editors' attitudes toward Garcia's articles, we will examine the communications between him and various editors during this period. In 1965, with no previous problems publishing in *Science, Nature,* or APA journals, Garcia sent two critical manuscripts off to APA's *Journal of Comparative and Physiological Psychology.* Both were promptly rejected, at a time when *JCPP* was rejecting 51% of the manuscripts submitted.[52] The editor, learning theorist William Estes, cited comments of an anonymous reviewer who doubted "whether your results are of general theoretical relevance" and listed a series of methodological complaints, such as unsuitability of experimental design, lack of temporal control of stimuli, lack of pseudoconditioning controls, and an alternative explanation of conditioned nausea. Estes conveyed the consultant's suggestion that "this research could be better reported in one of the journals which customarily deals with studies of an applied character having to do with the effects of irradiation."[53]

Garcia, however, wrote a lengthy rebuttal of the consultant's criticisms, and pointed out the inconsistency of rejecting both papers for lack of *the-*

oretical relevance when in fact all the specific remarks pertained to *methodology*.[54] Disputing the reviewer's arguments, he suggested that this form of associative learning "probably occurs in many situations, e.g. when a vitamin-deficient animal learns to select a compensatory diet or when a wild rat which has survived a poisoning attempt, develops 'bait-shy' habits." From the two articles and the correspondence exchange, it would seem that Garcia had by now become aware of the epistemological implications of his anomalous findings. Estes promptly responded, defending his consultant as someone well versed in the literature of conditioning and aware of relevant Polish and Russian studies, "although I'm not sure you are."[55] He commented on the unusual nature of Garcia's findings and suggested that conditioning theorists would find that "your results are not particularly surprising but also they are difficult to interpret" in light of lack of knowledge about the exact nature of the unconditioned response to irradiation and about the conditioned response. Estes did, however, offer to consider a new manuscript, although this would be sent to the same consultant, as well as to one other.

Garcia had made some rather telling arguments.[56] He (1) disputed the pseudoconditioning explanation, citing the pattern of data for nine experimental groups; (2) questioned certain of the reviewer's ad hoc hypotheses about nausea; (3) cited findings in the literature about temporal relations; (4) disputed the label of classical conditioning because of the long stimulus intervals, and (5) suggested that the findings were broadly generalizable to other learning situations. Shortly thereafter, an Estes-trained learning theorist, Sam Revusky, acquainted with Garcia's work, wrote to his former mentor that "the implications for conditioning theory are fundamental and revolutionary," and that "while there have been many hints of a stimulus-reinforcement belongingness in the literature, Garcia really proves it."[57]

At this point, Garcia did not choose to let the data linger in a file drawer, nor did he decide to submit them again to *JCPP* and the awaiting hostile reviewer. Completely rewritten and with additional data about delays of reinforcement of an hour or more, the manuscripts went to *Science,* where Garcia had never before had any problems publishing his ideas. This time both papers were refused. Although the reviewer found the data and hypotheses quite interesting, they were rejected on the grounds that Garcia did not know *how* the X-ray reinforcement produced its effect. Garcia's response was twofold. Wanting to get these novel ideas into print, he sent studies reporting the findings to *Radiation Research,* and, in extremely abbreviated form, to physiological psychologist C. T. Morgan's maverick journal, *Psychonomic Science.*[58] Next, he and his colleagues conducted conceptual replications that completely supported the earlier, criticized studies; sent to *Science,* they were both quickly published.[59]

Table 3-3. Publication patterns of John Garcia and fifteen APA Distinguished Scientific Contribution Award winners in related areas.[a]

| | Pre-award period[b] | | | | | | | | | | Post-award period | | | | |
| | First half | | | | | Second half | | | | | | | | | |
	APA[c]	S/N	O. Jrn	C & B	Total	APA	S/N	O. Jrn	C & B	Total	APA	S/N	O. Jrn	C & B	Total
John Garcia[d] (1979 award winner)															
% pages	23.2	9.7	45.2	21.9	N = 155	1.2	4.6	33.3	60.8	N = 666	35.9	0.8	36.5	26.7	N = 359
% articles	21.7	30.4	34.8	13.0	N = 23	1.8	15.8	49.1	33.3	N = 57	34.6	3.8	42.3	19.2	N = 26
% articles of 8 contemporary APA award winners (1977–1980)	35.9	3.3	33.1	27.8	N = 245 $\bar{x} = 30.6$	15.4	3.1	40.8	40.8	N = 422 $\bar{x} = 52.8$	26.9	5.4	46.3	21.5	N = 93 $\bar{x} = 11.6$
% articles of 4 neo-behaviorist winners (1956–1975)	46.2	0	42.9	10.9	N = 119 $\bar{x} = 29.8$	2.0	25.0	28.9	44.1	N = 152 $\bar{x} = 38.0$					

% articles of 3 Tolmanian winners (1956–1970)	57.3	0	39.5	3.2	N = 124	33.5	7.5	35.0	24.0	N = 200		
					$\bar{x} = 41.3$					$\bar{x} = 66.7$		
% articles of 15 above winners	43.9	1.6	37.1	17.4	N = 488	25.7	4.0	36.2	34.1	N = 774		
					$\bar{x} = 32.5$					$\bar{x} = 51.6$		

[a] *Source:* bibliographies published in *American Psychologist* (January) at time of award announcements; post-award data for 8 contemporary winners compiled from *Psychological Abstracts* and *Social Science Citation Index*; data for John Garcia updated from curriculum vitae, 1985, permitting calculation of number of pages published; page data missing for chapters and books published by 8 others, so articles only are counted.

[b] Key to award winners' publication periods (first half and second half pre-award; post-award): **J. Garcia** (1951–65; 66–79; 80–85). Eight recent award winners: **G. Bower** (58–68; 69–79; 80–84); **A. Bandura** (53–66; 67–80; 81–84); **R. DeValois** (50–63; 64–77; 78–84); **P. Teitelbaum** (54–66; 67–78; 79–84); **R. Atkinson** (52–64; 65–77; 78–84); **J. Hochberg** (49–63; 64–78; 79–84); **M. Posner** (63–71; 72–80; 81–84); **A. Liberman** (44–62; 63–80; 81–84). Four neo-behaviorists: **C. Hovland** (34–45; 46–57); **K. Spence** (31–43; 44–56); **N. Miller** (34–46; 47–59); **R. Sears** (32–48; 49–75). Three Tolmanians: **E. Tolman** (17–36; 37–56); **D. Krech** (32–51; 52–70); **D. Campbell** (47–58; 59–70).

[c] APA journals; *Science* or *Nature*; other journals; chapters and books.

[d] Publications for Garcia exclude one-page abstracts.

Garcia then prepared a theoretical review of the literature based on the accumulating series of anomalous findings, and sent it to the APA's *Psychological Review,* which had published an earlier review article by him. However, this time the article was rejected on the grounds that it was too discursive, too long, and not theoretical. Garcia disputed this evaluation, and after further discussion and delay, the paper appeared elsewhere.[60] It was a strong theoretical attack on two major principles underlying S-R learning theory: (1) the law of contiguity, which postulated the necessity of immediate (primary or secondary) reinforcement, usually in seconds or fractions thereof; and (2) the principle of stimulus equipotentiality, whereby any neutral stimulus was thought capable of becoming a conditional stimulus (CS).[61] The article went on to suggest limits on the organism and specificity "in the formation of 'molar associative habits' traditionally studied in the learning laboratory." However, this essentially subversive article, calling into question long-established principles, appeared in a biologically oriented journal, and probably did not circulate within the S-R learning theory community as effectively as articles appearing in APA journals.

Garcia's rejections did not come only from the mainstream neo-behaviorists, but from the Skinnerian operant world as well.[62] A paper was submitted to the *Journal of the Experimental Analysis of Behavior (JEAB),* resubmitted in July 1966, incorporating suggested revisions, rejected in October by the new *JEAB* editor, then independently reviewed again only to receive "criticisms which were directed towards changes suggested by the original referees (which) raise the question of the reliability of the referee method."[63] It was then withdrawn and published elsewhere, after having been delayed almost a year by the Skinnerians.[64]

Instructive is Garcia's evolving strategy of confronting mainstream editors about the accountability of their rejection decisions and then eventually finding alternative publication outlets. Undaunted by rejections, Garcia continued to hone his critique of learning theory.[65] Garcia's choice of radiation as a stimulus may have ultimately insured the longevity of his career. During the period of the cold war and the dawn of the nuclear age, there was intense interest from the U.S. government, the military, the Atomic Energy Commission, and others about the behavioral effects of post-atomic-attack radiation, fallout, and so on. For research linked to such questions of practical national interest, there was relatively little difficulty obtaining funding.[66]

NEO-BEHAVIORIST REACTIONS TO ANOMALY AND THE CONSEQUENCES FOR THE DISSEMINATION OF IDEAS

Garcia's 1965 epistemological breakaway implied a major modification of the neo-behaviorist tradition and perhaps a complete paradigm shift. It was immediately followed by a long period of difficulty in publishing his ideas in mainstream outlets. Responses from the paradigm/community to such an attack will be varied: (a) delaying or preventing the publication of the findings; (b) publishing them, but then ignoring or neutrally acknowledging them; (c) refuting or counterattacking the findings with arguments or data collection, or (d) deciding eventually to change the paradigm/exemplar. Let us look at some of the consequences of the editor-author frictions evolving around these anomalous findings and how they are disseminated.

Long delay of reinforcement – publication lag

Authors may feel frustrated with the speed of getting their ideas into print, especially if one's research is breaking new ground in competition with other groups. Only a small number of papers – about 10% of those submitted to *JEP* during the long editorship of Melton – are published without much revision or delay.[67] A rejection, it is estimated, adds 10 to 12 months to the publication process.[68] Publication lag, caused by a backlog of accepted papers, contributes additional delays, often in the range of six to 24 months. Garcia (and others) waited 15 to 17 months for publication of articles in *JCPP* in the late 1950s, although some APA journals, including *JEP* and *JCPP,* permitted one to jump the publication queue for a fixed fee – $20 per page in *JEP* in the 1950s, $30 in 1967, and $45 in 1970. We have discussed above how some of Garcia's articles were delayed between one and three years.[69] These delays sometimes led to decisions to publish in non-mainstream outlets, perhaps increasing the speed of publication at the cost of breadth of diffusion and even detail of discussion. (*Psychonomic Science* had a two-page limit on articles.) The question of speed of publication is important when considering the priority of a discovery. Within the paradigm/community, unpublished manuscripts and knowledge about work in progress circulate informally. We have no comparable data for speed of publication for other learning theorists with more direct access to mainstream journals (e.g., Seligman, Revusky, Rozin) but note that they always acknowledged Garcia's priorities of discovery. However, we have examined materials showing that on one occasion it took over six months of correspondence on the part of Garcia and other knowledgeable paradigm workers to convince a chapter author and an editor of a prestigious book series, both of whom had attachments to the *JCPP* editorial board, to correct the record about the priority of Garcia's work.

Editorial decision making and Type II incompetence

According to Revusky, Type II incompetence (T2) is demonstrated in editorial decision making when spurious criteria are used to deny that facts have been demonstrated. It is an active process, employing irrelevant criteria to reject otherwise sound manuscripts, sometimes to the advantage of the rejecting reviewer. Revusky suggested that perhaps "unreasonable application of standards of rigor" kept flavor-aversion studies out of the prestigious journals for some time.[70] From 1965 onward, Garcia began increasingly to receive "noxious" editorial responses to his submissions of anomalous findings, and this continued even as Garcia began to receive prestigious awards for his scientific contributions. Many of these evaluations stuck quite closely to the rules of the scientific game, but invoked additional and/or spurious scientific criteria.

As an example, we consider a paper Garcia submitted to *Science* that described a novel set of findings contradicting the classical conditioning concept of overshadowing. The article received two short reviews, one positive and one neutral, as well as a longer, negative one. The editor suggested revising the manuscript to take care of the negative reviewer's comments about clarity and procedure. In June 1977, the manuscript was revised by Garcia and resubmitted; in July came word that the original negative reviewer now demanded still more revisions. Again, Garcia revised the manuscript and included a detailed list of all the changes made, citing lines in the text where each of the reviewer's criticisms had been answered.[71] But the negative reviewer *still* refused the changes. Another consultant was now brought in, the fourth. This reviewer found that the paper had "interesting conclusions" and "provocative guesses" but criticized the figures as obscuring information and stated that "the communication is technically deficient, and portions of the research are clumsily designed." Based on two negative reviews out of four solicited, the paper was now rejected.

Further correspondence with the editor produced a response from one of the anonymous negative referees. The reviewer argued for highest standards of rigor in the case of novel and unique findings, because of the amount of follow-up work that will be stimulated. If the original work is not "an excellent description of and (sic) obviously well-designed and executed study . . . then a great deal of time and effort on the part of other investigators will be lost in pursuing false criticisms." Then, referring to work *more than a decade old,* the reviewer continues "I do not mean to be unkind, but that other work on toxicosis, particularly on the cue-to-consequence feature of it, was seriously flawed both in design and execution." Such research had wasted "the time of many competent and careful investigators trying to evaluate these flaws." After over a year's delay, this research appeared in a nonpsychology journal. Here, the use of extraneous criteria invoked to reject anomalous findings involved the carryover of a dislike for research done a decade earlier.

Another form of T2 incompetence may involve *ad hominem* evaluations of the scientist rather than objective judgments of the scientific work. Garcia himself noted a consultant who suggested "that one of our recent manuscripts would not have been acceptable even as a term paper in his learning class."[72] There are further examples of this sort of editorial response from such journals as *JCPP, PR,* and *JEAB,* during the period after 1965.[673] One anonymous reviewer sent an evaluation in 1978 which seemed to call into question Garcia's very credentials as a scientific researcher – apparently, he had done just about everything wrong in this paper:

> My impression of this manuscript is unfavorable. The paper suffers from a lack of operational definitions that allow one to distinguish between key concepts ... it also suffers from an excessive use of subjective terms and phrases ... The failure to operationalize the concepts under investigation resulted in the problem being ill-defined. Ill-definition of the problem led, in turn, to a poor experimental design, procedural inadequacies, and inappropriate, as well as insufficient, statistical analyses, all of which disallow any meaningful interpretation of the results. As a consequence, the experiment contributes little that is of theoretical or empirical value, and, in my opinion, does not merit publication.

Although we have heard some informal anecdotes, we have no systematic data about whether some of Garcia's problems were linked to prejudice. The overall success Garcia had in other aspects of his career, with the exception of mainstream publications, belies this, at least on the surface. Garcia may have been the first Hispanic psychologist to become a department chairperson in a U.S. university and receive prestigious professional awards. Some of his publications as a psychologist have also dealt with problems faced by minority group members. It is beyond the scope of the present study to look at the question of the history of professional prejudice in psychology. However, the social psychologist of science might well take an interest in collecting more systematic and verifiable data on any possibility of a causal connection between discriminatory (racist, sexist) verbal behavior and prejudicial decision making affecting dissemination of ideas and career progress.

Exclusion of anomalous researchers from the journal refereeing process

We have elsewhere shown that almost 30% of the articles contributed to one APA journal in 1965 came from that year's group of editors and reviewers.[74] Although there is some literature that suggests that referees chosen by editors do not always agree, it does not seem very probable that consultants are chosen who are in basic *disagreement* with the dominant paradigm/exemplar and community.[75] While we have no systematic data on this issue, Revusky reported that as of 1974, Garcia had

never been asked to referee a paper for *JCPP,* in which many of the flavor-aversion studies appeared.[76] Garcia believed that he had received no
more than two requests from *JCPP* and no recent requests from *JEP, PR,*
and *PB.*[77] Our search located one paper refereed for *JCPP* in August 1976
and one in *PR,* 1971. During this time of exclusion from mainstream
APA journal editorial consulting, however, he was quite active as a referee for non-APA journals and granting agencies. Revusky suggested that
this exclusion of "the single most qualified man in the area" from the
review process and nonuse of his expertise to aid the research of others
was unfair "to people submitting flavor aversion papers to journals of the
American Psychological Association or to readers of those journals."[78]

As we saw in Table 3-3, during the period of awards following 1978,
there was an increase in the presence of Garcia's articles in APA journals.
He was also increasingly asked to referee. Garcia reported that in addition
to joining the board of editors of *Behavioral and Neural Biology,* a non-
APA journal, he had also become a consulting editor with *Journal of
Comparative Psychology* and more recently with *Behavioral Neurosci-
ence,* two APA journals formed in 1982 after the split of *JCPP.*[79]

Dissemination of ideas in the secondary literature

Our discussion thus far has focused on problems of the primary scientific
literature, the journals regularly used by scientists to chart progress in
their specialty area. However, there are also a number of informal and
formal secondary channels through which scientific ideas are disseminated to members of a paradigm/community, and to their current and
potential apprentices, graduate and undergraduate students. Among
informal secondary channels we might include circulation of unpublished
manuscripts, correspondence, conference papers, colloquia, lectures, and
seminars.[80] Among formal secondary channels we would include the
printed literature that summarizes primary journal findings for an audience of professionals not specifically working in the area of the paradigm/
exemplar. Examples would include the *Annual Review of Psychology,*
handbooks, chapters in edited books, summary review articles, textbooks, continuing series on learning and motivation. Such secondary
sources often serve as the content base for nonspecialists; they are important in shaping the general knowledge base of students and incoming
members of the paradigm/community before they become active
researchers.

Space constraints limit us to an extremely cursory consideration of the
presentation of Garcia's novel findings within formal, secondary channels. Our preliminary assessment of the literature, by no means systematic or exhaustive, suggests that at least four categories can be
distinguished.

In the first category, that of *neutral or no response,* we would place authors who simply ignore Garcia's work or treat it somewhat neutrally. This includes many introductory textbooks of the 1960s and 1970s.[81]

In the second group, we find a defensive reaction from learning theorists who support the dominant paradigm/exemplar and who *reject or counterattack* against the anomalous findings. As an example, we may cite articles by animal learning theorist M. E. Bitterman that strongly attacked the work of Garcia and others in *Science.* Bitterman rejected ethological or ecological approaches that included notions of organismic constraints, species-specific capabilities and the denial of general learning laws as "simply . . . not persuasive." He later suggested that the taste aversion work of Garcia and others, although "indeed voluminous," contained "some serious methodological shortcomings," in a tone bordering almost on the *ad hominem.*[82] Revusky's detailed critique of the first article suggested that Bitterman may have "repressed" information on pseudoconditioning known to most learning theorists; this article was rejected by *Science* and appeared elsewhere.[83] Unexpected findings that strongly threaten a paradigm/exemplar and the basic beliefs of a paradigm/community, it appears, can unleash both strong public criticism and strong anonymous (T2) reactions. Rejoinders, even if only the second-to-last word, are possible in periodic media. A textbook may well disseminate only one side of a story for many years to numerous students, until a revised edition appears.

A third category of reactions to Garcia's work involves those who wish to *reform the paradigm/exemplar* in the light of an anomaly. The neo-behaviorist paradigm/exemplar had already undergone much reform from within by the 1960s.[84] Perhaps the work of Rozin and Kalat can be viewed within this reformist tradition. They maintained that apparent anomalies in imprinting and feeding, and Garcia's work on "belongingness" and "delay," can all be explained by adding an additional concept, a general adaptation principle to S-R learning theory. While describing the "revolutionary nature" of Garcia's work, Rozin and Kalat were able to maintain their peace with the dominant paradigm/exemplar, and optimistically hoped to formulate "laws of some degree of generality taking ecological factors into account."[85] A curious entry in the "reformist" literature is the toned-down article of Revusky and Garcia, which appeared in a series originated by the leading neo-behaviorist, Kenneth Spence, in collaboration with Janet Spence.[86] However, the symbolic breeching of the S-R paradigm/community's fortress had little carryover effect. Aside from this 84-page chapter, there is little other mention of Garcia's work in the remaining 3,808 pages of the first 12 series volumes; up to the end of 1978, only D'Amato and Berkeley-trained Bolles together offer three citations.[87]

Some recent introductory textbooks now seem to be taking a reformist attitude toward the neo-behaviorist paradigm, often adding a paragraph on the work of Garcia at the end of a traditional chapter on learning theory. Generally, such texts indicate that there may be some limits to the generalizability of classical principles and laws.

A fourth reaction to Garcia's work involves the acceptance of the radical epistemological consequences, even if this leads to a Kuhnian *paradigm shift* or "scientific revolution," and hence a challenge to the stability of the dominant paradigm/exemplar. For example, Seligman's critique of general process learning theory, relying heavily on Garcia's anomalous findings, goes well beyond that of the reformists.[88] Other paradigm dissidents, radicals, or "revolutionaries" have begun to emerge in the past decade. A conference organized by Hank Davis and Harry Hurwitz has provided transcripts of informal, spontaneous discussions in which prominent classical and operant learning theorists, including Garcia, questioned some of the basic definitions of their discipline.[89] Some of the questions raised may imply that paradigm reform is no longer satisfactory, and that rather an abandonment of, or breakaway from, the old S-R paradigm/exemplar is indicated. In fact, cognitivist conceptions of learning have been increasingly appearing in both primary and secondary literature.

SOME CONCLUDING THOUGHTS ON SCIENTIFIC PROGRESS

The social psychology of science approach offers an alternative assessment of scientific progress to the idealized psychology textbook accounts of science as a self-correcting set of ideas, governed by rules for determining "truth" or "falsifiability." In this latter view, the personalities and characters of scientists and editors are of no overall consequence, and the veracity of anomalous findings will inevitably be recognized, although sometimes belatedly or even posthumously. Our social psychological analysis focuses on social influences determining scientific outputs, especially those involving asymmetric power relations. In this case history, we have looked only at anomalous discovery, rather than "normal science," and we have concentrated specifically on just one asymmetric relation, the mechanisms of editorial gatekeeping. Our examination of reactions to Garcia's anomalies in both primary journals and in formal secondary diffusion outlets indicates that there was, at least until the late 1970s, a certain inertia about, indeed a willful resistance to, the free circulation of these ideas and an acceptance of their full epistemological consequences.

From the moment that Garcia implied the necessity of abandoning the old paradigm/exemplar, a variety of defensive gatekeeping mechanisms came into play to maintain the paradigm/community's status quo. It would appear from this case history that articles reporting normal science may have the smoothest going, while those with anomalous findings squeezed into the language and conceptual framework of the dominant paradigm/exemplar are also readily acceptable. The more difficult road is that of the paradigm revolutionary. It may well be that the various institutionalized asymmetric power relations of the paradigm/community can forestall challenges to its consensus or authority for a relatively long period, promote business-as-usual normal science additions to the exemplar, and even contribute to its persistence long after its heuristic value has declined.[99]

We have treated Garcia's research career both as a relative success story and as a case of impeded scientific progress. Although certain mainstream publication channels were blocked for a long period of time, his ideas did find other outlets and his work was cited by other specialists, although not all secondary sources conveyed the full impact of this work to students who would become the next generation of psychologists. The relevance of his research for control of livestock predators, radiation safety, and addiction treatment, ensured that his funding sources were not obstructed. And a small number of talented research associates and graduate students have been able to collaborate with him over the years on his research projects. The publication hindrance, although time and energy consuming, was eventually surmounted by Garcia's strategy of confrontation, persistence, and, when necessary, finding an alternative channel. He circumvented the paradigm/community's gatekeeping, and continues to glean professional awards as he approaches retirement.[91]

Although this case history seems to be drawing to a close on a successful note, we are still left with some questions about scientific progress that the social psychology of science might address. What of other researchers who are thwarted in one or more aspects of their scientific careers – publication, research funding, training students, career security – and cannot develop a resourceful strategy to surmount such problems? What will be the fate of other scientists – marginal or maverick, independent or isolated, unfunded, untenured or unemployed, reform- or revolution-minded – whose research findings are bypassed by their discipline's mainstream? How much creative research, and how many gifted researchers, we wonder, go unrecognized in their field or have disappeared from science – lost in the interplay of social dynamics and asymmetric power relations between paradigm/community and paradigm/exemplar?

NOTES

1 On the development of this research area, see, e.g., the internalist historical accounts of W. K. Estes, et al., *Modern Learning Theory: A Critical Analysis of Five Examples* (New York: Appleton-Century-Crofts, 1954); G. A. Kimble, *Hil-*

gard and Marquis' Conditioning and Learning, 2nd ed. (New York: Appleton-Century-Crofts, 1961); and the externalist accounts and/or historical reconstructions of D. Campbell, "A Tribal Model of the Social System Vehicle Carrying Scientific Knowledge," *Knowledge: Creation, Diffusion, Utilization* 1:2 (1979):181–200; I. Lubek, "Fifty Years of Frustration and Aggression: Some Historical Notes on a Long-lived Hypothesis," in K. Larsen (ed.), *Dialectics and Ideology in Psychology* (Norwood, NJ: Ablex, 1986):30–84; J. M. O'Donnell, *The Origins of Behaviorism: American Psychology, 1870–1920* (New York: New York University Press, 1985); F. Samelson, "Struggle for Scientific Authority: The Reception of Watson's Behaviorism, 1913–1920," *Journal of the History of the Behavioral Sciences* 17 (1981):399–425; L. D. Smith, *Behaviorism and Logical Positivism: A Reassessment of the Alliance* (Stanford: Stanford University Press, 1986).

2 J. Garcia, D. Kimmeldorf, and R. Koelling, "A Conditioned Aversion towards Saccharin Resulting from Exposure to Gamma Radiation," *Science* 122 (1955):157–158.

3 E.g., C. R. Gustavson, J. Garcia, J. Hankins, and K. W. Rusiniak, "Coyote Predation Control by Aversive Conditioning," *Science* 184 (1974):824–831 and J. Garcia, K. W. Rusiniak, and L. P. Brett, "Conditioned Food-illness Aversions in Wild Animals: *Caveat canonici,*" in H. Davis and H. M. Hurwitz (eds.), *Operant-Pavlovian Interactions* (Hillsdale, NJ: Erlbaum, 1977), 273–316, demonstrated swift conditioning of predatory animals to avoid eating their natural prey; ranchers could see the applicability of this for protecting their sheep from wolves, coyotes, etc.

4 E. Wyers, personal communication, 17 October 1983.

5 J. Garcia, "Tilting at the Papermills of Academe," *American Psychologist* 36 (1981):149–158.

6 T. S. Kuhn, *The Structure of Scientific Revolutions,* 2nd ed. (Chicago: University of Chicago Press, 1970).

7 S. Revusky, "Interference with Progress by the Scientific Establishment: Examples from Flavor Aversion Learning," in N. W. Milgram, L. Kramer, and T. M. Alloway (eds.), *Food Aversion Learning* (New York: Plenum Press, 1977), 53–71.

8 One of the journal editors we contacted, who had been involved in the events reported, was less cooperative, maintaining that publicly citing brief excerpts from the correspondence between a journal editor and an author was not "good practice," and that portions of an earlier draft of our case history smacked of Hearst smear tactics or yellow journalism.

9 S. Koch, "Epilogue," in S. Koch (ed.), *Psychology: A Study of a Science* (New York: McGraw-Hill, 1959), Vol. 3, 729–788. For the development of the Hull-Spence perspective, see, e.g., C. L. Hull, *Principles of Behavior* (New York: Appleton-Century-Crofts, 1943); *Essentials of Learning* (New Haven: Yale University Press, 1951); and *A Behavior System* (New Haven: Yale University Press, 1952). See also K. W. Spence, *Behavior Theory and Conditioning* (New Haven: Yale University Press, 1956).

10 Hull disseminated lengthy mimeographed lists of hypotheses in need of testing. See Lubek, "Fifty Years of Frustration and Aggression" and S. Koch, "Clark L. Hull," in W. Estes, et al., *Modern Learning Theory,* 1–2.

11 Some questioned whether to be a Hullian you needed to have conducted your

PhD under him; in this regard, the names of Kenneth Spence and Neal Miller (supervised at Yale by Yerkes and Miles, respectively) were often suggested as Hullians. Miller, for example, annotated his thesis listing (acknowledging W. Miles, and also R. Dodge, and Hull) as follows: "ideas grew out of Hull's theories and seminar -- was assistant in research to Miles and Dodge" (Personal communication, 30 October 1984).

12 E. R. Hilgard, "Kenneth Wartinbee Spence: 1907–1967," *American Journal of Psychology* 80 (1967):347–350.

13 K. W. Spence, "Clark Leonard Hull: 1884–1952," *American Journal of Psychology* 65 (1952):639–646; N. Guttman, "On Skinner and Hull: A Reminiscence and a Projection," *American Psychologist* 32 (1977):321–328.

14 B. F. Skinner, *The Behavior of Organisms: An Experimental Analysis* (New York: Appleton-Century-Crofts, 1938).

15 D. L. Krantz, "Schools and Systems: The Mutual Isolation of Operant and Non-operant Psychology as a Case-study," *Journal of the History of the Behavioral Sciences* 8 (1972):86–102.

16 Guttman, "On Skinner and Hull," 322; Krantz, "Schools and Systems."

17 E. C. Tolman, *Purposive Behavior in Animals and Men* (New York: Century, 1932); E. C. Tolman, "Principles of Purposive Behavior," in S. Koch (ed.), *Psychology: A Study of a Science*, Vol. 2 (New York: McGraw-Hill, 1959), 92–157.

18 See E. Brunswik, *Perception and the Representative Design of Psychological Experiments* (Berkeley: University of California Press, 1956); K. R. Hammond (ed.), *The Psychology of Egon Brunswik* (New York: Holt, Rinehart and Winston, 1966); L. Petrinovich, "Probabilistic Functionalism: A Conception of Research Method," *American Psychologist* 34 (1979):373–390; L. Postman and E. C. Tolman, "Brunswik's Probabalistic Functionalism," in S. Koch (ed.), *Psychology: A Study of a Science*, 502–564; E. C. Tolman and E. Brunswik, "The Organism and the Causal Texture of the Environment," *Psychological Review* 42 (1935):43–97.

19 In Ian Lubek and Erika Apfelbaum, "Analyse psycho-sociologique et historique de l'emprise d'un paradigme: l'apprentissage S-R, l'hypothèse frustration-agression, et l'effet Garcia," *Recherche de Psychologie Sociale* 1 (1979):112–120, 123–149, we mapped, somewhat primitively, the diffusion of learning theorists across 17 important American universities from the 1930s until the 1970s. We found a small number of Tolmanians huddled largely at Berkeley, a larger dispersion of Skinnerian researchers through a Minnesota, Indiana, Harvard, Columbia, Duke axis; the largest core of researchers by far were the Hull-Spence neo-behaviorists in the Yale, Iowa, Stanford, Wisconsin, Texas grouping.

20 See S. Koch, "Epilogue," 736–737; E C. Tolman, "Principles of Purposive Behavior," J. Garcia, "I. Krechevsky and I," in J. McGaugh and L. Petrinovitch (eds.), *Knowing, Thinking and Believing* (New York: Plenum Press, 1976), 71–84.

21 See E. R. Hilgard and G. H. Bower, *Theories of Learning,* 3rd ed. (New York: Appleton-Century-Crofts, 1966), 220. For a comparison of the "tribal leadership" of Spence and Tolman, see D. Campbell, "A Tribal Model," and D. L. Krantz and L. Wiggins, "Personal and Impersonal Channels of Recruitment in the Growth of Theory," *Human Development* 16 (1973):133–156.

22 See C. A. Boneau, "Paradigm Regained? Cognitive Behaviorism Restated," *American Psychologist* 29 (1974):297–309, for an indication that cognitive formulations may be returning in force. For evidence of the decline in researchers in experimental learning theory, see Lubek and Apfelbaum, "Analyse psycho-sociol-

ogique." For the rise after World War II of learning as a central core in the teaching of psychology, see R. R. Sears, "Graduate Training Facilities," *American Psychologist* 1 (1946):135–150, who found about 20% of doctoral programs having an experimental area. But compare P. F. Merenda, "Current Status of Graduate Education in Psychology," *American Psychologist* 29 (1974):627–631, who found that of 30 PhD programs with "core" requirements almost half (14) required one or two learning courses, three required various experimental courses, while 14 required physiological, comparative, and motivation courses. For evidence of some decline in the 1970s, see G. M. Pion and M. W. Lipsey, "Psychology and Society: The Challenge of Change," *American Psychologist* 39 (1984):739–754, who observed that between 1972–1973 and 1979–1980, experimental, comparative, and physiological programs declined from 36.7% to 31.0% of 1,200 specialty areas examined. But see L. V. Annis, G. H. Tucker and C. A. Baker, "APA Certification of Terminal Master's Degree Programs," *American Psychologist* 39 (1984):563–566, who showed 50% of respondents still concerned about having a "core" course in learning.

23 J. Ziman, "Information, Communication, Knowledge," *American Psychologist* 26 (1971):338–345; M. J. Mulkay, "Conformity and Innovation in Science," *Sociological Review Monographs* 18 (1972):5–23; D. Crane, *Invisible Colleges: Diffusion of Knowledge in Scientific Communities* (Chicago: University of Chicago Press, 1972).

24 D. Lindsey, "Distinction, Achievement, and Editorial Board Membership," *American Psychologist* 31 (1976):799–804; "Participation and Influence in Publication Review Proceedings: A Reply," *American Psychologist* 32 (1977):579–586; and *The Scientific Publication System in Social Science* (San Francisco: Jossey Bass, 1978).

25 See the discussion in Lubek and Apfelbaum, "Analyse psycho-sociologique," 130–132, of favoritism in these journals toward publications emanating from universities with editorial board representation (24.9 articles per year), compared with nonrepresented universities (13.7), and the reanalysis of data from W. M. Cox and V. Catt, "Productivity Ratings of Graduate Programs in Psychology Based on Publications in the Journals of the American Psychological Association," *American Psychologist* 32 (1977):793–813.

26 Lubek and Apfelbaum, "Analyse psycho-sociologique," 130–132.

27 Our thanks to Janet Spence, Nancy Innes, Emily Cahan, Harry Hurwitz, B. F. Skinner, and 22 Yale PhDs for their assistance with this project.

28 For discussions on author-editor relations, see D. Crane, "The Gatekeepers of Science: Some Factors Affecting the Selection of Articles for Scientific Journals," *American Sociologist* 2 (1967):195–201; R. S. Broadhead and R. C. Rist, "Gatekeepers and the Social Control of Social Research," *Social Problems* 23 (1976):325–336; Lindsey, *The Scientific Publication System;* W. B. Lacy and L. Busch, "Guardians of Science: Journals and Editors in the Agricultural Sciences," *Rural Sociology* 47 (1982):429–448. For a more social psychological perspective, see Lubek and Apfelbaum, "Analyse psycho-sociologique." For a discussion of whether social stratification occurs because of universalistic recognition of merit or through elites who "control the social institutions of science . . . to perpetuate their own ideas and assure the social mobility of their intellectual children," see J. R. Cole and S. Cole, "The Ortega Hypothesis: Citation Analysis Suggests that Only a Few Scientists Contribute to Scientific Progress," *Science* 178:368; on favoritism versus elitism see D. L. Schaeffer, "Do A.P.A. Journals Play Professional Favorites?" *American Psychologist* 25 (1970):362–365; D. D. Bowen, R.

Perloff and J. Jacoby, "Improving Manuscript Evaluation Procedures," *American Psychologist* 27 (1972):221–225.

29 Further data collection, now underway, seems to show that including "second generation" learning theorists may double the representation on an APA editorial board of that group, at least in more recent times.

30 J. Garcia, 6 September 1975, tongue-in-cheek, cited by H. Davis and H. M. B. Hurwitz (eds.), *Operant-Pavlovian Interactions* (see note 3), xvi.

31 R. Christie and J. Garcia, "Subcultural Variation in Authoritarian Personality," *Journal of Abnormal and Social Psychology* 46 (1951):457–469.

32 J. Garcia, personal communication, 29 November 1978.

33 Garcia, "I. Krechevsky and I."

34 Garcia, personal communication, 19 July 1986. See also R. Garcia y Robertson and J. Garcia, "X-rays and Learned Taste Aversions: Historical and Psychological Ramifications," in T. G. Burish, S. M. Levy, and B. E. Meyerowitz (eds.), *Cancer, Nutrition and Eating Behavior: A Biobehavioral Perspective* (Hillsdale, NJ: Erlbaum, 1985), 11–41.

35 Garcia, Kimmeldorf, and Koelling, "Conditioned Aversion towards Saccharin" (See note 2).

36 J. Garcia and D. J. Kimmeldorf, "Temporal Relationships within the Conditioning of a Saccharin Aversion through Radiation Exposure," *Journal of Comparative and Physiological Psychology* 50 (1957):180–183; see 181.

37 J. Garcia and D. J. Kimmeldorf, "The Effect of Ophthalmectomy upon Responses of the Rat to Radiation and Taste Stimuli," *Journal of Comparative and Physiological Psychology* 51 (1958):288–291; J. Garcia, D. J. Kimmeldorf, and E. L. Hunt, "The Use of Ionizing Radiation as a Motivating Stimulus," *Psychological Review* 68 (1961):383–395.

38 J. Garcia and N. A. Buchwald, "Notes on Furchtgott's 'Behavioral Effects of Ionizing Radiations: 1955–1961'," *Psychological Bulletin* 61 (1964):234–235; E. Furchtgott, "Behavioral Effects of Ionizing Radiations: 1955–1961," *Psychological Bulletin* 60 (1963):157–199.

39 J. Garcia, "X-ray Aversions: Quality of the Test Stimulus" (Unpublished manuscript, University of California at Berkeley, 1965); J. Garcia, "X-ray Aversions: Quality of the Reinforcer" (Unpublished manuscript, University of California at Berkeley, 1965).

40 Garcia y Robertson and Garcia, "X-rays and Learned Taste Aversions," 25.

41 Garcia, "Quality of the Reinforcer," 11–12.

42 Our thinking about a social psychology of science analysis, initially applied reflexively to social psychology, took form between 1974–1977. See, e.g., I. Lubek, "Some Tentative Suggestions for Analysing and Neutralizing the Power Structure in Social Psychology," in L. Strickland, F. Aboud, and K. Gergen (eds.), *Social Psychology in Transition* (New York: Plenum, 1976):317–333; I. Lubek, "Towards a Social Psychology of Social Psychology: An Analytical Attack on the Aggression Paradigm" (Paper presented at the 21st International Congress of Psychology, Paris, July, 1976; and I. Lubek, "The Psychological Establishment: Pressures to Preserve Paradigms, Publish Rather than Perish, Win Funds and Influence Students," in K. Larsen (ed.), *Social Psychology: Crisis or Failure?* (Monmouth, OR: Institute for Theoretical History, 1980):129–157. For the key notion of asymmetric power relations, see E. Apfelbaum, "Relations of Domination and Movements for Liberation: An Analysis of Power Between Groups," in W. G. Austin and S. Worchel (eds.), *The Social Psychology of Intergroup Relations* (Belmont, CA: Brooks/Cole, 1979):188–204 (translated by I. Lubek). For prior exhortations to use a social psychological perspective, see I. Lubek, "A Brief Social Psychological Analysis of Research on Aggression in Social Psychology," in A. Buss (ed.), *Psychology in Social Context* (New York: Irvington, 1979):282. Social psychological analyses of scientific enterprises, although not always explicitly identified as such, may be viewed as operating in D. Campbell, "Tribal Models"; I. I. Mitroff, *The Subjective Side of Science: A Philosophical Inquiry into the Psychology of the Apollo Moon Scientists* (Amsterdam: Elsevier, 1974); and M. Mahoney, *Scientist as Subject: The Psychological Imperative* (Cambridge, MA: Ballinger, 1976). Sociologists of science also draw on social psychological levels of analysis; see, e.g., G. Lemaine, et al. (eds.), *Perspectives on the Emergence of Scientific Disciplines* (Chicago: Aldine, 1976).

43 See Kuhn, *Structure of Scientific Revolutions,* 175 and I. Lakatos, "Falsification and the Methodology of Scientific Research Programmes," in I. Lakatos and A. Musgrave (eds.), *Criticism and the Growth of Knowledge* (Cambridge: Cambridge University Press, 1970), 176. For previous work addressing problems of scientific progress in contemporary research situations, see Lubek, "A Brief Social Psychological Analysis," Lubek and Apfelbaum, "Analyse psycho-sociologique." For case histories, see E. Apfelbaum and I. Lubek, "Augustin Hamon aux origines de la psychologie sociale," *Recherches de Psychologie Sociale* 4 (1982):35–48; I. Lubek and E. Apfelbaum, "Early Social Psychological Writings of the 'Anarchist' Augustin Hamon" (University of Guelph: Unpublished paper, 1982, 39 pages). For an analysis of progress involving both historical and contemporary sources, see Lubek, "Fifty Years of Frustration and Aggression."

44 J. Ziman, *Public Knowledge* (Cambridge: Cambridge University Press, 1967).

45 See, e.g., K. J. Gergen, *Toward Transformation in Social Knowledge* (New York: Springer-Verlag, 1982); K. J. Gergen, "The Social Constructionist Movement in Modern Psychology," *American Psychologist* 40 (1985):266–275; K. D. Knorr-Cetina, "The Constructivist Programme in Sociology of Science: Retreats or Advances?" *Social Studies of Science* 12 (1982):320–324.

46 For an early discussion of these differences, see Kuhn, *Structure of Scientific Revolutions,* and Lakatos and Musgrave, *Criticism and the Growth of Knowledge,* therein especially T. S. Kuhn, "Logic of Discovery or Psychology of Research?" 22–23; T. S. Kuhn, "Reflections on My Critics," 231–278; and Lakatos, "Falsification," 91–93, 155, 177–180. See R. K. Merton, "The Sociology of Science: An Episodic Memoir," in R. K. Merton and J. Gaston (eds.), *The Sociology of Science in Europe* (Carbondale: Southern Illinois University Press, 1977):68–75, for a thoughtful differentiation of Kuhnian and Popperian positions and their relationship to the Mertonian and other perspectives in sociology of science.

47 See Lubek and Apfelbaum, "Analyse psycho-sociologique"; Lubek, "Psychological Establishment." Up to this point, we have loosely used the term paradigm in several senses, as Kuhn originally did, until taken to task by critics about the imprecision of this useful concept. See Kuhn, *Structure of Scientific Revolutions;* and M. Masterman, "The Nature of a Paradigm," in Lakatos and Musgrave, *Criticism and the Growth of Knowledge,* 59–90.

48 D. J. de Solla Price, *Little Science, Big Science* (New York: Columbia University Press, 1963); Crane, *Invisible Colleges.*

49 Apfelbaum, "Relations of Domination"; Lubek, "The Psychological Establishment."

50 Asymmetric relations involving funding of research, apprenticeship training, career and employment decisions are discussed in Lubek, "Toward a Social Psychology of Social Psychology" and "Psychological Establishment."

51 We suspect that this citation data has also been affected by the changing degree of overlap of journal coverage of *SSCI* and *SCI*, and the extent to which their coverage is complete. For example, in recent years, *Science, Nature,* and *JCPP* are only selectively searched by *SSCI*.

52 See "Journal Operations," *American Psychologist* 21 (1966):1139–1145. For other APA journal rejection rates between 1951–1973, see Lubek and Apfelbaum, "Analyse psycho-sociologique," 132.

53 W. Estes, letter to Garcia, 26 May 1965.

54 Garcia, letter to Estes, 4 June 1965.

55 Estes, letter to Garcia, 8 June 1965.

56 Garcia, letter to Estes, 4 June 1965.

57 Revusky, in his letter to Estes, 8 July 1965, noted that "even though Garcia's results are very different from most of those obtained by American learning psychologists, they are very compatible with those obtained by ethologists and with Russian interoceptive conditioning." He took strong exception to the reviewer's remarks: "The reaction of your consultant is a fine example of one reason conditioning theory is getting less important in the U.S. The man knows the rules, Garcia's result has violated the rules, and therefore something is wrong. The first thing the consultant wants is the use of experimental designs to obscure the effect . . . and the pseudoconditioning objection is stupid." According to M. E. P. Seligman and J. Hager (eds.), *Biological Boundaries of Learning* (New York: Appleton-Century-Crofts, 1972), 8, the debate about the rejection of Garcia's paper by *JCPP* had a final word in 1968, when Estes, in a letter to Garcia, graciously regretted his earlier negative decision.

58 J. Garcia and R. A. Koelling, "A Comparison of Aversion Induced by X-rays, Drugs, and Toxins," *Radiation Research Supplement* 7 (1967):439–450; J. Garcia and R. A. Koelling, "The Relation of Cue to Consequence in Avoidance Learning," *Psychonomic Science* 4 (1966):123–124; J. Garcia, F. R. Ervin, and R. A. Koelling, "Learning with Prolonged Delay of Reinforcement," *Psychonomic Science* 4 (1966):121–122.

59 J. Garcia, F. R. Ervin, C. H. Yorke and R. A. Koelling, "Conditioning with Delayed Vitamin Injections," *Science* 155 (1967):716–718; J. Garcia, B. K. McGowan, F. R. Ervin and R. A. Koelling, "Cues: Their Relative Effectiveness as a Function of the Reinforcer," *Science* 160 (1968):794–795.

60 J. Garcia and F. R. Ervin, "Gustatory-visceral and Telereceptor-cutaneous Conditioning: Adaptation in the Internal and External Milieus," *Communication in Behavioral Biology* Part A, 1 (1968):380–415.

61 Kimble, *Hilgard and Marquis' Conditioning and Learning;* M. E. P. Seligman, "On the Generality of the Laws of Learning," *Psychological Review* 77 (1970):406–418.

62 Lubek and Apfelbaum, "Analyse psycho-sociologique."

63 Garcia, letter to Associate Editor Harrison, 27 January 1967.

64 J. Garcia, F. R. Ervin, and R. A. Koelling, "Bait-shyness: A Test of Toxicity with N-2," *Psychonomic Science* 7 (1967):245–246.

65 J. Garcia, B. K. McGowan, and K. F. Green, "Biological Constraints on Conditioning," in A. Black and W. Prokasy (eds.), *Classical Conditioning, II* (New

York: Appleton-Century-Crofts, 1972). Reprinted with other "classic" Garcia papers in Seligman and Hager, *Biological Boundaries of Learning.*

66 Garcia y Robertson and Garcia, "X-rays and Learned Taste Aversions."

67 A. W. Melton, "Editorial," *Journal of Experimental Psychology* 64 (1962):553–557.

68 W. D. Garvey and B. C. Griffith, "Scientific Communication: Its Role in the Conduct of Research and Creation of Knowledge," *American Psychologist* 26 (1971):349–362.

69 See also Lubek and Apfelbaum, "Analyse psycho-sociologique."

70 Revusky, "Interference with Progress," 61.

71 Garcia, letter to Assistant Editor of *Science,* 5 August 1977.

72 Garcia, "Tilting at the Papermills" (see note 5).

73 Lubek and Apfelbaum, "Analyse psycho-sociologique."

74 Ibid.

75 E. O. Smigel and H. L. Ross, "Factors in the Editorial Decision," Paper presented at the Sixth World Congress of Sociology, Evian, 9 September 1966; W. A. Scott, "Interreferee Agreement on Some Characteristics of Manuscripts Submitted to the *Journal of Personality and Social Psychology,*" *American Psychologist* 29 (1974):698–702; C. Hendrick, "Editorial Comment," *Personality and Social Psychology Bulletin* 3 (1977):1; S. Scarr and B. L. R. Weber, "The Reliability of Reviews for the American Psychologist," *American Psychologist* 33 (1978):935.

76 Revusky, "Interference with Progress."

77 Garcia, personal communication, 29 December 1978.

78 Revusky, "Interference with Progress," 64.

79 Garcia, personal communications, 18 December 1984 and 19 July 1986.

80 Garvey and Griffith, "Scientific Communication"; Crane, *Invisible Colleges.*

81 Cf. A. W. Melton (ed.), *Categories of Human Learning* (New York: Academic Press, 1964); Hilgard and Bower, *Theories of Learning;* J. F. Hall, *The Psychology of Learning* (New York: Lippincott, 1966); C. N. Cofer, "Motivation," *Annual Review of Psychology* 10 (1959):173–202; H. H. Kendler, "Learning," *Annual Review of Psychology* 10 (1959):43–88; W. K. Estes, *Learning Theory and Mental Development* (New York: Academic Press, 1970); J. Arbit, "Avoidance Conditioning Through Irradiation: A Note on Physiological Mechanisms and Psychological Implications," *Psychological Review* 65 (1958):167–169; E. Furchtgott, "Behavioral Effects of Ionizing Radiations," *Psychological Review* 53 (1956):321–334; E. Furchtgott, "Postscript to 'Behavioral Effects of Ionizing Radiations: 1955–1961'," *Psychological Bulletin* 61 (1964):236–238; M. E. Bitterman and W. M. Schoel, "Instrumental Learning in Animals: Parameters of Reinforcement," *Annual Review of Psychology* 21 (1970):367–436; M. A. D'Amato, "Delayed Matching and Short-term Memory in Monkeys," in G. Bower (ed.), *The Psychology of Learning and Motivation,* Vol. 7 (New York: Academic Press, 1973):227–269; and A. Dickinson and N. J. Mackintosh, "Classical Conditioning in Animals," *Annual Review of Psychology* 29 (1978):587–612.

82 See M. E. Bitterman, "The Comparative Analysis of Learning: Are the Laws of Learning the Same in All Animals," *Science* 188 (1975):708; and his later "Technical Comment on: Flavor Aversion Learning," *Science* 192 (1976):266. The response to the first article, J. Garcia, W. C. Hankins and K. W. Rusiniak,

"Flavor Aversion Studies," *Science* 192 (1976):265–266, written immediately, did not appear until 10 months later, accompanied by Bitterman's "Technical Note."

83 Revusky, "Interference with Progress."

84 See, e.g., Kimble, *Hilgard and Marquis' Conditioning and Learning,* for basic revisions of Hull and Spence and accommodation by the neo-behavioristic paradigm/exemplar of such new concepts as "rg-sg" expectancy mechanisms, drive stimuli, and conditioned frustration. For more far-reaching paradigmatic reforms, see N. E. Miller, "Liberalization of Basic S-R Concepts: Extensions to Conflict Behavior, Motivation and Social Learning," in S. Koch (ed.), *Psychology: A Study of a Science,* Vol. 2. (New York: McGraw-Hill, 1959), 196–292; O. H. Mowrer, *Learning Theory and Behavior* (New York: Wiley, 1960) for a revision involving two-factor theory; and W. K. Estes, "Stimulus-response Theory of Drive," in M. R. Jones (ed.), *Nebraska Symposium on Motivation,* Vol. 6 (Lincoln: University of Nebraska Press, 1958), 35–69, for a redefinition of stimulus and response.

85 P. Rozin and J. W. Kalat, "Specific Hungers and Poison Avoidance as Adaptive Specialisation of Learning," *Psychological Review* 78 (1971):459–486.

86 S. Revusky and J. Garcia, "Learned Associations over Long Delays," in G. H. Bower (ed.), *The Psychology of Learning and Motivation: Advances in Research and Theory,* Vol. 4 (New York: Academic Press, 1970), 1–84. Revusky explained how an article co-authored by Garcia could find a place in the important series on *Psychology of Learning and Motivation* founded by Spence and Spence in 1967. The first two volumes planned by the Spences were monopolized by the Yale-Iowa-Texas axis. When Kenneth Spence died in 1967, his editorship passed to Yale-trained Gordon Bower, who invited Revusky, a previous acquaintance, to contribute a chapter. Revusky insisted on Garcia's inclusion, as a pioneer researcher in the area. Revusky was responsible for the major share of the writing, and reported that he kept an even keel, taking some of Garcia's bolder ideas and couching them "in a reasonably conservative way. It was precisely because of my traditional background that I was able to have an impact on learning theorists." Personal communication, 1 December 1978; see also Revusky, "Interference with Progress," 64.

87 R. C. Bolles, "The Avoidance Learning Problem," in G. Bower (ed.), *The Psychology of Motivation and Learning,* Vol. 6 (New York: Academic Press, 1972), 97–145; D'Amato, "Delayed Matching." Despite the series' increasing emphasis on human cognitive learning under editor G. Bower, there were some additional citations following Garcia's professional recognition. In the 2615 pages published between 1979 and 1986, seven articles were cited in which Garcia was senior author and five in which he was junior author. See chapters by M. Domjan, vol. 17; P. C. Holland, vol. 18, and R. M. Colwill and R. A. Rescorla, vol. 20.

88 Seligman, "On the Generality of the Laws of Learning." See also Seligman and Hager, *Biological Boundaries of Learning;* and S. J. Shettleworth, "Constraints on Learning," in D. S. Lehrman, R. A. Hinde, and E. Shaw (eds.), *Advances in the Study of Behavior,* Vol. 4 (New York: Academic Press, 1972), 1–68.

89 Davis and Hurwitz, *Operant-Pavlovian Interactions* (See note 3).

90 See Lubek and Apfelbaum, "Analyse psycho-sociologique," and Lubek, "Fifty Years of Frustration and Aggression" on the longevity of paradigms.

91 Garcia recently reported that such confrontations with APA editors still occur; personal communication, 19 July 1986.

4

ON THE MARGINS: WOMEN AND THE PROFESSIONALIZATION OF PSYCHOLOGY IN THE UNITED STATES, 1890–1940

LAUREL FURUMOTO

Historians Joan Jacobs Brumberg and Nancy Tomes have recently called attention to a neglected area of inquiry in the development of the modern professions. Although the topic has been at the center of historical analysis for over two decades, these authors charge that the debate has not incorporated a crucial aspect: "the entry of middle class women into the professional milieu."[1] Surprisingly, professional women have also been largely overlooked in the current wave of historical writing on women and work. Brumberg and Tomes attribute this semiexclusion in part to the personal conflicts of women historians regarding the issue of professionalism in their own lives. They also implicate the recent emphasis on social history which has led a generation of men and women historians to rewrite history from the bottom up.

As a corrective the authors propose a research agenda that stresses the importance of a comparative approach, in which "separate histories of individual professions . . . constitute a crucial first step."[2] This chapter is offered as a contribution to this effort and describes in necessarily broad strokes the participation of women in the American psychological profession from the emergence of the modern discipline in the 1890s until the approach of World War II. The need for such a study is clear, for virtually nothing has been written about the professionalization of women in American psychology. In fact, as yet there is not even a full history of the professionalization of the men in the field.[3]

An account of the women is complicated in that there came to be two distinctly different working branches of the psychological profession: academicians and practitioners, with the situation for women different in each. Psychology originated as an occupation within academia, and by shortly after the turn of the century was firmly established there with good prospects for future growth. The practitioner branch of psychology, which would not experience any appreciable development until after World War I, used academia as its staging area. From the point of view of one historian, who has chronicled the development of psychology as a profession in the United States, this pattern was unique in its time. Applied psychologists, Donald S. Napoli claims, were the first occupational group to emerge directly from the university en route to professionalism. They had no nineteenth-century predecessors who engaged in volunteer work or apprenticeships before shifting to more formal training. On the contrary, the practitioners held college degrees from the inception of applied psychology. As Napoli indicates, this situation provoked conflict with academic psychologists, whose professional identity was that of college professor: "The academicians controlled psychological associations, journals, and graduate programs. They outnumbered the practitioners until the end of World War II, and they were reluctant to endanger their prestige as scholars by promoting the desires of their nonacademic colleagues."[4]

Within the academic sector, the employment opportunities for women psychologists were severely limited. Margaret Rossiter's assessment of the plight of women scientists in general from the late nineteenth century up to World War II also applies to women psychologists in particular: "Those very institutions that would educate them and award them doctorates would not hire them for their faculties. Until the women could find a way around that dichotomy, their positions in science and academia would remain marginal."[5] Thus women, who by the 1890s were gaining access to advanced training and taking PhDs in psychology, would find their employment opportunities restricted almost entirely to positions in women's colleges. And the availability of even these was confined to women who remained unmarried.

THE FIRST GENERATION OF WOMEN PSYCHOLOGISTS

In 1906, psychologist James McKeen Cattell published *American Men of Science* (hereafter *AMS*), the first comprehensive biographical directory of scientists in North America. Of more than 4,000 individuals who had engaged in scientific research or were members of scientific societies, the volume listed 186 who identified themselves as psychologists either by field or subject of research; 22 of them were women.[6] Although a few early women psychologists, for example, five women who were members of the American Psychological Association (hereafter APA) by 1906, were omitted from the directory, and some other included women were only tenuously related to the field, the 22 constitute a fairly complete group of early American women psychologists for whom basic biographical information is available.[7] These women shared with the men psychologists listed in the first edition of *AMS* the experience of being pioneers in what

Cattell had hailed as "the newest of the sciences."[8] Women participated in the discipline from the beginning, joining the APA soon after it was organized in 1892 and presenting papers at its annual meetings thereafter. They also published regularly in the newly founded psychological journals contributing original research, reviews, and commentaries.

However, the life histories of the early women psychologists are far from uniform in the degree of professional involvement they reveal. Approximately half of the women remained unmarried, and most of these had life-long careers as psychologists. Among them at least two – Mary Whiton Calkins and Margaret Floy Washburn – became acknowledged by their male and female peers as eminent psychologists. For the remainder who truncated their careers by choosing to marry, several, for example, Christine Ladd-Franklin, Helen Thompson Woolley, and Ethel Puffer Howes, struggled with varying degrees of success to remain professionally and scientifically active without the advantage of a regular academic appointment. A few of the women who married seem to have abandoned any attempt to continue in a professional role or to resume it later.

Perhaps the newness of the discipline and its resulting need to swell its numbers explains at least in part why women comprised a larger proportion of psychologists during the early years of the field than they did of physicists and chemists in the same period. By the time APA observed its 25th anniversary in 1917, women constituted 13% of the membership, and Cattell boasted in an address given to celebrate the occasion that the percentage of women in psychology surpassed that of any other science. Basing his claim on a count he had made of the number of women in the second edition of *AMS* published in 1910, he reported the following percentages of women among the sciences: psychology, 9.8; zoology, 7.5; chemistry, 2.1; physics and geology, 1.3.[9] The relatively high proportion of women persisted throughout the decades covered in this chapter. In 1921 and 1938, for example, the proportion of women psychologists listed in *AMS* was 20.4 and 21.7%, respectively. Of the fifteen sciences compared by Rossiter, the proportion of women was higher only in nutrition.[10]

Returning to the 22 women identified as psychologists in the first edition of *AMS,* some obvious questions arise. Who were they, and how comparable were their lives and experiences to those of male psychologists? The women can be described generally as Anglo-Saxon Protestants of privileged middle-class backgrounds, in this respect quite similar to the men. In fact, the similarities extend to place of origin, date of birth, and educational attainments. Most were born in the Northeastern or Middlewestern United States; though some were Canadians and among the men a few were European born, several were children of missionaries born abroad. The median age of both the women and the men in the directory in 1906 was about 39. However, the birth dates of the men extended back almost two decades earlier than those of the women (1830 as compared to 1847). This reflects the women's later access to higher education, for the women psychologists in the first edition of *AMS* were in the vanguard of women who sought a collegiate education equivalent to that of men in the decades following the Civil War.[11]

The median age at which both men and women completed their baccalaureate degree was approximately 22. Almost half of the women had earned their degrees from women's colleges; the remainder studied at a variety of coeducational institutions both public and private. Only two of the women reported no graduate work, approximately one-third had studied in Europe at some point, and 18 had completed the requirements for the PhD. The women were somewhat older than the men by the time they completed their graduate training, with the median ages of 31 for the women and 29 for the men. The difference does not seem to result because the women took longer to complete the work for their advanced degrees once they began, but rather is due to a longer hiatus between completing undergraduate work and entering graduate study. In all likelihood this delay reflects the ambivalence many of these women experienced as they contemplated embarking on a course that departed so radically from the traditional middle-class feminine role. Their indecision was no doubt compounded by the fact that in the 1890s, when the majority of the women in the group entered graduate study, the institutions that were most popular among the men for advanced work in psychology (Clark, Columbia, Leipzig, and Harvard) were closed to women.[12]

Overall, the early group of women psychologists were strikingly similar to their more numerous male colleagues in origins, age, and educational attainments. The similarity extended as well to their areas of specialization and research interests. A 1904 article in *Science* assessing the status of American psychology noted that the field had become differentiated into a host of subfields, including – besides experimental psychology – educational, comparative, and a wide variety of other specialty areas.[13] The women were involved in virtually all of the subfields. Furthermore, their research interests were distributed in a pattern indistinguishable from that of the men.

The women were also regular contributors to the psychological literature. Evidence of this comes from a comparison of the publication rates of a group of 25 early women psychologists, including 19 of the 22 women in the first edition of *AMS,* with an equal number of men selected randomly from the APA membership in 1907. Although the women, on the average, published fewer papers and books than the men, they nevertheless contributed substantial numbers of publications to the literature. From 1894 to 1958 the women published an average of 16 items (the number of publications ranging from 0 to 83), while the men had published an average of 26 items (the number of publications ranging from 0 to 100).[14]

Women were invited into the national professional organization almost from the very beginning. At the APA's second annual meeting in 1893, the first two women were elected to membership, and their numbers and participation increased steadily thereafter. This early acceptance of women psychologists stands in stark contrast to the situation of women in some other professional groups. For example, women doctors were excluded from the American Medical Association and women lawyers from the American Bar Association until 1915 and 1918, respectively.[15]

Thus, the early women psychologists were comparable in many respects to their male peers. Furthermore, several became recognized as eminent psychologists as signified, among other things, by being awarded a star in *AMS*. Yet, in occupational status the women were relegated to a distinctly inferior position. This can be documented by comparing employment rates and place of employment within academia for the men and women psychologists appearing in the first edition of *AMS*. The comparison is limited to academic institutions, because, as already mentioned, employment opportunities prior to World War I were confined almost exclusively to that setting. Whereas 65% of the men were college or university presidents or full, associate, or assistant professors in 1906, this was true for only 50% of the women. Comparing those in this sample who appeared in the third edition of *AMS* some fifteen years later, the differential continues: 68% of the men and only 46% of the women held a presidency or professorial rank.[16]

All the women who reached the rank of assistant professor or higher were unmarried, an issue that will be discussed later in the chapter. The institutions that employed them were predominantly women's colleges, and almost without exception only in these settings could the women hope to become a president or full professor. The only known exceptions to this generalization among the women psychologists in the first edition of *AMS* were one woman who was promoted to the rank of professor at Stanford University five years before she retired at age 65 in 1916, and another who held the rank at a normal school in Montana. Normal schools, teacher preparatory institutions whose students were almost exclusively females, constituted another type of institutional setting, lower in prestige than the college or university, in which some early women psychologists found academic employment.

Jobs in women's colleges were clearly not considered desirable appointments for new male PhDs. Among their drawbacks were low salaries, low prestige, heavy teaching loads, and little support for research. William James expressed his incredulity to a colleague in 1898 when a recent Harvard PhD in whom he saw promise accepted an appointment at a women's college: "Palmer tells me that Bakewell is going to Bryn Mawr – *why*, I can't imagine, for I should myself hate to be under that petticoat regime."[17] Cornell's E. B. Titchener wrote to one of his recent PhDs in 1919 about the disadvantages of a post at another women's college in a similar vein: "There is also a minor place at Randolph Macon Woman's College, Lynchburg, Va., but I don't suppose you'd care for that; lots of teaching and no chance of research."[18]

Despite their shortcomings, for those of the first generation of American women psychologists who sought employment, women's colleges were the only institutions where they could realistically hope to be considered for a position and, if hired, to be promoted to a professorial rank. Positions within the normal schools, which also provided some women psychologists with employment, exhibited, perhaps to an even greater degree, the professional drawbacks associated with teaching at the women's colleges. On the positive side, in these institutions women who were required to forgo marriage and family to pursue their academic careers often found themselves part of a female friendship network that provided them with emotional support and life-long companionships.[19]

Educational historian Patricia Palmieri's collective portrait of the women at Wellesley College richly portrays faculty life there, focusing on those who had been on the faculty for more than five years and held the rank of associate or full professor by 1910; five were among the group of 22 women psychologists in the first edition of *AMS*. The origins of the Wellesley professoriate as described by Palmieri sound remarkably similar to those of the early women psychologists as a group. The faculty came mainly from close knit New England families notable for the love and support given to their bright daughters, and were "strikingly homogeneous in terms of social and geographic origins, upbringing, and sociocultural world view."[20]

Palmieri claims, however, that the experience of these women scholars, in which *community* was a central theme, contrasted sharply with that of men at the research universities. In her view, the male academic of the period was an isolated specialist, while the female academic lived within a network of relationships: "These academic women did not shift their life-courses away from the communal mentality as did many male professionals; nor did they singlemindedly adhere to scientific rationalism, specialization, social science objectivity, or hierarchical association in which vertical mobility took precedence over sisterhood."[21]

There were other sources of difference as well, such as the obligations of a daughter to her family labeled the "family claim" by social reformer Jane Addams.[22] Another was the necessity, already mentioned, for an educated woman in the late nineteenth century to opt for either marriage or a career, a decision commonly referred to in the literature of the day as "the cruel choice." In a 1906 article titled "The Passing of Matrimony," feminist writer Charlotte Perkins Gilman described the unenviable situation confronting educated women who, unlike men, were forced to choose between finding self-realization in a career and the personal fulfillment of family life.[23] The lives of two of the Wellesley faculty included in Palmieri's study who were also among the early group of psychologists in the first edition of *AMS* provide particularly compelling examples of these gender-specific themes. One of the women was Mary Whiton Calkins (1863–1930), the other Ethel Puffer (1872–1950).

Calkins and Puffer exemplify the homogeneity already described in the early women academics and psychologists. Besides their shared Protestant New England heritage, both were first-born children in middle-class families, received their undergraduate education at Smith College, and did their doctoral work in the Harvard philosophy department under the guidance of psychologist Hugo Münsterberg. Both women were strongly attracted to academic careers and obtained appointments at Wellesley, where Calkins founded a psychological laboratory and introduced the new scientific psychology into the curriculum in the early 1890s. Puffer joined the Wellesley faculty in 1901, teaching courses in philosophy and in aesthetics, her area of specialization in psychology. Colleagues for several years in the department of philosophy, their life-courses diverged dramatically after 1908, when Ethel Puffer married an MIT-trained civil engineer, Benjamin A. Howes. Calkins remained on the Wellesley faculty, where she continued to teach, publish, and be involved in professional activities for two more decades until her retirement in 1929. She was recognized as an eminent psychologist and philosopher in her time, serving as president of the APA in 1905 and the American Philosophical Association in 1918.[24]

Puffer's career in psychology, in marked contrast, was derailed by her decision to marry. In fact, the mere news of her engagement was enough to squelch her chances for an academic position in New York City, where she and her husband were to reside after their marriage. The president of Smith College, L. Clark Seelye, wrote concerning her candidacy for a position at Barnard College, "I fear the rumor which reached me concerning your engagement may have . . . affected the recommendation which I . . . sent, and that a candidate has already been selected to present to the trustees of Columbia."[25]

Ethel Puffer Howes and her husband settled in Scarsdale, New York, a few years after their marriage where, when Howes was in her forties, she gave birth to two children. She never returned to an academic position in psychology. By the early 1920s, long privately tormented by what she viewed as a conspiracy of silence that operated to mislead talented young women about what they could expect of their future if they chose to marry, she felt impelled to address the issue publicly. In the first of two 1922 articles in the *Atlantic Monthly* Howes reflected on what she called "the persistent vicious alternative" confronting women: "Marriage *or* career – full personal life versus the way of achievement."[26] Admitting that marriage implied motherhood for most women, and believing that mothers needed to be "on call" for their children, Howes was forced to reach a disheartening conclusion. Women suffered an insurmountable disadvantage in careers where they competed with men who accepted the fact that they could not expect to achieve "without the most intense and most ruthless concentration."[27] As long as the culture defined careers as all consuming, and as long as women were expected to bear all the responsibility for the nurturing of children, there could be no way out of this dilemma.

Acknowledging both "the well-trained woman's need of carrying on after marriage [and] the mother's inability for an output of a certain quantity, deliverable without interruption," Howes suggested a means of coping with this predicament in her second article.[28] She exhorted women to forgo careers in the traditional sense in favor of professional work that could be accomplished on a flexible schedule as their primary duty of mothering permitted. How to enable "the trained woman, who finds her professional activities coming to a full stop in marriage and motherhood" to achieve what she referred to as "continuity" became a central concern in Howes' life throughout the 1920s.[29]

Her articles aroused the interest of influential people, leading in 1925 to the founding of the Institute for the Coordination of Women's Interests (hereafter ICWI) at Smith College, with Howes as director and supported by a three-year grant from the Laura Spelman Rockefeller Foundation. Despite an impressive array of projects carried out by Howes and the ICWI staff during the tenure of the grant, funding was not renewed and the institute was phased out by the end of the 1920s.

Presumably, it was the foundation's view that the efforts of the ICWI had been directed too much toward developing demonstration programs such as a cooperative nursery school and a food service that delivered hot meals to families, and that it had neglected the task of working out a theoretical framework for coordinating women's interests. Furthermore, the foundation's hope to see the ICWI integrated into Smith College and its aims reflected in the curriculum had not been realized. There was strong opposition to the institute among the faculty, many of whom believe it signalled a trend toward vocationalism or home economics and posed a threat to the liberal arts ideal. Finally, it has been suggested by one historian that Howes' efforts to reduce women's domestic responsibilities to free them for other vocations was ill-timed. Dolores Hayden argues that the institute was a casualty of a larger societal phenomenon, the need of defense industries after World War I for new markets which turned out to be domestic appliances such as refrigerators, vacuum cleaners, and washing machines. By the late 1920s, advertisers were portraying women as avid consumers, rather than producers, housewives busy buying and running appliances who had plenty to do at home without a career.[30]

After the demise of the institute and perhaps changed by her experience as its director, Howes was less sanguine about the ability of "special devices" and "personal adjustments" to enable women to "participate in both professional and family life." In her last published utterance on the topic, she insisted instead on the "necessity of transforming the whole social setting and the inner attitudes of men and women to accept the two fold need of women as fundamental."[31]

Even if a career-minded woman of the late nineteenth century steered clear of marriage and motherhood, she would still be subject in all likelihood to other gender-specific family demands. As mentioned earlier, Jane Addams called these obligations of daughters "the family claim." Mary Calkins spoke quite candidly about this in an address she presented to a group of undergraduate women in 1913. The notes for her talk, "The Place of Scholarship in Life," describe a situation which was for her, as eldest child and sole surviving daughter in her family, entirely familiar.

She pointed out that every scholar was confronted by the necessity of reconciling "the often conflicting claims of scholarship and life in its social relations." While acknowledging that this task was seldom easy for anyone, Calkins maintained that it was particularly difficult in the lives of most women, because they had more exacting social and especially family obligations than men. Moreover, she believed this to be true for unmarried women as well as mothers: "The chances are, for example, that the unmarried daughter rather than the unmarried son, if a choice became necessary, should undertake the responsibility for their parents' home."[32]

These words contain a very personal message, for Calkins herself never married and lived her entire life in her parents' home. As her three brothers married and moved away, and her parents became elderly, she assumed more and more responsibility for running the household and looking after her parents' welfare. These duties were to occupy her throughout her life – she outlived her father by just six years and was survived by her mother.

The struggle of educated women in the late nineteenth and early twentieth centuries to forge professional identities has been examined by historian Joyce Antler. She contends that women who entered careers in that era experienced intense conflict as they attempted to reconcile their gender-identity with the masculine model of professional behavior. In her view, "in the absence of a consensus among women as to appropriate directions, and in the face of severe personal, familial, economic and political barriers, the inchoate attempt of educated women to generate a redefinition of female roles was doomed to failure."[33]

Scrutiny of the lives and careers of the early women psychologists does not challenge Antler's basic conclusion. Although it is true that the women were present in the discipline at an early date and in relatively large numbers, nevertheless their gender marginalized them dramatically. Not only were they severely restricted in their employment opportunities, they were also subject to powerful societal norms defining women's role that often contradicted the requirements of the professional role.

WOMEN AND THE BURGEONING OF APPLIED PSYCHOLOGY

The practitioner branch of the profession had not yet been launched when the first-generation women psychologists were completing their graduate training and seeking employment in the late nineteenth and early twentieth centuries. Although the idea of applying psychology had a certain amount of currency and gained in popularity as the century advanced through the efforts of promoters such as James McKeen Cattell, G. Stanley Hall, and Hugo Münsterberg, very few psychologists were earning a livelihood as practitioners prior to World War I.

Both the promise that psychologists saw in the field of applied psychology and the small number of psychologists who were actually full-time practitioners are attested by statements commemorating the 25th anniversary of the American Psychological Association in 1917. Commenting favorably on the growth of applied psychology, Joseph Jastrow prophesied that the day of the psychological practitioner was coming. And G. Stanley Hall pointed to waves of new interest in the applied areas. There was hope for the future of experimental applied psychology, Margaret Floy Washburn thought, because of the able leadership of men such as E. L. Thorndike, Harry Hollingworth, and Walter Dill Scott. Though Cattell counted only sixteen members of APA "connected with boards of education, hospitals, laboratories of reformatory and charitable institutions and the like" compared with 272 academics, he suggested that it was "not impossible that this group, now so small, may at our fiftieth anniversary surpass in numbers those engaged in teaching."[34]

The trend of the field in the next two decades was in line with Cattell's prophecy. Between 1916 and 1938, the number of APA members in teaching positions grew from 233 to 1,229, a somewhat more than five-fold increase; but the numbers in applied jobs increased nearly twenty-nine times, from 24 to 694.[35] Many of those moving into applied work were women.

In trying to piece together the career patterns of women practitioners in psychology, the historian is confronted, as is often the case in women's history, by the problem of locating pertinent information. The female past, for a variety of reasons, has not been well preserved. There is reason to believe that only a small minority of women practitioners belonged to APA in the 1920s and 1930s, and few of them would have been included in directories such as *American Men of Science*. Thus two major sources helpful for identifying women academic psychologists provide only the tip of the iceberg for the practitioners.

A great deal of painstaking work, much of which involves tracking down and collecting material from scattered and obscure sources, remains to be done. Not until this task has been carried out will we have an information base adequate to attempt a reconstruction of the career patterns and professional experience of the second generation of women psychologists who came to predominate in the practitioner role in the 1920s and 1930s. What follows in this section is a preliminary exploration outlining women's move into the service branch of the discipline between the two world wars.

World War I

With the advent of World War I, many psychologists were eager to find ways in which psychology could aid in the war effort. Robert M. Yerkes, then president of the American Psychological Association, spearheaded the campaign to offer the profession's services to the military, which eventually came to involve several hundred psychologists either in uniform or as civilian consultants. Two major tasks were assigned to psychology: determining the occupational skills and testing the intelligence of new recruits.

Involvement of women psychologists in this effort was practically non-existent. Margaret Rossiter has commented on the underutilization of women psychologists in World War I, pointing out that only two of the psychologists among the large staff of the Army Psychological Testing Program that Yerkes directed were women. Moreover, "Mabel Fernald and Margaret Cobb, both staff psychologists at the . . . Social Hygiene Laboratory of the Bedford Hills Reformatory in New York State . . . were listed as mere 'assistants.'"[36] Rossiter maintains that this exclusion later had serious consequences for women in psychology, because most of the scientific leadership in the postwar period, for example at the National Research Council, built upon contacts established during the war in Washington.

Various accounts of psychology's involvement in the war effort concur in observing that there were gains for the youthful profession.[37] None of them, however, addresses the issue of the wartime situation of women psychologists. Franz Samelson, for example, notes that the war work brought psychology into public view, established it as a legitimate empirical science in the eyes of scientists in other disciplines, and notes that "the war experience had created a network of interpersonal contacts" among psychologists who were to go on to hold key positions in the APA and chairs at prestigious universities.[38] What he neglects to mention, perhaps because it is so obvious, is that this was an exclusively male network.

The 1920s: decade of expansion

American psychology received a tremendous developmental impetus as a result of World War I. According to Michael M. Sokal, "psychologists of the period shared a confidence possibly not seen at any other time in their science's history."[39] The field also experienced dramatic growth; in 1930 there were twice as many PhD psychologists as there had been in 1920.[40]

The expansion of academic departments during the same time period made it possible to absorb most of the new male psychologists. New academic positions for women psychologists, however, did not keep pace with the rate at which they received doctorates. In this same period, a change in the places where women received their doctorates indicates a fundamental shift away from training in the experimental areas characteristic of the earlier period toward the applied fields.[41]

A survey by an economist of 1,025 women who received the PhD between 1877 and 1924 highlighted the inadequate opportunities for women in the academic profession. The results of the study, published in 1929, reaffirmed the obvious fact that women were rarely admitted to the higher professorial ranks in the universities. In addition, many respondents referred to being discriminated against in matters of appointment, promotion, and salary. A section containing respondents' comments directed to prospective candidates for the degree was included in the report. The reply of one, identified as an associate professor at a university who had taken her PhD between 1915 and 1924, offers a personal perspective on the lack of opportunity for women psychologists in the academic sector:

> The factor of sex makes a noticeable difference in securing university teaching positions, and unless a woman intends to make practical use of her psychological training in clinical, vocational, or other lines I would not advise her to get a Ph.D. for the purpose of teaching in a university.[42]

The variety of practical uses to which women who had the PhD in psychology were putting their training was revealed in another section of the report. One woman was a psychologist in a juvenile court and had previously worked as a mental examiner in a private school. Another was with a child guidance clinic, prior to which she had had experience in three different positions in a state reformatory for women, a hospital, and a county child guidance clinic. A third held a position as a consultant in office management with a life insurance company, having previously worked as assistant director of a bureau of personnel research.[43]

Observing that by 1930 "men comprised over two-thirds of all American psychologists . . . but they made up a distinct minority of applied psychologists," Napoli points out that this situation "did not augur well for the professionalization of applied psychology."[44] It is necessary to qualify such generalizations about applied psychology, however, because the field was not homogeneous, but was made up of at least three sub-fields – industrial, school, and clinical – each of which had its own pattern of professionalization. Each also had differing proportions of women in its ranks. By 1938 women outnumbered men by 3 to 1 in school psychology, there were about equal numbers of men and women doing clinical work, and men outnumbered women in the industrial area.[45]

Industrial psychology remained the most closely tied to academia; few psychologists in the 1920s left college or university posts to take up full-time work in industry. Instead, industrial psychologists engaged in part-time work, usually studying job requirements, vocational selection, and merchandising. For example, Walter Dill Scott, a leading industrial psychologist, remained a professor at Northwestern University while he was organizing a consulting firm after World War I. By 1923, the Scott Company was working with more than 40 industrial firms to develop special tests for particular jobs and to promote efficient practices. Several other prominent academic psychologists, including James R. Angell, E. L. Thorndike and Robert M. Yerkes, were connected with the company as "Associates."[46]

School psychology thrived with the widespread use of intelligence testing in public school systems and in higher education following World War I. However, a deepening gulf came to separate the professionals with whom the tests originated and the "mental testers" who administered them. Educational psychologists tended to be situated in academic settings and to enjoy considerably more occupational prestige than practitioners. J. E. Wallace Wallin, a male applied psychologist who was active in efforts to improve the status of the practitioner branch of the profession as early as 1917, recalled "that school administrators (*ca.* 1915) considered practically anyone with a Binet test qualified to measure and diagnose mental and educational deviations and to differentiate among children for instructional purposes." Thus, although some psychologists working in the schools had doctorates and extensive experience (and were grossly underpaid), in general "the early school psychologists were not held in very high esteem."[47]

Clinical psychologists in the 1920s worked almost entirely in institutional settings and were in persistent conflict with another professional group struggling to establish itself, psychiatrists.[48] There was also a deep division between clinical and academic psychology, indicated by the fact that only about one-fifth of the country's clinical psychologists belonged to the APA. Academic psychologists tended to view "clinical psychology as menial work done in a subservient role," as John J. B. Morgan of Northwestern University observed; it was "'not the work for a man.'"[49] A revealing episode about the attitude of academic psychologists toward psychologists working in clinical settings is described in the reminiscences of Phyllis Blanchard, who took her MA and PhD at Clark University in the 1910s with G. Stanley Hall. Lacking other job offers, she spent a post-doctoral year (1919–1920) as a research assistant to Hall and then accepted a position as a psychologist on the staff of the New York State Reformatory for Women in Bedford Hills, New York. She distinctly remembered her mentor being worried about her taking the job, because he feared that she would become "just a mental tester"; and when she was interviewed, in her eighties, she still regretted that Hall had died before he could see her "become something more than a 'Binet tester.'"[50]

Wallin, whose comments on the low status of school psychology have already been noted, claimed, based on his own experience in the New Jersey State Village for Epileptics and on correspondence with other psychologists in similar settings, that "the psychologist enjoyed no professional prestige" comparable to that of staff members who held medical degrees. Rather, the psychologist was regarded as "a mere technician," was "over-regimented," "humiliated," and not invited to staff meetings. This repressive institutional atmosphere, Wallin observed, "did not stimulate one toward professional achievement or attract professional workers."[51]

The pattern that emerged as jobs in applied psychology continued to proliferate in the 1920s and beyond was for women psychologists to predominate in the lower status practitioner roles as mental testers and clinicians, while men psychologists retained their hegemony over the higher status academic areas—applied as well as pure—of the discipline.

The depression years

The depression had a profound effect on the academic job market for psychologists. Napoli reports that the squeeze began to be felt in the early 1930s, as the production of new PhDs outstripped academic openings. Soon "the shriveling of the academic marketplace affected psychology departments throughout the country."[52] New men PhDs in psychology found themselves confronting a situation the women had experienced a decade earlier: diminishing expectations for employment in higher education as the number of candidates far exceeded available positions. Men graduate students and their professors looked toward the applied areas of psychology, as the women had previously done, for a solution to their professional difficulties. During the 1930s, many psychologists were unemployed and various attempts were made to create jobs for them outside academia, including seeking support through the Works Progress Administration.[53]

Women psychologists, it seems, suffered less than the men from the dismal academic job situation, because their access to jobs in higher education had always been severely restricted and because they had been taking jobs as practitioners in increasing numbers since the 1920s. Some support for this conjecture is provided by statistics from the *American Men of Science* directories for 1921 (3rd edition) and 1938 (6th edition). Whereas in 1921, there were 15% of the women psychologists in the directory unemployed, in 1938 the percentage was 10.5.[54]

Although some men psychologists may have looked for jobs in applied fields in the 1930s because academic positions were scarce, at the end of the decade academic psychology was still seen as men's work and applied psychology as women's. Even within the more highly feminized branch of the discipline women did not attain leadership roles commensurate with their numbers. In the 1930s, women, not surprisingly, held virtually no offices in the APA, which was dominated by academicians. Women were better represented in the American Association for Applied Psychology, organized in 1937, as division chairs, journal editors, and administrative officers. Yet, in the seven years of this professional society's existence, with approximately one-third of its membership women, no woman was elected to the presidency and only two served on the 29-member founding board.[55]

Two articles that appeared in 1939, one by a male academic psychologist and the other by a woman with a PhD in psychology and an MD degree, testify to the dual labor market that existed in the field. The woman, Gladys D. Frith, directed her article in a newsletter called "Women's Work and Education" to women who might be considering psychology as a profession. She began by pointing out that while "it was formerly thought that if one entered the field of psychology he (sic) was limited to a life of teaching or of research which in both instances usually required that he (sic) be connected with some institution of higher learning," this was no longer the case.[56] She informed her readers that presently "the practice of psychology or applied psychology is coming decidedly to the front" and backed up her assertion with statistics from a recent article on employment trends in the applied fields.[57] The article stated that among the APA membership the number of applied jobs had increased from 9.3% of the total jobs reported in 1916 to 36.1% in 1938. Quoting another woman psychologist, Gertrude Hildreth, Frith maintained that "'As a teaching profession, psychology was, and still is largely a man's field, but the growth trends in the profession show that among the persons who have recently entered the consulting and applied fields, the women out-number the men.'"[58]

Frith and Hildreth were not alone in perceiving better opportunities for women in applied than in academic psychology. Samuel W. Fernberger, an experimental psychologist and professor at the University of Pennsylvania, who incidentally took a condescending view of applied psychologists, agreed.[59] In fact, when a woman graduate student decided to seek an academic career in psychology because she was not interested in an applied position, Fernberger reported that he "held out small hopes for success and told her that he suspected that there were much better opportunities for a woman in a career in applied psychology."[60] In response to his argument and much to Fernberger's surprise, the student discovered that more than 250 of the 688 women who were members or associates of the APA in 1938 held academic positions. His curiosity aroused, Fernberger decided that a "more detailed analysis of the situation seemed advisable" and reported the outcome in an article in the *Psychological Bulletin* entitled "Academic Psychology as a Career for Women."[61]

What he found reconfirmed his original belief. It was true, as his student had shown, that women, who comprised 30% of the APA, were employed in academic positions in substantial numbers. However, if employed in universities, they were likely to remain in the lower ranks and were not usually employed at all in colleges other than those for women. Furthermore, in terms of percentages the men did have a far better chance for academic employment than the women. Among the APA membership 75.3% of the men listed academic positions, while only 37.6% of the women did so. If Fernberger's attitude is representative of what was being communicated to women in graduate programs in psychology during the depression years, it is little wonder that they would be looking for employment opportunities where the odds were more favorable for them than in academe. Given the prejudice against women psychologists in higher education and the dismal job market, a career in applied psychology probably appeared preferable to unemployment.

WOMEN PSYCHOLOGISTS AND THE PROFESSIONAL HIERARCHY

This chapter began with a reference to Joan Brumberg and Nancy Tomes' call for more research on the history of women in the professions. It ends by discussing the model they propose for understanding the status of women in the professions and considering how it might be applied to women in psychology during the period covered by this chapter. Brumberg and Tomes hold that "the structuring of women's participation in the professional work force must be seen as a complex process in which gender distinctions are an organizing principle."[62] They go on to suggest that a comparative approach is essential in analyzing this complex process. In their view, it is necessary to study women's entry into both the feminized service professions (e.g., teaching, nursing, social work, librarianship) and the classically male dominated professions (e.g., medicine, law, engineering, the academy, the clergy) to shed light on the relationship between gender roles and the occupational structure. In this respect, the profession of psychology, which they do not mention, becomes an interesting case study since it comprises both a feminized service branch and a classically male dominated, academic branch.

To begin to make sense of both the pattern of women's participation across the gamut of the professions and their status within any given profession, Brumberg and Tomes borrow a conceptual model of "professional purity" developed by sociologist Andrew Abbott. Abbott claims that within a given profession, the highest status professionals deal with issues that have already had their human complexity and difficulty removed by other colleagues. The lowest status professionals, on the other hand, deal with problems from which the human complexities are not or cannot be removed.[63] Brumberg and Tomes maintain that historically women have been relegated to the bottom of the professional hierarchy, to "the 'dirtiest' areas of professional service ... those involving the most human contact with all its attendant complexities."[64] More specifically, during the nineteenth century, women assumed primary care of such problematic clienteles as the young, the poor, the immigrant, the intemperate, and the sick. The best employment opportunities for women thus came to be found in the so-called helping professions, such as social work and public health, which were created to treat the social ills stemming from immigration, poverty, and labor exploitation.

The low status, or in Abbott's terms, the lack of purity of the helping professions, can be understood as a consequence of the close contact with clients and all the unavoidable human complexity this involves. Women have become concentrated in these fields, Brumberg and Tomes maintain, precisely because the work is unappealing to men. The high status, male-dominated professions, by contrast, do not maintain close contact with their clients and are characterized by philosophical abstraction, isolation, and distance from human complications. How this model of the structure of women's participation in the professions applies to psychology must, by now, be obvious. The high status branch of the field, academic psychology, abstract and isolated within its ivory tower, was never welcoming to women, and few were able to find a place there outside of the women's colleges.

Why psychology's entry into the ranks of the helping professions happened precisely in the 1920s invites speculation. One historian has argued persuasively that a shift was occurring in American society during this period in which expertise came to be directed toward individuals rather than general problems as had been the case in the preceding Progressive era. John C. Burnham maintains that from the 1920s on, social salvation was seen to lie in the psychiatric treatment of everyone. The goal was to adjust the individual to the environment, taking the world as given, rather than attempting to effect desirable social change.[65] Obviously, a vast army of mental health practitioners, including applied psychologists, had to be recruited to achieve this aim. When jobs in the applied branch started to proliferate following World War I, new employment opportunities emerged for women especially in the lower status areas dealing with unruly clientele (e.g., school and clinical psychology). Thus, between the two world wars a gendered occupational hierarchy took shape in psychology: Men continued to predominate in the higher status, more professionally pure academic realm of the discipline, while women found their place in the lower status, less pure practitioner roles.

NOTES

1 J. J. Brumberg and N. Tomes, "Women in the Professions: A Research Agenda for American Historians," *Reviews in American History* 10 (1982):275–276.

2 Ibid., 277.

3 D. S. Napoli's book *Architects of Adjustment: The History of the Psychological Profession in the United States* (Port Washington, NY: Kennikat Press, 1981) provides a helpful overview up until about 1960, but is too brief to treat the subject with the scope and depth it warrants. Other works with material relevant to the professionalization of American psychology are T. M. Camfield, *Psychologists at War: The History of American Psychology and the First World War* (PhD Dissertation: University of Texas at Austin, 1969), and "The Professionalization of American Psychology, 1870–1917," *Journal of The History of the Behavioral Sciences* 9 (1973):66–75. Also helpful are M. Hale, Jr., *Human Science and Social Order: Hugo Münsterberg and the Origins of Applied Psychology* (Philadelphia: Temple University Press, 1980); D. Ross, *G. Stanley Hall: The Psychologist as Prophet* (Chicago: University of Chicago Press, 1972); J. O'Donnell, *The Origins of Behaviorism: American Psychology, 1870–1920* (New York: New York University Press, 1985); and his article "The Crisis of Experimentalism in the 1920s: E. G. Boring and his Uses of History," *American Psychologist* 34 (1979):289–295. Of the works cited only Napoli's addresses, albeit briefly, the role of women in the professionalization of the field.

4 Napoli, *Architects of Adjustment,* 9.

5 M. W. Rossiter, *Women Scientists in America: Struggles and Strategies to 1940* (Baltimore: Johns Hopkins University Press, 1982), 50.

6 J. McK. Cattell (ed.), *American Men of Science: A Biographical Directory* (New York: Science Press, 1906).

7 For a complete list of the 22 women psychologists and additional biographical data on each including date of birth, academic degrees, marital status, subject of

research, and professional positions, see L. Furumoto and E. Scarborough, "Placing Women in the History of Psychology: The First American Women Psychologists," *American Psychologist* 41 (1986):35–42.

8 J. McK. Cattell, *"Homo scientificus Americanus:* Address of the President of the American Society of Naturalists," *Science* 17 (1903):562.

9 J. McK. Cattell, "Our Psychological Association and Research," *Science* 45 (1917):278.

10 Rossiter, *Women Scientists in America,* 136.

11 For an engaging and scholarly account of women's entry into higher education in the United States, see B. M. Solomon, *In the Company of Educated Women: A History of Women and Higher Education in America* (New Haven: Yale University Press, 1985).

12 On the struggle to gain access to graduate training and advanced degrees for women in the late nineteenth and early twentieth centuries, see Rossiter, *Women Scientists in America,* Chapter 2.

13 B. G. Miner, "The Changing Attitude of American Universities toward Psychology," *Science* 20 (1904):299–307.

14 E. Scarborough and L. Furumoto, *Untold Lives: The First Generation of American Women Psychologists* (New York: Columbia University Press, 1987).

15 P. M. Hummer, *The Decade of Elusive Promise: Professional Women in the United States, 1920–1930* (UMI: Research Press, 1979), 23.

16 J. McK. Cattell and D. R. Brimhall (eds.), *American Men of Science: A Biographical Directory,* 3rd ed. (Garrison, NY: Science Press, 1921).

17 William James to George Holmes Howison, 18 May 1898. George Holmes Howison Papers, Bancroft Library, University of California, Berkeley, California.

18 E. B. Titchener to P. T. Young, 24 May 1919. Edward Bradford Titchener Papers, Cornell University, Ithaca, New York.

19 For a portrayal of faculty life at women's colleges in the late nineteenth and early twentieth centuries, see H. L. Horowitz, *Alma Mater: Design and Experience in the Women's Colleges from their Nineteenth Century Beginnings to the 1930's* (New York: Alfred A. Knopf, 1984), Chapter 12.

20 P. A. Palmieri, "Here was Fellowship: A Social Portrait of Academic Women at Wellesley College, 1895–1920," *History of Education Quarterly* 23 (1983):197.

21 Ibid., 209–210.

22 For an account of the impact of family bonds on the lives of educated women in the late nineteenth century, see J. Antler, "'After College, What?': New Graduates and the Family Claim," *American Quarterly* 32 (1980):409–434.

23 C. P. Gilman, "The Passing of Matrimony," *Harper's Bazar* 40 (1906):495–498.

24 For additional biographical information on Calkins see L. Furumoto, "Mary Whiton Calkins (1863–1930): Fourteenth President of the American Psychological Association," *Journal of the History of the Behavioral Sciences* 15 (1979):346–356; L. Furumoto, "Mary Whiton Calkins (1863–1930)," *Psychology of Women Quarterly* 5 (1980):55–68; and Scarborough and Furumoto, *Untold Lives,* Chapter 1.

25 L. Clark Seelye to Ethel D. Puffer, 29 April 1908. Morgan-Howes Papers, Schlesinger Library, Radcliffe College, Cambridge, Massachusetts.

26 E. P. Howes, "'Accepting the Universe'," *Atlantic Monthly* 129 (1922):444.

27 Ibid, 449.

28 E. P. Howes, "Continuity for Women," *Atlantic Monthly* 130 (1922):736.

29 E. P. Howes, "True and Substantial Happiness," *Woman's Home Companion* (Dec. 1923):32.

30 D. Hayden, *The Grand Domestic Revolution: A History of Feminist Designs for American Homes, Neighborhoods, and Cities* (Cambridge, MA: MIT Press, 1981), Chapter 12.

31 E. P. Howes, "The Meaning of Progress in the Woman Movement," *Annals of the American Academy of Political and Social Sciences* 142 (1929):6.

32 From handwritten notes in the Mary Whiton Calkins papers, Wellesley College Archives, Wellesley, Massachusetts.

33 J. Antler, *The Educated Woman and Professionalization: The Struggle for a New Feminine Identity, 1890–1920* (PhD Dissertation: State University of New York at Stony Brook, 1977), vi.

34 J. Jastrow, "Varieties of Psychological Experience," *Psychological Review* 24 (1917):256; G. S. Hall, "A Reminiscence," *American Journal of Psychology* 28 (1917):300; M. F. Washburn, "Some Thoughts on the Last Quarter Century in Psychology," *The Philosophical Review* 26 (1917):48; J. McK. Cattell, "Our Psychological Association and Research," *Science* 45 (1917):278.

35 F. H. Finch and M. E. Odoroff, "Employment Trends in Applied Psychology," *Journal of Consulting Psychology* 3 (1939):118.

36 Rossiter, *Women Scientists in America,* 119.

37 See Camfield, *Psychologists at War;* D. J. Kevles, "Testing the Army's Intelligence: Psychologists and the Military in World War I," *Journal of American History* 55 (1968):565–581; and F. Samelson, "Putting Psychology on the Map: Ideology and Intelligence Testing," in A. R. Buss (ed.), *Psychology in Social Context* (New York: John Wiley, 1979), 103–168.

38 Samelson, "Putting Psychology on the Map," 154.

39 M. M. Sokal, "James McKeen Cattell and American Psychology in the 1920s," in J. Brozek (ed.), *Explorations in the History of Psychology in the United States* (Lewisburg, PA: Bucknell University Press, 1984), 274–275.

40 Napoli, *Architects of Adjustment,* 47.

41 L. J. Finison and L. Furumoto, "Status of Women in American Psychology, 1890–1940, Or on How to Win the Battles yet Lose the War" (Unpublished manuscript, 1980).

42 E. J. Hutchinson, *Women and the Ph.D.: Facts from the Experience of 1,025 Women Who Have Taken the Degree of Doctor of Philosophy since 1877* (Greensboro, NC: The North Carolina College for Women, 1929), 189.

43 Ibid., 71.

44 Napoli, *Architects of Adjustment,* 47.

45 Finch and Odoroff, "Employment Trends," 121.

46 M. M. Sokal, "The Origins of the Psychological Corporation," *Journal of the History of the Behavioral Sciences* 17 (1981):56.

47 J. E. W. Wallin, "A Red-Letter Day in APA History," *The Journal of General Psychology* 75 (1966):112.

48 J. C. Burnham, "The Struggle between Physicians and Paramedical Personnel in American Psychiatry, 1917–41," *Journal of the History of Medicine and Allied Sciences* 29 (1974):93–106.

49 Napoli, *Architects of Adjustment,56.*

50 N. Golden, "Phyllis Blanchard Lucasse: Life of an Early Woman Clinical Psychologist" (Unpublished manuscript, 1983).

51 Wallin, "A Red-Letter Day," 111.

52 Napoli, *Architects of Adjustment,* 65.

53 For the impact and consequences of unemployment among psychologists during the Great Depression, see L. J. Finison, "Unemployment, Politics, and the History of Organized Psychology," *American Psychologist* 31 (1976):747–755 and "Unemployment, Politics, and the History of Organized Psychology, II: The Psychologists League, the WPA, and the National Health Program," *American Psychologist* 33 (1978):471–477.

54 Rossiter, *Women Scientists in America,* 140.

55 On the organizational efforts of women psychologists and their status in the profession during the World War II era, see M. R. Walsh, "Academic Professional Women Organizing for Change: The Struggle in Psychology," *Journal of Social Issues* 41 (1985):17–28, and J. H. Capshew and A. C. Laszlo, "'We would not take no for an answer': Women Psychologists and Gender Politics During World War II," *Journal of Social Issues* 42 (1986):157–180.

56 G. D. Frith, "Psychology as a Profession," *Women's Work and Education* 10 (1939):1.

57 The statistics come from Finch and Odoroff, "Employment Trends in Applied Psychology." In Frith's article she incorrectly states the number of applied jobs as 257 in 1916 and 1,923 in 1938. In fact these were the figures given by Finch and Odoroff for the *total* number of psychological jobs in those years.

58 Frith, "Psychology as a Profession," 1.

59 O'Donnell describes Fernberger as an intimate friend of Boring, whose self-ordained duty was to serve as gadfly to the scientific consciences of his Pennsylvania colleagues, whom he condescendingly referred to as "the Witmerian applied bunch"; "The Crisis of Experimentalism," 292.

60 S. W. Fernberger, "Academic Psychology as a Career For Women," *Psychological Bulletin* 36 (1939):390.

61 Ibid., 393.

62 Brumberg and Tomes, "Women in the Professions" (see note 1) 287.

63 A. Abbott, "Status and Status Strain in the Professions," *American Journal of Sociology* 86 (1981):823–824.

64 Brumberg and Tomes, "Women in the Professions," 287–288.

65 J. C. Burnham, "The New Psychology: From Narcissism to Social Control," in J. Braeman, R. H. Bremner, and D. Brody (eds.), *Change and Continuity in Twentieth-Century America: The 1920s* (Columbus: Ohio State University Press, 1968), 351–398.

5

FROM ACT PSYCHOLOGY TO PROBABILISTIC FUNCTIONALISM: THE PLACE OF EGON BRUNSWIK IN THE HISTORY OF PSYCHOLOGY*

DAVID E. LEARY

> In the coming years, Egon Brunswik will hold an ever increasingly
> significant and important position in the history of psychology.
> (from Edward C. Tolman's eulogy, 1956)

Despite Tolman's prediction, Egon Brunswik's place in the history of psychology has yet to be firmly established. Although his name and his concepts are frequently invoked, they are rarely used in defense of positions that he would have recognized as his own. And although most contemporary psychologists have failed to comprehend either the details or the underlying rationale of his psychological theory, historians of psychology have done even less to clarify the context, development, and import of his life and work.[1]

This neglect is unfortunate. Brunswik deserves much greater attention, not only because he was one of the major twentieth-century theorists on the psychology of perception, or because he was unusually prescient about later developments in psychology, but because his life and work constitute an extremely useful case history for the study of a variety of

---

* This chapter is based on a much larger study of Egon Brunswik's life and work, which was partially supported by grants from the History of Psychology Foundation and the National Science Foundation. Different versions have been presented to the American Psychological Association, the Department of Psychology at the University of California at Berkeley, and Cheiron: The International Society for the History of the Behavioral and Social Sciences. I thank Kenneth R. Hammond for the invitation that initiated this research project; Marion White McPherson, John Popplestone, and John Miller of the Archives of the History of American Psychology, Akron, Ohio, for their help in locating materials relevant to this project; and the many former colleagues and students of Brunswik who shared letters, lecture notes, and memories of Brunswik. I also thank David Devonis for his assistance in drafting the two diagrams used in this chapter. I dedicate this essay to Leonard Krieger, in gratitude for his guidance of my first attempts to understand the German-language psychology of the past.

critical historical issues, including topics of interest to both intellectual and social historians.

My primary concern in this chapter will be the conceptual and methodological development of Brunswik's psychology over the course of his career and in the context of his migration from Vienna to Berkeley. Without discussing the individual doctrines of his psychological system in extensive detail, I will describe its basic foundations and the historical sequence by which it was constructed. In doing so, I will show how Brunswik's psychology was based on a very unusual blending of intellectual and scientific traditions.

In addition to reviewing the foundations and historical development of Brunswik's psychology, I will also review its historical impact and consider why it has not been more influential. In the course of this analysis I will discuss some factors intrinsic to his psychology, the significance of his migration from Europe to the United States, and the means by which he tried to disseminate his ideas. Together with the preceding analysis of his psychology, these considerations should help us understand why Brunswik's legacy remains undefined over thirty years after Tolman's eulogistic prediction.

AN OVERVIEW OF BRUNSWIK'S CAREER

Egon Brunswik was born in Budapest on March 18, 1903. From the age of eight he was educated in the best schools in Vienna. Then, in 1923, after two years as an engineering student, he transferred to the University of Vienna where he began to study psychology under Karl Bühler. At the time Bühler was one of the foremost psychologists in the world. In the exciting atmosphere of Bühler's Psychological Institute, Brunswik was immediately swept into his newfound discipline and became an active participant in Bühler's famous Wednesday evening discussion group.

As if this were not stimulation enough, Brunswik was soon a frequent participant in a Thursday evening discussion group held by Professor Moritz Schlick. During the years of Brunswik's participation this group was the seedbed from which the Vienna Circle of logical positivists emerged, and for the rest of his career Brunswik maintained personal, professional, and intellectual ties with the logical positivists and with the Unity of Science Movement that grew out of logical positivism. So from the very beginning of his career, we can see the formation of distinctive philosophical as well as psychological interests. The integration of these interests became an implicit goal of Brunswik's lifework.

Brunswik received his PhD in psychology in 1927, and he immediately became an assistant in Bühler's Institute. For the next seven years, with the exception of a year spent teaching in Ankara, Turkey, Brunswik directed research at the Psychological Institute and continued his own research in the area of perception. In 1934 he published a major book, *Wahrnehmung und Gegenstandswelt,* which was based on his research of the preceding seven years. At the same time he became an associate professor, and soon thereafter he was invited by Edward C. Tolman to spend the 1935–36 academic year as a visiting lecturer and research fellow at the University of California, Berkeley. This invitation came as the result of a sabbatical that Tolman spent in Vienna in 1933–34. During this sabbatical he and Brunswik discovered that their psychological ideas were quite compatible and even complementary – so much so that the 47-year-old Tolman and 30-year-old Brunswik had co-authored an important theoretical article entitled "The Organism and the Causal Texture of the Environment."[2]

Brunswik's one-year stay in Berkeley was apparently mutually satisfactory, for in 1937, after an intervening year in Vienna, Brunswik returned to Berkeley as an assistant professor. He remained at Berkeley, advancing through the academic ranks, until his untimely death in 1955. Thus his career at Berkeley coincided almost exactly with the classical period in that department's history. During this time Brunswik was widely acknowledged to be, in essence, the department's intellectual conscience. His deep scholarship and meticulous research provided an exacting model of intellectual and methodological integrity for several generations of students and faculty.

THE FOURFOLD BASIS OF BRUNSWIK'S PSYCHOLOGY

This brief chronology has alluded to three primary bases of Brunswik's psychology, namely, the European functionalist tradition, represented by Bühler; the logical positivist movement, generated by and around Schlick; and American neo-behaviorism, as set forth by Tolman. The second and third of these bases – the positivist and behaviorist traditions – served to modify and extend the first. In turn, the psychology constructed on all three of these bases was extended and modified during Brunswik's years in the United States by a fourth and final tradition – the Anglo-American statistical tradition. As embodied in a succession of research assistants, such as Rheem Jarrett and Robert Rollin, this tradition helped Brunswik articulate a more sophisticated methodology for his emerging psychological system. With the elaboration of this methodology, Brunswik's psychology reached its mature form in the decade before his death.

The most important factor in the development of Brunswik's psychology was clearly the first of the four traditions I have pointed out – the European functionalist tradition as advanced by Karl Bühler and amended, as we will see, under the influence of Fritz Heider.

The ancestry of Bühler's psychology extended back through Oswald

Külpe, his mentor at Würzburg, to Franz Brentano, the founder of so-called act psychology. The fundamental postulate of Brentano's psychology is well known, even if the scope of its impact is not. The basic fact about psychological activities, according to Brentano, is that they always include a reference to some object. Consciousness, to take the most general case, is always consciousness *of something*. The practical result of this basic postulate was the dissolution of the philosophically worrisome dualism of subject and object, or knower and known. Külpe, Bühler and others accepted this postulate as a basic statement of a functional, or relational, theory of mind.[3]

Bühler's contribution consisted in pointing out and providing experimental corroboration of the fact that the fundamental unity of subject and object is not so definitive that each and every aspect of the object-world is related to one and only one psychic experience. Quite the contrary, in his groundbreaking studies in Gestalt psychology, he showed that the relationship between particular aspects of the object-world (sensations) and the experiential awareness of the subject (perception) is *fundamentally ambiguous*. Any given sensory stimulus, he showed, will be perceived differently when placed against a different contextual background.[4] Furthermore, Bühler found that the same principle could be applied in the study of language: no word has a single fixed meaning; rather, all words receive their meaning from the sentence and paragraph in which they are embedded. Any given word can mean several or more things, depending on the context in which it is uttered. Thus, the hearer of language must interpret – must infer the probable meaning of a word – based on the word's relation to its linguistic setting. This interpretation by the hearer is, of course, usually unconscious.

Over several decades, based on such research, Bühler formulated his well-known principle of "representation" – a principle he applied to all psychological phenomena, but most explicitly to language. Words, Bühler maintained, represent things or thoughts; they are not the things or thoughts themselves. Just as words can have different meanings and thus represent different objects, so too can objects be represented by different words. There is, in other words, no invariant one-to-one relationship between representations or signs (whether these be perceptual cues or words) and the things they represent.[5]

This was the state of affairs when Brunswik became Bühler's student in 1923. He soon began to follow up on Bühler's previous work on perception, and in particular on perceptual constancy. The influence of Bühler on Brunswik was profound and lasting. Between 1927 and 1929 Brunswik confirmed and extended Bühler's previous research, showing that perception is not a simple function of sensation, that there are fundamental ambiguities in stimulus information, and that the perceiver can and usually does learn to resolve most of these ambiguities in a fairly stable and reliable fashion. As a basic premise in all this work, Brunswik accepted Bühler's notion of perception as a subject-object relationship.[6]

Then, in 1929, Brunswik read Fritz Heider's paper on "Ding und Medium," and his thinking took a significant step forward. Heider, as a student of Alexius Meinong, was a member of the same functionalist tradition extending back to Brentano.[7] Not surprisingly, his article corroborated the relational framework Brunswik had inherited from Bühler. However, it also directed Brunswik's attention more forcefully toward the *object* side of the subject-object continuum. It did so by pointing out that most objects are not in immediate contact with the subject; rather, they are separated from the subject by a "medium" through which perception has to be *achieved*. The real issue for the psychology of perception, Brunswik came to see, was how the subject could use "proximal" (immediate) sensory cues to infer the nature of the "distal" (distant) objects that these cues represent. From this point on, Brunswik referred to his psychology as a "psychology in terms of the object." By this he meant that it was the task of psychology to determine how and to what degree individuals establish veridical contact with the world of objects. In his subsequent work, Brunswik understood proximal sensations (stimuli impinging directly on the sense organs) as representations of certain aspects of the distal object world, and he sought to discover how it is that perceivers achieve perceptions of objects on the basis of these representative sensory cues.[8]

At this point in the development of his psychological system, Brunswik's affiliation with the logical positivist group had a significant impact on his work. The impact was somewhat paradoxical. To date he had accepted the general conceptual framework of the European functionalist tradition and had begun to articulate his own distinctive version of functionalist theory, but he had not yet been converted to the probabilist assumptions that were to characterize his mature psychology. He came to accept these assumptions – and here is the paradox – through his allegiance to the logical positivist movement, and, specifically, as a result of a grave challenge posed by this movement to his Bühlerian heritage.

To understand this, we must recall that one of the major doctrines of the Vienna Circle was a theory of meaning and truth that was based on the contention that scientific language should and could be reducible to invariant sense-data referents.[9] Each term of scientific discourse, they claimed, must have one and only one sense datum (or set of sense data) as a referent. The problem was that Brunswik had corroborated Bühler's finding that the relationship between sense data and their objects – or between words and their referents – is fundamentally ambiguous, that is, uncertain. Not surprisingly, this contradiction between the epistemological premises of the Vienna Circle and the empirical results of his own experiments created an intellectual crisis for Brunswik, who was equally attracted to both of the ventures – philosophical and psychological – in which he was a privileged participant.

Brunswik resolved this tension through the discovery of the work of Hans Reichenbach, the leader of the Berlin school of logical positivists, who proposed a probabilistic theory of human knowledge in opposition to the Vienna Circle's stipulative and nomothetic approach.[10] This theory allowed Brunswik to resolve the fundamental conflict between his psychological *findings* and his desire to achieve a philosophically sound psychological *theory*. Utilizing Reichenbach's argument that all human knowledge is probabilistic, Brunswik was able to rationalize the ambiguous relationship between sensory cues and their objective referents by speaking of this relationship as probabilistic in nature. In principle, he was able to argue, objects can be perceived and therefore known only probabilistically. There is no one-to-one relationship between sense data and the objective world, nor can there be a one-to-one relationship between sense data and language, as the Vienna Circle claimed at that time.

Because Reichenbach was so widely respected among members of the Vienna Circle, Brunswik was thus able to maintain his allegiance to the general logical positivist movement while also remaining true to the premises and results of his psychological research. At the same time, the self-conscious designation of functional relations as probabilistic *in principle* – and not simply in relation to our imperfect means of knowing about such relations – constituted a major step towards his eventual system of "probabilistic functionalism."

The next state in the development of Brunswik's psychology occurred under the influence of the American behaviorist Edward C. Tolman, who corroborated the logical positivist insistence on objectivistic methodology, and particularly on verifiable, physicalistic measurements. This insistence led Brunswik – ironically, in view of Tolman's own use of "intervening variables" – to begin thinking in terms of a "psychology without an organism." As a result, the subjective pole in the functional relationship between the subject and object receded from Brunswik's psychology for more than a decade.[11]

Tolman also stimulated Brunswik to broaden his psychological system to include behavioral as well as perceptual events. In this regard Brunswik had an equally important reciprocal influence on Tolman, who simultaneously expanded the scope of his psychological metatheory to treat sensation and perception more specifically than before. These mutual influences were first explicated in their classic article on "The Organism and the Causal Texture of the Environment."

At the beginning of this article Tolman and Brunswik noted that they had composed their joint publication because they discovered that "our previous separate investigations had led us quite independently of one another to a common point of view as to the general nature of psychology." Indeed, the parallels in their "common point of view" were remarkable. These resulted, they said, from a shared vision of psychology as "primarily concerned with the methods of response of the organism to two characteristic features of the environment" – first, that the environment is a "causal texture" in which different events are regularly (but not invariably) linked with one another and, second, that these "causal couplings," because they are not absolutely invariant, are in any given instance "to some degree equivocal" or uncertain. The first characteristic, the regular linkages between different environmental events, had led each of them to the conclusion that certain events can serve as "signs" (Tolman) or "cues" (Brunswik) or "local representatives" (Tolman and Brunswik) from which other events or entities or goal states could be inferred and responded to, either behaviorally or perceptually. The second characteristic, that "local representatives" are "not connected in simply one-one univocal ... fashion" with these represented events, entities, and goal states, had led them to emphasize the significance of the "differing frequencies" – the relative probabilities – that characterize these relations and, therefore, characterize the "attainment" of behavioral "ends" (Tolman) and of perceptual "objects" (Brunswik).[12]

In other words, Tolman and Brunswik had independently arrived at the conviction that organisms operate on the basis of "hypotheses" that have "only a certain probability of being valid." Whether it is a rat trying to reach the food chamber of a T-maze (Tolman) or a human being trying to estimate the actual size of a distant object (Brunswik), the organism acts to achieve its distant goals by means of the immediate "signs" or "cues" at its disposal, and it continually adjusts its assumptions about the referents of these "local representives" on the basis of ongoing experience. The organism's task, Tolman and Brunswik said, "is to correct whatever hypotheses it brings with it to fit the real probabilities of the actually presented setup."[13]

At this point two diagrams will help clarify and summarize the basic structure of Brunswik's perceptual theory and the expanded metapsychology that he produced together with Tolman. Under the impact of Heider's notion of mediated perception, Brunswik had developed what he called a "lens model" of perception (see Figure 5-1). The illustration of this model crystallizes the core of Brunswik's perceptual theory.[14]

According to Brunswik's lens model, the distal object occasions various proximal sensations in the peripheral senses of the organism. These peripheral senses serve as a "lens" that collects the various cues and directs them to a central "focal point" where they are selectively utilized by the organism in the production of a "central response." In the typical Brunswikian experiment, this response was a visual perception of an object's size, objectively measured by the subject's verbal estimate of the

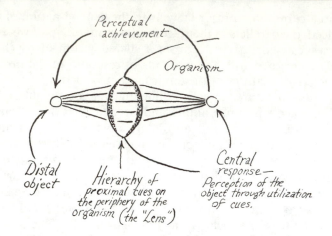

Figure 5-1. Bunswik's lens model of perception.

object's actual size. The degree of veridical accuracy of a given perception was, for Brunswik, the measure of its achievement, or what he later called its "functional validity."

The organism's perceptual achievements, according to Brunswik, depend on the selective use of an array of cues. In the course of experience, the organism learns that some cues are more likely than others to represent a given dimension of the external world. As a result, the organism places greater trust in these cues. (In Brunswik's later terminology, it comes to realize that these cues have greater "ecological validity," and it therefore gives them preeminence in its "hierarchy of cues.") However, since the relation between the organism and its environment is never completely static, the organism's expectations about the validity of cues are never absolutely certain and are continually subject to revision.

An expanded lens model can be used to represent the broadening of Brunswik's psychology that took place in collaboration with Tolman (see Figure 5-2). The extended portion of this model is a symmetrical, mirror image of the earlier model. On the new "motor" side of the diagram, an array of habits – alternate behaviors leading to any given goal – take the place of the hierarchy of cues on the sensory side of the model. Each potential behavior – each of the means at the organism's disposal – has a differential probability of leading to the intended goal. As in perception, the organism's behavioral responses are guided by hypotheses regarding the probable success of each of these alternative means. And again, the achievement of the organism's ends – for instance, the reaching of a food chamber in a T-maze – can be objectively measured. For the phenomena

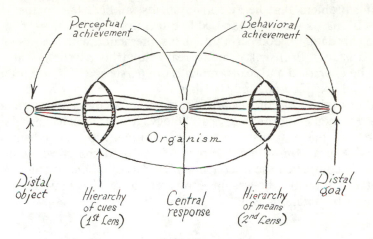

Figure 5-2. Extension of the lens model to behavior.

represented by this side of the diagram, Tolman's research on purposive behavior served as the prototypic illustration.[15]

Although their own investigations up to the mid-1930s had focused on a more restricted set of topics, Brunswik and Tolman concluded their classic article with the suggestion that

> *all* the problems of psychology — not only those of visual percep-
> tion and of learning — but all the more general problems of instinct,
> insight, learning, intelligence, motivation, personality, and emotion
> all center around this one general feature of the given organism's
> abilities and tendencies for adjusting to these actual causal textures
> — these actual probabilities as to causal couplings.[16]

Thus, by the time he came to the United States in 1935, Brunswik had developed a distinctive theory of perception and had extended that theory, in collaboration with Tolman, to cover – at least in principle – the entire domain of psychology. But a theory, however comprehensive in scope, is one thing; a fully articulated psychology with an appropriate methodology and an adequate stock of data is something else. Up to this point Brunswik's research had concentrated almost exclusively on selected topics in the psychology of perception, and in this research he had utilized relatively unsophisticated modes of quantitative analysis. For instance, he used simple ratios, comparing estimated to actual object size, as a gauge of the accuracy of perception. This was an effective way to describe the phenomena of size constancy, which was the typical experimental problem that he and his students studied, but in the United States Brunswik was soon exposed to much more powerful ways of interpreting his data. In good part through his interaction with a series of graduate assistants, Brunswik came to realize that his psychological theory could be expressed and tested much more persuasively through the language and use of correlation statistics.

Although the addition of statistical means of analysis may seem a trivial amendment of Brunswik's psychology, it was actually quite significant, for in matching his theoretical commitment to probabilism with a methodological commitment to probability-based analytical techniques, Brunswik completed the interlacing of a conceptual and methodological foundation on which he was now prepared to erect his mature system of probabilistic functionalism.

BRUNSWIK'S PROBABILISTIC FUNCTIONALISM

During his one-year stay in Berkeley in 1935–36, prior to his permanent move to the United States in 1937, Brunswik started to redeem his claim that behavioral as well as perceptual phenomena are probabilistic in nature. In a study of "Probability as a Determiner of Rat Behavior," Brunswik investigated behavioral-response learning in the context of varying probabilities of reward (or "goal achievement"), a context which as he said was more representative of "the natural environment of a living being" than the all-or-none reward schedules used in previous behavioral studies. When it was published in 1939, this study was noteworthy for its use of partial reinforcement and for being the first publication in which Brunswik applied correlation statistics.[17]

From this point on, Brunswik's distinctive approach to the study and understanding of psychological phenomena – and his realization of its far-reaching implications – unfolded at a rapid pace. Returning to the area of perception, he extended his use of correlation statistics in "Thing Constancy as Measured by Correlation Coefficients," published in 1940. This study advanced Brunswik's investigation of size constancy, demonstrating through a complex set of correlations that perceivers utilize sensory cues of relatively low degrees of reliability – having nowhere near one-to-one correspondence to reality – in the process of attaining remarkably high degrees of veridical perception (or "object achievement"). In other words, this study showed that the overarching functional relation between subject and object – the correlation between "central responses" and "distal objects" – was much greater than the correlation between "mediating proximal cues" and "distal objects." The clear implication was that perceivers make inferences about the object-world that go beyond the information provided by cues apparently on the basis of past experience with similarly ambiguous cues and distant objects.[18]

As important as this study was, it still relied on traditional experimental procedures. However, even before this study was in print, Brunswik realized that his psychological premises demanded a much more radical departure from traditional modes of investigation, and he set about designing a study of perceptual size constancy that would take place in a natural environment rather than a laboratory. Furthermore, instead of randomly varying subjects in this study, as was and still remains the standard procedure in experimental psychology, Brunswik opted to investigate the perceptions of only one individual across a variety of real-life situations, allowing the objects to be perceived to be randomly selected according to their chance occurrence in the subject's perceptual field at any given time.[19]

Clearly this was a radically new way of doing psychological research, and not surprisingly it aroused attention and debate among psychologists. In fact, as a result of a major address by Brunswik at the Sixth International Congress for the Unity of Science in 1941, the debate was under way long before he published his monograph-length report on this project in 1944. The original antagonists in this debate were Clark Hull and Kurt Lewin, Brunswik's distinguished co-symposiasts at the Congress. Their critical comments, published in 1943 along with Brunswik's address, started a controversy that continued throughout the final decade of Brunswik's life.[20]

We are already familiar with the fundamental notions underlying the position Brunswik advocated in his address, which he titled "Organismic Achievement and Environmental Probability." As we have seen, these notions were rooted deeply in Brunswik's intellectual history, but he expressed them now more forcefully than ever before. As in his classic article with Tolman, Brunswik emphasized that organismic achievement involves either the perception of distal objects or the attaining of behavioral goals, that the cues and means that facilitate perceptual and behavioral achievements are always "ambiguous," and that therefore the achievement of veridical perception and of behavioral goals is always to a certain degree probabilistic. Furthermore, Brunswik argued that such achievements are the result of the organism's "focusing" on distal objects and goals, albeit through the media of cues and means. This focusing of the organism on the ends of psychological processes – on distal objects and goals rather than on proximal cues and means – warrants, Brunswik said, a "molar" approach to psychological investigation. In other words, the primary concern of a functionalist psychology should be the correlation of the organism's perceptions and behaviors with their targeted objects and objectives, not the designation of less probable and replaceable "molecular" events.

To this molar functionalism Brunswik now added a thoroughgoing statistical probabilism. Psychology, he said, as long as it wishes to deal with the vitally relevant molar aspects of adjustment and achievement, has to become statistical throughout, instead of being statistical where it seems hopeless to be otherwise, and cherishing the nomothetic ideals of traditional experimental psychology as far as relationships between geographic stimulus variables and response variables are concerned.[21]

This was the challenge to which Brunswik's critics responded most vociferously. They realized that granting Brunswik's contentions would necessitate "the extension of such an instrument as correlation statistics from individual differences to stimulus-response relationships," the "representative sampling" of both perceptual objects and behavioral objectives, and the acceptance of statistical generalizations as the ultimate type of regularity that can be discovered by psychology.[22] For if the objects of perception and the objectives of behavior are the proper concerns of a functionalist or molar psychology, and if these objects and goals vary as much as – or even more than – the organisms that achieve them, then it is as important to sample the population of relevant natural objects and goals as it is to sample the population of relevant organisms – and for one and the same reason, so that individual differences among objects and goals can be taken into consideration, just as individual differences among organisms must be taken into consideration, in a properly statistical, which is to say, a thoroughly probabilistic analysis. Only then can psychologists make the kind of generalizations – statistical generalizations – that are worthy of a truly functionalist psychology.

The critical response to these contentions illustrated both the misunderstanding and the resistance that were to plague Brunswik in his remaining years. Clark Hull's critique can serve as an exemplar. After setting up a contrast between probability and natural law, he argued that "scientific theory is concerned with natural laws. These are conceived as being uniform. Do such isolable uniformities exist in the field of behavior? . . . Lewin and I believe they do; Brunswik, on the other hand, is convinced that no such uniformities exist."[23] The confirmation of one or the other of these beliefs, Hull said, must await "prolonged effort directed specifically to this task" of discovering uniform natural laws. Brunswik, he implied, had given up the quest as hopeless before he had devoted adequate effort to the "laborious and time-consuming" task at hand. In any case, even an ideal science like physics must accept certain errors of measurement that are bound to occur because "it is impossible to know the exact conditions" surrounding a given phenomenon. As a result, even in physics empirical correlations among phenomena are bound to be less than 1.00. It should not be surprising, then, if correlations in psychology are less than perfect. Even more than in physics "we always lack absolutely exact knowledge concerning [the] *conditions*" surrounding psychological phenomena. But this does not mean that psychologists are doomed to live with probability rather than natural law, any more than it means that physicists are.[24]

Hull's response showed how much he "cherished the nomothetic ideals of traditional experimental psychology," as Brunswik had put it. It also showed a fundamental confusion that Brunswik had to suffer for the rest of his life. Brunswik was not concerned that "we" who observe someone else's behavior cannot make precise predictions because "we" lack complete information about the organism's environmental conditions; rather, as he put it in a later publication, Brunswik was convinced that "so long as *the organism* does not develop, or fails in a given context to utilize completely, the powers of a fullfledged physicist observer and analyst, his environment remains for all practical purposes a semierratic medium [*for him*]; it is no more than partially controlled and no more than probabilistically predictable" *from the point of view of the organism; and it is the organism* that must respond on the basis of its own, necessarily probabilistic knowledge.[25]

To give Hull his due, this rejoinder relies on an aspect of Brunswik's thought that had been de-emphasized – even suppressed – since 1934, when he had chosen to develop a "psychology without an organism." I am referring to the cognitive role of the subject in the subject-object relationship that formed the basic foundation of his approach. Under the influence of the logical positivist and behavioral movements, Brunswik had rejected the use of "intervening variables" and the study of mediational processes as a valid concern for a "psychology in terms of the object." But it is not easy to shuck basic aspects of a system of thought, and the later elaboration of his system demanded the resurrection of its "missing dimension."

Interestingly, Hull sensed the inconsistency of Brunswik's critique of intervening variables, or as Hull called them, "symbolic constructs," and he noted that Brunswik himself seemed "at certain moments at least to introduce perception as a variable intervening between the physical stimulation of his subjects and their verbal responses."[26] A glance at the lens model diagrams that portray the basic structure of Brunswik's theory (see Figures 5-1 and 5-2) confirms what Hull said. Even if Brunswik preferred to focus on organismic achievements, he had to admit that the achievements depended on some sort of mediational processes that he had represented, however schematically, in this model. In his desire to remain as objectivistic as possible, however, he had renounced further discussion of these processes. But his whole point about the organism actively calculating its own behavior, actively responding according to its own perceptual and behavioral expectations – its "hypotheses" about the objects, events, and possibilities in its environment – implicated a recognition of the organism as a cognizing subject.

Whether in response to Hull's point or not, Brunswik began in the early 1940s to reinsert into his research a distinction he used years before in Vienna, a distinction between "perception" and "thinking," or more specifically, between the kind of cognition that occurs when a subject is in a relaxed, uncritical mental attitude and the kind of cognition that occurs when a subject is in a "betting" or calculating mental attitude. He also began to think of the organism as "an intuitive statistician" that routinely makes probabilistic inferences about its surrounding environment without being self-conscious about it, and he became one of the first psychologists to note the relevance of cybernetics and communications theory for psychology, well before the wholesale revival of cognitivism in psychology.[27]

Still, Brunswik was clearly uncomfortable speculating about organismic processes, and it was not until he could offer a "statistical separation of perception, thinking, and attitude" in 1946 that he became more comfortable with this aspect of his metatheory.[28] Although his "statistical separation" was not adopted by other researchers, he continued to elaborate his "ratiomorphic models of perception," for which he was subsequently designated a forerunner of the cognitive movement in psychology. Fittingly, one of the last pieces that he completed before his death was a posthumously published paper on the "Scope and Aspects of the Cognitive Problem." True to his original functionalist insight, he concluded this paper by saying that "only by detailed analysis of ecological [i.e., environmental] textures can the cognitive problem be restored from mere utilization problems [regarding how organisms use cues and means] to its full scope of achievement problems and thus again become the key to the core problem of psychology, that of the adjustment of the organism to a complex environment."[29] For Brunswik the cognitive problem, like all other psychological problems, had to be approached within the context of the primary relationship between subject and object – between the organism and its environment.

Whether or not Hull's critique sparked Brunswik's reassertion of the organism's role in psychological dynamics, it did provide an incentive for a longer, more formal statement about probabilistic functionalism. Brunswik made that statement in 1947 in a monograph entitled *Systematic and Representative Design of Psychological Experiments*.[30] This treatise, one of the most remarkable works in twentieth-century psychology, is properly considered Brunswik's major manifesto. However, it is remembered primarily for its critique of traditional psychology and for various of its concepts that have been borrowed and used in other contexts. It has rarely been used as Brunswik intended – as a blueprint for a methodological revolution in psychology.

The central distinction that Brunswik drew in this work was between the "systematic" and "representative" design of psychological experiments. In the systematic experiments typical of experimental psychology, Brunswik said, the organisms that serve as the subjects of investigation are sampled because their idiosyncratic characteristics cannot be separated and controlled, and their responses are then treated statistically so that generalizations can be made to other organisms that did not participate in the experiment. However, the environmental stimulus variables used in systematic experiments are typically separated and controlled to keep them constant or independent of one another, irrespective of how they covary, probabilistically, in the natural environment of the organism under investigation. As a result, many of these variables are artificially "tied" during the course of the experiment, and this "unnatural covariation of independent variables" destroys the grounds for logical inferences about the generalizability of experimental results. Consequently, it should not be surprising that generalizations from systematic experiments tend to break down across a variety of natural environments, just as they would for other organisms if the subject population had not been adequately sampled. In representative design, on the other hand, stimulus conditions would not be "unnaturally covaried," but would be sampled representatively just as subjects are in traditional experiments. Then the same logic of induction and the same statistical procedures could be performed on situational variables as are now performed on responses, and a thoroughgoing probabilism would establish psychology as a science of properly general results.

Rightly or not, Brunswik's arguments did not stimulate sustained attention, much less the conversion of large numbers of psychologists. In the absence of such success, Brunswik tried a different mode of publication. After many years of work, he completed and published his long-overdue historical treatise on *The Conceptual Framework of Psychology* in 1952.[31] This brilliant, if eccentric, work shows that Brunswik was not only a psychologist and philosopher of science; he was also a preeminent historian of psychology. Though his historical account is what we might call "presentistic" in that it leads inevitably up to his own probabilistic functionalism, his historical analyses are both profound and provocative, and they convey the rich historical context in which Brunswik situated his own work. Still, although it contributed to his reputation, Brunswik's monograph did not convert many psychologists to his point of view.

In July 1953, at the Berkeley Conference for the Unity of Science, Brunswik made his last major attempt to explain and defend probabilistic functionalism. Subsequently published in May 1955, Brunswik's exposition and reply to his critics – specifically to Herbert Feigl, Ernest R. Hilgard, David Krech, and Leo Postman – was literally his last stand.[32] Two months after its appearance, he committed suicide. Although ill health and several other factors were important incentives, there is little doubt that his final act was the tragic consequence of his deep depression over his inability to convince his contemporaries that what he had to say was of fundamental importance.

BRUNSWICK'S LEGACY

No major psychologist fails to have some effect on the course of psychology, and by any account Egon Brunswik was a major psychologist. Still, the situation at the time of his death was pathetic. Kenneth Hammond, a former student of Brunswik recalled that

> During the spring of 1954 [a year before Brunswik's death], I visited Brunswik in his office at Berkeley. . . . During the visit, Brunswik opened a file drawer and showed me two folders – one labeled Hammond, the other, Smedslund – and with unmistakable pride indicated that there were now two psychologists who were doing Brunswikian research. . . . Apparently there was no one else.[33]

But Hammond persevered, and over the years the number of legitimately called Brunswikians has grown. It is still a relatively small body of researchers, but they form an active and dedicated group with remarkably diverse interests, covering the entire range of topics falling between the end-terms in Brunswik's double-lens model (see Figure 5-2). According to Hammond's count,

> Over 200 studies have been carried out within the Brunswikian framework since 1964 [up to 1980]. They include numerous studies of clinical judgment; multiple-cue probability learning, which produced the concepts of cognitive feedback in contrast to conventional outcome feedback, as well as cognitive control, and cognitive skill; studies of interpersonal learning and interpersonal conflict; the effects of psychotherapeutic drugs on all of these processes; interactive judgment analysis that provides immediate cognitive feedback regarding judgments, and thus makes it possible to apply the Brunswikian tradition to the study of policy formation, policy implementation, and the study of expert judgment, as well as animal behavior.[34]

It is symptomatic that Hammond's count of Brunswikian research begins in 1964, almost a decade after Brunswik's death. Before and even after that time, most of the influence that might be accorded to Brunswik has been of a more general sort, or of such a specific type that it does not constitute the benefactor a Brunswikian in any exacting sense. But even in these cases, the influence has sometimes been quite significant. Donald Campbell may serve as a prime example. Although his work has followed its own trajectory, he acknowledges that its distinctive thrust has come from the early inspiration he received as a student and assistant of Brunswik at Berkeley. This inspiration, Campbell has written, was focused "at the levels of general perspective and of stating the problems which psychology must face." Furthermore, although Campbell has not been able to follow Brunswik on many points that Brunswik regarded as important, Brunswik's "stand" on such matters has served as "a major reference point" in Campbell's clarification of his own, different position. Beyond that, Campbell notes that his "total indebtedness to [Brunswik] is hard to estimate, since I learned from him primarily through lectures and conversations." He illustrates this point by reviewing several "discoveries" he made years after leaving Berkeley, only to find out later – when reviewing class notes from Brunswik's courses – that he had heard about these discoveries long before he made them.[35] Many other Berkeley students say the same thing.[36]

The list of those who were inspired by Brunswik in general, but meaningful ways could be extended to include those whose relation to Brunswik was mediated through his publications rather than through personal contact. Roger Barker and Jerome Bruner are only two of many well-known psychologists who have acknowledged some sort of "distal" debt to Brunswik – for general or partial inspiration rather than for his psychology as a whole. Similarly, references to Brunswik can be found scattered throughout the literature of recent decades on methodology, learning, thinking, decision processes, perception, communication, and psychological ecology. In addition, probabilism and the basic metaphor of the mind as an intuitive statistician have been gaining in popularity. But in most of the cases where Brunswik's work is cited as a precedent, it is generally a fairly routine citation, meant to confer a sense of authority and legitimacy to current theory and practice rather than to acknowledge an actual intellectual debt. As Herbert Simon has noted, Brunswik was a forerunner of a number of developments, but "did not, in fact, have much influence on what developed."[37]

Influence is an elusive thing. Even to corroborate some new developments – to serve as a legitimizing reference – is not without its significance. But it is clearly not what Brunswik had in mind. Given his generally acknowledged brilliance, why has so much of Brunswik's "influence" been of this nebulous, unfocused sort? And why have so many psychologists been uninfluenced by Brunswik, even in this rather generously construed form?

Even if Brunswik was properly understood – and this was frequently not the case – a number of reasons internal to his psychology help account for his limited, ambiguous legacy. Perhaps the major reason is that it is virtually impossible to implement Brunswik's methodology without some qualification. Even Brunswik never attempted, much less accomplished, a completely Brunswikian study. His groundbreaking 1944 monograph on "Distal Focussing of Perception" was only "a methodological demonstration" of his approach, not a fully realized study based on representative design. As Brunswik himself admitted, he had not scrutinized the situational generality of this study's results, nor had he checked the representativeness of the subject's choices of objects to be perceived.[38]

Demonstration or not, however, this study took a great deal of effort beyond that demanded by a typical laboratory experiment, and so it did not help his case – at least for those who were reading closely – when Brunswik noted that "the general trend and proportion of results" in more traditional experiments "is quite similar to those of the present study." As a result, he conceded, "the major results of our study may seem commonplace. A checkup of this kind is, however, a methodological requirement."[39] If in fact Brunswik's admittedly more cumbersome approach confirmed the general results of much simpler laboratory experiments, it was certainly not clear that the extra effort was necessary, except perhaps as an occasional "checkup" on the validity of experimental methodology.

The other major study that might seem to qualify as a definitive application of Brunswik's methodology is the second part of *Perception and the Representative Design of Psychological Experiments,* entitled "Perception: The Ecological Generality of its Distal Aim." This was Brunswik's final, summary treatment of his research on the psychology of perception. But in the Preface to this work, written just five months before his death, Brunswik admitted that it had become increasingly clear to him that "hybrid designs combining features of both systematic and representative deisgn are likely to continue and even to increase in frequency within the near future"; and in fact his own research in this study reflected this move toward "such an intermediate area."[40]

Beyond the practical difficulties that led to this sort of methodological compromise were emotional and intellectual difficulties that had to be faced. It may seem odd to speak of emotional difficulties when considering the application of scientific method, but in this case, as in others, emotional factors seem to have played a very tangible role. In the 1940s and early 1950s the nomothetic ideal of discovering universal and absolute natural laws through the use of carefully controlled experiments was deeply ingrained in the cultural ethos of the scientific community. Perhaps nothing, other than complete intellectual and methodological anarchy, could have been so threatening to that community – and especially to the self-conscious subculture of scientific psychology – as Brunswik's espousal of a thoroughgoing probabilism combined with his radical critique of experimentalism. How difficult it could be to deal with Brunswik's probabilistic functionalism is poignantly conveyed by Brunswik's own confession:

> The present writer has in himself experienced the required shift of emphasis as very slow going and hard to maintain, especially so far as consistent concrete application is concerned. The difficulties he encountered ... have given him the impression of resistances approaching in intensity those encountered in the opening up of emotionally highly loaded topics, such as those dealt with in psychoanalysis.[41]

And so:

> It takes a certain courage, a neglect of some of the attitudes sacred to scientific tradition, to give up the safety of molecular correlations, cheap as they are, in favor of the equivocalities or "vaguenesses" of molar correlations. But we have to prefer vagueness focused upon essentials to security and strict univocality focussed upon non-essentials.[42]

Brunswik was not exaggerating his own personal difficulty. For someone as rationalistic as he was, it had taken an enormous amount of courage to follow the path he felt compelled to take. He did not *want* probabilistic "explanations" of psychological phenomena; rather, psychological phenomena – it seemed to him – *demanded* such treatment, in total disregard of his temperamental inclinations.[43] But, as we have seen, Brunswik's realization of this need for a thoroughgoing probabilistic functionalism took many years to develop and grew out of a unique interplay of intellectual and scientific traditions. Perhaps he should not have expected others, who had the benefit of neither the same amount of time nor the same intellectual context, to respond in the affirmative when he called for fundamental change in psychology. In addition to all else, he was making this call during one of the most self-assured and dogmatic periods in psychology's history. It was hardly a time when the dice were loaded in his favor.

Such factors account for some of the obstacles that Brunswik's psychology faced: His methods were "formidable"; his theory was "at variance with the more traditional notions"; and his probabilism was bound to elicit some "emotional resistance."[44] We might be satisfied with them as an explanation for Brunswik's clouded legacy *except that* so many psychologists seemed not to *understand* his methodological, theoretical, and probabilistic convictions. They did not reject Brunswik's psychology for emotional or even clearly defined intellectual reasons. They simply let it slip by, in ignorance of its meaning and import. These psychologists include not only those who lived beyond Brunswik's orbit, but also many of his own students and colleagues. Here is the rub: Why have so many people simply not understood what Brunswik was saying? Why did Donald Campbell have to write in 1954 that "too few of us Berkeley students got what [Brunswik] had to say," even after attending his lectures and working with him as teaching and research assistants?[45] It is hardly surprising that others have failed to understand Brunswik's message if his own students and colleagues have admitted a considerable degree of incomprehension.

Derivation, Migration, Dissemination: Situating Brunswik in the History of Psychology

Three interrelated factors have contributed significantly to the misunderstanding and incomprehension from which Brunswik's psychology has suffered. These factors are, first, the constitution of Brunswik's psychology; second, the effects of Brunswik's move to the United States; and, third, the ways in which Brunswik tried to communicate his psychology.

Brunswik's psychology, as we have seen, was derived from a unique blend of intellectual and scientific traditions. The functionalist premises that Brunswik received from the European act-psychology tradition and the probabilist assumptions that he derived from a branch of the logical positivist movement were far from familiar to the majority of American psychologists. In addition, Brunswik's application of the statistical tools of differential psychology to the traditional subject matter of experimental psychology clashed with the mindset of American psychologists who had come to think of differential and experimental psychology as two quite distinct "disciplines" within psychology.[46]

The upshot, in colloquial terms, was that most American psychologists had difficulty understanding where Brunswik was coming from. At the same time most European psychologists, until the Anglo-American statistical tradition made greater inroads on the Continent in the 1960s and 1970s, had trouble comprehending, and so were not persuaded by, Brunswik's mature system of probabilistic functionalism.

In referring to the American and European situations I have already trespassed on my second point, that Brunswik's migration from Vienna to Berkeley affected more than the final theoretical articulation of his psychology. In making the move to the United States, Brunswik lost an audience that shared much of his intellectual background, the aid of a number of talented and committed research assistants, and a professional context in which perception was seen as an important and attractive research problem. In the United States during the 1940s and early 1950s, perception was not a highly regarded research topic and did not attract the number of able young investigators that it had in Vienna. As a result, despite the general influence he had on many students, Brunswik never played the active role in directing student research that he had enjoyed previously in Vienna. In all his years at Berkeley, he directed only four doctoral dissertations. Even Kenneth Hammond, his one true "disciple" at Berkeley, did not do his major research under Brunswik's direction. This loss of an institutional basis for a large-scale research program made it difficult for Brunswik to implement his theoretical insights as quickly and completely as he would have liked. As a result, he left behind much less research and fewer disciples than he might have in a more supportive context.[47]

The third factor I want to consider is Brunswik's style of communication – the means by which he sought to disseminate his ideas. I have not yet emphasized the number of important theoretical papers that Brunswik presented at philosophical conferences and published in philosophical journals. Never cutting his tie to the logical positivist and subsequent Unity of Science movements, Brunswik continued to scrutinize his psychological theory and methods – and to invite scrutiny – from the point of view of philosophical analysis. Although some American psychologists, such as Tolman and Hull, had peripheral associations with these movements, the majority of American psychologists were insulated from them and were therefore insulated from a certain number of Brunswik's important theoretical presentations.[48]

In addition, as mentioned previously in the brief discussion of his *Conceptual Framework of Psychology,* Brunswik was a careful student of the history of psychology, and he used his distinctive historical analyses to provide a context for explaining and defending his own probabilistic functionalism. Although his publications in this area were few in number, Brunswik frequently utilized historical analysis in his teaching, and his history of psychology course was one of the major means of communicating his approach to many Berkeley students. Unfortunately, there is evidence that these students were unprepared to profit from these analyses and hence missed the opportunity to learn what Brunswik was trying to convey.[49]

Matters were not helped by the fact that Brunswik was such a widely read scholar who continually referred to new developments in other sciences and disciplines that might have some significance for psychology. Many students heard for the first time about cybernetics, communications theory, econometrics, open system thermodynamics, biological systems theory, time series analysis and other developments in Brunswik's courses. His enthusiastic discussions of how these developments might be of service to psychologists were not always matched by the students' ability to follow what he was talking about.[50]

If the channels of communication that Brunswik used and the content of what he had to say often extended beyond the ken of his students and of most psychologists, Brunswik's writing style did little to balance the situation. In lectures and in personal conversation he was more expansive, which was often a problem in its own right, especially when his listeners were unable to follow the connections he would make. But in his writings, Brunswik's style was brutally precise, succinct, and demanding. As Tolman put it, Brunswik "was never willing to oversimplify or restrict the actual complexities of the relationships with which he was concerned. This always makes the reading of whatever he wrote a difficult task but an exciting and stimulating challenge [at least for the sympathetic Tolman]."[51]

Perhaps the scale of difficulty is best conveyed by the "good news" and "bad news" comments made by Julian Hochberg and Gustav Bergmann on Brunswik's *Conceptual Framework of Psychology.* Hochberg noted that a "decrease in Brunswik's customary condensation [in this book] makes for an increase in ease of reading." True, but the increase in ease was relative to Brunswik's own austere standard, as indicated by Bergmann's assessment that "physically this is a slim volume, hardly a book, rather, a monograph of barely a hundred pages. Intellectually this is the equivalent of three books or, to put it conservatively, of one well-sized book and two monographs of about one hundred pages each."[52]

There is no question that the style of Brunswik's communication – his uncompromising efforts to say things just right and just once – had a deleterious effect on the understanding of his message.[53] Few readers were able to muster the time and effort to enjoy the "exciting and stimulating challenge" that Tolman promised. Those few who did – for instance, Robert Leeper – were likely to find Brunswik's work "more impressive and persuasive" with prolonged study. But as Leeper himself noted, "in an age like ours, where rapid reading is praised, his [work] is altogether unsuited to the mode of approach that most readers would tend to bring."[54] In other words, it was not likely that many readers would choose to slowly and laboriously decode Brunswik's full message, and they have not. Instead many have turned to Brunswik's work for brief periods of time and have taken away this or that piece of his message, either ignorant or uncaring about the larger, systematic context from which that piece was removed.

Where does that leave us – or rather, where does it leave Brunswik? It is too soon to say what place he may be assigned in the larger sweep of the history of psychology, but in his own period of time, as I have tried to show, he was clearly situated at a number of crossroads – between various intellectual and scientific traditions (European functionalism, logical positivism, American behaviorism, and Anglo-American statisticalism), between various cultures and national traditions (European and American) and between various modes of scholarly endeavor (philosophical, historical and scientific).

Perhaps because he was situated at so many crossroads, Brunswik was more sensitive than most psychologists to the directions in which psychology was going. It may seem odd to suggest that Brunswik, the proponent of such a distinctive system, was representative of mid-twentieth-century psychology, but it is nevertheless the case that his system represented many of the major trends that have emerged more clearly into view in the years since Brunswik's death. Brunswik foresaw and advocated the emergence of probabilism, psychological ecology, perception, and cognition as key areas of psychological interest, increased scrutiny of the validity and reliability of psychological knowledge, greater historical and philosophical awareness, and the recognition of the "inextricable entanglement" of theory and method.[55] Brunswik was more than a weathervane, but he was that par excellence. If he did not create the weather patterns, he had an uncanny sense of which way the fresh breezes were blowing. Against the gales of opinion, he sought to give the breezes their due attention.

Edwin G. Boring, as the editor of *Contemporary Psychology,* appended the following quotation from John Morley to a 1957 review of Brunswik's posthumous *Perception and the Representative Design of Psychological Experiments:*

> There are some books which cannot be adequately reviewed for twenty or thirty years after they come out.[56]

In this instance at least, I believe that Boring was more prophetic than Tolman, whom I quoted at the beginning of this chapter. Thirty years after Brunswik's death, the time does seem ripe for more adequate reviews of Brunswik's life and works. I hope that this chapter will serve as a helpful starting point.

NOTES

1 The best sources on Brunswik's life and work are K. R. Hammond (ed.), *The Psychology of Egon Brunswik* (New York: Holt, Rinehart and Winston, 1966); K. R. Hammond, "Introduction to Brunswikian Theory and Methods," in K. R. Hammond and N. E. Wascoe (eds.), *Realizations of Brunswik's Representative Design* (San Francisco: Jossey-Bass, 1980), 1–11; L. Postman and E. C. Tolman, "Brunswik's Probabilistic Functionalism," in S. Koch (ed.), *Psychology: A Study of a Science,* vol. 1 (New York: McGraw-Hill, 1959), 502–564; and E. C. Tolman, "Egon Brunswik: 1903–1955," *American Journal of Psychology* 69 (1956):315–342 (reprinted in Hammond, *Psychology of Egon Brunswik,* 1–12).

2 E. Brunswik, *Wahrnehmung und Gegenstandswelt: Grundlinien einer Psychologie vom Gegenstand her* (Leipzig: Deuticke, 1934); E. C. Tolman and E. Brunswik, "The Organism and the Causal Texture of the Environment," *Psychological Review* 42 (1935):43–77.

3 Brentano is treated as the forerunner of the phenomenological movement in H. Spiegelberg, *The Phenomenological Movement,* 2nd ed., vol. 1 (The Hague:

Martinus Nijhoff, 1978), 27–52, and is placed within the European "movement toward objectivity" in J. Passmore, *A Hundred Years of Philosophy* (Harmondsworth: Penguin, 1968), ch. 8. Külpe is nicely treated in D. Lindenfeld, "Oswald Külpe and the Würzburg School," *Journal of the History of the Behavioral Sciences* 14 (1979):132–141. An introduction to Bühler's life and work is provided in J. F. T. Bugental (ed.), "Symposium on Karl Bühler's Contributions to Psychology," *Journal of General Psychology* 75 (1966):181–219. On the history of Bühler's institute, see Mitchell G. Ash, "Psychology and Politics in Interwar Vienna: The Vienna Psychological Institute, 1922–1942," in this volume.

4 Bühler gathered his research together in *Die Gestaltwahrnehmungen: Experimentelle Untersuchungen zur psychologischen und ästhetischen Analyse der Raum- und Zeitanschauung* (Stuttgart: Spemann, 1913).

5 K. Bühler, "Über den Begriff der sprachlichen Darstellung," *Psychologische Forschung* 3 (1923):282–294; *Die Krise der Psychologie* (Jena: Fischer, 1927), ch. 6; and *Sprachtheorie: Die Darstellungsfunktion der Sprache* (Jena: 1934). See R. E. Innis, *Karl Bühler: Semiotic Foundations of Language Theory* (New York: Plenum, 1982).

6 This research was integrated with subsequent work by Brunswik and his students in Brunswik's *Wahrnehmung und Gegenstandswelt;* Brunswik provided a list of all these research projects on pp. vii–viii. A typical study in which Brunswik followed up on Bühler's earlier research is "Das Duplizitätsprinzip in der Theorie der Farbenwahrnehmung," *Zeitschrift für Psychologie* 3 (1929):307–320.

7 F. Heider, "Ding und Medium," *Symposion* 1 (1927):109–127. On Meinong see D. Lindenfeld, *The Transformation of Positivism: Alexius Meinong and European Thought, 1880–1920* (Berkeley: University of California Press, 1980).

8 Brunswik, like Hermann von Helmholtz, approached perception as an achievement accomplished by making inferences from available cues. However, Brunswik came to differ from Helmholtz on the form of these inferences, which Brunswik took to be "ratiomorphic" rather than "rational." See E. Brunswik, *Perception and the Representative Design of Psychological Experiments* (Berkeley: University of California Press, 1956), 141.

9 For a succinct review of the history and major doctrines of the Vienna Circle, see J. Joergensen, *The Development of Logical Empiricism* (Chicago: University of Chicago Press, 1951).

10 H. Reichenbach, "Metaphysik und Naturwissenschaft," *Symposion* 1 (1927):158–176. Interestingly, this key article is in the same issue as Heider's "Ding und Medium." On Reichenbach see W. C. Salmon, "The Philosophy of Hans Reichenbach," in W. C. Salmon (ed.), *Hans Reichenbach: Logical Positivist* (Boston: Reidel, 1979), 1–84. The work of Richard von Mises was also important to Brunswik as a general corroboration of probabilism.

11 See E. Brunswik, "Organismic Achievement and Environmental Probability," *Psychological Review* 50 (1943):271.

12 Tolman and Brunswik, "The Organism," 43–44 (italics deleted).

13 Ibid., 47, 75.

14 Brunswik's first rendition of his analogical lens model appeared in his *Wahrnehmung und Gegendstandswelt,* in a section translated by L. W. Brandt in Hammond, *Psychology of Egon Brunswik,* 519. Over the years Brunswik elaborated the model, adding more and more details. Figure 5-1 is an adaptation of Brunswik's standard rendition in many of his later works. (See Hammond, "Introduction," 6.) Figure 5-2 is an adaptation of R. W. Leeper's expansion of Brunswik's single-lens model in R. W. Leeper, "A Critical Consideration of Egon Brunswik's Probabilistic Functionalism," ibid., 423. I believe that Leeper was correct in representing Brunswik's thought in this way.

15 See E. C. Tolman, *Purposive Behavior in Animals and Men* (New York: Century, 1932).

16 Tolman and Brunswik, "The Organism," 73 (italics added).

17 E. Brunswik, "Probability as a Determiner of Rat Behavior," *Journal of Experimental Psychology* 25 (1939):175–197.

18 E. Brunswik, "Thing Constancy as Measured by Correlation Coefficients," *Psychological Review* 47 (1940):69–78.

19 A preliminary report of this study was made at a Western Psychological Association meeting, as summarized in E. Brunswik, "A Random Sample of Estimated Sizes and Their Relation to Corresponding Size Measurements," *Psychological Bulletin* 37 (1940):585–586. The definitive report is E. Brunswik, "Distal Focussing of Perception: Size-constancy in a Representative Sample of Situations," *Psychological Monographs* 56 (1944):1–49.

20 The revised symposium papers were E. Brunswik, "Organismic Achievement"; C. L. Hull, "The Problem of Intervening Variables in Molar Behavior Theory," *Psychological Review* 50 (1943):273–291; and K. Lewin, "Defining the 'Field at a Given Time,'" ibid., 292–310.

21 Brunswik, "Organismic Achievement," 262. It was in the context of Brunswik's move to the United States and his espousal of a molar approach to psychological investigation that he began to speak of his functionalist approach as "biological" or "Darwinian" rather than "physiological," that is concerned with the adjustment of the organism to its environment rather than with the physiological processes that mediate this adjustment. This later, overlaid "American" functionalism has sometimes obscured Brunswik's earlier and more fundamental "European" functionalism. Although the two functionalisms coexist peacefully in most instances, some of Brunswik's functionalist pronouncements make better sense if understood within a Bühlerian ("European") rather than Darwinian ("American") framework.

22 Ibid.

23 Hull, "The Problem on Intervening Variables," 273.

24 Ibid., 274.

25 E. Brunswik, "Historical and Thematic Relations of Psychology to Other Sciences," *Scientific Monthly* 83 (1956):158 (italics added).

26 Hull, "The Problem of Intervening Variables," 280.

27 Brunswik studied the perceptual results of the two mental attitudes in "Distal Focusing." He advanced the concept of "the perceptual system as an intuitive statistician" in *Perception and the Representative Design of Psychological Experiments,* 80; and he discussed cybernetics and communications theory in *The Conceptual Framework of Psychology* (Chicago: University of Chicago Press, 1952), ch. 5, sect. 23.

28 E. Brunswik, "Statistical Separation of Perception, Thinking, and Attitudes," *American Psychologist* 3 (1948):342. Brunswik elaborated the distinction in "Reasoning as a Universal Behavior Model and a Functional Differentiation Between 'Perception' and 'Thinking'" (paper read at the International Congress of Psy-

chology in Montreal, 1954), in Hammond, *Psychology of Egon Brunswik*, 487–494; see also *Perception and the Representative Design of Experiments*, ch. 14.

29 E. Brunswik, "Scope and Aspects of the Cognitive Problem," in H. Gruber, R. Jessor and K. R. Hammond (eds.), *Cognition: The Colorado Symposium* (Cambridge, MA: Harvard University Press, 1957), 30.

30 E. Brunswik, *Systematic and Representative Design of Psychological Experiments* (Berkeley: University of California Press, 1947). This work was reprinted in 1956 as Part One of *Perception and Representative Design of Psychological Experiments*.

31 This work was published as part of the *International Encyclopedia of Unified Science* (vol. 1, no. 10).

32 Brunswik's "Representative Design and Probabilistic Theory in a Functional Psychology" (pp. 193–217) and his "In Defense of Probabilistic Functionalism: A Reply" (pp. 236–242) appeared as the first and last contributions to a "Symposium on the Probability Approach in Psychology," *Psychological Review* 3 (1955):193–242.

33 Hammond, "Introduction," 9.

34 Ibid., 9–10 (reference citations interspersed throughout the original passage have been dropped). Hammond's *Realizations* contains seven reports on recent Brunswikian research projects as well as many further references to Brunswikian research. See also L. Petrinovich, "Probablistic Functionalism: A Conception of Research Method," *American Psychologist* 34 (1979):373–390.

35 D. T. Campbell, "Addendum: A Personal Appreciation of Egon Brunswik's Psychology," unpublished addendum to D. T. Campbell, "Pattern Matching as an Essential in Distal Knowing," in Hammond, *Psychology of Egon Brunswik*, 41, 47.

36 Norma Haan, Nanette Heiman, Julian Hochberg and Daniel Levinson are representative of those students whose later psychological views, though not Brunswikian in any narrow sense, nevertheless reflect Brunswikian points of view. Personal communications to the author from N. Haan, 26 March 1980; N. Heiman, 15 April 1980; J. Hochberg, undated (May 1980); and D. J. Levinson, 12 August 1980.

37 Personal communications to the author from R. G. Barker, 25 March 1980; J. Bruner, 26 March 1980; and H. A. Simon, 25 March 1980.

38 Brunswik, "Distal Focusing," 3, 38.

39 Ibid., 37.

40 Brunswik, *Perception and the Representative Design of Psychological Experiments*, viii.

41 From Brunswik, *Systematic and Representative Design of Psychological Experiments*, reprinted in *Perception and the Representative Design of Psychological Experiments*, 39.

42 From E. Brunswik, "The Conceptual Focus of Some Psychological Systems," *Journal of Unified Science* 8 (1939):36–49, reprinted in M. H. Marx (ed.), *Psychological Theory* (New York: Macmillan, 1951), 137.

43 J. J. Gibson, who knew Brunswik personally, noted that "Brunswik himself could not rest comfortably in the lap of uncertainty. Nevertheless he disciplined himself to make virtue of what he considered a necessity." See J. J. Gibson, "Survival in a World of Probable Objects," *Contemporary Psychology* 2 (1957):34.

44 Brunswik, *Perception and the Representative Design of Experiments,* viii, 143; "Organismic Achievement," 270.

45 Personal communication to K. R. Hammond from D. T. Campbell, undated (May 1954), confirmed by personal communications to the author by many former students at a special commemorative symposium on Brunswik at the 88th annual meeting of the American Psychological Association, Montreal, 3 September 1980.

46 The exception proves the rule: E. C. Tolman, the one American psychologist who resonated instantly and steadfastly to Brunswik's tune, was one of the few American psychologists who shared a similar intellectual background by means of the neo-realism he absorbed from R. B. Perry and E. B. Holt at Harvard. See L. D. Smith, "Purpose and Cognition: The Limits of Neorealist Influence on Tolman's Psychology," *Behaviorism* 10 (1982):151–163. Not only are there common roots from Brentano to Bühler to Brunswik, and from Brentano to Perry and Holt to Tolman, but the homologous conceptual framework of these two traditions is nicely shown in Brunswik's easy shift from referring to Bühler in Europe to referring to Holt in the United States. See, e.g., Brunswik, "Representative Design," 194–201. On the "two disciplines" distinction, see G. Gigerenzer, "Survival of the Fittest Probabilist: Brunswik, Thurstone, and the Two Disciplines in Psychology," in G. Gigerenzer, L. Krüger and M. Morgan (eds.), *The Probabilistic Revolution,* vol. 2 (Cambridge, MA: MIT Press, 1987), and L. J. Cronbach, "The Two Disciplines of Scientific Psychology," *American Psychologist* 12 (1957):671–684.

47 Brunswik's doctoral students were Max Levin (1946), Murray Jarvik (1952), Thomas Nichols (1955), and William Sickles (1955). I should also note that Vienna after 1937, when Brunswik left, would not have been very supportive either: the Nazis were soon to arrive and change the complexion of Viennese life and scholarship. See Ash, "Psychology and Politics in Interwar Vienna." Brunswik was not Jewish, but he was engaged to Else Frenkel, a Jew, who emigrated to the United States in 1938 and soon thereafter became Else Frenkel-Brunswik. She too had a notable career as a psychologist, and her life and work were interwoven with Brunswik's in ways that, unfortunately, I have been unable to discuss here. Relatedly, I have had to omit Brunswik's relationship to psychoanalysis from the present discussion. For an introduction to her life and work, see N. Heiman and J. Grant (eds.), *Else Frenkel-Brunswik: Selected Papers* (New York: International Universities Press, 1974).

48 E.g., E. Brunswik, "Psychology as a Science of Objective Relations," *Philosophy of Science* 4 (1937):227–260; "Die Eingliederung der Psychologie in die exakten Wissenschaften," *Einheitswissenschaften* 6 (1938):17–34; and "The Conceptual Focus of Some Psychological Systems."

49 To be sure, very few faculty members would have been prepared for Brunswik's course, in which he presented material that he was pulling together for *The Conceptual Framework of Psychology.* I have reviewed the syllabus, handouts, and lecture notes from this course (courtesy of K. R. Hammond), and I am amazed at how intensive and demanding it was. Brunswik worked on *Conceptual Framework* for more than a decade, presenting early versions of his thematic analyses in "The Conceptual Focus of Some Psychological Systems" and "Points of View," in P. L. Harriman (ed.), *Encyclopedia of Psychology* (New York: Philosophical Library, 1946), 523–537. After *Conceptual Framework* appeared, Brunswik published a remarkable condensation of its thematic core in "Historical and Thematic Relations of Psychology to Other Sciences." An offshoot of Brunswik's research, presented as a speech in 1939, was published in somewhat revised form as "Ontogenetic and Other Developmental Parallels to the History of Science," in H. Evans (ed.), *Men and Moments in the History of Science* (Seattle: University of Washington Press, 1959), 3–21.

50 The final sections of *The Conceptual Framework of Psychology* exemplify Brunswik's wide-ranging interests and integrative skills. So too does Brunswik's "Historical and Thematic Relations of Psychology to Other Sciences."

51 E. C. Tolman, "Egon Brunswik, Psychologist and Philosopher of Science," *Science* 122 (1955):910. The relationships of Brunswik, Tolman, and Hull to the Unity of Science Movement, and of Brunswik to Tolman, are treated critically in L. D. Smith, *Behaviorism and Logical Positivism: A Reassessment of the Alliance* (Stanford: Stanford University Press, 1986).

52 J. Hochberg's review of Brunswik's *The Conceptual Framework of Psychology* appeared in *American Journal of Psychology* 67 (1954):386; G. Bergmann's in *Psychological Bulletin* 49 (1952):654.

53 Ironically, Brunswik's excessively terse style violated his own theoretical understanding of the need for "redundancy" in communication. See the very last section of his *Conceptual Framework of Psychology,* entitled "Redundancy as an Antidote to Equivocation." Brunswik's contentions in this regard exemplify a basic principle of probabilistic functionalism: the more redundant the cues or means (stimuli, words, behavioral options) the greater the probability of accurate or appropriate achievement (perception, communication, goal attainment).

54 Personal communication to K. R. Hammond from R. W. Leeper, 2 July 1962, Robert Leeper Papers, Archives of the History of American Psychology, Akron, Ohio.

55 Brunswik, *Perception and the Representative Design of Psychological Experiments,* 144.

56 Gibson, "Survival in a World of Probable Objects," 35.

6

PSYCHOLOGY AND POLITICS IN INTERWAR VIENNA: THE VIENNA PSYCHOLOGICAL INSTITUTE, 1922–1942*

MITCHELL G. ASH

When historians seek links between ideas and society, they often find institutions. Especially since the emergence of science as a profession, historians have inevitably become interested in the institutions in which science is created. These often bear the personal and intellectual stamp of their leaders, but they also have discoverable relationships to their social and political environments. Because these relationships change, it is worthwhile to follow the history of individual scientific institutions through succeeding periods, and especially important to examine their development under different political regimes. In this chapter the continuity of institutionalized science under changing political conditions will be considered by examing the history of the Vienna Psychological Institute from its founding in 1922 to 1942, using archival and other sources.[1] This institute is a fitting subject, because of the unusual political circumstances that led to its founding and the politically decided fates of its leading members during the Dollfuss-Schussnigg regime (after 1934) and following the Nazi takeover of Austria in 1938.

The archival sources for this account illuminate mainly the institute's connections with the Austrian state and Vienna city governments. But the research done there will not be ignored; for this case reveals particu-

*This is a revised and considerably expanded version of a paper delivered at the University of Essen in November 1984 and published in German under the title, "Die Entwicklung des Wiener Psychologischen Instituts 1922–1938," in A. Eschbach (ed.), *Karl Bühler's Theory of Language* (Amsterdam: John Benjamins B. V., 1987). Material from the German text is used here by permission of John Benjamins B. V. The English version was presented at the annual meeting of the American Historical Association in New York in December 1985. Research for the German version was supported by grant number Fr 132/16-1 of the Deutsche Forschungsgemeinschaft, "Psychologie im Exil" (Project Director: Werner D. Fröhlich, Psychological Institute, University of Mainz). Research and writing of the English version were supported by National Science Foundation grant SES-8511230.

larly clearly the complex variety of relationships between the aims and content of science and the goals of its patrons. This account may also supplement commonly accepted views of intellectual life in interwar Vienna, which sometimes discuss psychology, but usually emphasize psychoanalysis.[2]

BACKGROUND

As recent research has shown, the founding of the first laboratory for experimental psychology in Leipzig did not lead to the institutionalization of an independent discipline in Germany or Austria. Instead, experimental psychology remained a subfield of philosophy in the German-speaking universities until 1941. Until World War I, at least, this was so in part because neither the German state governments nor the authorities in Vienna saw experimental psychology as a discipline with sufficient potential for social utility, as they defined it, to justify funds for the requisite professorships and laboratories. It is also true, however, that academic psychologists did not always campaign vigorously for independence from philosophy, because many of them believed that empirical research in psychology could help resolve long-standing philosophical disputes, especially in epistemology and logic.[3]

Optimism on this score was visible in Vienna as early as the 1890s. In an 1893 article, for example, the philosopher Wilhelm Jerusalem cited the high enrollment in Wilhelm Wundt's Leipzig lectures as evidence that an important change was occurring: Philosophical principles would henceforth be based not on "armchair speculation," but on empirical research.[4] Though his views were not so empiricist as Jerusalem's, Franz Brentano, a precursor of phenomenology and one of Freud's teachers, was also convinced that empirical psychology could contribute to philosophy. Among his *Last Wishes for Austria,* published when he vacated his Vienna professorship in 1895, was the establishment of a psychological laboratory there. The year before, Alexius Meinong, a student of Brentano's, set the relevant precedent by founding the first such laboratory in Austria at the University of Graz.[5]

However, Brentano's wish was not so quickly fulfilled. The year it was expressed, Franz Hillebrand, a young philosopher who had established his scientific *bona fida* by working closely with the famous sensory physiologist Ewald Hering, applied to the Royal Ministry of Education for funds to set up a psychological laboratory at the University of Vienna. Ministry documents show that the authorities were willing to grant this request, but only if another laboratory (e.g., the Zoological Institute) could be moved to other quarters. Not surprisingly, nothing came of Hillebrand's proposal.[6] In 1902, the university's Philosophical (Arts and Sciences) Faculty referred to this in a public complaint to the Ministry about the general lack of adequate salaries and research facilities.[7] If the experience of German universities at the time is any guide, an underlying factor in this situation may have been Hillebrand's junior status. The major laboratories in Würzburg, Berlin, and Frankfurt were all founded, and those in Bonn and Munich expanded, when already successful experimenting psychologists being recruited for philosophy chairs in those places made such a step a condition of their appointment.[8] Precisely this was the way the Vienna institute, too, would be founded in 1922.

In the meantime, it could not be said that Vienna philosophers were hostile to psychology. Three of them, Wilhelm Jerusalem, Friedrich Jodl, and Adolf Stöhr, offered courses and published textbooks in general psychology between 1896 and 1917.[9] Jerusalem tended more toward empiricism than the others, but all three were careful to emphasize the autonomy of the psychical realm, meaning its nonreduceability to physics or physiology – a position that would not inflame conservative opinion or irritate the politically influential Roman Catholic clergy. Jerusalem tried to take an independent course between the so-called critical idealism of the German neo-Kantians and the neopositivism of Ernst Mach, who had been brought to Vienna in 1895, under a more liberal regime.[10] There were also courses in applied psychology and other areas, but philosophical aims clearly remained dominant.

The founding of the institute

The situation changed significantly after the fall of the Dual Monarchy in 1918. When Stöhr died in that year, the pedagogue Alois Höfler proposed as his successor the Munich philosopher and psychologist Erich Becher. The Philosophical Faculty nominated him to the Ministry as its only candidate in June 1921.[11] With an established reputation as a philosopher of science and a defender of an independent, "psychical causality," Becher seemed to his colleagues to have the credentials for the position.[12] However, he had succeeded Oswald Külpe as director of one of the largest psychological laboratories in Germany, and he asked that an institute of comparable size be set up for him in Vienna. At this point the negotiations ended; the Ministry of Education regretted that the Finance Ministry could not permit such an outlay, given the horrendous fiscal situation caused by rampant inflation.[13] One year later, however, an appointment was made and an institute funded.

The appointee was Karl Bühler. After receiving his first degree in medicine, Bühler had taken up psychology, working first in Berlin and then at the Würzburg institute under Oswald Külpe.[14] There he had become embroiled in the so-called imageless thought controversy, drawing harsh criticism from Wundt and others for allegedly perverting the experimental method in his search for new contents of consciousness, which he called simply thoughts. He remained loyal to Külpe, working as his assistant in Bonn and Munich. In his research, however, he returned to more orthodox topics and methods, becoming one of the first investigators to apply psychophysical measurements to form perception.[15] Following his marriage in 1915, he and his wife, Charlotte, who had been his student, began work on the mental development of young children. The resulting book, *Die geistige Entwicklung des Kindes (The Mental Development of the Child)*, appeared in 1918 and was rapidly accepted as one of the leading texts in the field.[16] The next year Bühler was appointed professor of philosophy and psychology at the Technical Academy in Dresden.

Bühler's productivity and accomplishments were not in doubt, but his appointment to the Vienna chair nearly failed for the same reasons that Becher's did. Bühler, too, asked for a psychological laboratory with adequate space and a full complement of the latest equipment.[17] At that point another actor came on the scene – Otto Glöckel, President of the Vienna School Board and founder of the already famous Vienna school reform movement. Through an intermediary, Viktor Fadrus, an official in the Ministry of Education, Glöckel offered to provide Bühler with the laboratory space he required – ten rooms in the School Board building itself, on the famous Ringstrasse – to pay the salaries of an assistant and a maintenance worker, and to supplement his salary by engaging him and Charlotte Bühler to teach psychology at the Pedagogical Academy of the city of Vienna, which was about to be reorganized. The Ministry, for its part, agreed to provide the institute's operating budget, to pay an additional assistant, and to finance the institute library and instrument collection. Further, the Ministry "acknowledged" Bühler's additional teaching at the Pedagogical Academy without objecting, and allowed him to officially designate the laboratory's researches as products of the university, although they would not be carried out on university property.[18]

When Bühler signed the requisite papers late in the summer of 1922, a collaboration began that was unique in both the history of psychology and in the history of Vienna university politics. Never before had the Ministry of Education allowed another government body such a role in an area of its jurisdiction. Since the Vienna city government was controlled at the time by the Social Democratic Party of Austria, while the same party had already lost control of the national government in 1920, the collaboration appears all the more remarkable.

THE INSTITUTE IN "RED VIENNA" 1922–1934: EXPECTATION AND REALITY

The expectations of the Vienna school reformers for the new institute and its founder were clear from the beginning. Glöckel and his co-workers sought not revolutionary change, but a social democratic republic, with equal opportunity for all regardless of social, ethnic, or religious background. Thus one of the first national school reform laws, passed in 1919, stated that the new system would be constructed on "'on the basis of the unified school (instead of the previous three-class school system), work-based instruction and the fastest possible elimination of educational privilege.'"[19]

After the Social Democrats handed over control of the central government in 1920, their reform plans were necessarily limited to the city of Vienna, which became an independent Austrian province the same year and remained a Social Democratic stronghold until 1934.[20] The general aims of the movement, however, remained as before: (1) to secularize first the Viennese, then the rest of the Austrian schools; (2) to reconstruct education first in Vienna, then throughout Austria on the basis of a "child-centered" pedagogy, as they called it, turning away from rote memorization of isolated intellectual data and toward the development of both intellectual and manual skills under the slogan, "from the drill-school to the learning and work school"; (3) to professionalize pedagogy by making the teacher's certificate equivalent to a university degree, or, failing that, to reorganize teacher training on a scientific basis.[21]

The Bühlers' work appeared to fit well into the second and third parts of this program. In *The Mental Development of the Child* and elsewhere, Karl Bühler described the development of children as a three-stage, evolutionary progression from the control of instincts to the training of sensory and motor skills to true, intelligent learning through the medium of language – a sequence which, he thought, paralleled the evolution of the intellect across species.[22] Clearly, such a view aligned well with both the child-centered perspective of the reformers and their emphasis on active, hands-on learning over rote memorizing in the early school years. In any case, the reformers accepted evolutionary theory as a matter of course. In a 1922 review of recent literature, Viktor Fadrus recommended *The Mental Development of the Child* as "one of the most significant publications in the field of child psychology," and added that "we consider ourselves fortunate to have the author in Vienna."[23] Bühler, for his part, openly advocated school reform, which led to criticism from his largely clerical-conservative professorial colleagues.[24]

By offering this perspective at the new Pedagogical Academy in Vienna, the Bühlers could take a long step toward fulfilling the third of the reformers' general aims, the professionalization of teacher training, thus winning adherents for the reform movement among Vienna teachers. Viktor Fadrus, who became the director of the Academy and editor of the reformers' journal, *Die Schulreform,* emphasized this point in his programmatic essay on the Academy's aims and in his annual summaries of its achievement. It was a cause for particular pride for Fadrus that the Bühlers made the Pedagogical Academy into "a place for research"; for this brought not only potentially relevant pedagogical knowledge but also an increase in status for the pedagogues.[25] The Bühlers were not the only people expected to fulfill such expectations. Alfred Adler taught at the Pedagogical Academy for a number of years as well, and is reputed to have had a significant impact particularly in the field of educational counseling.[26] The Bühlers, however, were the only regular, salaried staff in psychology.

How did the actual work of the Vienna Psychological Institute compare with these expectations? Karl Bühler's research was clearly not limited to pedagogical or even developmental psychology. His general approach in this period is best reflected in his book, *Die Krise der Psychologie* (1927). There he attacked all narrowly based "schools" of psychology, including behaviorism, Gestalt psychology, psychoanalysis, and so-called "humanistic" or *Geisteswissenschaftliche Psychologie,* and tried to develop a point of view that could unite them: "In the great house of psychology there is room for all," he wrote.[27] This methodological and theoretical openness was mirrored in the administrative structure of the institute. In its heyday, in the late 1920s and early 1930s, there were three divisions, or "departments," each with its own head, different sources of funding, and even different locations. As one of them, Paul Lazarsfeld, later recalled, the division heads had a great deal of freedom to organize research as they wished. Regular contact with Bühler was assured through the institute's weekly colloquium, but the director imposed no rigid methodological or theoretical straitjacket. The organization of the institute "guaranteed, on the one hand, that the spirit of the leadership influenced all of its parts, and at the same time allowed the assistants to freely develop their own interests."[28]

Perhaps it is already clear that one cannot easily draw a direct line from the political intentions of the school reformers to the work of the Vienna institute. The research of each of the three departments of the so-called Vienna school could easily be the subject of a separate chapter. The following paragraphs give only a brief idea of the variety of intellectual and social interests and institutional connections involved.

Experimental psychology

The experimental psychologists in the narrower sense worked under the direction first of the assistant Helmut Boksch, then from 1929 on under Egon Brunswik in the Department of General Psychology, located in the institute's rooms in the School Board building. There they used standard methods of self-observation *(Selbstbeobachtung)* to work on problems that Bühler had already raised in his earlier research on form perception. Particularly important issues were the perception of objects and the related problem of the so-called perceptual constancies – why we see objects as being nearly the same size, shape, color, etc., despite variations

KARL BÜHLER
Photograph taken in the late 1920s. Reproduced by permission of Achim Eschbach.

in their distance from us or in the surrounding field.[29] Viewed in historical context, this research was a continuation of pre-World War I, cognitively oriented experimental psychology. The most important members of this research group, Brunswik and Ludwig (later Lajos) Kardos, emphasized this continuity in historical essays in which they pointed to the the philosophical roots of their research issues.[30]

Karl Bühler gave this work a more general theoretical framework and secured its continued philosophical relevance by extending and reshaping the intentional model of mind originally proposed by Franz Brentano and developed by Edmund Husserl and Alexius Meinong. According to that model, consciousness is a fundamentally active, directed process. In his attempt to give this idea a biological foundation, Bühler developed a general theory of language and expression, in which perceptions were described as signs, by analogy with the biological concept of signals.[31] Clearly this was a continuation of experimental psychology's original project – philosophically relevant laboratory research. Although the work was done in the School Board building, it seems to have had no immediate pedagogical or political relevance. This was basic research, not applied psychology. The only potential connection with the aims of the school reformers was work by Brunswik and others on the development of memory and Brunswik's dissertation on color perception in children. But the relevent publications made little or no reference to pedagogical applications.[32]

Child and youth psychology

The child and youth psychologists were led by Charlotte Bühler, who held the rank of assistant until 1929, when she was given the title of Associate Professor.[33] She was assisted from 1925 to 1931 by Hildegard Hetzer, a child-care worker assigned to the institute by the city. They were located from 1926 on in a two-room suite in the city's Adoption Center *(Kinderübernahmstelle)*. The Center was a special project of City Councilor Julius Tandler, an anatomist by training who had become a specialist for social policy. Tandler is best known for his leadership of the immense workers' housing projects that made "Red Vienna" internationally known. However, this was only part of an all-encompassing social welfare concept that also included city-supported pregnancy counseling, maternity aid, and child care. In line with this concept, the city took over legal guardianship of all children who, because of economic difficulties or conflicts at home or with the law, could not be cared for by their parents. The Adoption Center was a clearing house, where these wards first underwent physical examinations to check their general health and guard against infectious diseases. After this the authorities decided whether the children should go to one of the city's children's homes, to private foster homes, to institutions for special education, or back to their parents. In an essay called "The Psychology of Welfare," Tandler called all this "the administration of the organic capital of society" and emphasized the dimension of social control involved: "welfare is more than accidental aid, more than provision of material help, more than social service; it is psychological investigation, mental influence, true education and becomes a holy mission especially where people are still educable."[34]

With its capacity of more than 2,500, the Adoption Center offered an ideal opportunity to observe children's behavior, especially since the subjects were kept in glass-walled rooms and thus could easily be seen from the hallways despite quarantine orders. According to Lotte Schenck-Danziger (then Lotte Schenck), who succeeded Hetzer as Charlotte Bühler's assistant in 1931, students were taught to keep exact, minute-to-minute records of their observations, which later became data for dissertations. In return, the psychologist who oversaw the students had to carry out intelligence or development tests with some of the children in the institution's care.[35]

On the scientific side, the investigators, most of them women, utilized a wide range of methods, including the interpretation of diaries, statistics, and experiments with free play, with the aim of creating a unified scheme of psychological development from birth to early adulthood. This research program, like that of the experimentalists, pursued issues raised earlier by Karl Bühler, here in *The Mental Development of the Child*. From him Charlotte Bühler took the basis of her scheme, the parallelism and mutual interaction of psychological and biological development. However, the research done under her direction emphasized the cognitive and personality structures considered characteristic of each developmental stage.[36]

From 1926 on this work was also supported by the Laura Spellman Rockefeller Memorial, the leaders of which had the year before conceived a huge program of research with similar aims in mind. In the academic year 1924–1925 Charlotte Bühler went to the United States as a Rockefeller Fellow to learn about American research in child and youth psychology from Edward Thorndike at Columbia University's Teachers College, Arnold Gesell at Yale University, and others. Her stay coincided with the construction of the largest research program in the history of the social sciences up to that time by Beardsley Ruml and Lawrence K. Frank. The Vienna Institute was the only one outside the United States selected for funding. The money was used mainly for doctoral dissertation scholarships, which made the Vienna Institute one of the most productive in Europe.[37]

Given its location and alternative sources of support, perhaps it is not surprising that even this department, the one we would expect to be most closely connected with the aims of the school reformers, did not become so tightly linked. In their introduction to the monograph series, "Vienna Research on Pedagogical Psychology," co-editors Charlotte Bühler and Viktor Fadrus said the series would have three goals: (1) to produce psychological research that would be the basis of a practical and scientifically secure pedagogy; (2) to determine the extent to which pedagogical goals and the developmental characteristics of each stage could be coordinated; (3) to view development from the perspectives of biological function and cultural value, of society and the individual.[38] Comparing the first two points already reveals a certain tension between the projected linkage of psychological research with pedagogy and more general research aims. Later, Charlotte Bühler and Hildegard Hetzer published an essay on the history of child psychology in which they made it clear that their priorities were indeed somewhat different from those of the reformers. There they presented the development of child psychology as a successful struggle to protect pure psychology from incorporation by pedagogy.[39]

In fact, in a retrospective survey of the group's achievements, Hetzer reported that the largest group of studies – 46% – dealt with preschool children, of which the Adoption Center had plenty. The most important of these were studies by Bühler, Hetzer, and others on the first year of life and the so-called small childrens' tests *(Kleinkindertests)* for diagnosing developmental problems in early childhood.[40] This work had clear practical relevance, but mainly for the Adoption Center. Hetzer reported that the group did little or no classroom research; the only exceptions were isolated studies on the social structure of school classes and of the process of instruction in language courses. As a result, there were occasional mutterings that the Psychological Institute was misusing its funding from the School Board.[41] True, this research still fit, in a broad sense, into the second of the school reformers' aims; a comprehensive scheme of psychological development could be described as an essential prerequisite to a scientifically grounded, child-centered pedagogy. But the tension between the reformers' sociopolitical project and Charlotte Bühler's more general scientific goals was undeniable.

This is not to say that the work of this department of the institute had no political importance. The opposite is particularly true for the department's work in youth psychology. The general interest of political authorities in youth issues, already great at the turn of the century, increased noticeably in the 1920s.[42] The Bühlers were aware of this before they came to Vienna; Charlotte Bühler's research on youth psychology began with a request from the Dresden city government, originally addressed to her husband. The most significant Vienna studies in the field were published in a volume whose title, *Jugend und Beruf (Youth and Occupation),* already points to the social policy issues involved. The volume's chief author, Paul Lazarsfeld, had the cooperation of Socialist youth groups, and thus reached young workers without diaries. He then supplemented Charlotte Bühler's diary evaluation method with statistically evaluated questionnaires and demographic data, concluding that "occupational wishes of urban youth in their statistical distribution reflect the economic structure" of the cities investigated.[43]

However, for this field, too, the work of the institute had at best an indirect connection with the school reform movement. In 1929, Charlotte Bühler desribed the relationship between youth research and pedagogy as follows:

> It is becoming clearer that we in youth psychology, as in psychology in general, cannot proceed from single investigations, but must ask ourselves: how does the growing person gradually gain his relationships to the world, its laws, tasks, and possibilities? . . . One sphere after the other opens itself to them, some of them through the school; that is its psychological significance.[44]

Clearly, in youth psychology, too, school-related research was embedded from the beginning in a much broader research program. This implied at least a relative reduction in the importance of the reformers' goals.

Charlotte Bühler and her co-workers tried to achieve a variety of political, pedagogical, and scientific aims. They do not seem to have always succeeded to their complete satistifaction. In 1930, for example, Charlotte Bühler confessed to a visiting Rockefeller Foundation official that she felt constrained by the institute's political linkages. Understandably, the majority of the Adoption Center's children came from working or lower-class families; she, however, wanted to interview children from better-off families, but was having difficulty gaining access to them.[45]

Economic and social psychology

The economic and social psychologists, headed first by Paul Lazarsfeld, then by Herta Herzog and Marie Jahoda-Lazarsfeld, reveal a rather different disalignment between research and policy interests. The work of this department was done at the Research Center for Economic Psychology *(Wirtschaftspsychologische Forschungsstelle)*, founded in 1927 and located in various rented offices separate from those of the other two divisions. Funding came first from privately commissioned market research, for example, on coffee consumption, and then, after 1931, from the institute's Rockefeller Foundation grant of $4,000 per year. However, according to participants' memoirs, the funds were used for politically motivated social research. Lazarsfeld, Jahoda, and many of their co-workers (e.g., Hans Zeisel and Hilde Weiss) came from the socialist youth movement and had connections with Austrian socialist leaders, such as Bruno Bauer. They used statistical, survey, and interview techniques to create what they called a sociography of working class districts in Vienna, hoping to discover, among other things, whether, as Marxist theory predicted, economic crisis fostered revolutionary class consciousness.[46]

Their most important study, *Die Arbeitslosen von Marienthal (The Unemployed of Marienthal)* (1932), remains a classic of its kind.[47] Employed here to study the repercussions of unemployment for community and family life were life histories, time budgeting studies, statistics on participation in local clubs and party organizations, and consumer research methods. The main finding – that resignation and withdrawal, not revolution, was the more likely reaction of working class men to long-term crisis – was not what Austro-Marxist theory predicted. However, workers' feelings of community remained strong, and interpersonal relations proved remarkably resistant to change. Strong marriages, for example, became better under the pressure, while difficult ones grew worse.

That such studies were financed by the Rockefeller Foundation was not paradoxical; the Foundation's Social Sciences division evidenced here, as elsewhere, an interest in the problem of social control. The enthusiastic, indeed envious assessment of the Marienthal study by the definitely non-Marxist German sociologist Leopold von Wiese seems also to have impressed Foundation officials.[48] Important here, however, is that the relationship between political and research interests in the case of the Research Center for Economic Psychology was ironically reciprocal to that of the child and youth psychologists. Charlotte Bühler and her co-workers, supported by politically interested sources, tried to carry out what they took to be politically disinterested research. Lazarsfeld and his co-workers – if their memoirs can be believed – took funding from sources with interests running in one direction and used it to support research with rather different political aims.

Clearly, the Vienna school reformers' expectation that important, policy-oriented psychological, pedagogical, and social research would emerge from the unique institutional matrix that was the Vienna Psychological Institute was fulfilled. But it was fulfilled in ways that were not foreseen by either the institute's founders or their original patron.

THE VIENNA INSTITUTE UNDER AUSTRO-FASCISM, 1934–1938

By the time Charlotte Bühler made her comment to the Rockefeller Foundation official, in the early 1930s, Vienna Social Democracy, and the taxes introduced to support it, had already come under increasingly heavy attack from the city's clerical-conservative opposition. Among the signatories of a statement against such attacks, which appeared during an election campaign in the Vienna *Arbeiter Zeitung* on April 20, 1927, were Karl Bühler, Alfred Adler, and Sigmund Freud.[49] When Vienna fell under the dictatorship of Engelbert Dollfuss in May 1934, after a workers' uprising was bloodily suppressed in February, the cooperation of state and city officials that had been the basis of the institute's support seemed threatened. Viktor Fadrus was one of the first officials dismissed by the new regime. In the fall of 1934, as a result of the "reorganization" of the School Board, the institute was moved from the Board's building on the Ringstrasse to the rooms near the University where it is still located today.[50] At the same time, the title of the reformers' journal was changed from *Die Schulreform* to *Der pädagogische Führer (The Pedagogical Leader)*. The new slogan for the schools was to be, not "from the drill school to the learning and work school," but "Vaterland und Familie" (Fatherland and Family).

However, the School Board continued to contribute to the institute's budget, though in smaller amounts. The Bühlers still taught at the Pedagogical Academy. Though a teacher surplus in the later 1920s and funding cuts during the Depression had already ended the special teacher training programs in which the Bühlers had participated, the new regime seems to have had as much need of support from schoolteachers as the old. The institute itself seems to have continued working much as before. The only obvious changes in its research structure were the establishment of a new department for "Life Psychology" *(Lebenspsychologie),* announced by Charlotte Bühler in the first volume of *Der pädagogische Führer,* and a new series of studies by her and co-workers in "family research."[51] In 1935, a lecture by Karl Bühler entitled "The Future of Psychology and the School" appeared in a series that also included a talk on "Patriotic Education" by teacher Ludwig Hänsel and political speeches by Richard Schmitz, the new mayor of Vienna, Archbishop Cardinal Theodor Innitzer, Minister of Education Hans Pertner, and members of the new school administration.[52] However, Bühler took no obvious political position.

In February 1934, immediately after the workers' uprising was put down, Sigmund Freud assessed the situation as follows: "The future is uncertain: either an Austrian fascism or the twisted cross. In the latter case we will have to leave: we will endure some things from the local fascism, since it will hardly treat us so badly as its German cousin. It wouldn't be pleasant, of course; but life in a foreign country is not so pleasant, either."[53] Perhaps the Bühlers' views were similar. Their adaptive moves, however, were necessarily more public than Freud's, since they were nearly completely dependent on state support.

Two other events of 1935 and 1936 posed more direct threats to the institute. In the summer of 1935, the Rockefeller Foundation notified Karl Bühler that it planned to cut the institute's grant for the next two years by 50%, and then to end its support altogether. Bühler wrote to the Ministry that the reasons given for the move were "the uncertain political situation in Europe and the failure of the (Austrian) state to provide support even nearly comparable to the Foundation's assistance."[54]

Another reason behind the decision may or may not have been known to Bühler. In 1934 the Foundation reorganized its operations, and the officials of the Medical Sciences division, to which the institute was then assigned, apparently had a different view of the quality of the research, especially of Charlotte Bühler and her associates, than their social science counterparts had had. The report they presented to the Foundation's Paris office reveals their ambivalence. On the one hand, they noted, "Professor Karl Bühler's interests, as that of a medically-trained man, link the psychological side of his work with activities in the medical sciences. Dr. Charlotte Bühler, his wife and associate, while not medically-trained, has had a wide experience in child psychology . . . both are talented teachers and both of them are eminent in their ability to create an atmosphere of real enthusiasm." However, they added, "criticism from competent observers would indicate that the present level of activity at the Institute is undesirable. Amongst the workers, particularly from foreign countries, there has crept in too large a percentage of students of inferior quality."[55]

To deal with the situation, Bühler petitioned the Ministry in July 1936 for supplemental appropriations. Pointing to "the scientific and propaganda significance of the Psychological Institute abroad," he wrote that after the "suppression" *(Zurückdrängung)* of psychological research in Germany, only the Vienna institute has, "alone among the German-speaking countries, an important position among the similar institutions in the world."[56] The Ministry granted the institute 2,000 Schillings – less than one-fifth of the Foundation's grant – in 1936, and 1,000 Schillings the next year.[57]

To make up the rest, the Bühlers organized a patrons' group, the "Friends of the Vienna Psychological Institute." The names of the "honor committee" and the advisory board of this group read like a directory of the Viennese social and political establishments. Titled nobility abounded. High government and church officials included, in addition to Cardinal Innitzer, Minister for Culture and Propaganda von Hammerstein-Equord, State Councilor Seyss-Inquart (later Reich Plenipotentiary under Hitler), and School Inspector Antonin Simonic.[58] This shows how far the Bühlers were prepared to go to adapt to political circumstances. It is not clear how much money this group raised. However, the institute's altered finances do not seem to have affected its work in the short run. Many of the research papers listed in 1935 as "in preparation," including some of the "family research" mentioned above, appeared by 1938.[59]

A rather more direct threat came on November 17, 1936, when security police raided the Research Center for Economic Psychology and arrested four staff members. Marie Jahoda-Lazarsfeld and a young co-worker were subsequently interrogated and charged with using the Center as a blind to maintain a secret mail drop for the Social Revolutionaries, the Social Democrats' underground organization. Both went on trial in May 1937; Jahoda was found guilty and sentenced to three months in prison in July. After intervention from abroad, she was released on the condition that she emigrate immediately; she went to England.[60] She later said that she felt at least partly responsible for the arrest of Karl Bühler after the German takeover. At the time, however, the security forces admitted that they had no evidence that the work of the Research Center as such was subversive, and it continued operating under the direction of Hans Zeisel until 1938.[61]

Under the Austro-fascist dictatorship, the Vienna institute was threatened in specific ways, but continued to operate. Charlotte Bühler wrote in her autobiography that, when Fordham University offered professorships to her and her husband in 1937, "Karl was disinclined, because he had become firmly entrenched in Vienna and hoped that Austria would hold out against Hitler. However, he finally gave in and we accepted the appointments for autumn 1938. This proved to be too late."[62]

THE "ANSCHLUSS" AND AFTER

In March 1938, just after German troops entered Vienna, Karl Bühler was arrested. On April 9, his name appeared on the first list of professors to be dismissed "for political and world-view reasons" because their views were considered dangerous to the "peace and public order of the (Philosophical) Faculty."[63] Available documents do not indicate whether Bühler's earlier links with the Social Democrats or his more recent ties with the Dollfuss-Schussnigg regime were meant. Charlotte Bühler, who had one Jewish parent, was listed soon afterward among the professors to be dropped on "racial" grounds.[64] Thus Nazi racism was not the primary reason for Karl Bühler's dismissal; previous accounts had mentioned only his "non-Aryan" wife in this connection. However, since the Nuremberg Laws called for the release of civil servants who were married to Jews, Bühler would surely have been dropped for this reason in any case.

Within a week of submitting the first list of professors marked for dismissal, the Dean of the Philosophical Faculty wrote confidentially to Otto Tumlirz, a Graz professor and Nazi party member known for his work on "characterology" and "psychological anthropology," and asked him to take over Karl Bühler's courses for the summer semester, which was about to begin.[65] Tumlirz replied that he would be happy to come to Vienna, but that teaching Bühler's courses would be out of the question:

> Continuing Professor Bühler's courses is not possible, first of all because I cannot prepare a four-hour lecture with a wave of the hand, and also because I view the tasks of German psychology differently than Mr. Bühler – which is surely the more decisive factor. What I could do here in recent years only under camouflage, anthropological holistic psychology, race psychology, etc., must now be supported in Vienna also.[66]

However, Tumlirz taught in Vienna for only one semester, and was never named director of the institute. That task fell temporarily to Friedrich Kainz, a philosopher who, among other actions, began the addition of part of Karl Bühler's private library to the institute's collection.[67] In the autumn of 1938, Bühler's chair and the institute directorship were assumed by Günther Ipsen, a proponent of the so-called Leipzig school of "holistic" or *Ganzheitspsychologie* and like Tumlirz a party member. The university catalogues for 1938 to 1940 reflect the changes Tumlirz and Ipsen intended to make. Announced for summer 1938 were the following courses by Karl Bühler: "The Psychological Bases of Language Theory"; "Psychological Practicum – Biological Models in Psychology"; and "Psychological Colloquium for Advanced Students." Instead of these courses, Tumlirz may have offered titles similar to those he announced for 1938–1939, which included a psychological practicum entitled "Race and Character." For the first trimester 1940, Ipsen announced "Folk Theory" *(Volkslehre)*,"Introductory Praktikum in Youth Studies" and "Race and History – in the Psychological Institute."[68]

However, Ipsen's tenure, too, was short. With the outbreak of war in September 1939, he entered the Wehrmacht's psychological service. The institute was again led by Kainz on a temporary basis until 1942, when Hubert Rohracher was appointed Associate Professor and institute director. Rohracher was known, both then and later, for solid research in physiological psychology and personality theory, but had no obvious political leanings. He continued as director after the war.[69] Thus, the institutional history of psychology in Vienna proved similar to that of its major rival, the Psychological Institute of the University of Berlin, in one important respect. In both places it proved possible to drive out the psychology that had been propagated before the Nazi takeover, but not to replace that psychology with an institutionally stable, Nazified version.[70]

When Karl Bühler was released from confinement in May 1938 he faced the choice of forced retirement or emigration.[71] Charlotte Bühler, who held a visiting professorship in Norway at the time, wrote frantically to colleagues in England and the United States seeking positions for herself and her husband, but without success.[72]

Completely unhelpful were their erstwhile supporters at the Rockefeller Foundation. Egon Brunswik, who had already gone to the University of California at Berkeley in 1937 with partial support from the Foundation, wrote on behalf of the Bühlers to colleagues Gordon Allport at Harvard and Henry Beaumont at the University of Kentucky. When Beaumont, who had studied with the Bühlers in Vienna, wrote to the Foundation for assistance, he was coolly informed that Foundation policy was to provide only one-half salary for emigrés, and then only if assurances were forthcoming of permanent employment to follow – a policy that was not consistently applied before 1938, but was more rigorously enforced in response to the sudden rush of emigrés in that year. Leonard Carmichael of Tufts University received the same answer when he applied to the Foundation later for a one-year professorship for Karl Bühler.[73]

In October 1938, Luton Ackerson, a member of the newly organized Emergency Committee in Aid of Displaced Foreign Psychologists of the American Psychological Association, found a position for Karl Bühler at tiny St. Scholastica College in Duluth, Minnesota. This had to suffice as the basis for his emigration to the United States in 1939. Charlotte Bühler followed the next year.[74]

CONCLUSION

Life in the United States proved kinder to Charlotte than to Karl Bühler. After initial difficulties in academic psychology, she shifted to the clinical field and eventually became one of the founders of the so-called human-istic psychology movement. Her husband's American career ended shortly after it began.[75] However, the events of 1938 in Vienna changed much more than the lives of two of the leading psychologists of their time. They also put an end to a multifaceted set of linkages between psy-chological theory and research and constructive social change.

The fact that the so-called Vienna school was not a classical, that is, dogmatically centralized "school" of psychology, and the fact that fund-ing came from several different sources made it possible for the research-ers of the Vienna Psychological Institute to pursue a wide variety of agen-das, both scientific and political. The results were not always pleasing to all parties; tensions between political and scientific interests ran in var-ious directions. Much of the research that emerged, however, has endured. Charlotte Bühler's work, for example, was reissued after World War II, and had a significant impact on German research in what came to be called life-span developmental psychology; Karl Bühler's language theory is now seen as an important forerunner of modern semiotics.[76] The institute's unusual structure, and its even more unusual combination of scholarly and policy-oriented research, were copied by Paul Lazarsfeld when he built up the Center for Applied Social Research at Columbia University in the 1940s and 1950s.[77] In Vienna, however, the model had already come under heavy pressure before 1938; after that it had no successor.

NOTES

1 Archival materials are used by permission of the holders and come from the following sources: papers of the Federal Ministry for Instruction (Bundesminis-terium für Unterricht), Österreichisches Staatsarchiv und Allgemeine Verwal-tungsarchiv, Vienna (hereafter ÖSA); personnel files of Karl and Charlotte Bühler and files of the Philosophical Faculty, Universitätsarchiv der Universität Wien (hereafter UAUW); files of the Dokumentationsarchiv des Österreichischen Wid-erstandes (hereafter DAÖW); files of the Rockefeller Foundation Archives, North Tarrytown, New York (hereafter RFA). Unfortunately, unpublished documents in the Vienna University Archives were accessible only for the years to 1933.

2 See, e.g., B. Janik and S. Toulmin, *Wittgenstein's Vienna* (New York: Simon and Schuster, 1973) and W. Johnston, *The Austrian Mind: An Intellectual and Social History 1848–1938* (Berkeley: University of California Press, 1972).

3 M. G. Ash, "Academic Politics in the History of Science: Experimental Psy-chology in Germany, 1879–1941," *Central European History* 13 (1980):255–286; "Wilhelm Wundt and Oswald Külpe on the Institutional Status of Psychology: An Academic Controversy in Historical Context," in W. G. Bringmann and R. D. Tweney (eds.), *Wundt Studies* (Toronto: Hofgrefe, 1980), 396–421.

4 W. Jerusalem, "Über die Zukunft der Philosophie," in *Gedanken und Denker. Gesammelte Aufsätze* (Vienna: Braumüller, 1905), 15–16.

5 On Brentano and on Meinong's laboratory, see D. Lindenfeld, *The Transfor-mation of Positivism: Alexius Meinong and European Thought, 1890–1920* (Berkeley: University of California Press, 1980).

6 ÖSA, K. u. K. Ministerium für Cultus und Unterricht, Dept. V, 4 G Phil, Psychologisches Institut, Nr. 2715 (29 February 1895), 10425 (20 May 1895), 17826 (27 July 1895).

7 *Denkschrift über die gegenwärtige Lage der Philosophischen Fakultät der Universität Wien* (Vienna: Holzhausen, 1902), 13.

8 Cf. Ash, "Academic Politics."

9 W. Jerusalem, *Lehrbuch der Psychologie,* 3rd, rev. ed. (Vienna: Braumüller, 1902); F. Jodl, *Lehrbuch der Psychologie* (Stuttgart: Cotta, 1896); A. Stöhr, *Psychologie* (Vienna and Leipzig: Braumüller, 1917).

10 Jerusalem, "Ernst Machs Analyse der Empfindungen" (1900), in *Gedanken und Denker,* 194–202; *Der kritische Idealismus und die reine Logik. Ein Ruf im Streite* (Vienna and Leipzig: Braumüller, 1905). On Mach's views and his teaching in Vienna see F. Stadler, *Vom Positivismus zur 'wissenschaftlichen Weltauffassung' am Beispiel der Wirkungsgeschichte von Ernst Mach in Österreich von 1895 bis 1934* (Vienna: Löcker, 1982).

11 Alois Höfler to Ministry, 2 July 1921. ÖSA Unterrichts-Ministerium, 4 Phil (K. Bühler), Nr. 12561 (1921); Dean of the Philosophical Faculty to Ministry, 1 June 1921. UAUW, D.Z. 531; Ministry to Erich Becher, 8 June 1921. ÖSA, Nr. 11377 (1921).

12 See, e.g., E. Becher, *Gehirn und Seele* (Heidelberg: Winter, 1911).

13 Becher to Ministry, 12 June 1921. ÖSA, Nr. 12561 (1921), 18331 (1921).

14 For the following see G. Lebzeltern, "Karl Bühler – Leben und Werk" in K. Bühler, *Die Uhren der Lebewesen und Fragmente aus dem Nachlass,* ed. G. Lebzeltern (Vienna: Böhlau, 1969).

15 K. Bühler, *Die Gestaltwahrnehmungen* (Stuttgart: Spemann, 1913).

16 K. Bühler, *Die geistige Entwicklung des Kindes* (Jena: Fischer, 1918; 6th ed. 1930); *The Mental Development of the Child: A Summary of Modern Psychological Theory* (New York: Harcourt Brace, 1930).

17 Bühler to Ministry, 25 May 1922. ÖSA, Nr. 10257 (1922).

18 Ministry to Bühler, 9 May 1922. ÖSA, Nr. 10257 (1922); Bühler to Ministry, 22 July 1922, ÖSA, Nr. 15652 (1922); Ministry to Bühler, 24 September 1922, ÖSA Nr. 19511 (1922). The city of Vienna's involvement is particularly clear in the Ministry report of 12 July 1922, which is appended to the first document above. See also V. Fadrus, "Professor Dr. Karl Bühlers Wirken an der Wiener Universität im Dienste der Lehrerbildung, Lehrerfortbildung und der Neugestaltung des österreichischen Schulwesens," *Wiener Zeitschrift für Philosophie, Psychologie und Pädagogik* 7 (1959):3-25.

19 Cited in E. Weinzierl, "Sozialdemokratische Schulpolitik und 'Einheitsschule' in der Ersten Republik," in R. Olechnowski and E. Weinzierl (eds.), *Neue Mittelstufe. Skizze eines Modells für die Sekundarstufe I.* (Vienna: Herder, 1981), 64. Cf. R. Olechnowski, "Schulpolitik," in E. Weinzierl and K. Skalnik (eds.), *Österreich 1918–1938* (Graz, Vienna, Cologne: Styria Verlag, 1983), vol. 2, 592 ff.

20 On the history of Austrian social democracy, see C. Gulick, *Austria from Hapsburg to Hitler* (reprint ed., Berkeley: University of California Press, 1980) and Fritz Kaufmann, *Sozialdemokratie in Österreich. Idee und Geschichte einer Partei von 1889 bis zur Gegenwart* (Munich: Amalthea, 1978).

21 Olechnowski, "Schulpolitik," 595; cf. M. Jahoda-Lazarsfeld, "Autorität und Erziehung in der Familie, Schule und Jugendbewegung Österreichs," in M.

Horkheimer, et al., *Studien über Autorität und Familie* (Paris: Alcan, 1936), 706–725.

22 K. Bühler, *Die geistige Entwicklung,* passim.; cf. Bühler, "Der Ursprung des Intellektes," *Die Naturwissenschaften* 9 (1921):144–151.

23 Fadrus, review of *Die geistige Entwicklung, Die Schulreform* 2 (1922):88.

24 R. Knoll, G. Majce, H. Weiss, and G. Wieser, "Der österreichische Beitrag zur Soziologie von der Jahrhundertwende bis 1938," in M. R. Lepsius (ed.), *Soziologie in Deutschland 1919–1945 (Kölner Zeitschrift für Soziologie und Sozialpsychologie,* Sonderheft 24; Opladen: Westdeutscher Verlag, 1981), 90f.

25 Fadrus, "Das Pädagogische Institut der Stadt Wien," *Die Schulreform* 5 (1926):1–42, here:23.

26 A. Bruder-Bezzel, *Alfred Adler: Die Entstehungsgeschichte einer Theorie im historischen Milieu Wiens* (Göttingen: Vandenhoeck and Ruprecht, 1983), 142–143. Cf. J. Reichmayr, "Sozialistische Erziehung und Psychoanalyse in der Ersten Republik," in E. Adam (ed.), *Die österreichische Reformpädagogik 1918–1938* (Vienna, Cologne, Graz: Böhlau, 1981).

27 K. Bühler, *Die Krise der Psychologie* (Jena: Fischer, 1927), 142.

28 P. Lazarsfeld, "Amerikanische Beobachtungen eines Bühlerschülers," *Zeitschrift für experimentelle und angewandte Psychologie* 6 (1959):69.

29 See, e.g., L. Kardos, *Ding und Schatten (Zeitschrift für Psychologie,* Ergänzungsband 23; Leipzig: Barth, 1934); E. Brunswik, *Wahrnehmung und Gegenstandswelt* (Vienna: Deuticke, 1934). For further discussion of Brunswik's views and their relation to Bühler's, see D. Leary, "From Act Psychology to Probabilistic Functionalism: The Place of Egon Brunswik in the History of Psychology," this volume.

30 Kardos, "Die 'Konstanz' phänomenaler Dingmomente: Problemgeschichtlicher Darstellung," in E. Brunswik, et al., *Beiträge zur Problemgeschichte der Psychologie. Festschrift zu Karl Bühlers 50. Geburtstag* (Jena: Fischer, 1929), 1–77; Brunswik, "Prinzipienfragen der Gestalttheorie," ibid., 78–149.

31 K. Bühler, *Ausdruckstheorie. Das System an der Geschichte aufgezeigt* (Jena: Fischer, 1933); *Sprachtheorie. Die Darstellungsfunktion der Sprache* (Jena: Fischer, 1934). Cf. A. Eschbach, "Wahrnehmungen und Zeichen: Die Sematologischen Grundlagen der Wahrnehmungstheorie Karl Bühlers," *Ars Semiotica* 4 (1981):219–235.

32 E. Brunswik, "Zur Entwicklung der Albedowahrnehmung," *Zeitschrift für Psychologie* 109 (1928):40–105; Brunswik, L. Goldschneider and E. Pilek, *Die Entwicklung des Gedächtnisses (Zeitschrift für angewandte Psychologie,* Beiheft 64; Leipzig:Barth, 1932).

33 ÖSA, Nr. 24535 (1929), Blatt 6.

34 J. Tandler, "Zur Psychologie der Fürsorge," *Jahrbuch des Wiener Jugendhilfswerks* (1926), 6, 11.

35 L. Schenck-Danziger, "Zur Geschichte der Kinderpsychologie: Das Wiener Psychologische Institut," *Zeitschrift für Entwicklungspsychologie und Pädagogische Psychologie* 14 (1984):88–89.

36 C. Bühler, *Kindheit und Jugend: Genese des Bewusstseins* (Leipzig: Hirzel, 1928); *Der menschliche Lebenslauf als psychologisches Problem* (Leipzig: Hirzel, 1933); *From Birth to Maturity: An Outline of the Psychological Development of the Child* (London: Kegan Paul, Trench, Trubner, 1935).

37 For Charlotte Bühler's fellowship see Rockefeller Foundation Archives (RFA), LSRM, Box 57, Folder 51. On the plans of Ruml and Frank, see F. Samelson, "Organizing for the Kingdom of Behavior: Academic Battles and Organizational Policies in the Twenties," *Journal of the History of the Behavioral Sciences* 21 (1985):33–47.

38 Summarized in H. Hetzer, "Kinder- und Jungendpsychologische Forschung im Wiener Psychologischen Institut von 1922 bis 1938," *Zeitschrift für Entwicklungspsychologie und Pädagogische Psychologie,* 14 (1982):201.

39 C. Bühler and H. Hetzer, "Zur Geschichte der Kinderpsychologie," in E. Brunswik, et al., *Beiträge zur Problemgeschichte der Psychologie* (see above, note 30), 204–224.

40 C. Bühler, H. Hetzer, and B. Tudor-Hart, *Soziologische und psychologische Studien über das erste Lebensjahr* (Jena: Fischer, 1927); Bühler and Hetzer, *Kleinkindertests: Entwicklungstests für das erste bis sechste Lebensjahr* (Leipzig: Hirzel, 1932); cf. Hetzer, "Kinder- und Jugendpsychologische Forschung," 199.

41 Hetzer, "Kinder- und Jungendpsychologische Forschung," 204. Hetzer's successor reports that "interest shifted somewhat from preschool to school-age children" after 1930. Schenck-Danziger, "Zur Geschichte der Kinderpsychologie: Das Wiener Institut" (note 35), 94.

42 L. Rosenmayr, *Geschichte der Jugendforschung in Österreich 1914–1931* (Vienna: Österreichisches Institut für Jugendkunde, 1962).

43 P. Lazarsfeld, et al., *Jugend und Beruf* (Jena: Fischer, 1931), 7.

44 C. Bühler, "Jugendpsychologie und Schule," *Süddeutscher Monatshefte* 27 (1929):186.

45 C. Bühler to J. B. Van Sickle, 17 June 1931. RFA, RF 1.2, 705S, R 1116 (University of Vienna Psychological Institute), Folder 1930–1931.

46 P. Lazarsfeld, "An Episode in the History of Social Research: A Memoir," in D. Fleming and B. Bailyn (eds.), *The Intellectual Migration: Europe and America, 1930–1960* (Cambridge: Harvard University Press, 1969), 270–337; M. Jahoda, "Ich habe die Welt nicht verändert. Gespräch mit Marie Jahoda," in M. Greffrath, *Die Zerstörung einer Zukunft: Gespräche mit emigrierten Sozialwissenschaftlern* (Reinbek: Rowohlt, 1979), 103–144; Hans Zeisel, "Paul Lazarsfeld und das Wien der 20er Jahre," in M. R. Lepsius (ed.), *Soziologie in Deutschland 1919–1945* (see note 24), 395–403.

47 M. Jahoda, P. Lazarsfeld, and H. Zeisel, *Die Arbeitslosen von Marienthal: Ein soziographischer Versuch* (1932; 2nd ed., reprint. Frankfurt a.M.: Suhrkamp, 1978).

48 J. B. Van Sickle, memorandum of 18 September 1933. RFA, RF 1.2, 705S, R 1116, Folder 1932–1933.

49 A. Eschbach, "Einige kritische Notizen zur neuesten Bühler-Forschung," *Historiographia Linguistica* 11 (1984):149–158.

50 Ministry to University Rector, 8 September 1934. ÖSA, Unterrichtsministerium, Nr. 34102-I/1 (1934); Ministry to the Mayor of Vienna, 6 October 1934, ÖSA, Nr. 29380-I/1 (1934); Mayor of Vienna to Ministry, 23 October 1934. ÖSA, Nr. 33237 (1934). ÖSA, Nr. 39757 (1934).

51 C. Bühler, "Das Wiener Psychologische Institut," *Pädagogische Führer* 2 (1935):96.

52 K. Bühler, *Die Zukunft der Psychologie und die Schule* (Schriften des Pädagogischen Instituts der Stadt Wien, Heft 11; Vienna: Verlag für Jugend und Volk, 1935).

53 Sigmund Freud to Ernst Freud, 20 February 1934, in *Sigmund Freud – Briefe,* ed. E. L. Freud (Frankfurt A.M.: Fischer, 1960), 412. The translation is my own.

54 K. Bühler to Ministry, 8 July 1936. ÖSA, Nr. 25391 (1936).

55 Detail of Information. Medical Sciences, Paris. Research Aid Professors Karl and Charlotte Bühler," n.d. Copy in RFA, RF 1.2, 705S, R 1116, Folder 1950–1955.

56 K. Bühler to Ministry, 8 July 1936 (see note 54).

57 ÖSA, Nr. 25391 (1936), 32119 (1937).

58 Aufruf des Vereins der Freunde des Wiener Psychologischen Instituts. Supporting document for K. Bühler to Ministry, 4 November 1937. ÖSA, Nr. 20424 (1937).

59 C. Bühler, et al., *Kind und Familie* (Jena: Fischer, 1937).

60 Anklageshrift gegen Maria (sic!) Jahoda-Lazarsfeld und Marie Schneider, 28 May, 1937. Copy in Dokumentationsarchiv des Österreichischen Widerstandes (DAÖW), 6414. On foreign intercession for Jahoda's release, see State Secretary in Chancellor's Office for Foreign Affairs to Ministry of Justice, 20 July 1937, copy in DAÖW, 3423, and J. Messner to Hofrat Dr. A. Pilz, Ministry of Justice, 26 June 1937, copy in DAÖW, 6414.

61 Jahoda, personal communication to A. Eschbach, in Eschbach, note 49; cf. Provincial Criminal Court Vienna I, Dept. 26c to Ministry of Justice, 4 June 1937, copy in DAÖW, 6414.

62 C. Bühler, "Charlotte Bühler," in L. Pongratz, W. Traxel and E. Wehner (eds.), *Psychologie in Selbstdarstellungen,* Vol. 1 (Bern: Huber,1972), 28.

63 Dean of the Philosophical Faculty to Ministry, 9 April 1938, G.Z. 1937/1938:659. Copy in DAÖW, 68026. On measures against university professors during and after the "Anschluss," see W. Weinert, "Die Massnahmen der Reichsdeutschen Hochschulverwaltung im Bereich des österreichischen Hochschulwesens nach der Annexion 1938," in H. Konrad and W. Neugebauer (eds.), *Arbeiterbewegung-Faschismus-Nationalbewusstsein: Festschrift zum 20-jährigen Bestand des Dokumentationsarchivs des Österreichischen Widerstandes und zum 60. Geburtstag von Herbert Steiner* (Vienna: Europaverlag, 1983), 127–134.

64 Dean to Ministry, 14 April 1938. Copy in DAÖW, 68026.

65 Dean to Otto Tumlirz, 15 April 1938. Copy in DAÖW, 68026.

66 Tumlirz to Dean, 20 April 1938, ibid.

67 Friedrich Kainz to Dean's office, 22 November 1938; Ministry to Dean's office, 9 December 1938; Kainz to Ministry, 7 January 1939; Viktor Kraft and Kainz to Ministry, 19 January 1939. ÖSA, Nr. 46205 (1938).

68 *Vorlesungsverzeichnis der Universität Wien* (Universitätsarchiv), Summer semester 1938, 48; Winter semester 1938–1939, 31–32; 1. Trimester 1940, 44.

69 H. Rohracher, *Kleine Einführung in die Charakterkunde* (Leipzig: Teuber, 1934); *Die Vorgänge im Gehirn und das geistige Leben* (Leipzig: Barth, 1939). Cf. K. F. Heiser, "Notes on the Psychological Institute of the University of Vienna," typescript in Walter Miles papers, Archives of the History of American Psychology, Akron, Ohio.

70 Cf. U. Geuter, "'Gleichschaltung' von Oben? Universitätspolitische Strate-

gien und Verhaltensweisen in der Psychologie während des Nationalsozialismus,"
Psychologische Rundschau 35 (1984):198–213; M. G. Ash, "Ein Institut und eine
Zeitschrift: Zur Geschichte des Berliner Psychologischen Instituts und der Zeit-
schrift 'Psychologische Forschung' vor und nach 1933," in C. F. Graumann (ed.),
Psychologie im Nationalsozialismus (Berlin, Heidelberg, New York, Tokyo:
Springer Verlag, 1985), 113–137.

71 Ministry to University Rector, 28 May 1938. Copy in DAÖW, 68026.

72 Cf., e.g., C. Bühler to Lawrence K. Frank, 6 May 1938, Lawrence K. Frank
papers. National Library of Medicine, Bethesda, Maryland.

73 Henry Beaumont to Edward E. Day, 7 October 1938; Sydnor Walker to Beaumont, 15 October 1938; Leonard Carmichael to Frank B. Hanson, 20 March
1939; Hanson to Carmichael, 23 March 1939; Carmichael to Hanson, 29 March
1939. RFA (see note 55), Folder 1937–1939.

74 M. G. Ash, "Aid to Emigré Psychologists: A Research Note," in H. Carpintero
and J. M. Peiró (eds.), *Psychology in its Historical Context: Essays in Honor of
Josef Brozek* (Valencia: Monografias de la Revista de Historia de la Psicología, 1,
1985).

75 For further information see J. M. Mandler and G. Mandler, "The Diaspora
of Experimental Psychology: The Gestaltists and Others," in Fleming and Bailyn
(eds.), *The Intellectual Migration* (See note 46), 371–419. See also L. Coser, *Ref-
ugee Scholars in America: Their Impact and Their Experiences* (New Haven: Yale
University Press, 1983), 37–41, 110–120.

76 On the reception of Charlotte Bühler's work after 1945, see L. Schenck-Dan-
ziger and H. Thomae (eds.), *Gegenwartsprobleme der Entwicklungspsychologie.
Festschrift für Charlotte Bühler* (Göttingen: Hogrefe, 1963). On Karl Bühler and
semiotics, see R. E. Innis, *Karl Bühler: Semiotic Foundations of Language Theory*
(New York: Plenum Press, 1982); C. -F. Graumann and T. Herrmann (eds.), *Karl
Bühler's Axiomatik der Sprache* (Frankfurt a.M.: Klostermann, 1984); and A.
Eschbach (ed.), *Karl Bühler's Theory of Language* (Amsterdam: John Benjamins
B. V., 1987). Eschbach is preparing an edition of Karl Bühler's writings, to appear
with Suhrkamp Verlag.

77 Lazarsfeld, "Amerikanische Beobachtungen eines Bühler-Schülers" (see note
28) and "An Episode in the History of Social Research" (note 46). Cf. K. Pawlik,
"Das Wiener Psychologische Institut: Historische und persönliche Reflexionen
zur 'Wiener Schule',"*Bericht über den 34. Kongress der Deutschen Gesellschaft für
Psychologie* (Göttingen: Hogrefe, 1985).

7

GERMAN PSYCHOLOGY
DURING THE NAZI PERIOD*

ULFRIED GEUTER

INTRODUCTION: GERMAN AND AMERICAN DISCUSSION
OF THE TOPIC

For decades the image that the international scientific community had of
the history of German psychology under National Socialism was shaped
by the dismissal and emigration of Jewish professors, by the shift of leading Gestalt psychologists to the United States, or by National Socialist
attacks on psychoanalysis. At times it was also noted that the Nazi period
saw a flourishing of typologies and of race psychology. But the whole
development of psychology during the Nazi period was little known. For
example, it was not part of the standard view that the discipline advanced
to professional status precisely in this period, achieving previously
unheard of state recognition through the introduction of an official
diploma.

In postwar Germany this period in the history of psychology was not
discussed for a long time. The Swiss psychologist Franziska Baumgarten's
attack on the political stance of German psychologists during World War
I and throughout the Nazi period remained largely unanswered.[1] Questions from postwar students were deflected by older psychologists with
the statement that they did not want to deal with those "dark times."[2] If
the Nazi period was mentioned at all by psychologists in the 1950s, the
only purpose was to gain an advantage in current academic controversies

* Unless otherwise noted, information in this chapter is taken from my book, *Die Professionalisierung der deutschen Psychologie im Nationalsozialismus* (Frankfurt am Main:
Suhrkamp, 1984). An English translation is in preparation and will be published by Cambridge University Press. I wish to thank Jill Morawski, Franz Samelson, and Mitchell Ash
for their comments on an earlier version of this chapter. Mitchell Ash assisted with the
preparation of the final version.

by associating opponents with it, openly or by implication. Genuine discussion of psychology and National Socialism did not occur.[3] This finally began to change when the journal *Psychologie- und Gesellschaftskritik,* a publication located on the critical fringe of the discipline, published two issues on "Psychology and Fascism" containing several studies on psychology in Nazi Germany and on postwar treatment of the period.[4] These publications, however, did not reach a broad academic audience. In 1982 the question was dealt with for the first time at a congress of the German Society for Psychology, and in succeeding years research appeared that shed new light on the place of the Nazi period in psychology's history.[5]

The only comprehensive study on psychology and National Socialism in English was published in 1944 by two emigrants, Frederick Wyatt and Hans Lukas Teuber. For decades this was the only work available on this topic.[6] A central interest of Wyatt and Teuber was to establish how certain traditions of German psychological and philosophical thinking made the fusion of psychology with Nazi ideology possible.[7] At the time the study was written, moral concern with Nazism moved many North American psychologists to some political actions, such as pressure against holding the 12th International Congress of Psychology in Vienna in 1940, and to a few publications denouncing the Nazification of psychological theory in Germany, like Boder's challenge of racism in Erich Jaensch's pro-Nazi typology.[8] Other psychologists, however, were more cautious. In his presidential address to the American Psychological Association in 1939, for example, Gordon W. Allport mentioned but did not criticize Erich Jaensch's typology.[9]

During the war and the first postwar years, however, the interest of American psychologists in German psychology of this period changed. Sometimes engaged by the U.S. army, they tried to observe developments in Germany to explore the possibilities of adopting German psychological methods, and attempts were made by Henry Murray and others to introduce the methods of personnel selection used by psychologists in the German army to the American army.[10] This work was extended after the war, when the U.S. army even engaged former German military psychologists.[11] Also conducted were studies of the methods used in German industry and in the German Labor Front commissioned by governmental and military institutions.[12] These studies introduced American readers to the wide practical use of psychology in Nazi Germany. Their authors criticized German methods on methodological grounds only, or recommended their use.

Heinz L. Ansbacher, a Jewish emigrant from Germany who had come to the United States in 1924 and worked for the Psychological Warfare Division from 1943 to 1945,[13] pointed in one of the wartime studies on German psychology to the continuity of German psychology through the Nazi period. He concluded "that when and as psychology is employed, even within a totalitarian state and dealing with forced labor, it still is essentially the same psychology one would find in a voluntary situation within a free society, thus indicating that the same set of psychological principles holds universally."[14] Since he did not find anything fascist or repressive in the psychological selection of foreign workers in German war industry, Ansbacher implied that psychology must be universal as well as democratic. This statement led to a criticism by Epstein that Ansbacher was a Nazi-defender. But the critic was one-sided as well. From the fact that traditional methods were used, Ansbacher had inferred that this use must have been humane. His critic, in turn, inferred from the general National Socialist context of psychology's use that all psychologists were "Nazi psychologists."[15] Neither author evaluated fully the character of psychology's methods, the political context of their use, and the intricate situation of professional psychologists who applied psychology in the National Socialist state.

But neither Ansbacher's nor Epstein's viewpoint ultimately affected the standard evaluation of the development of psychology during the Nazi period. Looking at the theoretical development of German psychology, the emigration of the Gestaltists, or the disastrous history of the psychological institutes from which the famous emigrants came, North American authors have charted a decline. Mary Henle, for example, has spoken of the "destruction of German psychology by Hitler."[16] German psychologists commonly asserted that psychology as a subject had been discriminated against by the Nazis.[17] At the International Congress of Psychology in Washington, D.C., in 1963, for example, Wolfgang Metzger, a representative of Gestalt psychology and pupil of Wolfgang Köhler, went so far as to maintain that "autocratic regimes . . . are, without exception, full of distrust and aversion against this science."[18] In contrast to Ansbacher, Metzger thus presupposed a politically forced discontinuity in the development of German psychology. This widely shared assumption of discontinuity can also be found in the writings of some West and East German psychologists who hold the entirely different opinion that the discipline was taken totally into the service of the Nazi regime.[19]

In each of these views – in Ansbacher's claim that the same psychological methods continued to be applied, and in the two opinions just stated – there is some truth. The thesis of psychology's decline does justice in particular to the immense loss of personnel that resulted from National Socialist civil service policy. The thesis of psychology's cooptation can point to numerous attempts to link psychology with National Socialist ideology. These two aspects of psychology's development will be treated in the following sections. I will then discuss psychology's practical applications under the Nazi dictatorship, which occurred mainly in the military, and their results for the professionalization of the discipline.[20] However, only academic psychology and its practical applications will be considered here. This excludes both the Frankfurt School, which was not connected with academic psychology at the time, and psychoanalysis, which was then theoretically as well as institutionally separate from academic psychology.[21]

DISMISSALS AND EMIGRATION

The dismissals of psychology professors form possibly the most important part of the North American picture of psychology in the Nazi period. The so-called "Law for the Reconstitution of the State Civil Service" *(Gesetz zur Wiederherstellung des Berufsbeamtentums)* of April 7, 1933, decreed the dismissal of Jewish and politically unreliable civil servants. This law affected five of the then fifteen full professors who taught psychological subjects at the 23 German universities because of their Jewish origin. All lost their chairs: Adhemar Gelb in Halle, David Katz in Rostock, Wilhelm Peters in Jena, William Stern in Hamburg, and Max Wertheimer in Frankfurt. In 1937 the Munich professor Aloys Fischer, who was married to a Jewish woman, was also retired. At the Technical Universities *(Technische Hochschulen)* no full professor was definitely dismissed as a result of the law. Otto Selz, the only full professor who taught psychology at a business school *(Handels-Hochschule),* was dismissed in 1933; he was murdered ten years later in Auschwitz. Some famous associate professors and assistants were also dismissed, including Walter Blumenfeld in Dresden, Curt Bondy in Göttingen, Erich von Hornbostel in Berlin, and Heinz Werner in Hamburg. Kurt Lewin resigned from his position in Berlin before he could be struck by the same law.

German psychology lost additional professors for political reasons. Gustav Kafka in Dresden asked in 1933 for premature retirement at the age of 50. Wolfgang Köhler left his chair in Berlin in 1935 because he could no longer resist political interventions in his institute.[22] The Munich professor Kurt Huber supported the "White Rose" resistance group, and was executed in 1944. The Göttingen psychologist Heinrich Düker was arrested during the 1930s because of his left-wing political engagement; after a period of freedom, he was put in a concentration camp in 1944 and rescued by the Soviet army in 1945.

Most of the dismissed professors emigrated; among the full professors at the universities (without the Technical Universities), the loss by emigration was one-third. Katz first went to England, then to Sweden; Peters went to Turkey; Stern, Wertheimer, and later Köhler went to the United States. Gelb had offers from the universities of Istanbul, Kansas, and Stockholm, but he was very ill and died in 1936 after a short stay in the Netherlands. After the occupation of Austria by the German army in

1938, Karl Bühler, the head of the Vienna Psychological Institute, who was married to the half-Jewish Charlotte Bühler, was dismissed and arrested; he emigrated in 1939, also to the United States. Thus, at the level of full professors, psychology appears to have been struck hard by the dismissal policy, compared with the incomplete data we have for professors in other disciplines.[23] If, however, we consider all the members of the German Society for Psychology, regardless of rank, we find that 14.6% emigrated. Compared with available data for other disciplines and professional groups, this figure is below average.[24]

The conclusion that the Nazis aimed at the intellectual destruction of psychology, especially Gestalt psychology, with these dismissals seems to be supported by the fact that the leading Gestaltists Wolfgang Köhler, Kurt Lewin, and Max Wertheimer, and the famous professors William Stern and Karl Bühler were among the emigrants. A more accurate interpretation, however, would note that all dismissed psychologists were Jewish or married to Jewish women; they were dismissed for this racist reason and not because of their scholarly viewpoints. There is no proof that the Nazis especially wanted to strike Gestalt psychology as a theory. Indeed, when a new professorship was filled in Münster in 1942, the ideological watch office of the Nazi party, the *Amt Rosenberg,* even favored the Wertheimer pupil Wolfgang Metzger against the air force psychologist and characterologist Robert Heiss, arguing that Metzger's research was "very accurately done." The central office of the NS Professors' League *(Nationalsozialistischer Dozentenbund)* stressed that Metzger had developed Gestalt psychology "in an independent and productive way," and praised his book *Psychologie* of 1941 as a "remarkable discussion of the basic concepts of the subject."[25]

Only one psychologist publically raised his voice against Nazi dismissals. Wolfgang Köhler criticized this policy, albeit cautiously, in a newspaper article in April 1933 when the Jewish physicist and Nobel Prize winner James Franck resigned in protest against anti-Semitic Nazi policy.[26] The German Society for Psychology, in contrast, intervened nowhere on behalf of a dismissed psychologist. Instead, the Society's leadership urged the authorities to fill vacated chairs immediately to assure the discipline's continued representation. After the resignation from the executive committee of its two Jewish members, David Katz and William Stern, of Karl Bühler, and of Gustav Kafka in spring 1933, the Society oriented itself fully to the new political situation under the leadership of Felix Krueger. The October 1933 congress of the Society, which was moved from Dresden to Leipzig after Kafka's resignation from the executive committee, openly proclaimed the change. In his address, Krueger called on psychologists to join the politicians and achieve the "psychological renewal" of the German people.[27]

THE INSTITUTIONALIZATION OF PSYCHOLOGY AT THE UNIVERSITIES

Dismissals have often been seen as a sign that the Nazis wanted to expel psychology from the universities. At least, it has been maintained that psychology lost academic chairs during the Nazi period.[28] It is true that the chairs of Wertheimer in Frankfurt and Katz in Rostock were completely lost, and Köhler's vacant chair in Berlin was not filled until 1942. In Hamburg, William Stern's chair was lost, and a new psychology professorship was not reestablished until 1942. Earlier, the Ministry for Science and Education had asked the university to propose a psychologist to succeed Stern; the faculty, however, opposed this, since they wanted to have a race biologist instead. Thus, in this case, it was not the policy of the state administration that hampered the filling of psychological chairs.[29]

In fact, during the entire Nazi period the central science administration followed a policy of supplying the universities with chairs of psychology and filling vacant ones. Thus, several chairs formerly designated for philosophy or pedagogy were now specified for psychology. In addition, the universities of Giessen and Kiel raised the status of the professorship in psychology, and five new psychological chairs were established: Breslau in 1937, Erlangen in 1939, and Freiburg, Münster, and Cologne in 1942. Thus, if we compare the representation of the discipline between 1932 and 1942 by chairs, we find that psychology's institutional status improved at 13 of the 23 universities in the Reich. The dismissals brought about a loss in the intellectual representation of the discipline, and, during the first years of the Nazi period, in its institutional representation as well. However, institutionalization advanced in the period as a whole.

This fact clearly runs counter to the assumption that the existence of psychology at the universities was menaced by the Nazis. Not only the science administration, but even party authorities were active in supporting psychology professorships. In 1941, for example, a high-ranking party official, the *Stabsamtsleiter* of the *Gauleitung* Hessen-Nassau, called on the University of Frankfurt to finally fill Wertheimer's long-vacant chair.

An important reason for the advancement of psychology's institutionalization was the use of psychological methods for personnel selection in the German army, which will be discussed. When, for example, the new chairs in Breslau and Erlangen were to be established, the authorities argued that the universities should offer training opportunities for future army psychologists. In Breslau, the Wehrmacht even intervened directly by letter, as General Hans von Voss, the military chief of army psychology, did in the case of Leipzig, where in 1938 he called for the prompt filling of Wilhelm Wundt's vacant chair. The interest of the Wehrmacht corresponded to a change in National Socialist science policy. After a first phase of ideological and political "coordination" of the teaching staff at the universities, scientific disciplines were supposed to supply knowledge and experts to support preparation for war and fulfill the requirements of a war economy. By offering usable diagnostic methods and training future army psychologists, psychology was able to meet these needs.

A further reason for the advancement of psychology's institutionalization was the weakness of philosophy and pedagogy in relation to psychology. The Ministry for Science and Education followed a policy of equipping each university with two philosophical chairs, one of them for psychology and pedagogy. Since pedagogy was still a mainly theoretical subject, chairs defined for both subjects were dominated by psychology. For example, the Munich chair previously defined for pedagogy and held by Aloys Fischer changed with the appointment of Oswald Kroh in 1938 to a chair for "Psychology and Pedagogy with special regard for Army Psychology."

THE SERVICEABILITY OF PSYCHOLOGICAL THEORY: PSYCHOLOGY AND POLITICAL IDEOLOGY

The adaptation of psychological theory to National Socialist ideology supports the view that psychology was fully coopted by the regime, or presented itself for cooptation. There were a variety of attempts to use psychology to legitimize racist throught, to orient research toward topics that could be considered politically desirable, or to connect existing psychological theories with basic Nazi beliefs. It is interesting, however, to note that no document has yet been found in which party authorities tried to formulate concrete ideological expectations for psychology. Nonetheless, there was a general framework of ideological beliefs that could not be openly opposed, including anti-Semitism, the biologically based superiority of the Nordic "race," the need of that race for "living space," or the organization of society according to principles of race and leadership.

Even without official directives for psychology's theoretical development, psychologists took ideological expectations of the subject for granted and attempted by themselves to show the compatibility of their approaches with Nazi ideology. More than anything else, psychologists' shift to the topic of race gives the Nazi period its special place in the history of German psychology. Especially during the first years of the regime, this shift helped establish a climate of intellectual acceptance for racist thought that was necessary for Nazi hegemony. There were, for example, attempts to employ psychological studies to work to show differences between so-called "Nordic," "Falic," and "Ostian" people, and thus to legitimate Hans F. K. Günther's semiofficial system of racial classification. Research projects on the subject were proposed. Johann Baptist Rieffert planned one such project at the Psychological Institute of the University of Berlin on the "characterology" and modes of expression of Jews. The work was not performed, however, because Rieffert was dismissed for trying to conceal his earlier membership in the Social Democratic Party.[30] Many authors took advantage of the situation to claim the topic of race for psychology and for their own research, without necessarily building Nazi racism or anti-Semitism into their theories. Bruno Petermann, for example, outlined the principles of a hereditary psychology in 1935 under the title "The Problem of the Racial Soul."

Typological systems were now linked with race theory, either loosely, as in the case of Göttingen professor Narziss Ach, or systematically, as in the case of Tübingen professor Gerhard Pfahler. In the Nazi period, Pfahler attributed a personality type with firm attitudes, narrow, focused attention and consistent perseverence to "Nordic" people, and a type with fluid attitudes, broad, wandering attention, and lesser perseverance to "Ostian" people.[31]

Best known of those who tried to combine typology and race theory is Erich Jaensch.[32] He was the only psychologist who systematically attempted to introduce anti-Semitism into his psychological theory. Jaensch was already famous before 1933, especially for his research on perception and his related typological and philosophical writings. In 1933, in a political reversal, he presented himself as a defender of a psychology oriented to the goals of the National Socialist revolution. In the 1920s, Jaensch had done extensive research on the phenomenon of eidetic perception, the ability to produce subjective visualizations that are neither real perceptions nor mere imaginations, but which the subject experiences as being real. Jaensch held that this ability depended on personality types. Persons who could experience such visualizations as belonging to their ego he called "integrated" types. Opposed to them were so-called "synaesthetic" types whose psychical functions were supposed to be labile. Already before 1933, Jaensch had related the various subgroups of these types to certain European populations. But after 1933 he no longer regarded these subgroups as equal. Synaesthetics were now seen as inferior and the Jews as a prominent representative of this type, though not the only one. The subgroups of the integrated type were now related to the doctrine of Hans F. K. Günther, and the "Nordic" and "Falic" types of Günther were now seen as the firmest, psychologically. This concept was broadly described by Jaensch in his book *The Anti-Type*.[33] With this work, he wrote to the Ministry, he wanted to provide the scholarly underpinnings for what the Nazi movement was actually doing by feeling and instinct.[34] He could not have stated more clearly that he wanted to legitimize Nazi policies with so-called psychological-anthropological theory.[35]

Wyatt and Teuber have already pointed to the then dominant anti-rationalism in German psychology, which enabled its theoreticians to fit their ideas to certain aspects of the jumble called Nazi ideology. But as observers from the United States, they were not yet aware of all the publications and thus excluded the *Ganzheits*-psychology of Felix Krueger and the Gestalt psychologists from their account of attempts at political apology.[36] Both schools opposed associationism with the thesis that we directly perceive Gestalten or wholes *(Ganzheiten)*. Krueger also applied this view to social problems. During the Weimar period, writing in the vein of then-common conservative thinking, Krueger called for a renewal of society on the basis of original social communities *(Gemeinschaften)* like the family, youth groups *(Bund),* and the folk. He shared some viewpoints with the conservative ideology of folkish community *(Volksgemeinschaft),* but he did not attempt to apply his theory to actual Nazi organizations and politics. However, Krueger's former assistant, Friedrich Sander, went so far as to maintain that the National Socialist movement under the leadership of Hitler would realize the Gestalt of the German folk by letting the folkish whole follow its inner laws. In 1933, just when the first concentration camps were built and the political parties were prohibited, Sander claimed as a psychological law that a "threatened whole" excludes "everything alien to its essence." In 1937, Sander went even further, stating that the elimination of the Jews and of people with inferior genotype could be justified by the will toward the pure Gestalt of the German essence, which was at the same time the will to eliminate anything extraneous to that Gestalt *(Gestaltfremdes).*[37]

The Gestalt psychologist Wolfgang Metzger also tried to show the compatibility of dominant political theory with psychology. Metzger argued that holistic psychology related to the concept of the structural role *(Gliedhaftigkeit)* of the individual in a community. The political view of the natural order of the folkish state would correspond to a psychological view of the natural order of things under the Gestalt principle of *Prägnanz*. In contrast, he saw "hedonistic psychoanalysis" and "atomistic behaviorism" as equivalents to the parliamentaristic view of the community as an "aggregation" of individuals, found in the traditionalist "order of pure chance" in England *(traditionalistische Zufallsordnung)* or the rationalist "order of compulsion" in France *(rationalistische Zwangsordnung).* Metzger even compared the "Gestalt laws," according to which similarity and proximity determine the formation of perceived groups, with the formation of social entities according to the principles of "race" and "enclosed living space" *(geschlossener Lebensraum).* Gestalt psychology thus stood the test of being a loyal theory.[38]

There might have been various reasons for producing such theories. Some psychologists, like Pfahler, were convinced Nazis even prior to 1933. Others put on the new style, like Sander and even Jaensch. They were *Märzgefallene,* as those people were called who quickly joined the party in March 1933, before access to membership was closed.[39] While Jaensch did a double somersault into the Nazi camp, Sander and Metzger only tried to show the compatibility of their theory with Nazi ideology here and there, and in nonscholarly journals. In the case of Sander we do not know the reasons, but Metzger's article of 1942 and another, rather political article of 1938 appeared when Metzger was proposed for professorships first in Halle and then in Münster.

The aim of such statements was to demonstrate the political usefulness or desirability of particular theories, and thus of their proponents. Psychologists intended to show their ideological conformity to the party and state authorities. They also wanted psychology to legitimize the political system by asserting that this system was formed according to scientific knowledge.

THE ARMY, THE WAR, AND THE RISE OF THE NEW PROFESSION

In the face of such obvious efforts at political adaptation, and of the dismissals of prominent Jewish psychologists, one may well conclude that the Nazi period marked a break in the development of German psychology. But this was not the whole story. Numerous other facts reveal continuities in the theoretical, institutional, and professional development of psychology from the Weimar period through the Nazi era and into the postwar years. These facts are perhaps still more unsettling than those already described; for they reveal that the National Socialist system also supported a psychology that was and remained normal by international standards. The opening up of practical fields, cautiously begun in the 1920s, proceeded rapidly in the Nazi period; psychological knowledge that was relevant to professional diagnostic practice continued to be produced; and, with the first German diploma examination in 1941, professional university training in psychology was established. Thus the Nazi era was precisely the time in which psychology, previously a weak and insignificant academic field, became a profession with its own occupational role outside and its own professional training inside the university. This occurred primarily as a result of the demand in the military for trained psychologists to assist in the selection of officers and specialists.[40]

In the 1920s, psychology had not yet become a profession. In industry, psychological methods were applied, but mainly by engineers. In education, psychologists worked in teacher training colleges, but hardly anywhere else. In the health services, physicians dominated. According to an official count published in 1930, only about thirty psychologists worked professionally in public institutions in Germany, half of them in vocational guidance bureaus and twelve in the army.

This situation changed rapidly with the expansion of the military in the Nazi period. The psychological service of the army had been established in 1925, and in 1927 the psychological examination of officer candidates had been made obligatory. Psychologists also were responsible for the selection of certain specialists. These were their main tasks, and they remained so during the Nazi period. The number of full-time psychologists working in the army conspicuously demonstrates the impact of the army's expansion on the development of the profession, especially after the reintroduction of compulsory universal military service and the reestablishment of an independent air force and general rearmament in 1935. Thirty-three psychologists were working in the army in 1933, and 69 in 1935; the number jumped to 143 in 1937, and to 170 in 1938. These figures include the army and the navy. From 1938 onward, an independent air force psychological unit was established; it had at least 45 posts by 1940. Altogether, in 1942 around 450 psychologists were working in the military, either full-time or part-time. These people were not all trained in psychology. Due to the shortage of psychologists at that time, some were teachers or professors of philosophy or pedagogy. By then, however, the profession of psychologist had become nearly identical with that of diagnosing military psychologist. The Wehrmacht had created a new profession outside the university.

Other fields were not that important for the professionalization of psychology during the Nazi period. In industry, a few full-time working psychologists were engaged in the late 1930s. Psychologists continued to work in these years at vocational guidance bureaus, but there is no indication of an increase in their numbers. However, the German Labor Front, the Nazi successor organization of the trade unions, established the first German research institute for industrial psychology and pedagogy, which probably engaged seven psychologists. This institute worked as a service office making materials and counselors available to industry. During the war the institute offered test materials with which 400,000 deported foreign workers were examined, in order to place them in appropriate jobs in war production.

In the 1940s, psychologists started to work professionally in the field of educational guidance. Formerly, educational guidance had been conducted by psychiatrists in the state youth service and by psychotherapists in free clinics. The National Socialist Welfare Organization engaged psychologists for this purpose for the first time in its own child guidance service, which employed around 40 psychologists during the war. These psychologists were responsible, for example, for providing advice on custody decisions for so-called "children in need of proper upbringing." The moral intricacies of this work became clear when the SS sought to enlist the "cooperation" of a woman psychologist from the National Socialist Welfare Organization in its "selection" of Polish children, who were taken from their parents and distributed to German families, public foster homes, or camps. To decide the destiny of these children, which could mean not only the choice of their future quarters but also between life and death, the SS planned to have the psychologist carry out characterological assessments. However, the sources examined to date do not clearly indicate whether the psychologist in question was actually employed for this purpose.

CONTINUITIES IN PROFESSIONAL DEVELOPMENT: EXPRESSION ANALYSIS AND CHARACTEROLOGY

The rapid development of military psychology was possible because the discipline could offer theories, methods, and procedures that supported the claim that psychologists could carry out personnel selection more effectively than officers and staff physicians. For the selection of drivers in World War I, psychologists had developed methods of testing the reception and processing of simple sensory stimuli. For officer selection in the 1920s, new methods and theories determined personality characteristics, especially expression analysis and characterology. This was the psychological knowledge used in the military, not the typological systems or race-typologies discussed previously. At the same time, expression analysis and characterology played essential parts in the intellectual development of psychology in the Nazi period. After the war, they continued to form the core of German psychology until the late 1950s, and were considered the hallmark of German psychology by the international scientific community.[41]

The army needed methods for evaluating the character of officer candidates. Qualities of leadership, however, could not be gauged by psychotechnical apparatus. Because expression analysis stressed the meaning of bodily or facial expression for underlying mental idiosyncrasies, it was seen as an expedient means of determining character traits. Characterological systems then served to theoretically integrate and lend meaning to diagnostic findings.

It was mainly the work of Ludwig Klages and Philipp Lersch that helped to establish characterology and expression analysis. The books they wrote during the 1920s and 1930s were still used as textbooks after the war.[42] Philipp Lersch's book, *Face and Mind,* was probably the best known work in the field of expression analysis. In it the classification of the relation between facial expressions and their possible meanings was based on a variety of photos taken during the examination of officer candidates when Lersch worked as army psychologist (1925–1930). The 1930s spawned many studies on the meaning of gestures, pantomimics (meaning of body movements), mimics (facial expression), handwriting, or the human voice. All these studies derived from army diagnostics.

Subjects were given tasks in experimental situations, such as to stretch an expander or to make themselves up in front of a mirror, in which they then were filmed. The pictures, together with observations from other situations, were then interpreted by the psychologist.

Characterological models were used to order the diagnostic findings in the evaluations written by army psychologists. The most influential one was the model presented by Lersch in 1938 in his book *The Structure of the Person (Der Aufbau der Person)*. In this book Lersch was not interested in the development of human character or in the problem of social character as it was being approached by Erich Fromm at the same time. Since he wanted a model to integrate diagnostic findings, he focused on the structure of character and outlined a model consisting of different layers of feelings, which were dominated by a superstructure of will and thinking.

Evaluations had to serve the practical task of predicting the success of military leaders or military specialists. Race psychology and typology did not meet this special need. The typological method functions primarily to show the universal validity of a classificatory system. It enables the investigator to study distinct cases, assuming that what is distinct in several selected cases may exist to a diminished extent in all cases. For the problem of aptitude evaluation, however, the psychological or racial type to which a candidate belonged was not of great interest, as long as any relation of this type to the required military qualification had not yet been demonstrated. At this point, army diagnostics were fairly pragmatic. The army even used psychotechnical apparatus, which Jaensch and his followers called "Jewish." Especially in the selection of specialist personnel, psychotechnical methods, such as tests of sensorimotor coordination or reaction speed were needed. Air force psychologists, for example, developed new methods for diagnosing the ability to retain spatial orientation independent of vestibular sensations or visible points of orientation, which were taken up after the war by NASA.[43]

Thus, some fields of psychology that began to develop before the Nazi period flourished during this period and were pursued after it. In the new examination regulations of 1941, characterology and expression analysis were defined as independent subfields of the discipline, and they remained as examination fields until the late 1960s. That these fields received recognition is also indicated by the fact that in 1939 Lersch, though apparently not a Nazi party member, was called to succeed Krueger in the most famous psychology chair in Germany, that of Wundt in Leipzig, with the argument that he had applied new methods in psychology.[44] Characterology and expression analysis became important because they met demands on psychology from outside. They were also able to meet these demands because their concepts concurred with military ideals. Examples of this are the idea that strained muscles indicate will power, which can be found in expression analysis, or the concept that will and intellect dominate feelings and emotions in Lersch's personality model.

THE FIRST PROFESSIONAL DEGREE IN GERMAN PSYCHOLOGY, 1941

The military's demand for trained psychologists and the problems posed by its career system led to an improvement of psychology's training conditions at the universities. The problem of army psychology with the current training system was twofold. The first difficulty was that training in psychology at the various universities was more oriented toward the psychological school of the local full professor and less toward training in practical fields, such as diagnostics; some universities did not even offer courses in these fields. The second difficulty was that the general career prescriptions for state civil servants which were also valid for civilians in the army, like psychologists, demanded a state examination and not the PhD offered by the university. But a state examination requiring all needed subfields could only be enacted and thus made obligatory for all universities, which were state institutions in Germany, by a ministerial order.

Until 1941, the only way to graduate in psychology was to write a PhD thesis on a psychological subject. But not all universities provided the opportunity to pass the doctoral examination in psychology as an independent subject; in 1926, only 11 of the 23 universities in the Reich did so. Elsewhere it was only possible to sit for philosophy or pedagogy. Because of the requirements of the army career system, in 1937 the military chief of army psychology, and then in 1939 the Ministry asked the universities to change their doctoral examination regulations in favor of psychology. In February 1940, the board of the German Society for Psychology took the initiative to set up a professional degree, the *Diplom,* and proposed appropriate examination regulations. A committee was established to outline a proposal including the definition of psychology's subfields. These subfields served as examination areas for an intermediate and a final examination, in which all oral examinations were concentrated. Because the Ministry for Science and Education was responsible for training regulations during the Nazi period, as the various state ministries are in West Germany today, the proposal was forwarded to the Ministry in September 1940. In a very short time and with only a few rather formal corrections the draft was adopted. After the party had declared its consent, it was enacted in June 1941, going into effect retroactively to April 1.

Psychology had now gained a status that it had not been successful in attaining, despite some efforts, during the Weimar period. The long-lasting conflict with philosophy was now resolved in favor of psychology.[45] With this decree psychology became an independent subject emancipated from philosophy and departmentalized in fields of examination that later formed the framework for scientific specialties.

Psychology thus gained in status and stability. The vacant Berlin chair was filled, in Hamburg an associate professorship was set up, and the new chairs in Freiburg, Cologne, and Münster were established in order to fulfill the requirements of the new order. The Cologne chair, however, was not filled. The examination order had a stabilizing effect internally, too. The German Society for Psychology gained new members. The Society's newsletter, written by chairman Oswald Kroh at Christmas 1941, triumphantly announced that the "requirements for the development of an organized and recognised psychological profession" had been created.[46] At that time, psychologists saw the new examination order as the discipline's greatest success in decades.

However, this success was challenged by another professional group, the psychiatrists, who did not want the examination regulations to include medical psychology and psychopathology. Leading professors of psychiatry did not admit psychology students to their courses, even if attending these courses was now an official part of their training. Psychiatrists were afraid of a new professional rival in their area. Thus they put pressure on the Ministry to eliminate medical subjects from the examinations; they succeeded in 1942.

THE CURTAILMENT OF ARMY AND AIR FORCE PSYCHOLOGY

Another challenge for the newly stabilized discipline was the curtailment of army and air force psychology in 1942. In April 1942, the chief commander of the training section of the air force decreed that aptitude tests for fliers were cancelled. Five weeks later the Supreme Command of the Army ordered that the psychology service be disbanded. Navy psychology was kept alive until the end of the war, but gave up psychological officer selection.

After the war, German psychologists used these actions to prove that psychology was opposed to National Socialism. Until the present some have reiterated the claim that the party's opposition was responsible for the dissolution of these services.[47] But there is not much evidence to support this opinion. A scrutiny of the literature and records only discloses one case in which a party authority openly, but not publically, attacked army psychology. In 1938, Hitler replaced the War Ministry with the Supreme Command of the Military *(Oberkommando der Wehrmacht)*. The psychological service, which had formerly been attached to the War Ministry, was reorganized and renamed, thus coming to the attention of the party's "brown house." The Berlin professor Alfred Bäumler, who was in charge of the party's ideological watch office, the *Amt Rosenberg,* answered a request from Martin Bormann of the bureau of Hitler's deputy Rudolf Hess by criticizing the basic world view epxressed in earlier publications of Max Simoneit, the scientific chief of army psychology. But he did not criticize the diagnostic methods used in army psychology, nor was any document located that affirmed concrete steps taken on behalf of the party against the army psychological service.

A detailed examination of the various arguments for the dissolution of army and air force psychology, of the development of demand and supply for officer candidates and fliers, and of the army's policy for engaging officers suggests a different reason for the curtailment. Early in the war, the air force had already confronted a severe shortage of fliers, especially after the air war against England in the fall of 1940. Because passing the psychological examination was a prerequisite for candidacy as flier, every rejection worked against the needed expansion. Later the air force wanted to engage nearly anybody who applied to become a pilot. But selection is generally needless if there is nobody to select, or if the population to be drawn from no longer exceeds the numbers required. The army lacked officers in 1940, and again in 1942, after the German army was heavily defeated for the first time near Moscow in winter 1941–42. Moreover, war provided a chance to test the candidates' qualities in real life. Hence it is not astonishing that concomitant with the dissolution of army psychology was an order that the success of a corporal in the field was decisive for promotion to officer status, whereas up to June 1942 virtually only *Gymnasium* graduates could apply for officer training immediately on finishing school. After all, prognosis is no longer needed when real life provides a better test. In an ongoing war the most important task of army psychology, which had been to predict an officer candidate's worth for real war, became ancillary.

Navy psychology survived. The reasons for this are not revealed by the sources. Possibly the main reason is that Navy psychology focused more on the selection of military specialists, such as radio operators, signalmen, or ship mechanics, than on officers. Selection of specialist personnel by psychotechnic methods was also pursued by the army after the dissolution of the psychological service. Moreover, the Navy did not suffer from the supply problems of the army or the air force.

Despite the central role of army and air force psychology in German psychology as a whole, the discipline did not break down after this dissolution. There are three possible reasons for this. First, the new training regulations strengthened the position of psychology in the universities. Second, psychology could consolidate a new professional field within the child guidance service of the National Socialist Welfare Organization. Third, the dissolutions did not put pressure on the labor market, because most psychologists were state officials and thus had to be employed further by the state administration as long as they did not have to serve at the front.

During the war, some psychologists tried to prove the discipline's relevance in new areas, for example, by showing the relevance of animal psychology for the training of SS and army dogs, or of psychological diagnostics for settlement planning in the conquered areas. In Poland, the SS was interested in having empirical data from psychologist Rudolf Hippius for its brutal population planning. Race psychology had turned away from legitimizing Nazi ideology in an only theoretical way to become a hard, empirical subject, providing effective knowledge for Nazi crimes and striving to legitimize concrete Nazi politics. It could not yet be proved, however, whether the SS ever used these studies.

CONCLUSIONS

Psychology underwent a decline during the Nazi period. But that meant not only the loss of theoretical research potency caused by the dismissals. It was also a decline in the behavior of the psychologists who remained in Germany. Many were willing to legitimize Nazi power with psychology, or at least to offer their expert knowledge to the institutions of the Nazi state. This view of decline does not fit the apologetic claim that the history of psychology during the Nazi period was only a history of suffering. The leading representatives of the discipline acted relatively independently to orient the discipline toward new, politically required tasks. Psychologists were not forced to rewrite their theories according to Nazi ideology. Some scholars did not do so, and they did not suffer political repression. Thus the counter thesis mentioned at the beginning of this chapter does not meet the facts either. Psychology was not forced by the Nazi party to meet any specific political demands. The Nazi party had no concept for the discipline's theoretical development, nor did the party specifically suffocate psychology. The only constant factor of Nazi science policy was the persecution of Jewish and politically opposing scholars. Thus, racist dismissals hit psychology. But at the same time the party authorities and representatives who were responsible for science policy fostered the professional development of the field. The Nazi regime was not only interested in ideological legitimation. It was also interested in a science that was highly effective in a technological, or, as Jürgen Habermas has put it for the social sciences, in a "socio-technological" sense. This was true not only for psychology, but also for other disciplines.[48]

Psychology's professionalization largely shaped its development throughout the Nazi period. The discipline was able to prove its usefulness in the army and in other fields outside the university, and leading psychologists seem to have been guided primarily by a desire to do all that was worthwhile for the improvement of the discipline's institutionalization and professionalization. They did not reflect on the ends for which their knowledge was used, even when the German army, for which they were working, spread war and terror over Europe.

But the great importance of psychology in the military and the accelerating role of war in psychology's professionalization is not only a German phenomenon. This has already been stressed for the United States and Canada in World War I and World War II, and can surely be found in other countries as well.[49] In Germany, the requirements of the army for a great number of psychological experts pushed psychology's professionalization ahead and favored its orientation toward diagnostics. In this particular sense Ansbacher, who was quoted in this chapter's introduction, was right. Diagnostic methods used by the German army and psychotechnics used in industry were indeed the same as those used under different social and political conditions. Thus, psychology was successful in its professionalization by the normality of its application, as a discipline with expert knowledge, even under totalitarian conditions – a scandalous normality that might be thought provoking in our day.

Experts are sometimes blind. They offer their knowledge and their abilities as effective means of performing tasks whose aims they have neither set nor considered. Even after the war, psychologists did not discuss the role of their discipline during the Nazi period. Of course, in psychology the problems of self-reflection were different from those in medicine or law. According to our present knowledge, psychologists were not professionally involved in war crimes, though at least two came close to such involvement. They did not work in concentration camps and did not take part in criminal experiments in human beings, as far as can be determined from the inspected sources. Nor were psychologists engaged professionally in Nazi party propaganda.[50]

Even so, it is astounding how psychologists blurred or ignored the entire period after the war. They did not discuss why the discipline could meet the interests of the army, why it was supported and not oppressed by the rulers, and why its theories and methods suited the needs of public institutions of the Nazi regime. On the contrary, they still thought primarily about the validity of army diagnostics. They asked whether they did a good job, and left aside the ends for which the job was required. This narrow, limited perspective makes it understandable that Oswald Kroh, the chairman of the German Society for Psychology, could write at the end of 1941, after the enactment of the new examination regulations and in the middle of a terrible war, that the Society might look back on the last year with satisfaction.[51]

NOTES

1 This attack was first published in English and then in German; see F. Baumgarten, "German Psychologists and Recent Events," *Journal of Abnormal and Social Psychology* 43 (1948):452–465; *Die deutschen Psychologen und die*

Zeitereignisse (Zürich: Der Aufbau, 1949). For the replies cf. U. Geuter, "Institutionelle und professionelle Schranken der Nachkriegsauseinandersetzungen über die Psychologie im Nationalsozialismus," *Psychologie- und Gesellschaftskritik* 4:1/2 (1980):11 ff.

2 C. F. Graumann, "Psychologie im Nationalsozialismus. Eine Einführung," in C. F. Graumann (ed.), *Psychologie im Nationalsozialismus* (Berlin, Heidelberg, New York, Tokyo: Springer, 1985), 2.

3 Geuter, "Institutionelle und professionelle Schranken," 15–28; Ulfried Geuter, "The Uses of History for the Shaping of the Field: Observations on German Psychology," in L. Graham, W. Lepenies, and P. Weingart (eds.), *Functions and Uses of Disciplinary Histories* (Dordrecht: Reidel, 1983), 206–210.

4 P. Chroust, "Gleichschaltung der Psyche. Zur Faschisierung der deutschen Psychologie am Beispiel Gerhard Pfahlers," *Psychologie- und Gesellschaftskritik* 3:4 (1979):29–40; U. Geuter, "Der Leipziger Kongress der Deutschen Gesellschaft für Psychologie 1933. Ausrichtung, Anbieten und Arrangement einer Wissenschaft im nationalisozialistischen Staat," ibid., 6–25; P. Mattes, "Profession bei Fuss – Wehrmachtspsychologie nach 1945," *Psychologie- und Gesellschaftskritik* 3:1/2 (1980):40–46; S. Schunter-Kleemann, "Die Nachkriegsauseinandersetzung in der DDR über die Psychologie im deutschen Faschismus," ibid., 47–67; Geuter, "Institutionelle und professionelle Schranken."

5 U. Geuter, "Der Nationalsozialismus und die Entwicklung der deutschen Psychologie," in G. Lüer (ed.), *Bericht über den 33. Kongress der Deutschen Gesellschaft für Psychologie in Mainz 1982* (Göttingen: Hogrefe, 1983), 99–106; *Die Professionalisierung der deutschen Psychologie im Nationalsozialismus* (Frankfurt: Suhrkamp, 1984); "'Gleichschaltung' von oben? Universitätspolitische Strategien und Verhaltensweisen in der Psychologie während des Nationalsozialismus," *Psychologische Rundschau* 35 (1984):198–213; "Nationalsozialistische Ideologie und Psychologie," in M. G. Ash and U. Geuter (eds.), *Geschichte der deutschen Psychologie im 20. Jahrhundert. Ein Überblick* (Opladen: Westdeutscher Verlag, 1985), 172–200; C. F. Graumann, *Psychologie im Nationalsozialismus*, note 2.

6 F. Wyatt and H. L. Teuber, "German Psychology under the Nazi System – 1933–1940," *Psychological Review* 51 (1944):229–247.

7 One of their conclusions was that the more philosophical parts of psychology tended more to adopt the tenets of National Socialism. This was answered by Lerner, who in view of future reeducation policy warned against judging the political attitude of an author by Nazification of his or her theories. See E. Lerner, "A Reply to Wyatt and Teuber," *Psychological Review* 52 (1945):52–54.

8 In 1937 the Psychologists' League took steps to boycott the import of German test materials; in 1938 an editorial denouncing Nazi science was published; see "Boycott of German Test Material?" *Psychologists' League Journal* 1 (1937):13–14; "American Scientists Slam Nazi 'Science'," *Psychologists' League Journal* 2 (1938): 95. For the history of the 12th International Congress of Psychology, see U. Geuter, "The Eleventh and Twelfth International Congresses of Psychology. A Note on Politics and Science Between 1936 and 1948," in H. Carpintero and J. M. Peiró (eds.), *La psicología en su contexto histórico. Ensayos en honor del Prof. Josef Brozek* (Valencia: Monografías de la *Revista de la Historia de la Psicología*, 1984), 127–40; J. Whitmore, *American Psychology Responds to Nazi Germany* (Unpublished M.A. thesis, University of Akron, Ohio, 1969). For Boder's challenge to Jaensch's racism, see D. P. Boder, "Nazi Science," *Chicago Jewish Forum* 1 (1942):23–29; and "Nazi Science," in P. L. Harriman (ed.), *Twentieth Century Psychology* (New York: Philosophical Library, 1946), 10–21.

9 G. W. Allport, "The Psychologist's Frame of Reference," *Psychological Bulletin* 37(1940):1–28.

10 H. L. Ansbacher, "Murray's and Simoneit's (German Military) Methods of Personality Study," *Journal of Abnormal and Social Psychology* 36 (1941):589–592; "German Military Psychology," *Psychological Bulletin* 38 (1941):370–392; L. Farago (ed.), *German Psychological Warfare* (New York: G. P. Putnam's Sons, 1942); Heinz L. Ansbacher, personal communication, June 17, 1980, protocol in U. Geuter, *Gespräche zur Entwicklung der Psychologie in Deutschland von den 20er Jahren bis 1945. Eine Protokollsammlung. Mit einem Anhang: Jahresbericht des Instituts für Arbeitspsychologie und Arbeitspädagogik der Deutschen Arbeitsfront 1944*. Institut für Zeitgeschichte, Munich, Sammlung Zeugenschrifttum, ZS/A 37, 168–72.

11 H. L. Ansbacher, "Lasting and Passing Aspects of German Military Psychology," *Sociometry* 12(1949):301–312; J. W. Dunlap, *Training of Free Gunners in the German Air Force* (Washington, D.C.: U.S. Department of Commerce, Publ. Vol. No. 4364, 1946); D. D. Feder, H. Gulliksen and H. L. Ansbacher, *German Naval Psychology,* U.S. Naval Publication NavPers 18080 (Washington, D.C.: Bureau of Naval Personnel; Princeton, NJ: College Entrance Examination Board, 1948); P. M. Fitts, "German Applied Psychology during World War II," *American Psychologist* 1 (1946):151–61; cf. note 43.

12 H. L. Ansbacher, "German Industrial Psychology in the Fifth Year of War," *Psychological Bulletin* 41 (1944):605–614; "Testing, Management, and Reactions of Foreign Workers in Germany during World War II," *American Psychologist* 5 (1950):38–49; J. W. Dunlap and J. B. Rieffert, *Tests for Selection of Personnel in German Industry,* U.S. Naval Technical Mission in Europe, Report No. 300–45, Publ. Vol. No. 22933, Sept. 1945; M. S. Viteles and L. D. Anderson, *Training and Selection of Supervisory Personnel in the I.G. Farbenwerke, Ludwigshafen,* FIAT Final Report No. 930 (Washington, D.C.: U.S. Department of Commerce, 1947).

13 Geuter, *Gespräche,* 216.

14 Ansbacher, "Testing, Management, and Reaction of Foreign Workers," 48.

15 B. Epstein, "Cold War in Psychology," *Benjamin Rush Bulletin* 1 (1950):43–49; I thank H. L. Ansbacher for forwarding this article to me.

16 M. Henle, "One Man Against the Nazis – Wolfgang Köhler," *American Psycholgist* 33 (1978):939.

17 Geuter, *Professionalisierung,* 30–33.

18 W. Metzger, "The Historical Background for National Trends in Psychology: German Psychology," *Journal of the History of the Behavioral Sciences* 1 (1965):112.

19 C. Fritsche, *Untersuchung zur Krise der bürgerlichen Psychologie anhand ihrer zeitgenössischen Reflexion von 1897–1945* (Unpublished PhD dissertation, Karl-Marx-Universität Leipzig, Sektion Psychologie, 1981), 95; Schunter-Kleemann, "Die Nachkriegsauseinandersetzung in der DDR," 49.

20 Geuter, *Professionalisierung,* passim.

21 On the history of psychoanalysis during the Nazi period, see G. Cocks, *Psychotherapy in the Third Reich. The Göring Institute* (New York/Oxford: Oxford University Press, 1985) and R. Lockot, *Erinnern und Durcharbeiten. Zur Geschichte der Psychoanalyse und Psychotherapie im Nationalsozialismus* (Frankfurt: Fischer, 1985).

22 M. G. Ash, "Ein Institute und eine Zeitschrift. Zur Geschichte des Berliner

Psychologischen Institute und der Zeitschrift 'Psychologische Forschung' vor und nach 1933," in Graumann, *Psychologie im Nationalsozialismus,* 113–137; Geuter, "'Gleichschaltung' von oben?"

23 Cf. E. Y. Hartshorne, *The German Universities and National Socialism* (London: Allen and Unwin, 1937).

24 M. G. Ash, "Disziplinentwicklung und Wissenschaftstransfer – Deutschsprachige Psychologen in der Emigration," *Berichte zur Wissenschaftsgeschichte* 7 (1984):209.

25 Institut für Zeitgeschichte, Munich, Mikrofilmarchiv 116/10. In his book *Psychologie,* Metzger did not cite Wertheimer's or Lewin's name. For a broader evaluation of the book and other publications of Wolfgang Metzger during the Nazi period, see M. Stadler, "Das Schicksal der nichtemigrierten Gestaltpsychologen im Nationalsozialismus," in Graumann, *Psychologie im Nationalsozialismus,* 141–152.

26 Henle, "One Man Against the Nazis – Wolfgang Köhler;" Ash, "Ein Institut und eine Zeitschrift."

27 Geuter, "Der Leipziger Kongress der Deutschen Gesellschaft für Psychologie 1933."

28 H. Misiak and V. S. Sexton, *History of Psychology. An Overview* (New York and London: Grune and Stratton, 1966), 113.

29 Geuter, "'Gleichschaltung' von oben?" 200–202.

30 See Note 22.

31 Chroust, "Gleischschaltung der Psyche"; U. Geuter, *Psychologie in der Zeit des Nationalsozialismus* (Hagen: Studienbrief 'Problemgeschichte der Psychologie,' Kurseinheit 2, Fernuniversität Hagen, 1984) 43–44.

32 See Boder, "Nazi Science"; R. Stagner, *Psychology of Personality* (New York: McGraw-Hill, 1937), 213–216; Wyatt and Teuber, "Psychology under the Nazi System," 234 ff.

33 E. R. Jaensch, *Der Gegentypus. Psychologisch-anthropologische Grundlagen deutscher Kulturphilosophie, ausgehend von dem was wir überwinden wollen. (Zeitschrift für angewandte Psychologie und Charakterkunde,* Beiheft 75; Leipzig: Barth, 1938).

34 Zentrales Staatsarchiv der DDR, Potsdam, 49.01 REM 2606, f. 19.

35 For a detailed account of Jaensch and his work during the Nazi period see Geuter, "Nationalsozialistische Ideologie und Psychologie (note 5), 179–192.

36 Wyatt and Teuber, "Psychology under the Nazi System."

37 F. Sander, "Die Idee der Ganzheit in der deutschen Psychologie," *Der Thüringer Erzieher* 1 (1933):10–12; "Deutsche Psychologie und nationalsozialistische Weltanschauung," *Nationalsozialistisches Bildungswesen* 2 (1937):641–649. For a broader account of Krueger's *Ganzheits*-psychology and its relation to National Socialism, see U. Geuter, "Das Ganze und die Gemeinschaft – Wissenschaftliches und politisches Denken in der Ganzheitspsychologie Felix Kruegers," in Graumann (ed.), *Psychologie im Nationalsozialismus,* 55–87.

38 W. Metzger, "Der Auftrag der Psychologie in der Auseinandersetzung mit dem Geist des Westens," *Volk im Werden* 10 (1942):133–144. This and other publications of Wolfgang Metzger were mentioned for the first time after the war in Geuter, "Der Nationalsozialismus und die Entwicklung der deutschen Psychologie," 102 and 106, and later broadly discussed in Stadler, "Das Schicksal der

nichtemigrierten Gestaltpsychologen im Nationalsozialismus," and Wolfgang Prinz, "Ganzheits- und Gestaltpsychologie im Nationalsozialismus," in Graumann (ed.), *Psychologie im Nationalsozialismus,* 89–111.

39 Cf. M. G. Ash and U. Geuter, "NSDAP-Mitgliedschaft und Universitätskarriere in der Psychologie," in Graumann (ed.), *Psychologie im Nationalsozialismus,* 263–278.

40 This entire process has been documented in Geuter, *Professionalisierung,* and can only be briefly summarized here.

41 Cf. R. Maikowski, P. Mattes and G. Rott, *Psychologie und ihre Praxis. Materialien zur Geschichte und Funktion einer Einzelwissenschaft in der Bundesrepublik* (Frankfurt: Fischer, 1976).

42 L. Klages, *Ausdrucksbewegung und Gestaltungskraft. Grundlegung der Wissenschaft vom Ausdruck,* 3rd and 4th ed. (Leipzig: Barth, 1923); *Die Grundlagen der Charakterkunde,* 4th ed. (Leipzig: Barth, 1926); P. Lersch, *Gesicht und Seele. Grundlinien einer mimischen Diagnostik* (Munich: Reinhardt, 1932); *Der Aufbau des Charakters* (Leipzig: Barth, 1938).

43 See, e.g., English contributions by former German air force psychologists: S. Gerathewohl, "Psychological Examinations for Selection and Training of Fliers," in Department of the Air Force (ed.), *German Aviation Medicine in World War II* (Washington, D.C.: U.S. Government Printing Office, 1950), Vol. II:1027–1052; and K. Kreipe, "Evaluation and Procedure in the Characterological Selection of Fliers," ibid.,1053–1058. From 1946 onward, Gerathewohl worked for the American air force. He moved to the United States in 1947, and in 1960 became Chief of Operational Development, Office of Life Sciences, NASA; see Geuter, *Gespräche,* 235.

44. The sequence Wundt-Krueger-Lersch in the famous Leipzig chair clearly stands for the history of German psychology's ideas. For further information on Nazi party membership and academic advancement in psychology, see Ash and Geuter, "NSDAP-Mitgliedschaft und Universitätskarriere in der Psychologie."

45 Cf. M. G. Ash, "Academic Politics in the History of Science: Experimental Psychology in Germany, 1879–1941," *Central European History* 13 (1980): 255–286; Geuter, *Professionalisierung,* chapter II, esp. 85–87, 129–130.

46 Deutsche Gesellschaft für Psychologie, "An die inländischen Mitglieder der Deutschen Gesellschaft für Psychologie," Oswald Kroh, Weihnachten 1941; Universitätsarchiv Tübingen 148/24, Allgemeiner Briefwechsel, Psychologisches Institut.

47 See the interviews with ten former military psychologists in Geuter, *Gespräche;* see also Geuter, *Professionalisierung,* 32; and "Institutionelle und professionelle Schranken," 15 ff.

48 See, e.g., A. Beyerchen, *Scientists under Hitler, Politics and the Physics Community in the Third Reich* (New Haven: Yale University Press, 1977); Cocks, *Psychotherapy* (note 21); C. Klingemann, "Heimatsoziologie oder Ordnungsinstrument? Fachgeschichtliche Aspekte der Soziologie in Deutschland zwischen 1933 und 1945," in M. R. Lepsius (ed.), *Soziologie in Deutschland und Österreich 1918–1945 (Zeitschrift für Soziologie und Sozialpsychologie,* Sonderband 23; Opladen: Westdeutscher Verlag, 1981), 273–307.

49 See, e.g., T. M. Camfield, *Psychologists at War. The History of American Psychology and the First World War* (Unpublished PhD dissertation, University of Texas, 1969); D. S. Napoli, *Architects of Adjustment. The History of the Psycho-*

logical Profession in the United States (Port Washington, NY: Kennikat Press, 1981); F. Samelson, "Putting Psychology on the Map: Ideology and Intelligence Testing," in A. R. Buss (ed.), *Psychology in Social Context* (New York: Irvington, 1979), 103–168; M. J. Wright, "CPA: The First Ten Years," *The Canadian Psychologist* 15 (1974):112–131.

50 To a limited extent propaganda was a part of the task of military psychology. The Psychological Laboratory in the War Ministry included a study group on folk psychology that was responsible for evaluations of the psychological traits of different European nations. This group was separated from the Laboratory on December 1, 1938. For this group and other propaganda activities, however, the army typically engaged journalists or intellectuals other than psychologists.

51 See note 46.

8

L . S . VYGOTSKII : THE MUFFLED DEITY OF SOVIET PSYCHOLOGY*

DAVID JORAVSKY

In ideological declarations Soviet psychology is both Marxist and Pavlovian, and largely indifferent to the illogic of the combination. In concrete research and teaching Soviet psychology is neither Marxist nor Pavlovian, and never has been. The most important Soviet psychologists have formed a school of cognitive studies very like Piaget's, though few of them have been willing to acknowledge the affinity. That cluster of bizarre incongruities – a cognitive school like Piaget's enclosed within devotion to a uniquely Soviet Marxist Pavlovian science that transcends all "bourgeois" schools – grew out of the tensions between scholars and politicians following the Bolshevik Revolution of 1917. The politicians insisted on ideological devotion, which proved to be intellectually inane, rather like the religious devotion of Galileo or Pasteur.

All that seems quite foreign to Western psychologists, who coexist peacefully with their countries' political and ideological authorities. They pay scant attention to the implicit ideologies within psychological science that make such coexistence possible. Discovery of that inward accommodation is a major benefit of studying the strange history of Soviet psychology. It brings out what is otherwise too familiar to be noticed, the implicit ideologies that have eased the conflict with external authorities, helping Soviet psychologists achieve a measure of autonomy that is persistently denied to literary artists, who also claim knowledge of the mind. Built into psychological science is the unexamined assumption that scientific explanation of the mind is preferable to the imaginative under-

* This article is adapted from a book in progress, *Russian Psychology (And Our Own)*. Beginning in the 1860s and coming to the recent past, the book analyzes the academic discipline called psychology as it connects, or fails to connect, with psychologies implicit in neurophysiology, psychiatry, imaginative literature, and political ideology.

standing at work in everyday discourse and in literary art. I call that assumption an ideology, a form of scientism, and note a similar effect East and West, an accommodation between psychological scientists and the powers that be.

The knowledgeable reader may think that S. L. Rubinshtein (1889–1960) was the Soviet psychologist with the most to say on such fundamental problems. In actuality his life and work reveal more of what is past and foreign in Soviet psychology than what is continuing and similar to Western experience. He started out as a metaphysical philosopher, with a 1914 dissertation under Hermann Cohen and Paul Natorp at Marburg, on "Absolute Rationalism (Hegel)," and proved remarkably obstinate in that line of thought.[1] During the twenties, while Soviet psychologists were rather free of metaphysics and scholasticism in discussing the implications of Marxism for their science, Rubinshtein was almost entirely silent. In the 1930s, when Stalinists pushed the discipline toward destruction by demanding that all "bourgeois" schools be repudiated so that a uniquely Soviet psychology might emerge, Rubinshtein emerged, with a pile of quotations from Marx and heaps of scholastic argument on the compatibility of Marxism and empirical psychology.[2] He helped to appease the zealots and to save the discipline. During the anticosmopolitan campaign of the late 1940s he was put down for being insufficiently patriotic – code language for Jewish – but he rebounded after Stalin's death to produce his least stereotyped philosophizing on such fundamental problems as "Being and Consciousness."[3] Perhaps experimental psychologists should be interested, but for the most part they are not – unless they need some ideological references to reassure the Soviet ideological establishment.

L. S. Vygotskii (1896–1934) provides a revealing contrast. He also came to psychological science from humanistic scholarship; literary criticism in his case, which inclined him toward empirical studies of the mind as expressed in its works. He did not criticize twentieth-century psychology from without; he entered the profession, fully absorbed its antimetaphysical ethos, and exposed its basic problems with the persuasive power of a comrade. We aspire to a science, he noted, and we have created several of them; we have not overcome the crisis that Franz Brentano, one of our founding fathers, called attention to in 1874.[4] He challenged his colleagues to scorn the easy escape, which is to immure oneself in a single school and pooh-pooh the others. He laid out a most ambitious program of unification, with an "historico-cultural" approach as the central feature. Though tuberculosis cut him off at a very early age, Vygotskii left prolific disciples, most notably A. R. Luria (1902–1977) and A. N. Leont'ev (1903–1979), who founded the Vygotskii school of cognitive psychology, focused on brain damage and child development.

There is a great irony in that history: Preaching a comprehensive science, Vygotskii started one more school. Much of his work was actually concealed by his avowed disciples or by the censorship, or by some combination of timid disciples and fearsome censors. His major books were withheld from publication, for 40 years in one case, 55 in another.[5] When they finally appeared, his admirers had become thoroughly specialized adepts in one or two parts of his comprehensive project, conditioned to ignore the rest. There are peculiarly Soviet features in this ironic history, but there are also striking analogies to the fate of Wundt or James among Western psychologists, who also profess reverence for founding fathers and ignore their central ideas.

I

Like Luria, Vygotskii was obviously Jewish and defiantly indifferent to the ethnic fact.[6] The Bolsheviks in their early period campaigned against Russian nationalism, but it would be foolish to imagine that ethnic animosities were dissolved by a Communist campaign against them or by the consequent appearance of many Jews in prominent positions. Maybe Vygotskii was more stoical than defiant, as he carried into Russian academia the telltale combination of Russified Polish name and Mediterranean face. The usual photograph shows large dark eyes lit with gentle intensity rather than arrogance, reinforcing the disciples' talk of an "enchanting personality." We must make do with guesswork from bits of evidence, for extensive material is not provided. If he left an autobiography, it is still among his unpublished papers along with self-revealing letters, which must have been written, for he had a warm, outgoing nature. His disciples tell us that, but they themselves are utterly ungiving of documents, and closefisted even with elementary details of his life. They refuse to let Soviet readers know anything about family background beyond the bare fact that his father was a *sluzhashchii* (literally a person in service). That means a white-collar or salaried person, in contrast to a blue-collar or wage-earning person, and includes levels of status far above poor clerks or bookkeepers. Foreign readers are permitted to learn a little more; a recent biographical sketch, published only in English, acknowledges that Vygotskii's father was a bank officer, and gives a little reminiscence of the family's secular Jewishness.[7] The son was an outstanding student, who earned a joint degree at Moscow University in law and "philological studies" (read: imaginative literature and cultural history), and was making a name for himself as a literary critic by the time of the 1917 Revolution, when he was only 21.

That is another part of the legendary aura that radiates from Vygotskii: the incredibly young genius who had to do his enormous work at great speed, while tuberculosis was pushing him to periodic bedrest and early death, in 1934 at age 37. The admirers who stress the doomed youth's intense engagement with his calling are strangely vague about his path through the revolutionary storm.[8] He may have consorted with non-Bolshevik Marxists in 1917, for he published in two periodicals edited by Gorky, which were critical of the new dictatorship and were soon shut down by it.[9] Studied silences suggest unpleasant news. The disciples say nothing about his politics in 1917–1918; for the ensuing years of Civil War they tell us only that he taught at a pedagogical institute and advised a theatrical company in a small Belorussian town. They refrain from republishing or even from adequately describing the earliest articles he is known to have published in 1915–1923, though literary art was their topic. If he wrote anything on politics, it has been kept in the dark.

When we contemplate the skimpy accounts of Vygotskii's major intellectual transformation from literary critic to psychologist, one large fact quickly emerges. The accounts are skimpy because his distinctive ideas about literary art are not to the taste of his disciples in psychological science. They admire the psychologist that emerged from the literary critic in the period from 1915 to 1923, but they have been unwilling or unable to confront the critic, or the influence of the critic on the scientist. *The Psychology of Art,* the dissertation that summed up the emergence of one from the other, and earned Vygotskii a doctorate in 1925, waited 40 years to be published (heavily abridged in 1965, "corrected and enlarged" in 1968).[10] Editor A. N. Leont'ev asserts, without offering evidence, that Vygotskii himself withheld the book from publication, since he was acutely aware that he had not solved the problems he was struggling with.[11] That may be true, but it is much more obviously true that Vygotskii died in 1934, and his disciples – Leont'ev included – waited 30 years before they could bring themselves (and the ideological establishment) to set aside the master's perfectionist scruples and put the book before the public. Archival information would help, but one can discover the major reason why without the archives. One need only consider Vygotskii's argument concerning art, and compare the disciples' onesided summaries, when they have felt obliged, briefly and perfunctorily, to report it. He discovered antinomies in modern views of the expressive mind; they prefer to brush the antinomies aside, mumbling about the imperfect stage of psychological science in his day and hurrying back from the expressive imagination to the problem-solving intelligence.[12]

This was the basic antinomy: The belief that imaginative literature (or art in general) is merely a manner of signalling, like birdsong or rat-squeak, to be explained by its biological and social functions, versus the belief that it is also a thing in itself, to be not only explained but also understood as beautiful truths accumulating in a cultural process, which creates the human mind even as it is created by it. Vygotskii began with the second belief, was drawn against his aesthetic inclination toward the first, tried to fuse them, but did not succeed.

He started in particular with an intensive study of *Hamlet* and the critical controversies that have accumulated about it. He wanted to understand the appeal of art works called classic, a persistent appeal that must be evidence of some persistent structure of thought and feeling inherent in the human mind. If the fictive tragedy of *Hamlet* is a perennial stimulus of pleasurable feelings, and it is, whoever would explain that paradoxical fact – tragedy stimulating pleasure – cannot ignore either literary analysis of the drama or psychological analysis of author, actors, audience, critics. Until 1924 Vygotskii concentrated on the author's text and the critics' debate, with splendid results. His literary essays remain the most original and exciting part of his writing on the psychology of art, though ostensibly they only lead up to it, passing on to psychological science a problem that literary criticism cannot solve.

Literary analysis revealed to Vygotskii that *Hamlet's* dramatic tension derives from the opposition between the plot formula and the actual plot; what the audience expects to happen (criminal outrage corrected by vengeful justice) is opposed to what the audience actually sees (random violence, insanity, and vengeful justice dissolving into absurdity). Adult audiences know that there are such distressing incongruities between the expected and the actual pattern of life. Why their enactment in fiction pleases the distressed mind is a question that carries the critic from literary to social and psychological analysis. Vygotskii's response was a version of "catharsis," interpreted in Freudian fashion as the patterned discharge through dramatic fiction of suffering that would otherwise be destructive. That seems to be a functional, scientific explanation of tragic fiction. But Vygotskii also argued, with a rare combination of erudition and clarity, that the two types of analysis have been increasingly at odds with each other. As psychologists have separated their discipline from philosophy and modeled it on the natural sciences, they have moved toward a psychology of art "from below," functional analysis of stimulus and reaction that is primitively crude, incompatible with literary analysis of such texts as *Hamlet*. And vice versa. As critics have separated their discipline from metaphysical doctrines of "the soul" or "the mind," they have kept alive a psychology of art "from above," but increasingly deprived of a psychological theory that might justify it.[13]

Vygotskii turned to Marxism, not for a readymade theory of art or psychology or unification of the two, but for a methodology that might help him to overcome the antinomy he was struggling with. He emphasized that Marxism was not opposed to aesthetic theory "from above." Young Marx, he noted, asked the same question about the persistent appeal of Greek classics that he was asking about *Hamlet*.[14] How could it be that the beautiful works of a slaveowning society are still beautiful in a capitalist society and will be under socialism? The persistence of the appeal challenges the Marxist theory that social superstructures, mentalities included, change with transformations of the social base. Vygotskii had to emphasize that Marx recognized the problem, for Marxists tended to regard their doctrine as an approach "from below," a sociological analysis of the class feelings communicated and shaped by art.

The reductive inclination was reinforced after the Revolution by official disapproval of "formalism" in literary studies, a label of disapproval for emphasis on qualities that inhere in works of art regardless of changing social relations and psychological mutability.[15] In the postrevolutionary context a "formalist" approach seemed to imply the superior isolation of the artist, elevating the "engineer of human souls" above the leaders who tell engineers what needs to be constructed.[16] Vygotskii's brilliant internal or structural analyses of literary art came dangerously close to such "formalism," and his respectful attention to the chief bugbears of "formalist" theory (Potebnia and Shklovskii) must have inclined the ideological establishment against publication of *The Psychology of Art*.

But there were also professional reasons for his disciples' wary reluctance to confront his essential argument. Literary analyses of *Hamlet* seem as alien to psychologists who have no fear of Party ideologists as to those who do. The Western psychologists who came to admire Vygotskii in the post-Stalin era have shown no more interest in his psychology of art than have his Soviet disciples.[17] A complementary indifference to Vygotskii's psychology is observable among literary critics, East or West, who are unresponsive to suggestions that "the biological basis of art" may be found in "the possibility of releasing into art powerful passions which cannot find expression in normal, everyday life."[18] In support of that idea Vygotskii cited both Nietzsche and Sherrington, trying to combine intuitive understanding of bardic frenzy with physiological analysis of the nervous system, the poetic striving for harmonic order in our emotive thinking with the mechanistic image of art as a safety valve that relieves an overburdened steam boiler. (Yes, he used that reductive metaphor.)[19] Vygotskii has had no more success in the West than at home in his efforts to bridge the "two cultures," or rather to show that works of art may be used as such a bridge, since they are created by the mind in a dense context of social and biological functions, demanding both humanistic and scientific approaches to be fully understood and explained.

Vygotskii is known at home and abroad primarily as a cognitive psychologist, rather than a writer on literary art. His disciples have been persistently eager to tell at length about his investigation of problem-solving development in children, and to give lip service to his "historico-cultural" project for psychology, but they are not at all clear or convincing in their accounts of how he came to that work, or even how he came to the Institute of Experimental Psychology where he pursued it. They note his emergence from provincial seclusion in 1924, but do not say who invited him or why. We simply learn that he was a major speaker at the

Second Psychoneurological Congress in January of that year, the meeting that proclaimed the campaign for a Marxist reconstruction of psychology.[20] Vygotskii must have been known as a Marxist sympathizer in the psychology of art and of education, but the disciples do not say whether he chose or the organizers of the Congress chose for him a more elemental and sharply controversial topic: consciousness (*soznanie,* the thinking and feeling mind), as a problem for physiology and psychology.

Whether intended by the organizers or not, that is what he spoke about, with such eloquence and clarity that witnesses felt the excitement of attendance at an historical event.[21] Yet they have been persistently vague and inaccurate in recounting what he said and explaining why it constituted an historical event. The reporter who wrote a long account of the Congress for the major intellectual journal, *Red Virgin Soil,* thought that Vygotskii epitomized a brilliant young psychologist on the way to Marxism but hesitating en route.[22] Yet the reporter gave no evidence for that judgment, nor have subsequent admirers, who picture Vygotskii as a full-fledged Marxist. They imply that he was *the* Marxist hero of psychological science, who turned his errant colleagues away from an infatuation with reflexology to a proper interest in the conscious mind.[23] But they offer no evidence to support that legend, nor can they, for Vygotskii did not criticize fellow psychologists, who did not have an infatuation with reflexology. He criticized some physiologists, most notably Pavlov and Bekhterev, and refrained from naming Marxists who shared the assumption that consciousness is to be explained by physiological reduction.

Both the contemporaneous reporter and the subsequent admirers have been gesturing toward a kind of disagreement they may not speak of frankly: between academic professionals and Party leaders. It was not professional psychologists who were infatuated with reflexology, it was the Party's chief ideologists. After 1917 as before, K. N. Kornilov (1879–1957) deliberately included subjective elements in his "reactology," and the central Institute of Psychology, which he directed, sponsored no research of the purely objectivist kind, whether Pavlovian, Bekhterevian, or rat-running American behaviorist.[24] Bukharin and the other ideological leaders of the Party were either unaware of the psychologists' outlook or unsympathetic to it; either thoughtlessly or threateningly they equated scientific psychology with Pavlov's and Bekhterev's reduction of mind to reflexes.[25] From the tribune of the January 1924 Congress Vygotskii was arguing explicitly with Pavlov and Bekhterev, the non-Marxist leaders of physiology, but implicitly with the Party leaders who took it for granted that those physiologists had founded psychological science. His fellow psychologists were an enthusiastic audience, for they shared his conviction that subjectivity and consciousness are central to the science of the mind, but they had not known how to fit that conviction with Bukharin's Marxism.

In the Soviet as in the prerevolutionary period, nearly all of Russia's professional psychologists took it for granted that their disciplines must analyze consciousness, though they disagreed on the proper way to do that. With one or two exceptions, they did not polemicize against Pavlov or Bekhterev. They praised studies of conditioning as a physiological foundation for psychology, not a replacement of it, and they had cause to wonder whether the distinction was clear to laymen, especially the new rulers, who simply assumed that the study of conditioning was psychology *tout court*. The psychologists had been encouraged in 1923 by an article of Bukharin's ridiculing an extreme left version of Pavlov's doctrine – Enchmen's "theory of new biology," which predicted that conditioned grunts and gestures of the proletariat would replace the verbal culture of "bourgeois" society.[26] But soon after that encouraging article was published, the Party leaders gave psychologists new reason to be anxious, by their gentle response to Pavlov's ridicule of Marxism. In November 1923 *Pravda* published replies by Zinoviev and Trotsky, who limited their criticism of Pavlov to social theory and politics, while reverently accepting his reduction of psychology to conditioned reflexes.[27] In January 1924, while the Psychoneurological Congress was meeting, the first part of Bukharin's lengthy reply to Pavlov was either at the newsstands or on the way.[28] And Bukharin, the Party chief of ideology, pronounced Pavlov's doctrine of conditioned reflexes "a weapon from the iron arsenal of materialism."[29] He also repeated one of the reflexological figures of speech that he had put in his textbook of historical materialism: "If we consider the individual personality *(lichnost')* in its development, we see that it is in essence like a little sausage skin stuffed with the influences of the environment."[30]

That was the context that challenged Vygotskii when he rose to defend psychology as the science of the conscious mind. He opened with Marx's well-known contrast – it occurs in *Capital* – between the clumsiest human architect or weaver and the most unerring bee or spider. The human sees the intended construction in the mind's eye before physical eye and hand put a sketch on paper or a physical structure on the ground or the loom.[31] The bee and the spider are much simpler machines: They excrete their hives or webs in unchanging stereotypes without intentional preliminaries. So a passage from Marx himself disproved the widespread notion that radicals favor physiological reduction of the mind, while psychologies of the conscious mind are musty relics of old-regime metaphysics if not the church. Vygotskii made the ideological point all the more effective by abstaining from stereotyped use of such labels as mentalist or materialist; he showed, quite artfully, how the physiological materialism of Pavlov and Bekhterev forced them into dualist inconsistency. Nor did he indulge in flagwaving talk of "bourgeois" versus Marxist in psychological science. After citing Marx on the unsolved problem of consciousness, he set his analysis within the framework of classless science.

He noted, for example, that Pavlov's hypothetical brain processes were at odds with the findings of major neurophysiologists such as Sherrington.[32] He did not drag the audience into obscure technical issues, but brought the clash of basic concepts to vivid life by contrasting Pavlov's switchboard model of the working brain – random temporary associations as called for by external stimuli – with Sherrington's metaphors of highly structured organization: funnels collecting and concentrating neural energies, or better yet a big busy house with small doors controlling the flow of business in and out. Vygotskii also called Sechenov to witness against Pavlov, reminding the audience that the father of Russian physiology had defined thinking as an *interruption* of reflexive activity, which opens the way to a nonreflexive psychology of thinking.[33] By such appeals to physiological authority and by matter-of-fact argument he demonstrated the need to supplement neurophysiology with a psychology that analyzes "the structure of our [conscious] behavior . . . its composition and forms."[34] Obviously the Gestalt school was a major influence on this omnivorous consumer of all psychologies. He also had the literary flair to make everyone see the necessity of assuming inherent mental structure, the absurdity of Pavlov's opposite, associationist assumption: "A human being* is not at all a skin sack filled with reflexes, and the brain is not a hotel for a series of conditioned reflexes accidentally stopping in."[35]

That witty negation of Bukharin's sausage simile, to ridicule simple-minded faith in Pavlov's doctrine, was probably the reason why the reporter for *Red Virgin Soil* typed Vygotskii as a hesitant, incomplete Marxist; how else explain a scholar who quotes Marx and mocks Bukharin? But the reporter refrained from naming the butt of Vygotskii's witty thrust, as Vygotskii refrained in the printed record. Whether in extemporaneous speech he named the leaders who were too exalted to be engaged in public dispute with mere academics, archival records may some day reveal. His admirers did a little prevaricating shuffle to respect the leaders' exaltation above criticism. They pictured Vygotskii as challenging the vogue of reflexology among "Marxists." They carefully ignored the difference between Marxist Party ideologists like Zinoviev, Trotsky, and Bukharin, who shared in that vogue, and Marxist professional psychologists, who did not.

In a short time the prevaricating shuffle became a standard formula, which is repeated to this day in Western as well as Soviet histories:

---

* *Chelovek,* "man" in the generic sense, not the male "man," which is *muzhchina.* Russian separates the two meanings that English lumps into a single word.

Reflexology dominated Soviet psychology until the mid-1920s, when Vygotskii and his disciples called psychologists to the social or "historico-cultural" study of the conscious mind that is appropriate to Marxists.[36] In fact Kornilov, Luria, and the other Marxist psychologists were using subjective methods and studying consciousness before Vygotskii appeared at the Congress of January 1924 to defend such studies. He showed them how to justify their disagreement with reflexology and with the Party ideologists who favored it.

There was something much more important than a tactical evasion of scandal in Vygotskii's argument. He showed psychologists a sophisticated kind of Marxism, which went far deeper into their problems than the simplistic formulas of Bukharin or Trotsky or Lenin; he took Marxism into serious analysis of the war of schools. Of course his tactical smoothness was essential to that deep discussion. He had a style of argument that fit the mores of the 1920s, combining criticism with respect for such non-Marxist eminences as Pavlov and Bekhterev, on whom the government was lavishing favor, and artfully honoring the taboo on explicit criticism of Party leaders, while actually disagreeing with them. One must give credit to the administrator – Kornilov, in all likelihood – who recognized the value of such a thinker, and invited Vygotskii to join the Moscow Institute of Psychology soon after the Congress of January 1924.[37] One must also give credit to Bukharin, for keeping quiet. Indeed, in a 1924 speech to the Comintern, he even hinted possible disapproval of reflexology.[38] Given his power as Stalin's right-hand man, and that on this issue he expressed the superficial opinion common to Bolshevik ideologists, any further public statement of his views on psychology whould have had a stifling effect on professionals in the field. His forbearance enabled them to engage in fairly free discussion, though they constantly bore in mind the latent discord between themselves and the ideological establishment.

Within that cagey community Vygotskii had an exhilarating way of speaking clearly on basic issues while avoiding scandalous conflict. He named Bukharin and Trotsky only when ostensibly agreeing with them.[39] Toward lesser mortals he was courteous in a more forthright manner. He could, for example, write penetrating criticism of Luria's effort to mix Freudianism with Marxism, and still keep Luria's adoring friendship.[40] He could criticize his immediate chief, Kornilov, and still hold his favor.[41] He had by all accounts an unusually attractive personality, but he had a far more important intellectual advantage, which is obvious to the outside observer reading through the publications of those psychologists who called themselves Marxist. Vygotskii was the only one who had thoroughly absorbed Marxism. He had studied Marx, Engels, and Plekhanov – probably before the Revolution as his disciples claim. (I am inclined to believe them even though they offer no evidence; it would probably show some heretical form of Marxism.) He had studied "the classics of Marxism" for deeper reasons than political convenience or ideological fashion, as he studied Spinoza, his favorite philosopher. He was seeking unified understanding of human beings as natural objects with conscious minds.[42]

II

Vygotskii showed his exceptional intellectual breadth and seriousness of purpose most notably in his major book, written in 1926–1927, while he was committed to bedrest by an acute attack of tuberculosis. His title was ambivalent. *The Historical Meaning (smysl) of the Psychological Crisis* suggested not only significance in some functional sense – as in "the evolutionary significance (*znachenie*) of the grasp reflex" – but also meaning in the humanly goal-seeking sense – as in "the meaning (*smysl*) of life." Moreover, the curious phrasing at the end – psychological crisis rather than crisis of psychology – invited thought about psychology as mindset along with psychology as science, about a crisis in self-knowledge as reflected in a crisis of science. To be sure, that ambivalence was implicit rather than elaborated, in the body of the book as well as in the title. (I am assuming that the editors have not silently omitted substantial chunks of the text.)[43]

Vygotskii focused his explicit argument on psychological science, which had been in a chronic crisis since its emergence as a separate discipline, for each of its warring schools had hold of an indubitable truth, but all the partial truths together had formed a wrangle instead of a consistent science. He noted also, as an obvious truth, that literary art still provides far more important understanding of our minds than scientific psychology. Such truths seem to call for retreat from faith in a single psychological science to acceptance of "two psychologies" in permanence: "understanding" or humanist as opposed to "explanatory" or natural scientific.[44] But Vygotskii would not accept the permanence of that division. It implies a pluralist universe, in which human consciousness is an anomalous presence, to be *explained* by natural science but *understood* by artistic self-expression and by everyday forms of intuitive self-analysis.

Implicitly Vygotskii accepted that vision, as an accurate characterization of human understanding at odds with nature in past and present; explicitly he rejected such pluralism for the future. There would be no *permanent* division between the conscious mind and unconscious nature, he insisted. The tension between reality and aspiration resonated in the quotation from Spinoza that he had used as epigraph to his previous book, *The Psychology of Art*. He had quoted Spinoza defending monistic naturalism against the objection "that solely from the laws of nature considered as extended substance" one cannot "deduce the causes of buildings, pictures, and things of that kind which are produced only by human art; nor would the human body, unless it were determined and led by the mind, be capable of building a single temple."[45] That objection to the monistic vision is very like Marx contrasting the mindful architect or weaver to the mindless bee or spider, and indeed like countless others observing the obvious difference between a mind with intentions and a physical body without them. Spinoza's reply to the objection is that "the objectors cannot fix the limits of the body's power, or say what can be concluded from a consideration of its sole nature." Evidently Vygotskii liked Spinoza's philosophizing to prove that in principle mind and body *can* be explained by a single science of "extended substance," but his twentieth-century mind turned deliberately away from philosophizing about such a science to the concrete problems of building it.

A unified psychology was not in sight, even in the mind's eye; he showed that quite vividly by reviewing the war of schools. The psychologies rooted in natural science were persistently opposed to the psychologies rooted in literary and philosophical reflection on ourselves. He avoided going back to philosophy by affirming Marxist faith in the future. Evolving together in emergent unity, a new society and a new human being would create a new, unified science of psychology. That affirmation concludes *The Historical Meaning of the Psychological Crisis*. It seems almost certain that he used – and the editors have deleted – his favorite quotation from Trotsky: "Man is himself *stikhiia*," *stoicheion* or elemental chaos, which is yet to be shaped into an authentic human being or superhuman, as Kautsky predicted, in another quotation that has probably been deleted.[46] The editors have let stand the book's final paragraph, which drew again on Spinoza:

> In the future society psychology will be in actuality the science of the new man (*chelovek*). Without that perspective Marxism and the history of science would not be complete. But that science of the new man will still be psychology; we now hold in our hands the thread leading to it. Never mind that that psychology will resemble present-day psychology as little as – in Spinoza's words – the constellation Canis resembles the dog, a barking animal.[47]

With that the book ended. And somehow that futuristic yearning, pitting Spinozist faith against the incoherent pluralism of contemporary culture, had the acrid flavor of modernist absurdity. Psychologists aspiring to a unified science, a dog barking beneath the constellation named for him – that summed up *The Historical Meaning of the Psychological Crisis*.[48]

Perhaps the effect was not consciously intended, for the bulk of the text preceding the final paragraph was a respectful analysis of the contending schools in modern psychological science. Vygotskii classified them according to three basically different approaches. Psychologists proceeded either from analysis of the normal adult mind (e.g., in Gestalt), or from the pathological mind (e.g., in psychoanalysis), or from subhuman animal behavior (e.g., in Pavlov's doctrine of conditioned reflexes). At times those categories tended to blur and to fission, but it would take us too far afield to offer an adequate sampling of Vygotskii's subtle analyses. One must, however, note the resemblance between his views on the crisis of psychology and those offered by Karl Bühler and by William James.[49] He drew on them, and on many other Western scholars, in an open, generous spirit that seems unSoviet to those who know only the Soviet publications of the 1930s and after.[50] They have insisted on a heavyhanded distinction between Soviet and "bourgeois" scientists, who may not be trusted in ideologically sensitive matters. Vygotskii's *Historical Meaning of the Psychological Crisis* seems at first to be utterly different, showing what Soviet psychology was *not* until Stalin's "revolution from above" transformed it.

The most obvious contrast is between Vygotskii's sensitive cosmopolitan attitude and the crude secessionist rage of high Stalinism. He included Soviet Marxist psychologists within the worldwide discipline and thus within its crisis, for the obvious reason that he and his colleagues followed much the same lines of thought as the schools contending with each other in the West. He paid no attention to Lenin's talk of a crisis in science at large, the supposed result of its adepts' "bourgeois" ideology, their ignorance of dialectical materialism.[51] Stalinists in the 1930s would seize on that Leninist argument to hammer the point that Soviet scientists must separate themselves from "bourgeois" science by applying dialectical materialism to their disciplines.

The outside observer with the advantage of hindsight can see the secessionist spirit of Stalinist psychology emerging in the 1920s within talk of "Marxist psychology," or *Psychology Presented From The Viewpoint of Dialectical Materialism,* as Kornilov entitled his textbook in 1926.[52] Vygotskii opposed that kind of talk. He argued that it confused three different levels of knowledge: psychology as a specific science, which must be distinguished from the particular methodology appropriate to it, which in turn must be distinguished from the most general methodology of knowledge as a whole. Dialectical materialism, in his view, was the Marxist version of the most general methodology. It could be translated into specific methodological principles for psychology only in the context of protracted, concrete labor within the science, overcoming thus the war of schools: "Our science will become Marxist to the degree that it will become true, scientific; and we will work precisely on that, its transformation into a true science, not on its agreement with Marx's theory."[53]

Monism was one of the central assumptions of the truly scientific and therefore Marxist methodology: mind and body constitute a single reality in the functioning human being, and therefore a single science must ultimately describe and explain the unity. That assumption was shared not only by Marxists but by most specialists in the human sciences, in the West as well as the Soviet Union. That was a major reason why Soviet Marxists in the 1920s so confidently described their philosophy as "intrascientific." They were making explicit a methodology that was already implicit in the practical assumptions of scientists who did not yet think of themselves as Marxists.[54] Vygotskii took that familiar theme of reassurance to scientists and made it fearsome, by showing its dreamlike, futuristic contrast with reality. No existing school of psychology nor all of them lumped together achieved the monistic ideal of a single science of the mind-brain. What they were contradicted what they hoped to be. He nevertheless clung to reassurance by preaching patience: "That psychology of which we speak does not exist yet; it is still to be created, and not by a single school. Many generations of psychologists will labor on it, as [William] James said."[55] Such millennial calm is disturbing to specialists hoping for perceptible gains in their own lifetime. To the frantically impatient mentality that erupted in Stalin's revolution from above, such calm would be simply unthinkable. For those Stalinists the protracted tension of opposed schools would be plain evidence that they were in a "bourgeois" dead end, from which Marxists must effect a great leap forward, to a completely new, genuinely monistic science of psychology.

Am I therefore placing Vygotskii completely outside the drift to the psychology of Stalinism? I am not. He did, after all, collaborate in the furtive semi-concealment of his views, the public show of unity and progress that camouflaged the back-and-forth of opposed tendencies among Soviet Marxist psychologists as among their "bourgeois" colleagues at home and abroad. By withholding his most serious writing from publication, he was implicitly accepting for psychology the rule of secrecy that Stalin established for political discourse early in the 1920s: the most sensitive issues should be thrashed out within a small circle of wise initiates, and a unified front must always face the simpleminded public.[56] Vygotskii went further than mere withholding of troublesome debate. He prevaricated on occasion. It is startling to compare his semiprivate writing on "the psychological crisis" with the rah-rah review of Soviet psychology that he published in a 1928 volume celebrating the social sciences during the first decade of Soviet power.

He opened the review with his favorite theme: the problem of psycholog*ies* aspiring to be psycholog*y*. And he ended with the quotations from Trotsky and Kautsky on the new society and the new man that will emerge from past and present human *stikhiia,* elemental chaos, along with a new, unified, practically useful science of psychology. In that respect the essay was a condensed version of his unpublished book. But his tone was quite different; there was no breath of Jamesian resignation to many generations of labor toward an ideal that might possibly prove to be unrealistic. At some points he must have consciously doubted what he put on paper. For example:

> If in the doctrine of conditioned reflexes our psychology has found its *biological foundation,* and in materialist dialectics *its philosoph-ical formalization* [*oformlenie*], in psychotechnics – in the broadest sense of the word – it has found *its practice,* i.e. the mastery of human behavior in deed, the subordination of it to the control of reason.[57]

All three parts of that claim were at odds with Vygotskii's beliefs, as he had presented them elsewhere and at length. He had shown that Pavlov's explanation of conditioned reflexes clashed with neurophysiology. He had also observed that the would-be "foundation" did not match "the roof," that is, that conditioned reflexes could not explain higher nervous functions such as thinking and speaking.[58] He had argued that dialectical materialism is not a readymade philosophy for psychology, yet here he described it as the "philosophical *oformlenie,*" which means formaliza-tion in the bureaucratic sense of registering a marriage or drawing up a treaty, quite different from the openended emphasis of Vygotskii's pas-sages on Marxism in *The Historical Meaning of the Psychological Crisis.* And the enormous claim made for psychotechnics, that it had already found practical mastery of human behavior, was another incongruity. Like other Soviet writers on psychotechnics, Vygotskii normally stressed its embryonic or inchoate condition.[59]

Evidently the telescoping of aspiration and actuality, which comes so naturally at jubilees, took hold of Vygotskii on that occasion. It would hardly be worth mentioning, if it did not anticipate so clearly the Stalinist habit of requiring such a telescoping, of forcing present reality to collapse into future dream. To be sure, Vygotskii wound up his celebratory essay with a clear statement that "Marxist psychology" expressed a will to the future rather than a present achievement. His was a comparatively small step toward the collapse of present reality into future dream. But small as it was by comparison with the tubthumping extremes that were to come, it was still there in his published work, disturbingly at odds with the dominant theme of the major work that he had just finished, which was circulating in manuscript, and would remain unpublished until 1982, fifty-five years after he wrote it.

My account of Vygotskii has deliberately scanted the features of his work that have been habitually emphasized by his admirers, both Soviet and Western: his cognitive studies of children, his interest in cognitive disorders of mentally ill and braindamaged people, and his project for an "historico-cultural" approach to general psychology. That habitual emphasis distorts historical reality. Whether we judge quantitatively or qualitatively, Vygotskii's emphasis in the 1920s was on the issues that I have stressed: the psychology of art and the discord among rival schools of psychology. When he came to cognitive psychology, he did preliminary theorizing far more than experimental research. And when he came to preach "historico-cultural" psychology, his theorizing was quite thin and derivative.

He ostentatiously put the "historico-cultural" slogan at the center of his program for psychology, yet he worked at the subject only belatedly and briefly. His first published venture was a little survey that he and Luria brought out in 1930, mostly reviewing theories of Western psychologists: *Studies in the History of Behavior; Ape, Primitive, Child.*[60] Stalinists immediatey attacked the scheme of behavioral evolution that it presented as essentially "bourgeois."[61] Vygotskii's defensive and aggressive responses – restricting his freewheeling thought, attacking "bourgeois" elements in Piaget – belong to the Stalinist 1930s.[62] The point here, respecting the 1920s, is that even then, in a relatively liberal atmosphere, Vygotskii resembled most other Soviet psychologists in his paradoxical combination of insistence that social psychology be the center of the discipline and his evasion of serious work at that center. Even this extraordinarily venturesome thinker tended to stand clear of an area charged with ideological and political passion, while solemnly calling on Soviet psychologists to make it their focus.

Vygotskii dreamed of a psychological analogue to the "biogenetic law," that ontogeny recapitulates phylogeny.[63] He supposed that the individual mental development of the child recapitulates the mental development of humanity, with primitive and peasant adults somewhere on the evolutionary ladder between completely childlike and completely civilized. In their actual work as psychologists, he and his school got stuck in parts of ontogeny. The cognitive development of children and cognitive disruption in braindamaged people became, in the 1930s, the major area of their research and their main claim to world renown in the decades following the master's untimely death in 1934.[64] That prudently lopsided development of the school can be discerned already in the 1920s, if only in embryo. Vygotskii first became involved with problems of child development as early as the Civil War, while he was teaching at a pedagogical institute in a small Belorussian town. The practical emphasis of his earliest writing on the subject was never lost, even when it was nominally subordinated to the grand theorizing that preoccupied him after moving to Moscow. The link to teacher training would keep his school alive during the years of high Stalinist insistence on practicality, when the whole discipline of psychology was threatened with destruction. On the other hand, the link of child development studies to a general "historico-cultural" psychology never got very far beyond general pronouncements, not even in the 1920s.

At Kornilov's Institute there were colleagues working on comparative or animal or zoo-psychology (it was called all three names and not yet ethology). They were supposed to work out the levels of development below "historico-cultural" psychology, and they had a tendency to stay down there, avoiding upward comparisons with human behavior. In the 1930s Stalinists would denounce them for reducing human psychology to bestial patterns, but the denunciation was quite unmerited. If anything, they deserved praise for cautioning Pavlov and Bekhterev against simplistic reduction of human psychology to supposedly universal patterns of conditioned reflexes. They argued for emergent levels of increasingly complex behavior, with fullfledged consciousness emerging at the human level, and they tended to restrict their investigations to worms, fish, and apes, stopping short of serious inquiry into continuities and discontinuities with the human level.[65] The little book that Vygotskii and Luria offered in 1930, as a first effort at such inquiry, ran into a stone wall of ideological disapproval.

One major feature of Vygotskian studies in child development has been entirely overlooked by admirers and commentators, whether Soviet or Western, since it is common to the whole field. Within the race of Cyclops the single eye goes unnoticed. That feature is the concentration on problem solving, the virtual neglect of expressive understanding. Consider, for example, the report by Vygotskii and Luria, of a conversation between a five-year-old boy and his mother. She called his attention to the planet Jupiter. He wanted to know "For what (*zachem*) is Jupiter?" and refused to be turned away to naturalistic disregard of the question. His mother finally turned his question back upon him – "And you and I, for what are we?" – to which the child instantly replied: "For ourselves." When the mother surrendered – "Well, then, Jupiter also is for itself" – the boy was pleased and started a list: "And ants, and bedbugs, and mosquitoes, and nettles – are they also for themselves?" As his mother wearily agreed, he laughed with joy. William Blake might have turned that into a poem, but Vygotskii and Luria repressed any joy with their Gradgrind analysis: "In this conversation the child's primitive teleologism is quite characteristic. Jupiter must obligatorily exist for something. Precisely this 'for what' (*zachem*) most often replaces, for the child, the more complex 'by what rule' (*pochemu*)."*[66] And the two scientists pointed a warning finger at adults who continue such childlike thinking when they should have the scientific and practical turn of mind.

It is hard to believe that was written by the same scholar who began his investigation of the mind with sensitive analyses of imaginative literature, and had some familiarity with the philosophical tradition that pondered the difference between the thing in itself and the thing for itself.

---

* *Pochemu* parallels *zachem* in linquistic construction: literally "in accordance with what," contrasted to "for what." Both are usually translated into English as "why."

The further away from aesthetic studies, the deeper he went into psychology – even the part of the science that studies "consciousness" – the more Vygotskii tended to repress his original concern with expressive thought, to ignore the effort to understand humanly as well as explain scientifically.[67]

I am tempted to picture Vygotskii, like the best literary artists, as a person in search of the essential self, but one turned increasingly away from the search by his determination to find the self in psychological science. Some future biographer, with full access to his papers, will perhaps discover how close to the man's inward life this guess may be. For present purposes the important issue is the collective mentality that he was assimilating, the functionalist ethos of professional psychologists in the twentieth century. In their congregation the component elements of personality are explained by the functions they serve, the whole is the sum of those functions, efficiency is the measure of the integrating function, and any questions about an essential person are turned aside as relics of a bygone metaphysical inquiry into the spirit or soul.

All the subjects of my history were self-assertive individuals. Whether scientific psychologists or imaginative writers, neurophysiologists or political leaders, all sought to put themselves forward, to call attention to themselves, if only by publishing their individual names at the head of impersonal scientific studies. The anonymous labor of the toiling masses was not sufficient to express their sense of self. Yet each of these assertive types had a sharply different manner of self-expression.

The scientists put their names over works that claimed to exclude the subjective individual. Their proud assertion of authorship laid claim to impersonal knowledge of human beings as a natural species, not as subjective persons. Godlike arrogance inheres in such a claim. You may fancy yourself to be a person, the conscious center of your intentional life, but scientists know you to be an ephemeral specimen of replicating nervous systems and a replaceable part of an impersonal social system. There is an unwitting affinity here with the political leaders' claim to know the interests and the passions of the toiling masses better than subjective individuals within those masses know what they need and feel.

Both the scientific and the political claims seem to contrast sharply with the apparent humility of imaginative writers, who express the tormented or comic search for a self worth telling about. But the writers' overweening humility may contain an implicit challenge to godlike claims. Everyone can see that imaginative writers touch nerves of feeling and understanding that political leaders claim mastery of and scientific psychologists claim impersonal knowledge of. Writers and readers communing thus with each other implicitly push pretentious statesmen and scientists aside, toward irrelevance, maybe absurdity. Even if the whole business of that literary communion is imaginary, Soviet political leaders have taken far more interest, often alarmed or worried interest, in the apparently humble works of imaginative writers than in the apparently arrogant claims of psychological scientists.

I am groping for the reason why the boldest psychologists in the most liberal periods of Russian history – pre- as well as postrevolutionary – have been quite tame politically, have provoked only a little ideological controversy compared to the most creative imaginative writers. If one may indulge in antique language, the writers challenge politicians to struggle for our souls, while scientific psychologists turn away, striving to extricate themselves from any entanglement with the soul, the essence of a human being. The determined phenomenalism of modern science helps to win it acceptance – or toleration, or indifference – while the essentialism of imaginative writers keeps many people intensely interested, sometimes in awe, sometimes in anger.

Perhaps the oddest feature of these modern ways to knowledge of ourselves is the reverential credence widely given to neurophysiologists with sweeping claims. Pavlov and Bekhterev and Ukhtomskii were not content to work out neural circuitry, but made vaulting extrapolations to mental and social functioning. Yet Bolshevik ideologists were largely deferential, quite gingerly in criticism. Indeed Pavlov was canonized, elevated above criticism along with Marx, whose claim to scientific knowledge Pavlov ridiculed. But that absurd chapter in modern intellectual history belongs elsewhere, perhaps with the assimilation of behaviorism in the culture of God-fearing America.

NOTES

1 S. Rubinstein, *Absoluter Rationalismus (Hegel)* (Marburg, 1914). I wish to thank Mitchell Ash for getting me a copy. The title page promised a second half, on "Absolute and Dualist Rationalism and Transcendental Philosophy," but it never appeared.

2 S. L. Rubinshtein, "Problemy psikhologii v trudakh Karla Marksa," *Sovetskaia psikhotekhnika* 7 (1934), No. 1: 3–20. His most notable contribution was *Osnovy psikhologii* (Moscow, 1935), and *Osnovy obshchei psikhologii* (Moscow, 1940), which was awarded a Stalin Prize. For more information, see T. R. Payne, *S. L. Rubinštejn and the Philosophical Foundations of Soviet Psychology* (Dordrecht, 1968).

3 Rubinshtein, *Bytie i soznanie* (Moscow, 1957); and *Printsipy i puti razvitiia psikhologii* (Moscow, 1959).

4 L. S. Vygotskii, "Psikhologicheskaia nauka," in *Obshchestvennye nauki SSSR* (Moscow, 1928), 25, 44. See also Vygotskii, *Sobranie sochinenii* (Moscow, 1982), vol. 1, 374. He was referring to Brentano's declaration in the Preface to his *Psychologie vom empirischen Standpunkt* (Leipzig, 1874), vi: "We must strive to achieve here [in psychology] what mathematics, physics, chemistry and physiology have already accomplished, some earlier, others later: a nucleus of generally recognized truth to which, through the combined efforts of many forces, new crys-

tals will adhere on all sides. In place of *psychologies* we must seek to create *a psychology.*"

5 *The Psychology of Art* was withheld for 40 years, *The Historical Meaning of the Psychological Crisis* for 55. See below. For some of the evidence that his admirers wanted to publish the *Crisis* book much earlier, but were restrained by the censor (or by their fear of trouble with the censor), see V. N. Kolbanovskii, "Lev Semenovich Vygotskii," *Sovetskaia psikhotekhnika* 7 (1934), No. 4, especially 389–393, where the book is summarized, and 394, for the express hope that it would be published. Kolbanovskii was director of the major Institute of Psychology at the time.

6 For Luria's defiant indifference, see his autobiography, *The Making of Mind* (Cambridge, MA: Harvard University Press, 1979), 18: "My family was typical of what in Russia is called 'the intelligentsia.' We considered ourselves progressive and had no religious traditions." Cf. 198ff., for the editor, Michael Cole, unpacking the meaning of that remark.

7 K. Levitin, *One Is Not Born a Personality: Profiles of Soviet Education Psychologists* (Moscow, 1982), 24ff. I thank Alex Kozulin for telling me of this book.

8 See, e.g., the vague passage in Kolbanovskii "Lev Semenovich Vygotskii," 388. Luria was even less informative: *Sovetskaia nevropatologiia, psikhiatriia i psikhogigiena* 4 (1935), No. 1: 165–169. Cf. A. N. Leont'ev, "O tvorcheskom puti L. S. Vygotskogo," in Vygotskii, *Sobranie,* I, and the joint article by Leont'ev and Luria in Vygotskii, *Izbrannye psikhologicheskie issledovaniia* (Moscow, 1956), 4–36. For further references to Soviet writing on Vygotskii, see A. V. Petrovskii, *Istoriia sovetskoi psikhologii* (Moscow, 1967); A. A. Smirnov, *Razvitie i sovremennoe sostoianie psikhologicheskoi nauki v SSSR* (Moscow, 1975).

9 *Letopis'* and *Novyi put'.*

10 Vygotskii, *Psikhologiia iskusstva* (Moscow, 1965), and 2nd ed. (1968). The English translation, *The Psychology of Art* (Cambridge, MA: Harvard University Press, 1971), seems to be from the first edition.

11 Ibid., ix–x.

12 See studies of Vygotskii cited in preceding notes. Cf. the conference devoted to his thought: *Nauchnoe tvorchestvo L. S. Vygotskogo i sovremennaia psikhologiia* (Moscow, 1981), at which 3 of the 57 papers dealt with his views on art.

13 Vygotskii, *Psikhologiia iskusstva.*

14 See references to Marx in the Index, ibid.

15 See V. Erlich, *Russian Formalism,* 2nd ed. (The Hague, 1980).

16 In 1932 Stalin gave artists the job classification, "engineers of human souls." See his *Sochineniia,* vol. 13 (Moscow, 1951), 410, and explanation by A. A. Zhdanov, in the keynote address to the First Congress of Soviet Writers in 1934.

17 See, most notably, M. Cole, et al., "Introduction" and "Afterword," in Vygotskii, *Mind in Society* (Cambridge, MA: Harvard University Press, 1978); J. Wertsch (ed.), *Culture, Communication, and Cognition: Vygotskian Perspectives* (Cambridge, MA: Harvard University Press, 1984); and Jerome Bruner's introduction to the Vygotskii memorial issue of *Soviet Psychology,* 1967, No. 3. An illuminating cross-cultural review of Vygotskii is provided by A. Kozulin, *Psychology in Utopia* (Cambridge, MA: Harvard University Press, 1984).

18 Vygotskii, *Psychology of Art,* 246.

19 Ibid., 246–248. It must be noted that Sherrington did *not* have a reductive view of art.

20 The most detailed account is G. Daian, "Vtoroi psikhonevrologicheskii s'ezd," *Krasnaia nov'* 4 (1924), Nos. 2, 3.

21 From various accounts I infer that he spoke extemporaneously, at two sessions. At any rate, two of his articles appear to be subsequent written versions of what he said. See Vygotskii, "Soznanie kak problema psikhologii povedeniia," in *Psikhologiia i marksizm* (Moscow, 1925), and "Metodika refleksologicheskogo i psikhologicheskogo issledovaniia," in *Problemy sovremennoi psikhologii* (Moscow, 1926).

22 Daian, "Vtori psikhonevrologicheskii s'ezd," *Krasnaia nov'* 4 (1924), No. 2: 164–166.

23 See the writings of A. N. Leont'ev and A. R. Luria, cited above, and especially the chapter on Vygotskii in Luria's *The Making of Mind.*

24 See the *Uchenye zapiski* of the Institute. The first two volumes are cited in note 21. Volume 3 was also called *Problemy sovremennoi psikhologii* (Moscow, 1928). For an index of the Institute's publications, see Akademiia pedagogicheskikh nauk SSSR, Institut psikhologii, *Ukazatel' literatury vypushchennoi institutom psikhologii za 50 let* (Moscow, 1967).

25 The full evidence for this generalization is presented elsewhere in the book from which this article is drawn.

26 Bukharin, "Enchmeniada," *Krasnaia nov'* 3 (1923), No. 6.

27 Zinoviev, "Intelligentsia i revoliutsiia," *Pravda,* 25 November 1923, 27. Trotsky, "K pervomu s'ezdu nauchnykh rabotnikov," *Pravda,* 1924, No. 24.

28 Bukharin, "O mirovoi revoliutsii, nashei strane, kul'ture i prochem (otvet prof. I. Pavlovu)," *Krasnaia nov'* 4 (1924), Nos. 1, 2. Also published as a pamphlet, and included in Bukharin, *Ataka* (Moscow, 1924).

29 Ibid., No. 1.

30 Ibid., in a somewhat different version. The actual words quoted here are from Bukharin, *Historical Materialism* (Ann Arbor, Mich., 1969), 98.

31 Vygotskii, "Soznanie . . .," as cited in note 21.

32 Ibid., 179 et passim.

33 Ibid., 190.

34 Ibid., 179.

35 Ibid. For Vygotskii's views on Gestalt psychology see his "Strukturnaia psikhologiia," in *Osnovnye techeniia sovremennoi psikhologii* (Moscow, 1930), 178–205. Cf. E. Scheerer, "Gestalt Psychology in the Soviet Union I: The Period of Enthusiasm," *Psychological Research* 41 (1980): 113–132.

36 See, e.g., historical surveys cited in note 8. The pioneering study by R. Bauer, *The New Man in Soviet Psychology* (Cambridge, MA: Harvard University Press, 1952), offered a variant of that theme. See M. Thielen, *Sowjetische Psychologie und Marxismus; Geschichte und Kritik* (Frankfurt am Main, 1984), 87, for his agreeing with that theme, and disagreeing with J. McLeish, *Soviet Psychology: History, Theory, Content* (London, 1975).

37 Since Kornilov was the Director, I assume that he invited Vygotskii, as A. N. Leont'ev implies, in Vygotskii, *Sobranie,* vol. 1, 13. Luria implies that Kornilov opposed Vygotskii's outlook, and that he, Luria, was responsible for bringing

Vygotskii to Moscow. See *The Making of Mind,* 38–39. But Luria is too vague to be convincing, and is inaccurate in his picture of Kornilov.

38 See *Pravda,* 29 June 1924. Kornilov chose to interpret Bukharin that way. See *Problemy sovremennoi psikhologii,* vol. 3 (Moscow, 1928), 15–17.

39 See, e.g., the article reviewing the first decade of Soviet psychology, cited in note 4, 32, 45.

40 Vygotskii, *Sobranie,* vol. 1 (Moscow, 1982), 330–339. Luria read this work, *The Historical Meaning of the Psychological Crisis,* in manuscript, and cited it in admiration, both in the 1920s and in a 1935 commemoration of Vygotskii.

41 Vygotskii, ibid., 361–363, 422–423, 432. To be sure, the criticism is imbedded in praise – extravagant praise, in my reading – but Vygotskii does lump Kornilov with "eclectics," and explicitly disapproves of Kornilov's calling his psychology Marxist or dialectical materialist.

42 See references to Marx and Spinoza in Vygotskii, ibid., conveniently indexed.

43 The editors declare, ibid., 7, that they are "publishing the text of the original without alterations." I am willing to bet that they have omitted Vygotskii's quotations from presently proscribed authors, such as Trotsky, Bukharin, and Kautsky. (See below, note 46.) But they have published his presently proscribed arguments – against the notion of a Marxist psychology, most notably – with critical notes to such passages, warning the reader against heresy. See especially 472.

44 Vygotskii frequently repeated this fundamental distinction in works published during his lifetime. See, e.g., the opening passage of "Geneticheskie korni myshleniia i rechi," *Estestvoznanie i marksizm* 1 (1929), No. 16: 106–108, where he adds other synonyms to each side of the contrast; e.g., "phenomenological" alongside "understanding." The posthumous republication of that article in his best-known book, *Myshlenie i rech'* (Moscow, 1934) – 2nd ed. in his *Izbrannye* (Moscow, 1956) – silently omitted the crucial opening pages, and the omission is carried into the English translation, *Thought and Language* (Cambridge, MA: Harvard University Press, 1962), Chapter 4, and into his *Sobranie,* vol. 2. See ibid., 480–481, for the editors' implying that Vygotskii himself altered the text.

45 Spinoza, *Ethics,* Part III, Postulate 2, Scholion, translated by R. H. M. Elwes, as quoted in Vygotskii, *The Psychology of Art,* 1.

46 Compare Vygotskii, *Sobranie,* vol. 1, 436 – taking care to note the ellipsis points just before the final paragraph – with the close of Vygotskii's "Psikhologicheskaia nauka," cited in note 4, 45, where the quotes from Kautsky and Trotsky are highlighted. For the original of the quote from Trotsky see his *Sochineniia,* vol. 21 (Moscow, 1927), 110–111. For Kautsky's forecast of a superman, see David Joravsky, *The Lysenko Affair* (Cambridge, MA: Harvard University Press, 1970), 256.

47 Vygotskii, *Sobranie,* vol. 1, 436. His reference is to theorem 17 of Spinoza's *Ethics.* Cf. the closing paragraph of "Psikhologicheskaia nauka," cited in note 4.

48 For Vygotskii's sensitivity to modernist absurdity, see again his analysis of *Hamlet.* Cf. his review of Andrei Belyi's *Petersburg,* in *Letopis',* 1916, No. 12, 327–328.

49 The editors of Vygotskii, *Sobranie,* vol. 1, 449, observe that Bühler's *Die Krise der Psychologie* appeared "a year after Vygotskii completed the manuscript" of his book with a similar title. Whether he saw the preliminary article by Bühler in *Kantstudien,* 1926, is not clear. He did repeatedly cite the famous declaration that closes James's *Psychology,* on the hope of a science rather than the science itself.

50 Of course Vygotskii was also critical, markedly so after Stalinist attacks on "bourgeois" psychologies. See, e.g., his introduction to Bühler's *Mental Development of the Child,* reprinted in Vygotskii, *Sobranie,* vol. 1, 196–209.

51 The main texts are Lenin's *Materialism and Empiriocriticism* (1908) and his 1922 essay, "On the Significance of Militant Materialism." For an historical analysis, which explains why Lenin's talk of a crisis had little impact on Soviet science before the thirties, see David Joravsky, *Soviet Marxism and Natural Science, 1917–1932* (N.Y., 1961), Chapter 2 et passim.

52 K. N. Kornilov, *Uchebnik psikhologii, izlozhennoi s tochki zreniia dialekticheskogo materializma* (Leningrad, 1926); 2nd and 3rd eds., 1928.

53 Vygotskii, *Sobranie,* vol. 1, 434–435.

54 See Joravsky, *Soviet Marxism.*

55 Vygotskii, *Sobranie,* vol. 1, 436.

56 For a plain statement of that policy, see Stalin, *Sochineniia* (Moscow, 1950), vol. 5, 223–225.

57 Vygotskii, "Psikhologicheskaia nauka" (note 4), 40.

58 See especially Vygotskii, as cited in note 21. Those articles are conveniently republished in his *Sobranie,* vol. 1. For Vygotskii on Pavlov's achievement, see references to Pavlov in the index, ibid.

59 See, e.g., ibid., 388 et passim.

60 Vygotskii and Luria, *Etiudy po istorii povedeniia; obez'ian, primitiv, rebenok* (Moscow, 1930).

61 See *Psikhologiia,* 5(1931), No.1:3, and P. Razmyslov, "O'kul'turnoistoricheskoi teorii psikhologii' Vygotskogo i Luriia," *Kniga i proletarskaia revoliutsiia* 3 (1934), No. 4: 78–86.

62 These are dealt with in another chapter of the book from which this article is drawn. For the sudden attack on Piaget, see his introduction to Piaget, *Rech'i myshlenie rebenka* (Moscow, 1932), 3–54. Compare the previous admiration and very limited criticism, e.g., in *Etiudy po istorii povedeniia* and in "Geneticheskie korni myshleniia," cited in note 44.

63 Vygotskii, "Biogeneticheskii zakon," *Bol'shaia sovestskaia entsiklopediia,* 1st ed., vol. 6 (Moscow, 1927), 275–279. And see *Etiudy po istorii povedeniia.*

64 Dealt with elsewhere in the book in progress. For his earliest Western renown, see E. Hanfmann and J. Kasanin, "A Method for the Study of Concept Formation," *Journal of Psychology* 3 (1937): 521–540.

65 See especially the works of V. M. Borovskii, beginning with his "K voprosu ob instinkte v nauke o povedenii," in *Psikhologiia i marksizm* (Moscow, 1925), 161–174. A partial list of his works is in the index cited in note 24.

66 *Etiudy po istorii povedeniia,* 140–141.

67 For an intermediate stage, see Vygotskii, *Voobrazhenie i tvorchestvo v detskom vozraste* (Moscow, 1930), republished in 1967. For a rare criticism of Vygotskii – and Piaget – for failing to understand "what is specifically artistic," see S. L. Rubinshtein, *Problemy obshchei psikhologii* (Moscow, 1973), 125.

9

THE SOCIAL HISTORY OF CHINESE PSYCHOLOGY*

MATTHIAS PETZOLD

The Chinese case could be seen as proof of the special sensitivity of psychology to political and ideological influences. The fact is, however, that modern Chinese psychology is influenced by at least the following main sources: its own tradition arising from an old civilization and culture; modern Western thought, which included but is by no means limited to Soviet Marxism, and the present political structure. A thorough analysis of these influences should include political and historical research and future studies should be done cooperatively with Chinese historians of science. However, a more objective view from abroad can also be useful.

For an analysis of Chinese psychology one has to take up the threads of psychological thought in Old China. Against this background, the recent history of Chinese psychology will be outlined. The institutional history of psychology in China has been described in detail elsewhere,[1] and I will concentrate instead on the political impact of modernization as well as Maoist Socialism on Chinese psychology. This analysis yields four stages in the development of psychology as an independent academic discipline in China and places this development in both ideological and political context. Some comparisons with Western and Soviet psychology are attempted in the conclusion.

WESTERN AND CHINESE PSYCHOLOGY

China is the most populous nation and one of the oldest cultures in the world. It has had a highly diversified agricultural economy, a hierarchi-

* I would like to thank Professors Liu Fan and Jing Qicheng for helpful comments and important discussions on some crucial points of this paper. I am also grateful to Helen Petzold, Mitchell Ash, and Christiane Hartnack for critical remarks and corrections of stylistic and idiomatic mistakes.

cally organized state administration, and a rich and varied literature and philosophy since ancient times. Because of its indigenous philosophy and its many contributions to the sciences, European interest in Chinese culture was already strong in the sixteenth and seventeenth century, when European science was still making its breakthrough to modern thinking and scientific research. One of these European philosophers, Gottfried Wilhelm Leibnitz, introduced much of this Chinese thinking to the Occidental world and noted that Chinese science was already highly developed at that time.[2] But only after Joseph Needham again pointed out that the Chinese have contributed so much to science was it finally generally recognized, for example, that it was not a German monk but the Chinese who had invented gunpowder, albeit for amusement. Other examples worth mentioning are the magnetic compass and the letterpress, both of which were invented far earlier in China than in Europe.[3]

However, the course of the development of the sciences in China was not continuous. At the time of the rise of modern science in Europe, a period of stagnation had begun in China that is only being overcome in recent decades. A detailed discussion of the reasons for this stagnation is still going on among Sinologists, but it is a matter of fact that within the old system of Chinese science and philosophy a special discipline of psychology had not evolved.[4] Therefore, one cannot speak of a traditional Chinese psychology, because only some aspects within traditional Chinese empirical science and philosophy – according to the Western present standpoint – could be seen as psychological thinking.

Modern Western psychology has hardly ever made reference to Chinese psychology although public interest has increased suddenly in the course of recent political developments. Even though many Chinese students – among them psychologists – have studied in different parts of the Occidental world since the turn of the last century, Western psychologists have paid no attention to the work these scholars have done after returning home. It was only during the cold war that U.S. interest in what was going on behind the Iron Curtain increased, and against this background the first Western book on the work of Chinese psychologists was published.[5] With the exception of some minor articles, Chin and Chin's book was the only source to throw some light on the turmoil in psychology during the Chinese "Cultural Revolution." After the end of this campaign China itself became instrumental in making new contacts in the Western world, and Western visitors traveled to China, a number of psychologists among them.[6] In China, however, psychology was not considered one of the socially or scientifically relevant disciplines, and it was not until 1978 that Chinese psychologists resumed work in this field. Since then many new contacts to the West have been made and new reports, books, and analyses have been produced by Western observers.[7]

ANCIENT CHINA AND THE SCIENCE OF PSYCHOLOGY

Chinese psychologists themselves have not been very much concerned with discussions of traditional Chinese philosophy. Only in recent years have suggestions been made to use the treasury of ancient Chinese philosophy for the development of an indigenous modern Chinese theory of psychology.[8] This discussion is only beginning and I will not be able to refer to it in more detail, but I will analyze the main roots from an outside point of view.

The general problem area of interest is the concept of humanity and the notion of human development as it was outlined by the famous scholars Confucius, Lao Tse, and their followers. This conception in ancient and modern China has been analyzed by the Sinologist Donald Munro, who has also discussed the implications still relevant to China's modern society.[9] Taking into account his analyses as well as others, one might make the following points.

Pragmatic rationalism

The Chinese have retained their old, very specifically integrated view of knowledge and action. Whereas modern Occidental philosophy strictly separates the categories of *knowing* and *acting* as having no necessary logical relation to one another, since the time of the Enlightenment such a distinction has never been made in China. Of course, there is no absolute identification of these categories in traditional Chinese philosophy (e.g. Confucianism), but if the relation of acting and knowing is treated, it is considered from a pragmatic point of view insofar as acting is given first rank, and philosophical considerations that are not of use in practice are not followed up. This explains why the Chinese do not possess sophisticated philosophical and psychological systems to explain the "soul." This also has some effect on the absence of a category of the unconscious and of the distinction between consciousness and unconsciousness. Therefore, Chinese society has to be regarded as based on a pragmatic rationalism; Max Weber considered the traditional Confucian system even stronger in its pragmatic rationalism than Anglo-Saxon Protestantism.[10]

The Confucian notion of educability

Confucianism, one of the most influential schools of Chinese thought, has itself undergone development and cannot be thought of as a closed dogmatic system. It contains, rather, many contradictions in itself. Within Confucian philosophy the assumption of *innate traits* has often been contrasted with the view of an unlimited possibility of shaping and manipulating individuals. Confucianism on the one hand states that humans are formed by their innate traits and on the other hand sees far-reaching possibilities for educational adaptation. In Confucius' view people can be described in three categories. The upper class of the "wise" and the lower class of the "foolish" are both determined by their innate qualities. The broad middle class, however, can be promoted by education. This aspect has been called "the malleability of man," and it is a plausible assumption that the educational optimism in Mao-Zedong-Thought has been influenced by this aspect of Confucianism.[11] It could also be seen as one of the reasons for the great interest in cognitive processes in Chinese psychology.[12]

Dialectical philosophy

The philosophical principle of *dialectics* was already developed in ancient Greek philosophy, but is also a principle in traditional Chinese philosophy. In China, however, dialectics were not abandoned, as was the case in modern Western thought where linear causal-logical explanations have triumphed in public as well as scientific thinking. Dialectics already prevailed in the ancient natural philosophy of the five elements (earth, water, fire, air, and heaven) which emphasized the mutual interrelationship of these five sources of life. Another old and still known concept is the Chinese Yin-Yang principle. The Yin has been described as negative, cold, dark, and female whereas the Yang has been seen as positive, light, warm, and male. In general, Yin and Yang hold a balance in nature, enabling illness to be diagnosed as a preponderance of one element and treated by strengthening the other. The theory of the five elements and the Yin-Yang principle could be and were applied to psychical illnesses as well.[13] However, these dialectical principles have been discussed only with regard to traditional Chinese philosophy and traditional medicine. Although some of the many fashionable forms of psychotherapy in the West refer to such old Indian and Chinese techniques, a thorough analysis of the useful implications of ancient Chinese as well as Indian philosophy for modern psychology still remains to be carried out.[14]

Transfer of Western categories into China

The fundamental category of the *individual,* which has been of primary importance for modern Western society and its conception of human rights and the uniqueness of personality, is a specific product of the European Enlightenment and was not developed in traditional China. Only recently has it been introduced into modern China.[15] In this respect, China has a totally different social historical background. The question remains open whether a capitalist system did not develop in China because the concept of the independent individual had not been established, or whether one should assume that the concept of independent individuals could not develop in China because of the absence of a capitalist economy. In developed Western societies, this conception laid the foundations for an enhanced individualism and egoism that stress competition between individuals. Western psychology was only developed as a science against the background of this Western individualism, and became socially relevant in the form of psychotherapy as more and more individuals failed to master the fierceness of competition on their own. Contrarily, the Chinese emphasize that individuals belong to groups (clans and families in old China, families and working units in the socialist system), and for thousands of years altruistic behavior was a matter of course within these groups.

The different approach to psychology is also apparent in terminology. Whereas Descartes and other European philosophers assumed that the soul must be a part of the brain, it is a fundamental Chinese assumption that the seat of the soul is in the heart. Up to the nineteenth century the Chinese did not have a term for psychology, but only translated it after having come into contact with the modern industrial world. This is the reason why the Western term psychology has been translated as Xinli Xue (Xin = heart; li = rule, law; Xue = science, study of), as science of the laws of the heart.

THE INTRODUCTION OF WESTERN SCIENTIFIC PSYCHOLOGY IN CHINA

The discipline of psychology was only established in China after the introduction of modern Western thought and science there at the end of the last century. Although the Japanese Empire strengthened contacts with the newly industrialized nations as early as the beginning of the nineteenth century, the Chinese Qing dynasty, the last of the imperial dynasties, generally refrained from establishing contacts with the West and withstood ideological influences from colonial powers. However, Chinese students who had studied in the West brought back the ideas fundamental to psychology and began translating Western books. The first translation of a Western psychology book was Joseph Haven's *Mental Philosophy* (1857), which was translated in 1889 from a Japanese version by Yan Yongjing.[16] The most important of the many translations that followed was the translation in 1907 of Harald Höffding's *Psychologie in Umrissen auf der Grundlage der Erfahrung (Outline of Psychology on the Basis of Experience)*.[17]

At the turn of the century a strong republican movement arose in China based on modern ideas of democratization and public education.

After the fall of the Qing dynasty in 1911, this new movement fought to reform the country under the slogan "science and democracy." This movement was led by Chinese intellectuals who had studied in Europe or the United States and introduced many modern Western ideas on their return to China. These intellectuals invited Western democratic scholars such as Bertrand Russell and John Dewey to come to China.[18] In the public debate following the May Fourth Movement in 1918, scientific psychology was even seen as a means of democratizing and modernizing the country. One of the leaders of this democratic political movement, the educational reformer Cai Yuanpei, had studied at Wundt's laboratory in Leipzig and promoted the opening of the first psychological laboratory in China at Beijing University in 1917. Though Cai Yuanpei studied in Europe, most of the leading psychologists who followed him qualified at American universities, mainly at the University of Chicago and Columbia University.

Cai Yuanpei was later minister of education, and the reform of the educational system was considered the keystone for the reform of society. Although the old society only had schools for the education of royal administrators, a new education system for the broad masses was now set up. In this context there was a need for new insights into basic processes of education, and psychology was given primary importance both in the introduction of a large number of tests for selecting and evaluating pupils and in investigations of basic cognitive processes in children.[19] The educational reformers oriented themselves by referring to the latest Western research. In psychology this meant American functionalism and behaviorism from Chicago and Columbia, where many Chinese psychologists had studied. In comparison with Confucian thought, which had prevailed up to that time, the introduction of Behaviorism and Functionalism led to a more mechanistic and deterministic conception and stressed interindividual differences in cognitive processes. The most radical behaviorist position was even developed by a Chinese, Zing-yang Kuo, whose assumption that even instincts should be considered as results of learning processes was not shared by many of his Chinese colleagues. His later emigration to the United States, however, was caused by his general opposition to Chinese Socialism.[20]

The institutionalization of psychology began with the first independent department at Nanjing University in 1920. Universities in other major cities soon followed. The Psychological Society was founded as early as 1921 in Shanghai, and a research institute for psychology was opened in the Chinese Academy of Sciences (Academia Sinica) in Beijing in 1928.[21] In this first stage, however, Chinese psychology was at best a mere copy of Western psychology. To put it in the words of the most prominent Chinese psychologist, "it should be said that psychological work during this period was still imitative in nature."[22]

Chinese psychological research and teaching was, however, called to a halt after only two decades by the Japanese invasion in 1937, and universities and research institutes were closed. Many psychologists either went abroad or joined the National Front, a broad political coalition that supported the Communist resistance against the Japanese occupation. The leading psychologists Pan Shu and Chen Li, for example, took part in founding the Anti-Japanese Jiu-San-Society, a member organization of the National Front.[23]

FOUNDATION OF THE DISCIPLINE IN THE PEOPLE'S REPUBLIC

A second stage in the development of the discipline of psychology in China was made possible by the founding of the People's Republic, although the strong orientation toward the Soviet Union in the Republic's first decade hindered this development. Chinese intellectuals were not only attracted by Marxism because it was a radical kind of Western philosophy, but also because it was the ideology of an underdeveloped Asian country, the Soviet Union, which had gone through a radical social and educational reform that some Chinese intellectuals thought to be paradigmatic for China as well. For this reason, a few Chinese psychologists had already started to read Marxist literature in the 1920s.[24] However, most Western-educated Chinese psychologists did not know much about Marxism or Russian psychology.

During the first years of the People's Republic, psychology was not regarded as an important discipline in public debate. An educational scientist even wrote in an educational journal that psychology was useless; instead, psychologists ought to study Marxism and Leninism. This statement was representative of the dominant viewpoint at that time. However, many psychologists did not follow such a rigorous prescription; they suggested that psychology should be changed a little in content, orientation, or in theoretical points, but should still be considered as a branch of science. Traditionally, Chinese psychologists had been oriented toward the United States, England, and Germany, but now the general orientation was shifted toward the Soviet Union; therefore, psychologists learned Russian and began to read Russian psychology texts. In 1952–1953 He Baoyuan, a psychologist, and He Wanfu, a translator, as well as Zhao Biru translated Teplov's and Smirnov's textbooks. The Soviet Union also sent "experts" to help in and control the reconstruction of the country. The first one, A. Pushkin, came in 1953. However, he was not a psychologist but an educationalist. Pushkin taught in Beijing Normal University and asked teachers, lecturers, and professors to take his course. Following him were Petrushevski, Petrovski, and another child psychologist. They all came through the Ministry of Education and were engaged in teaching only.[25] In research at the Academia Sinica, however, there was no Russian expert for psychology, only visitors from other socialist countries who came for short visits, for example, the noted Gestalt psychologist Kurt Gottschaldt from East Germany in 1956.

In spite of this general orientation toward the Soviet Union, Chinese scientists fought for their own views, and psychologists succeeded in refounding their own Psychological Society, reopening the research Institute of Psychology at the Academia Sinica in 1956, even though their research colleagues in the Soviet Union did not enjoy an independent status as psychologists at that time.[26] However, research was generally forced to keep within the lines of reductionist Pavlovianism, and Chinese psychologists did not approach social problems. Instead, Chinese psychologists relied on the highly academic program formulated for the Twelve-Year Plan in 1958. Psychology was seen as a basic science and given five main areas of inquiry: "(1) origin and development of the mind; (2) basic stages of the mind; (3) psychology of individuality; (4) basic theories and history of psychology; and (5) special branches in education, medicine, art and literature, and physical culture."[27]

However, this platform became the target of the so called "Criticism Movement" in 1958. This was part of a "Campaign against Rightists" that followed the short period of liberalization known by Mao Zedong's saying that "hundred flowers should flourish and hundred schools of thought should contend." The "Criticism Movement" was directed against a so-called biologistic and physiologistic trend, which was seen as characteristic of the "bourgeois class character" and "bourgeois academism" of psychology. After the failure of the Great Leap Forward in 1959, more realism entered into Chinese politics and the harsh criticisms were stopped. However, vehement discussions on the nature of Marxist psychology in 1959 yielded three standpoints:

1. Some psychologists defined *psychology as a natural science* which could therefore not have any "class character," but should not touch on social problems and keep to pure experimental research.[28]
2. Social-science oriented researchers, especially teachers and students from pedagogical universities and colleges, referring to Marx's Feuerbach thesis that man is a "species-being," made the point that human beings are by nature social beings. Thus, psychology should be seen as a *social science based on Marxism.*[29]
3. The leading psychologists Pan Shu and Cao Richang formulated an integrative position, claiming that man is both a natural and a social being and that *psychology should dialectically combine social and natural science methods.* This third position has been officially recognized as the right one, and is maintained again today.[30]

The "Criticism Movement" did not succeed in destroying psychology as an academic discipline, but it forced Chinese psychologists to build a more solid theoretical basis for their discipline in accordance with the special form of Chinese Mao-Marxism. The main pillars of this theoretical framework, which is shared by most Chinese psychologists to this day, can be summarized in five points.[31]

1. *Marxist materialistic monism* is based on the principle of the identity of mind and matter. It thus rejects any kind of dualism as posited not only in Confucian thought, but also in most of the European psychological schools of thought at that time. This monism, however, corresponds to American behaviorism as well as Soviet Pavlovianism.
2. The *theory of reflection,* as elaborated by Lenin, considers human thought to be nothing more than a mirror of the outer world. This concept was also adopted in Chinese psychology. On the one hand, it promoted a reductionist viewpoint of the kind held by Russian Pavlovians, and on the other it stressed the role of ecological factors in psychic processes.
3. The Marxist principle that *humanity is a social being* was also upheld in Chinese Marxism, and some Chinese political cadres laid great emphasis on this aspect so as to counter the deeply rooted Confucian conviction of innate traits.
   Apart from these three basic elements drawn from classical Marxist theory, two further points were elaborated by Mao Zedong within the Marxist framework and might be characterized as the specific basis of Chinese socialism. Their implications for psychology are, however, not yet well worked out in Chinese psychology.[32]
4. Mao Zedong often stressed *dialectics* and referred to both the Hegelian approach he knew from Marx's writings and the traditional Chinese approach, often using stories for examples while explaining basic political ideas. Within the Marxist system of dialectics Mao not only created the concept of main contradictions versus subordinate contradictions, but also stretched the validity of dialectics by seeing contradictions as a working principle even for the Communist future, while Stalin rejected such a viewpoint.
5. The other specific contribution by Mao Zedong lies in his emphasis on *practice as the proof for all ideas.* Here we can see how Mao was influenced by traditional philosophy which did not make the Western distinction between knowing and acting. Mao always rejected purely logical solutions and stressed political struggle and practice. In doing this he opposed all dogmatic Marxists who relied more on the correctness of their system per se than on proof in practice. Such a view is, however, not especially fruitful for basic sciences such as the investigation of fundamental principles in psychology, and it was perhaps this particular Chinese viewpoint that led to Chinese psychology being disrupted by political campaigns such as the Cultural Revolution.

BLOSSOMING AND DECLINE IN THE 1960s

The third stage of the development of Chinese psychology saw a variety of new experimental research. This was possible in the political climate of the early 1960s, when China had to rely on its own resources after the Soviet Union had withdrawn all their specialists and advisors in 1960. The pragmatic Chinese government headed by Liu Shaoqi decided to promote industry, technology, and science. Thus, psychology had the chance to flourish as an experimental empirical science. Basic problems of perception and cognition, as well as questions of practical relevance in education and industry, were investigated.

In his 1965 Preface to the translation of Woodworth and Schlossberg's standard textbook on experimental psychology, Cao Richang resolutely defended the use of the experimental method in psychology but warned against using a too narrow approach.[33] In these years, developmental and educational psychology became the largest subdisciplines within Chinese psychology. Topics investigated included the child's conception of number and perceptual development. Such research was undertaken with a view to finding practical applications in curriculum reform in primary schools. The leading role of child psychology in a broad sense is also evident in the papers presented at the First Annual Meeting of the Chinese Psychological Society in 1963. From among 203 papers delivered, more than 75% dealt with educational and developmental psychology. Further fields reported on were labor psychology, clinical psychology and basic research in perception and physiology.[34]

However, all these fruitful beginnings were curtailed by the so-called "Cultural Revolution," a radical movement that might be interpreted as an attempt by Mao Zedong to avoid the failures of the Soviet model by making use of ultraleft and anarchist tendencies especially among students and youth. Western and liberal intellectuals were among the major targets of criticism. Starting as early as 1964, students and minor cadres launched attacks which, with regard to psychology, were based on the following two assumptions: Psyche and consciousness are "class determined" and typical products of bourgeois society; psychology is therefore of no use at all in a socialist system. Laboratory and experimental work were condemned as dangerous bourgeois metaphysics and Mao-Zedong thought was called the best psychology. The attacks against psychologists became stronger in the summer of 1965, and with the beginning of university courses in the autumn of that year the campaign came to a climax. The decisive criticism of psychology, however, did not evolve out of a mass movement, but was launched by the Communist Party's chief of propaganda, Yao Wenyuan, who attacked Chen Li's and Wang Ansheng's study on color and form preferences specifically in an article in the leading newspaper *Renmin Ribao* under the pseudonym "Ge Mingren" (=

The Revolutionist). The article singled out an outstanding psychologist for criticism and culminated in a denunciation of psychology as bourgeois metaphysical nonsense. His argument was based on the opinions that psychological experiments abstract from concreteness and reality, and that individual traits do not exist and could not be a subject of research. Because of this viewpoint he denounced Chen Li's and Wang Ansheng's studies as based on an abstraction from the social context.[35]

Although these arguments were in no way scientifically valid, Yao Wenyuan managed to use his high political position to issue an official prohibition of psychology on the eve of the Cultural Revolution. The consequences were evident by the spring of 1966. The publication of psychology journals and books ceased; psychology was banned as a university subject; the Institute of Psychology at the Academia Sinica was closed; and scientists, professors, and lecturers were sent to "work and reeducation camps" or put under house arrest. Psychology thus fell victim to the Cultural Revolution very early; its rehabilitation took more than a decade. However, the particularly strong effects of this political campaign on psychology cannot be explained only by referring to the Chinese situation itself; one must also take the special character of this science into account. Ridley, in analyzing this relationship, has pointed out that psychology is a science especially sensitive to political influences and thus was struck early by the Cultural Revolution.[36]

The Chinese themselves describe recent political history as having been determined by a "struggle of two lines" within the Communist Party. In regard to politicians' attitudes toward the sciences and the intellectuals, these two lines can be traced quite clearly and linked to specific Chinese politicians. Pragmatic political leaders, such as Zhou Enlai and Deng Xiaoping, represented the line that conceded the intellectuals a degree of independence and responsibility. This made it possible for scientists to elect the directors of their research institutes themselves, as was for a short time in the 1950s and is, with some restrictions, now again the case. The contrary attitude was taken up by the so-called ultraleftists, for example, Yao Wenyuan who banned psychology in the Cultural Revolution. They claimed that only the Communist Party could take the lead in science and research and sent political cadres with no academic expertise to occupy key positions as directors of institutes and universities. In the course of its development Chinese psychology was influenced by both of these political lines, and this goes a long way toward explaining the extreme ups and downs it experienced. However, a further issue is also of importance in this respect, namely the social relevance of Chinese psychology.

Whereas Western psychology developed out of an indigenous history, it was imported into China after the end of the old dynasties. It did not grow in answer to the specific needs of the Chinese society, but was applied to the needs of new, Western-based educational and industrial programmes. This application saw several attempts to solve the problem of the justification of psychology in China. The Western-trained Chinese psychologists interpreted psychology as a basic science within the natural sciences. They thought it could yield some general insights into the process of human cognition but, being a basic science, could not possess social relevance by itself. Ultraleft Chinese politicians, however, claimed that psychology could not be of use in any way because of its relation with bourgeois society out of which it had been developed. Under this political verdict, current during the Cultural Revolution, no psychological research was possible at all. Finally, called on by political leaders to contribute to the modernization program in the early 1960s and again after the Cultural Revolution, Chinese psychologists engaged themselves in many experiments on improvements in industry and education. However, they could not yet rely on detailed research results that took into account specific Chinese conditions. Therefore, their research was of limited social use. Their most urgent problem is still today to modernize and adapt psychology to the Chinese situation.

REBIRTH OF PSYCHOLOGY IN POST-MAOIST CHINA

The present fourth stage in the history of Chinese psychology has its general background in the newly developed Chinese contacts to the rest of the world. This "Ping-Pong-diplomacy" could only begin after the end of the Cultural Revolution. However, the political struggle between the so-called ultraleftists and the pragmatic leaders took several years; psychology, as a politically very sensitive discipline, had to wait until this struggle came to an end in 1976. Although efforts to rehabilitate psychology began as early as 1973, and some psychologists managed to keep working in university departments for philosophy or physiology, psychology was not re-established at universities and research institutions in the People's Republic until after the fall of the so-called Gang of Four. In spring 1977 a first article by a group of psychologists from Beijing University suggested the revival of psychology as an academic discipline. A few months later, plans were discussed at a conference at Penggu in August and September 1977. In May 1978 a special conference was held in Hangzhou on developmental and educational psychology, which resolved to reintroduce teaching and research in psychology at a few universities. The first post-Maoist congress of the Chinese Psychological Society was then held in Baoding in December 1978; Professor Pan Shu was reelected president.

Today, psychology is officially recognized as an important basic science, and tasks for psychologists have been integrated into the modernization program. Psychology is seen as having primary importance for the reform of education, the improvement of health services, for counseling in the birth control and family program, and for increasing labor efficiency. Furthermore, psychology has a growing role in giving advice about social problems such as juvenile delinquency. However, in university education, a full graduate academic course in psychology is offered by only six leading universities, which can each accept only around twenty full-time students per year. Besides this, there are plans to institute psychology as an obligatory minor field for all teacher and educational students, but not all normal universities are as yet able to offer adequate courses.

For their research work the universities have some minor facilities, but most research is done at the Institute of Psychology at the Academia Sinica in Beijing, which has about 100 scientific and about 50 nonscientific staff members.[37] The Institute also has a central library with about 40,000 volumes and subscriptions to 300 psychological periodicals from all over the world. The institute is directed by Professor Xu Liancang and is organized in six sections: developmental psychology; sensation and perception studies; physiological and medical psychology (including psychotherapy); ergonomics and labor psychology; basic theories and history of psychology; information and publication. Research in educational psychology is also conducted on a broad scale in a section of the central Educational Research Institute at the Ministry of Education in Beijing.

The Chinese Society of Psychology, refounded in 1978, had more than 2,000 members in 1984. It is concerned with the promotion and coordination of scientific studies, which are often undertaken by several cooperating teams in different cities. The Society is also responsible for scientific exchange with colleagues abroad. Much of the work of the Society, however, is carried on through the Institute of Psychology at the Academia Sinica which has better financial support. In 1980 the Chinese Psychological Society became a member of the International Union of Psychological Science (IUPsyS).[38] The Society is also the publisher of the official journal *Xinli Xuebao (Acta Psychologica Sinica)* which has an astonishing circulation (30,000 copies in 1980) and is read in many academic and teaching institutions throughout China. A second official Chinese psychology journal is the *Xinli Kexue Tongxun (Information on Psychological Science)* which is published by the East China Normal University at Shanghai on behalf of the Chinese Psychological Society. A third journal, *Psychology in Education,* with special reference to teachers and teacher students is scheduled for publication. Another journal, edited in Hangzhou, translates articles from Western psychology journals. This journal and the many small news gazettes in several cities are not available outside China. These include several regional psychology periodicals published by the respective regional branches of the Chinese Psychological Society. In April 1982 a new association, the Chinese Society for

Social Psychology, was founded by scientists from the Academy for Social Science. It plans to publish its own periodical, *Chinese Journal of Social Psychology*. This society investigates new fields with a demanding program covering such problems as the study of social customs, juvenile delinquency, family planning, and the education of the only child.

Since 1978, Chinese psychologists have been improving contacts with colleagues all over the world by inviting well-known psychologists to China and sending delegations to Australia, the United States, Europe, and Japan.[39] In recent years, a number of younger students have also been sent to these countries, most of them with grants from their hosts. Some international cooperative studies have been initiated, especially in the field of child psychology and cognition. A recent project has begun on educational questions revolving around the birth control campaign so as to be able to give full advice to one-child families. To this end, a new Child Development Center has been opened in Beijing with the help of the United Nations.[40]

The contemporary theoretical framework of Chinese psychology has not yet been finally established. Chinese psychologists are still in search of a new unified theory and see this task as one of primary importance. As they maintain, psychology can only be of service to the modernization of society if it becomes modernized itself.[41] A theoretical problem still under discussion in China is the old question of the mind-body relationship. Pan Shu recently outlined his dialectical and materialist view on this question:[42]

> From the dialectic materialist point of view, the mind-body problem is a substance-function problem. The body is the substance of the mind, and the mind is the function of the body. All material objects have their movements, actions, or functions. The relation between the mind and the body is also to be looked at like this. One form of the movements, actions, or functions of the human body is its mental activity. Human body and its mental activity, like any object and its movements, operation, or function, are completely and essentially united together and could not be separated, and therefore are actually and naturally monistic rather than dualistic. Only the theory which explains the relation between the mind and the body actually by this way can be called the materialistic and scientific mind-body monism.

This view may be regarded as a monistic approach that tries to integrate elements of Marxism with elements from American functionalism and Soviet psychology. It is, however, still too early to regard such statements as cornerstones of a new psychological theory. Nevertheless, the Chinese approach, taking elements from psychological theories from quite different systems trying to integrate them in a new theory, could be said to be unique. Such a view should not be regarded as helpless eclecticism but as an open-minded integrative approach. Learning from all the other theories in international psychology is not yet very widespread in the world, although communication in the West provides the best preconditions.

COMPARISONS WITH WESTERN AND SOVIET
APPROACHES

International communication in psychology has followed a general pattern of one-way systems. The reception of American psychology in Europe during the last decades, for example, has not been reciprocated at all by a discussion of German or other European psychology in the United States, with the exception of the Piaget boom in the 1960s. Chinese psychological research in psychology has only very recently been discussed in U.S. psychology. However, Western as well as Soviet psychology have been highly influential in China, to such an extent that the question arises as to whether one can describe Chinese psychology as a derivative of one or several of the schools of Western or Soviet psychology.

American and Chinese psychology

As I have noted above, in the early decades of this century, behaviorism and functionalism had a strong impact on the emergence of psychology as an independent discipline in China. Indeed, John Dewey has been called the midwife of Chinese psychology.[43] It was not by chance that a Chinese has been titled the most radical behaviorist. In the People's Republic the experimental paradigm of psychology was again upheld, and this paradigm dominated much of the research on learning and perception.[44] However, all in all, one cannot speak of behaviorism and functionalism as the governing models in Chinese psychology, because other approaches have also had a remarkable influence.

Soviet and Chinese psychology

In the years of the re-establishment of psychology in the newly founded People's Republic, official Soviet psychology doctrines initially dominated the theoretical landscape. The reductionistic, deterministic Pavlovian approach was not totally contrary to the experimental paradigm as it was promoted by those Chinese psychologists who had returned home after their studies in centers of behaviorism. At this time much emphasis was placed on the investigation of neurophysiological questions, which were then discussed in Pavlovian terminology.[45] After overcoming this reductionist viewpoint in Russia, S. I. Rubinstein and other scholars developed a more dialectically oriented approach. This was discussed with great enthusiasm in China in the early 1960s and has stimulated many studies on mathematics learning.[46] In the 1950s many Chinese students were sent to Russia and were fascinated by the first Russian research in labor psychology, which was based on integrating cybernetics into the concept of activity as outlined by A. R. Luria.[47] Thus it is clear that there is no one single Soviet school to the exclusion of all the others, but a broad variety of approaches that all have been influential in China. Although reductionist determinism was prevalent in China for a short time in the 1950s, it cannot be said that later Chinese psychology has been dominated by any one of the different Soviet approaches.

European and Chinese psychology

In the early years of Chinese psychology Wilhelm Wundt was one of the European imports brought to China by Cai Yuanpei. Chinese psychologists today still see themselves as following the tradition of Wundt.[48] A more essential influence comes from the German Gestalt psychology. A few Chinese scholars studied at Wolfgang Köhler's laboratory in Berlin, and a dissertation written by a Chinese at Tübingen university on a perceptual problem in 1928 is exemplary of a Gestalt approach.[49] This tradition was upheld in the 1960s in the experimentally based research on learning Chinese characters.[50] By far the most important European influence at present is the Piagetian school, which is discussed controversially among Chinese developmental psychologists. Piaget's "clinical method" has been widely used in China, although some alterations were suggested that led to results quite different from those found by Piaget and his followers. This was particularly true of a huge study on the development of number conception in Chinese preschool and primary school children. This showed, contrary to Piaget, that developmental stages are not fixed but are highly influenced by educational and other ecological variables.[51] Thus, though reference to Piaget seems to be quite strong in this field, one cannot say that this is the prevailing concept, even within the subdiscipline of developmental psychology.

Looking at all these different currents and cross-currents, it appears that no single one has come to dominate Chinese psychology. It is neither a pure derivative of any Western or Soviet school, nor has it found its own prevailing paradigm yet. After having lived through so many different political pressures, Chinese psychologists are nowadays cautious about clinging to one theory or one school of psychology. For this reason Pan Shu, who has gone through this history since the 1920s personally, considers an eclectic approach the most fruitful for establishing an indigenous Chinese psychology.

NOTES*

1 The most informative and authoritative Chinese source is Pan Shu (ed.), "Sixty years of Chinese Psychology," *International Journal of Psychology* 18 (1983):167–184. For a Western analysis see M. Petzold, *Entwicklungspsychologie in der VR China* (Saarbrücken and Fort Lauderdale: Breitenbach, 1983); and M. Petzold, "The History of Psychology in the People's Republic of China," *Asien – Journal of the German Association for Asian Studies,* Serial No. 12 (1984):55–71.

2 See G. W. Leibnitz, *Novissima Sinica* (Hannover: Förster, 1697) and the study by D. E. Mungello, *Leibnitz and Confucianism, the Search for Accord* (Honolulu: University Press of Hawaii, 1977).

3 A comprehensive survey of traditional Chinese science and its history is the still unfinished voluminous work by J. Needham, *Science and Civilization in China* (Cambridge, England: Cambridge University Press, 1954ff).

4 For an overview on these questions see J. Needham, "Human Law and the Laws of Nature," in *Clerks and Craftsmen in China and the West* (Cambridge: Cambridge University Press, 1970).

5 Ai-li S. and R. Chin, *Psychological Research in Communist China 1949–1966* (Cambridge, MA: MIT Press, 1969).

6 However, these Western psychologists were not allowed to meet their Chinese colleagues. See the report of the United States delegation in W. Kessen (ed.), *Childhood in China* (New Haven: Yale University Press, 1975).

7 Extensive information and many translations from Chinese articles are given in L. B. Brown, *Psychology in Contemporary China* (Oxford: Pergamon Press, 1981).

8 Such an integrated viewpoint is mentioned in Pan Shu, "Sixty Years of Chinese Psychology," and with regard to developmental psychology in Liu Fan, "Developmental Psychology in China," *International Journal of Behavioral Development* 5 (1982):391–411.

9 See the two volumes by D. Munro, *The Concept of Man in Early China* (Stanford, CA: Stanford University Press, 1969) and *The Concept of Man in Contemporary China* (Ann Arbor: University of Michigan Press, 1977).

10 See the detailed comparison of Chinese thought and Anglo-Saxon Protestantism in M. Weber, "Konfuzianismus und Taoismus," in *Aufsätze zur Religionssoziologie,* Vol. 1 (Tübingen: Mohr, 1920), 276–536.

11 See Munro, *The Concept of Man in Contemporary China.*

12 A detailed discussion of these implications is in Petzold, *Entwicklungspsychologie in der VR China,* 242–256.

13 A thorough analysis of traditional Chinese philosophy and its implications for psychiatry is J. J. Kao, *Three Millennia of Chinese Psychiatry* (New York: Institute for Chinese Medicine, 1979).

14 A noteworthy psychoanalytic approach is given by C. G. Jung in R. Wilhelm, *Das Geheimnis der Goldenen Blüte* (Zürich: Rascher, 1929).

15 See D. Munro, "The Concept of 'Interest' in Chinese Thought," *Journal of the History of Ideas* 41 (1980):179–198.

* References are limited primarily to sources available in English.

16 See Zhao Liru, "Research on 'Mental Philosophy'," *Acta Psychologica Sinica* 15 (1983):380–388 (in Chinese).

17 See C. C. Ching, "Psychology in the People's Republic of China," *American Psychologist* 35 (1980):1084–1085.

18 An extensive analysis is given by Tse-tsung Chow, *The May Fourth Movement* (Stanford, CA: Stanford University Press, 1960).

19 Probably the most extensive bibliography of psychological and pedagogical tests at that time was done by a Chinese, C. K. A. Wang, *An Annotated Bibliography of Mental Tests and Scales,* 2 Vols. (Peking: Catholic University Press, 1939 and 1940).

20 See Zing-yang Kuo, *The Dynamics of Behavior Development* (New York: Random House, 1967), and the biography by G. Gottlieb, "Zing-yang Kuo – Radical Philosopher and Innovational Experimentalist (1898–1970)," *Journal of Comparative and Physiological Psychology* 80 (1972):1–10.

21 See Academia Sinica (ed.), *The Academia Sinica and its National Research Institutes* (Nanking: Academia Sinica, 1931).

22 Pan Shu, "On the Investigation of the Basic Theoretical Problems of Psychology," *Acta Psychologica Sinica* 12 (1980):1–8; English translation in *Chinese Sociology and Anthropology* 12 (1980):24–42.

23 See Chu-yüan Cheng, *Scientific and Engineering Manpower in Communist China* (Washington, D.C.: U.S. Government Printing Office, 1965), 165.

24 See Pan Shu, "Sixty Years of Psychology in China."

25 One of these advisors reported remarkable difficulties with the "bourgeois Chinese psychologists"; see S. A. Petrushevski, "On the Status of Psychological Science in China and the Development of Contacts with Chinese Psychologists," *Voprosy Psichologii* 2 (1956):102–108 (in Russian).

26 It should be noted that this institute never belonged to the Department of Philosophy and Social Science, as Chin and Chin stated in *Psychological Research in Communist China;* see Petzold, *Entwicklungspsychologie in der VR China,* 59f.

27 Pan Shu, 1958, cited in Chin and Chin, *Psychological Research in Communist China,* 22.

28 See Tang Yue, "On Objects of Study in Psychology," *Guangming Ribao* (13 July 1959), 3, translated in *Joint Publications Research Service* No. 1017-D (1959):41–51.

29 See Kuo Itzen, "Old and Young Psychologists in the Capital Discuss Academic Problems Together," *Renmin Ribao* (10 June 1959), 3, translated in *Joint Publications Research Service* No. 1932-N (1959):48–58.

30 Ibid.; for the current opinions see Pan Shu, "On the Investigation of Basic Theoretical Problems of Psychology."

31 See C. C. Ching, "Psychology in the People's Republic of China," 1084.

32 See Mao Zedong's writings "On Practice" and "On Contradictions," in *Selected Works* (Peking: Foreign Languages Press, 1968).

33 See Cao Richang (= Ts'ao Jih-chang), "Preface to Experimental Psychology," translated in T. Tang, "A Preface to Experimental Psychology in China," *Psychologia* 18 (1975):30–34.

34 See C. Richang, "Upraising the Scientific Level of Psychological Research," *Acta Psychologica Sinica* 8 (1964):1–18 (in Chinese).

35 See Ge Mingren (= Ko Ming-jen), "Is This a Scientific Method and Correct Direction for Studying Psychology?" *Guangming Ribao* (28 October 1965), English translation in *Survey of Chinese Mainland Press* No. 3587 (1965):9–18.

36 C. P. Ridley, *China's Scientific Policies* (Stanford, CA: Hoover Institution Press, 1976), 61.

37 For more information on the institute see Petzold, *Entwicklungspsychologie in der VR China,* or Pan Shu, "Sixty Years of Chinese Psychology."

38 Ibid.

39 For the contacts up to 1980 see Brown, *Psychology in Contemporary China,* chap. 1.

40 The most important psychological research in this center deals with problems in one-child families. See C. C. Ching, "The One-Child-Families in China: The Need for Psychological Research," *Studies in Family Planning* 13 (1982):208–212.

41 See Pan Shu, "On the Investigation of Basic Theoretical Problems in Psychology."

42 Pan Shu, "On the So-Called Mind-Body Problem," *Xinli Kexue Tongxun* (Information on Psychological Sciences) 7 (1982):1–4 (author's translation in manuscript).

43 The beginning fruitful discussion between American and Chinese psychologists had its first highlight at a joint conference at the University of Michigan, Ann Arbor, in August 1983. See American Psychological Association, *Issues in Cognition: Proceedings of a Joint Conference in Psychology* (Washington, D.C.: American Psychological Association, 1984).

44 Chin and Chin, *Psychological Research in Communist China,* 7.

45 See Gottlieb, "Zing-yang Kuo."

46 See Petzold, *Entwicklungspsycholgie in der VR China,* 150ff.

47 See, e.g., the Moscow PhD Xu Liancang, et al., "Stimulus-response Compatibility and Efficiency of Information Transmission," *Kexue Tongbao* (March 1964):253–254; English translation in *Scientia Sinica* 14 (1964):1015–1017.

48 See Pan Shu and Chen Li, "Wilhelm Wundt and Chinese Psychology," in G. Eckardt and L. Sprung (eds.), *Advances in Historiography of Psychology* (Berlin: VEB Deutscher Verlag der Wissenschaften, 1983), 146–149.

49 See Kuo Itzen, "Vergleichende Untersuchungen über das Aubertsche Phänomen," *Zeitschrift für Psychologie* 108 (1928):49–84.

50 See Petzold, *Entwicklungspsychologie in der VR China,* 183ff.

51 See Petzold, *Entwicklungspsychologie in der VR China,* 97ff and 238ff.

10

BRITISH PSYCHOANALYSTS IN COLONIAL INDIA*

CHRISTIANE HARTNACK

The focus of this chapter is a lesser known application of psychoanalysis, not one that, with the aim of enlightenment, questions or even opposes dominant morals and at times politics, but one that conceals realities and legitimizes oppression. The work of two British army officers, Owen Berkeley-Hill and Claud Dangar Daly, the only foreigners in British India who published psychoanalytical articles, will be presented and their impact both inside and outside colonial India discussed.[1] Although Berkeley-Hill's and Daly's research was not commissioned by the British army, their identification with the imperial power that employed them was important to their work. Both men offered to advise the colonial administration in dealing with Indians who dared question British rule. In line with European thought at the time, they conceptualized a hierarchy with white men at the top and dependent people, women, infants, so-called primitives, and neurotics at or near the bottom. Their use of concepts of Freud, Jones, Abraham, and Ferenczi to elaborate these ideas provided seemingly scientific justification for British feelings of superiority to an alien people. This explicitly political appropriation of psychoanalytic theory is significant, as it came at a time when the newly formed Indian independence movement experienced its first successes.

In addition to their political writing, Berkeley-Hill and Daly took part in the psychoanalytic activities of Bengali intellectuals, and functioned as a link between them and the International Psychoanalytical Association. Especially Berkeley-Hill left his mark on the development of psychoanalysis and psychology in India. As a training analyst, he influenced the

* This chapter was written while the author was Visiting Research Fellow at the Center for International and Comparative Studies, The University of Iowa. Thanks to the members, and especially to Professor Paul Greenough, for support and guidance.

second generation of Indian psychoanalysts. Indeed, as president of the Indian Psychological Association and editor of the *Indian Journal of Psychology,* he was, with Girindrashekhar Bose, one of the leaders of institutionalized psychology and psychoanalysis in India. Though Daly was less influential institutionally, he was not without importance; some of his work was reprinted even after independence, in the Indian psychoanalytical journal *Samiksa.*

Beyond these political and institutional levels, a look into Berkeley-Hill's therapeutic work reveals previously little-known aspects of applied psychoanalysis and psychology under colonial conditions, illustrating the problems of transferring psychoanalysis and other Western therapies into differently structured cultures. As head of the most prominent psychiatric institution in British India, Berkeley-Hill developed treatment methods for mentally disturbed British subjects that were remarkably liberal compared with those in other colonial institutions. However, as will be shown, his attitude changed whenever he confronted Indian realities. Thus the apparent progressiveness of his approach was not consistently realized; Indian reality proved time and again to be a different one. Like an unnoticed, but overwhelmingly powerful intervening variable that destroys the nicely controlled conditions for which an experiment is designed, colonial reality devalued Berkeley-Hill's therapeutic experiments.

POLITICAL AND PSYCHOLOGICAL ASPECTS OF BRITISH LIFE IN INDIA IN THE 1920s

For British officials, attractive jobs, quick advancement, and the privileges of a "middle-class aristocracy" were often the motives for coming to India and for staying there. Over the years, these officials were able to create exclusive enclaves on the subcontinent, where they could compensate for the uncomfortable climate and the heavy workload by playing polo and developing hill stations into fancy resorts. With the growing British and Anglo-Indian population, the interaction with Indians became more and more indirect, with the Indians almost reduced to invisible servants. As Francis Hutchins writes, "Churchill – and he was typical of hundreds and thousands of others in this respect – spent three years in India without apparently meeting any Indian other than menial. . . . Indians for the British who lived in this protected world were little more than scenery; they had lost all individuality."[2] However, the political assertiveness of Indian, especially Bengali intellectuals contributed to their growing visibility among the British; and the independence movement, which was nationwide by the 1920s, disturbed Britons' emotional ease.

Official statements made in Parliament during the Great War had encouraged political India to expect a significant advance, perhaps even home rule, after 1918. However, the introduction of the Rowlatt Bills in early 1919, which restricted the liberties of Indians by permitting imprisonment without trial of persons suspected of subversion, shattered many hopes. Mohandas Karamchand Gandhi was one of the disillusioned. As Ainslie T. Embree writes, Gandhi's "commitment to action within the legal framework was shaken, for, as he put it, the government itself had moved outside this framework."[3] After the Rowlatt Bills were passed by the Viceroy's Council on February 6, 1919, Gandhi called for *hartals* (a kind of general strike) in western India, which led to the arrest of many, including himself. Rioting in the Punjab led to the deaths of two British citizens. Thereafter, all political activities were forbidden. Disregarding martial law restraints on public assembly, on April 13, 1919, the Punjabi New Year's Day, thousands of Indians gathered at Jallianwala Bagh, an enclosed square in Amritsar. The only exit from the enclosure was then used by General Dyer to let his troops fire into the people. More than 300 were killed and 1,200 wounded. This massacre is considered the turning point in the history of British India. From then onward the Non-Cooperation movement developed rapidly, leading to Hindu-Muslim alignments that challenged the colonial doctrine of "divide and rule."

The success of the independence movement, along with increasing isolation from life in England, made it more and more difficult to be both a liberal and a colonial official. Some began to doubt the justification for their stay in India. But they had to put themselves under pressure not to show any signs of doubt or resentment, as those who did not play the colonial game of mutual reinforcement were discredited. One colonial "drop-out," George Orwell, described these mechanisms in *The Road to Wigan Pier*:

All over India there are Englishmen who secretly loathe the system of which they are part; and just occasionally, when they are quite certain of being in the right company, their hidden bitterness overflows. I remember a night I spent on the train with a man in the Educational Service. ... Half an hour's cautious questioning decided each of us that the other was 'safe'; and then for hours ... we damned the British Empire – damned it from the inside, intelligently and intimately. It did us both good. But we had been speaking forbidden things, and in the haggard morning light, when the train crawled into Mandalay, we parted as guiltily as any adulterous couple.[4]

Orwell decided to leave India. The majority, however, had no intention of giving up their colonial privileges, but rather tried to silence their own doubts, and perhaps those of others, by legitimizing British domination.

OWEN BERKELEY-HILL (1879–1944)

Son of a wealthy and famous English physician, Berkeley-Hill was educated at Rugby and Oxford and studied in Göttingen and Nancy before receiving his medical degree at Oxford. He entered the elite Indian Medical Service in 1907 and stayed in India until his death in 1944, with an interruption of four and one-half years during World War I, when he joined the East Africa Corps. With characteristic self-depreciation he described his decision to come to India as a result of a quarrel with his mother:

> At that time I was an unpaid anaesthetist at the London Lock Hospital, learning something about anaesthetics and something about venereal diseases. . . . My mother suddenly burst out into a violent denunciation of my idleness and lack of interest in my future. . . . To placate my mother I said I would try for the Indian Medical Service. . . . Little did I then realize that I had committed the stupidest act in my life.[5]

Berkeley-Hill's first position was in the Venereal Hospital for British troops in Bangalore. From there he was transferred to several places, becoming Officiating Medical Superintendent of the Punjab Lunatic Asylum in Lahore in 1912. The next year, he was transferred to the Bombay Lunatic Asylum at Yeravda, near Poona. After his return from East Africa, from 1919 to 1934 he was head of the most prominent psychiatric institution in India, the European Asylum in Ranchi. He married an Indian Hindu, a Tiyyan by caste. This must have made him suspect to his class, for intermarriage between officers and native women was looked down on in British India at that time. However, in his autobiography, which, after a description of his childhood and adolescence, continues with his premarital sex life and ends with a detailed description of his horses, there is less mention of his wife than of extramarital affairs.

Berkeley-Hill had contact with the international psychoanalytical movement from its beginning. An old friend of Ernest Jones, a pioneer of psychoanalysis in the Angloamerican world, he was among the first members of the American Psychoanalytical Association, which he joined in 1911, and in 1913 he helped found the British Psychoanalytical Society.[6] Sigmund Freud mentioned him in his *History of the Psychoanalytic Movement* (1914), saying that, "an English neurologist in Central India (Berkeley-Hill) informed me, through a distinguished colleague who was visiting Europe, that the analyses of Mohammedan Indians which he had carried out showed that the aetiology of their neuroses was no different from what we find in our European patients."[7]

Berkeley-Hill remained alert to every opportunity to increase his knowledge of psychoanalysis. While in England during World War I, after he fell sick in East Africa, he attended Jones' lectures, and when a group of Bengali intellectuals led by Girindrashekar Bose started meeting regularly in Calcutta to discuss psychoanalytical publications, Berkeley-Hill got in contact with them. He thus became a founding member of the Indian Psychoanalytical Association in 1922, and was one of the most active members of this group. In addition to giving lectures, he offered theoretical and practical instruction in psychoanalysis to Indian candidates from 1931 onward at the Psychoanalytical Training Institute in Calcutta, and functioned as one of the Institute's training and control analysts.[8]

Berkeley-Hill was also active in psychological affairs. Between 1927 and 1938, he was president of the Indian Psychological Association, and he also initiated the Indian Association for Mental Hygiene, for which the British Association for Mental Hygiene served as a model. He was internationally known among psychiatrists as well. In 1922, Emil Kraepelin asked him to do research on the incidence of neuro-syphilis among "colored" people. Berkeley-Hill then designed a questionnaire that he sent to British psychiatrists in India and other British colonies.[9]

Early psychoanalytic work

Berkeley-Hill's early psychoanalytical essays were all published in the *Indian Medical Gazette*. In them, he tried to arouse interest in psychoanalysis in India by explaining its basic concepts. His early focus was on anal fixations. One publication was a replication of a study by Jones, in which Berkeley-Hill correlated the incidence of epilepsy with psychic disorders. One of the "two cases successfully treated by psychoanalysis" he described included the dilemma of a homosexual army officer who started having difficulties using his right hand for signing papers. In the psychoanalytic treatment, Berkeley-Hill found out that the use of this hand was related to masturbatory practices. The other case concerned a man who suffered from recurrent nausea sometimes followed by vomiting, which Berkeley-Hill attributed with the help of free association and other psychoanalytic techniques to a "father complex."[10] Montague D. Eder critically reviewed the case studies in the *Internationale Zeitschrift für Psychoanalyse*. The same journal also published short reviews by Eder and Jones of two other papers by Berkeley-Hill.[11]

The European mental asylum in Ranchi

Descriptions of the conditions in mental hospitals in British India provide views of colonial life that are quite different from the usual portrayals. The "Jewel of the Crown" was not always shiny and sparkling but had a dark side, which had to be denied. Among the patients were Indians and those British colonials who were not able to go back to England to live or die "in style." The latter were segregated from the colonial circle and disappeared into jail-like asylums. In 1922, when C. J. Lodge Patch took charge of the Punjab Mental Asylum, he wrote that there were no less than 600 cages for more than 1,000 patients.[12] As the death rates in these institutions were extremely high, and the British who were kept there were hardly treated any better than the Indians, complaints and investigations increased early in the twentieth century. To provide better facilities for the Europeans, the government of Bengal decided in 1915 that patients from the six northern provinces – Bengal, Punjab, Bihar and Orissa, United Provinces, Assam, and Central Province – should be admitted to a psychiatric institution for British and Anglo-Indians only.[13]

The newly built institution, inaugurated in 1918, was situated in a hilly region near Ranchi, about 275 miles northwest of Calcutta. Berkeley-Hill became superintendent in 1919. He later described his impression as follows: "It did not take me long to see that I had been asked to take charge, not of an asylum, but of a bear-garden. My heart sank . . . I felt so overcome with disappointment."[14] Finding that he could expect no support from the relevant officials, he talked to the editor of the *Statesman* in Calcutta, who then published a leading article describing the asylum as "worse than a kaffir's kraal."[15] The intended uproar led to investigations and finally to the introduction of changes that Berkeley-Hill advocated. With financial support from provincial governments and the central government, he employed a large number of Indians to care for the patients.

By 1921, the staff consisted of 73 Indians, 13 Europeans, and one Anglo-Indian for 186 patients. Of the patients, 118 were Eurasians and 52 were British. Others were non-British Europeans, Armenians, West-Indians, and Goanese. The male-female ratio was 106:80. The population of the asylum was almost entirely from the larger towns and cities. Berkeley-Hill wrote that the patients' social status generally would be lower middle class in England, "such as employees of the railways or telegraph departments and mechanics."[16] He added that 73, or 39.24% of the patients had syphilis. Of psychic disorders, *Dementia praecox* had the highest incidence in Ranchi: 86 patients, or 46.24%, were so diagnosed.[17]

The treatment in Ranchi was designed primarily to induce feelings of comfort and relaxation. To achieve this, Berkeley-Hill created a resort-like program, offering: rest, for at least a week and sometimes longer; prolonged bathing for patients who suffered from excitement so acute that they would not lie in bed; nutrition, with loss of weight corrected by a special diet, selected male patients allowed their own mess, and male and female patients allowed to dine together at small tables to improve table manners and deportment; occupational therapy; exercise, with outdoor games such as soccer, hockey, cricket, croquet, badminton, or tennis, and "Swedish drill" (a kind of calisthenics) for some male patients; and amusement, with recreation rooms open until 9 P.M. for reading, writing, card-playing, chess, dominoes, or for using a gramophone and, in the late 1920s, a cinematograph. In addition, as many patients as possible were given the privilege of going in and out of the hospital whenever they wished until 9 P.M. They were asked to sign a paper promising not to abuse their privilege. Berkeley-Hill stated that in the first three years only one patient who was on parole escaped.[18]

More explicitly psychological was Berkeley-Hill's therapy for "bad habits," such as copious salivating or masturbation. In 1928, he introduced charts consisting of four columns. In the first the bad habit was listed; in the second appeared his "prescription," the method deemed likely to correct the habit. The form was then given to the staff in charge, who were ordered to observe the patient's behavior. After doing this for one week, they had to fill in column three: results, if any. The occupational therapist was asked to add further remarks. Subsequently, it was inspected by Berkeley-Hill, who could describe disciplinary measures, such as barring the patient from dances or cinema shows. He stated that "out of a total of 58 patients treated along these lines, 41 patients have been cured of their bad habits."[19]

Even if Berkeley-Hill idealized conditions in Ranchi, it is obvious that he tried to turn the "bear-garden" into a club or cure-park, an extension of the elevated style enjoyed by the British elite under the Raj. Nevertheless, both his attempts to make the inmates feel comfortable and his therapeutic innovations are remarkable, especially compared with procedures at other psychiatric institutions in India.

Berkeley-Hill and psychoanalysis in Ranchi: a case study

A case of paranoid dissociation, published in 1922, illustrates both Berkeley-Hill's use of psychoanalytic methods and his role as a representative of the colonial power, who did not want his patients to show any disloyalty to British culture by interacting with Indians.

When the patient, a thirty-year-old British enlisted man in the Indian army, was admitted to Ranchi, he showed classical symptoms of schizophrenia, such as hallucinations, hearing voices, and weaving trivial matters into a complex scheme of persecution. The patient was convinced that Indian *Pandits* (Brahmin priests) were after his life, because they were jealous of his knowledge of astrology. He also believed that someone from the criminal investigation department watched him: "That is the Government: this is as far as I am concerned a fight to the finish with Government who are my greatest enemy."[20] The patient had constant hallucinations at first, but after six months' residence in the asylum they almost disappeared, and he began to show signs of adjustment. He was then asked to become an instructor in Swedish drill for the other patients, a task he took very seriously. Berkeley-Hill described this as the crucial turn in the treatment process.

After about eight months' residence, the patient consented to undergo psychoanalysis. Despite continuing competition between him and the "spycologist," as he called Berkeley-Hill, Berkeley-Hill claimed to have uncovered several traumatic events and complexes from the patient's past. The only reassurance of his potency and capability that the patient seemed to have gotten in England had come from astrology, and in India he had consulted Indian astrologers frequently. Although Berkeley-Hill's psychoanalytic interventions apparently helped the patient adjust to life in a colonial asylum, this issue remained between the two men. The analyst expressed his contempt for astrology openly: "In 1915 the patient seems to have got into touch with one of the numerous charlatans who profess to be psychologists, astrologers, and what not. This rogue wrote him a letter. . . . It appears that this persevering spider had at least caught his fly."[21]

Berkeley-Hill's description and analysis of this case reads in many respects like a battle for the patient's loyalties between two mutually exclusive authorities. On the one hand there was the potent father figure Berkeley-Hill, directly linked to the colonial army and government, and on the other hand the Indian *Pandits* and astrologers. The patient tried to fight against both. In his moments of guilt about having dealt with the *Pandits,* they became threatening to him, too. Unfortunately, we do not know what the patient finally decided to do, once the gates in Ranchi opened for him, if they did at all – whether he continued to adjust to the British colonial world, or whether he sought further help from the *Pandits* and therefore accepted being a renegade. After this experience in Ranchi, however, it seems that there was no chance for him to combine these two worlds.

Berkeley-Hill's feelings toward Indians

To protect the European inmates of the asylum against attacks by Indians, Berkeley-Hill was given a machine gun by the government.[22] But he also defended his interests and those of the patients in other, more subtle ways. He even went so far as to try to quiet the drums of an Indian troop that came regularly to a nearby village by arming himself with a long, sharp knife and hiding among the trees along the roadside.

> As soon as a party of drummers passed the point where I was concealed, I would leap out, and uttering blood-curdling yells, pursue them. The result was always the same. Believing themselves pursued by an evil spirit, the drummers would throw down their drums and run for dear life. As soon as they were out of sight, I fell upon the drums with my knife and cut out large pieces of the hide.[23]

Berkeley-Hill's autobiography contains several such stories, narrated in the style of hunters' tales of heroic fights against wild game. In stories like these, his basic attitudes toward Indian people came out. Thus, it is not accidental that G. Bose wrote in an obituary that he would be missed by many "mental sufferers," but did not mention that he himself, or any other Indian, mourned.[24] This reflected Bose's relationship toward Berkeley-Hill, which in turn reflected Berkeley-Hill's attitude toward Indians. This will be the focus of the next section.

BERKELEY-HILL'S PSYCHOANALYTICAL WRITINGS ON INDIANS

In a review of Berkeley-Hill's collected papers, Jones mentioned that many of them deal with racial problems, "as one might expect from an author who has done so much to lead Europeans and Asiatics to a better understanding of one another."[25] Jones considered Berkeley-Hill's essays, "The Anal-erotic Factor in the Religion, Philosophy, and Character of the Hindus," "A Short Study of the Life and Character of Mohammed" and "Hindu-Moslem Unity" to be among the most significant. These will be discussed here, focusing on their ideological functions in the colonial context.

"The Anal-erotic Factor in the Religion, Philosophy and Character of the Hindus" was written in 1919, during the aftermath of the Amritsar massacre. The timing of the article, at the climax of postwar mass mobilization against the British with demands for political freedom, is significant. However, it is also obvious that Berkeley-Hill was influenced by Jones' writings on anal-eroticism, a topic of his early psychoanalytical publications. It seems likely that he sought a way to apply these concepts. Like most of the British, he found some aspects of Hindus' behavior so astonishing that they demanded explanation. Given his background, it is not surprising that he tried to interpret them with the help of psychoanalysis. In this paper he gave a range of examples of what he considered to be sublimations of, or reaction formations against, anal-erotic impulses. In particular, the classic Vedic texts and Hatha Yoga were said to be preoccupied with control over the sphincter muscles. He claimed that in Brahmanism this "flatus complex" masquerades as a metaphysical spirit, *Atman,* and that in the excessive ritualism of Hinduism a classical pedantic-compulsive, anal-erotic component is evident. To prove this point he gave detailed descriptions of compulsive elements in Brahmanic rituals, for example, eighteen rules for answering the "call of nature," and nine for cleaning the teeth.[26]

In a second part, Berkeley-Hill discussed the character traits and the temperament of the Hindus. Referring directly to Jones' work on anal eroticism, he stated that the Hindu has all the disadvantageous traits of an anal-erotic personality, such as irritability, bad temper, unhappiness, hypochondria, miserliness, meanness, pettiness, slow-mindedness, a tendency to bore, a bent for tyrannizing and dictating, and obstinacy. This explained, to him, why people from all over the world developed antipathies toward Hindus. Further, he wrote, these traits are just the opposite to those of the Europeans, especially the English, to whom he ascribed positive characteristics, for example, determination, persistence, reliability, thoroughness, and individualism. He concluded by implying that British rule is justified, since the Hindus are neither interested in responsible leadership, nor do they have a psychological disposition for it, since they are, in addition to being obsessive-compulsive, also infantile.

In his review of this paper, Smith Ely Jelliffe basically agreed with Berkeley-Hill's analysis: "All these (negative characteristics) the author shows the Hindu possesses in great measure in a most convincing manner."[27] Jones and Bose recorded that the British authorities proscribed the publication of a book of Berkeley-Hill's papers containing this article, because they feared that such interpretations could lead to more anti-colonial resentment among Hindus.[28]

Whereas Berkeley-Hill's essay on the Hindus focused on their religion, philosophy, and character structure in general, his "Study of the Life and Character of Mohammed," published the same year, was directly aimed at a perceived political threat.[29] Writing when the anti-British Khilafat movement was rapidly gaining influence in India, Berkeley-Hill reacted to the rise of Muslim solidarity by warning his countrymen of the inherent power of Islam.[30] He apparently took Muslims more seriously than Hindus, because he considered their behavior and values to be more similar to the British. With the help of psychoanalytic concepts, however, he tried to show that the origin of Islam lay in an individual neurosis. Thus he implied that the foundations of that culture were not as solid as those of the Christian British. Following a line of thought from Karl Abraham's study of another religious leader, Amenhotep IV, Berkeley-Hill claimed that Islam could be traced to a neurosis of Mohammed, who suffered, among other things, from an all-pervasive father complex.[31]

As a posthumous child, Mohammed hated his grandfather, who in his case replaced his father, and attempted to replace both of them by himself, which led him into a life-long war against religious, political, and social authorities. Because his grandfather was patriarch of his tribe, the Coreish, Mohammed had to transcend him by creating a religion with a Divine Father as midpoint. He attributed to his creation unlimited power, such power, in fact, as the child supposes his father to have. Allah thus became the magnified reflection of Mohammed's wishes. Because of the – in his view – virile psychopathology on which Islam is based, Berkeley-Hill concluded, "Islam is . . . the only force able to hurl Asia upon the iron civilization of Europe." As a practical answer to this threat, he suggested a "rational and scientific attitude towards Muslims, which would again result in saving those responsible for the maintenance of law and order in countries inhabited by Muslims."[32]

Responses to this article came in reviews by Louise Brink and C. W. Forsyth. Forsyth focused on the academic aspect, noting that "the life-history and influences at work in forming the character of Mohammed are essentially the same as those of Amenhotep." Louise Brink, however, brought out the fundamental political issue: "The author sketches most interestingly the general ideas of religious faith and fanaticism as seen in the Mohammedan group psychology conditioned as it is upon the unconscious of its devotees. Here are lessons for the practical politician."[33]

A heritage from the time the Muslims conquered and ruled India were tensions between them and Hindus that led to occasional open clashes between the communities. The British made use of these conflicts, at times manipulating the underlying opposition between them. But in the early 1920s there was a sudden change, when a plea for Hindu-Muslim unity was initiated primarily by Gandhi, who was trying to align the anti-British sentiments of Muslims with the Hindu Non-Cooperation movement.[34] In 1925, Berkeley-Hill reflected on this much-discussed political issue in the paper, "Hindu-Muslim Unity."[35]

According to Berkeley-Hill, there could be no other explanation for the stubborn and vehement fights between Muslims and Hindus but their unconscious psychic structures, because there are neither racial nor language barriers between them. He uncovered two aspects that he thought could provide a useful explanation. First, he found some analogy to the situation in what Jones wrote about the feelings of the Irish toward the English. Jones maintained that the Irish associated the idea of Ireland in a very intimate way with ideas of woman, mother, virgin. Similarly, Berkeley-Hill argued, the "very ancient cult of mother-worship among Hindus has resulted in the production of an association of ideas between the 'mother' concept and the land in which they live. . . . [This] would inevitably lead to an expression by the Hindus . . . of bitter hatred against those who violated their beloved mother-land [namely the Muslim]."[36]

But Berkeley-Hill then left this line of thought to borrow Freud's construct of the totem. The core of the problem between Hindus and Moslems, he argued, is that the Hindu totem animal, the cow, is slaughtered by Muslims, after "Mother India," the Indian soil, was conquered by them. He therefore proposed that "any reconciliation between Hindus and Muslims would demand as a cardinal feature some form of ceremonial in which cows would be killed and eaten, either actually or symbolically, by Hindus and Muslims in conclave."[37]

When Berkeley-Hill read this paper to the Indian Psychoanalytical Association on August 11, 1924, the memoir recorded, "the meeting was attended by many eminent literary men and politicians besides the members, and keen interest was shown by the visitors."[38] And indeed, this paper must have left an impression on some Indian psychoanalysts, for members of the Association discussed his proposal with Gandhi in August 1925. His view, however, was that "there were many more factors involved in the problem, all of which could (not) be tackled from the stand-point of 'the unconscious'. The problem should be taken up by the individual workers with reference to different provincial conditions and not in an amateurish manner."[39]

In Europe, the article was reviewed by Otto Fenichel, who found Berkeley-Hill's suggestions "fantastical – at least to one who has no better knowledge of the Indian situation."[40] Indeed, it appears that Berkeley-Hill was so impressed by Freud's concept of the totem that he transferred it uncritically to this case.

It is important to note, however, that Berkeley-Hill claimed to contribute to Hindu-Muslim unity, and not to "divide and rule." Given the political events of the mid-1920s, which saw the collapse of Hindu-Muslim political *détente* and an upsurge of urban communal rioting, perhaps he felt that it was in the British interest to strive toward peaceful progress best assured by harmonious relationships between the two communities. This line of argumentation is similar to that of Berkeley-Hill's other psychoanalytical articles, where he more or less explicitly stated that reforms, not restrictions, will in the long run assure progress under the leadership of the "civilized." This attitude is related to the pattern of interaction and intervention with his patients in his clinical work in Ranchi, which allowed the inmates to express their interests and skills, but only so long as their actions did not challenge the given order, and they behaved like Englishmen or -women.

Concluding reflections on Berkeley-Hill

In a way similar to Aimée Césaires's later description of the relationship between colonizer and colonized, Berkeley-Hill had reduced his interaction with the Indian people to a kind of monologue.[41] Although he was less conventional than most of his fellow-countrymen, he was nevertheless a representative of the colonial system, which he apparently did not question. Thus, whenever Indians challenged the status quo, he defended it with his weapons, from the "drum cutting knife" to psychoanalytically based derogations. Despite the impressive changes that he introduced in Ranchi, including the application of psychotherapy, his thinking left out one essential element – conscious acceptance of being in a different culture, among different people. Because he negated this reality, he was not able to reflect on specific conditions that caused split perceptions and confusions among those who did not deny the existence of Indian culture.

Further, Berkeley-Hill burdened his Indian colleagues and students with his peculiar psychoanalytic views. Because the colonial conditions did not permit them to criticize these openly, it is not surprising that his authority remained unquestioned. Similarly, European psychoanalysts, though not enthusiastic, were also not critical toward him. They found in him a missionary, who was useful in spreading their basic message to far off lands, and in his writings a confirmation of their belief in that message's universality.

CLAUD DANGAR DALY'S PSYCHOANALYTICAL WRITINGS ON INDIA

There were worlds of difference between Berkeley-Hill, the upper-class renegade, and Claud Dangar Daly (1884–1950). Daly was born in New Zealand, where his father was a farmer. His parents separated when he was five years old, and he was educated in Newport, England. In 1899, he volunteered for the South African War by exaggerating his age, and between 1902 and 1905 he learned nursery gardening in England. At the age of twenty-one, he was commissioned in the Suffolk Regiment and was then transferred to the Indian Army. After fighting in France during World War I, he returned to India and stayed with some interruptions until 1936, when he retired from the British Army as Major in the Transport and Supply Corps.[42]

Daly came to learn about psychoanalysis after a nervous breakdown in France during the Great War and had a few months' analysis in London. In 1924, he was a patient of Sigmund Freud, and in 1928–1929 of Sandor Ferenczi. The problems that led him into analysis remain unclear, but it seems that by spending so much time with psychoanalysts in Europe he consciously sacrificed chances of promotion in his military career. After his retirement in 1936, he went back to Vienna to continue working with Freud, and took some patients himself.

Daly's writings focus on the implications of female sexuality, especially the menstruation complex. His publications related to India are: "Hindumythology and Castration Complex" (1927) and "The Psychology of Revolutionary Tendencies" (1930). The first was written not long after his analysis with Freud. In it he combined several areas of his interest in psychoanalysis, such as castration fears, incest wishes, anal eroticism, and his own reflections on menstruation, with aspects of Indian religion, mythology, and social behavior. Reading this article is something like being in a haunted house, a continuous confrontation with aspects of Hindu culture that appear strange to a European.[43]

Daly gave the central place in his interpretation to the Hindu goddess Kali. She is worshipped as the all-embracing mother, but is also the goddess of death, destruction, fear, night and chaos, of cholera and of thieves and prostitutes, the symbol of cemeteries, the destructress of time – in short, the source of all evil. Popular pictures depict her dancing wildly on the corpse of her husband Shiva, with the head of a giant whom she has just killed in her hand and everything dripping with blood. As Kali is completely covered in these pictures with phallic symbols – she wears, for example, a belt consisting of human arms with hands, and earrings in the shape of human beings – Daly saw in the decoration a symbolization of the gruesome appropriation of this desired object, representing the penis envy of all women. That explained, for him, the fear of this over-whelmingly powerful and castrating goddess. Daly interpreted the Hindu's retreat before and subjection to this castrating, killing super-mother as evidence for stagnation and fixation at an early stage of human development; he thought the castration fear of the Hindus to be paralleled only in isolated and pathological cases in Europe.

As one might expect, the reception of this article among Hindus was not enthusiastic. The memoir of the two meetings of the Indian Psycho-analytical Association at which Daly presented these ideas stated that the participants preferred to delay discussion until the next meeting, but the record of that meeting mentions no such discussion.[44]

The article, "The Psychology of Revolutionary Tendencies," was written when the organized anti-British movement had consolidated.[45] At the end of the 1920s the Indian National Congress openly proclaimed its struggle for independence, and the civil disobedience movement, led by Gandhi, became the most important factor in Indian politics. The activities of the Indian revolutionaries deeply upset colonial officials. Most puzzling for the British must have been that many revolutionaries belonged to the *Bhadralok,* the group of highly educated, westernized Bengalis, from which the British Government had selected its recruits for further training in England.[46] The difficulty of understanding and dealing with these phenomena was reflected in British officials' attempts to find easy explanations and to scapegoat and jail movement leaders.[47]

Some British officials, however, sensed that these were not solutions, and that a first step in the direction of countermeasures would be to understand the underlying motives of the Indian revolutionaries to prevent them from mobilizing the Indian masses. Daly's essay is one example of this. His information on the revolutionaries came mainly from Lord Ronaldshay's book, *The Heart of Aryavarta, a Study of the Psychology of Indian Unrest,* published in 1925.[48] Ronaldshay, formerly Lawrence J. L. D. Zetland, was a Conservative member of Parliament who became Governor of Bengal in 1917, replacing a Liberal. It was said that he was appointed to inject some "backbone" into the provincial administration. Ronaldshay thought that it was pointless to reason with the "terrorists," because a psychological gulf separated them from the Englishmen. But he showed an interest in Bengali history and culture, because he considered this necessary to effectively control, if not destroy, revolutionary activities.

Using Ronaldshay's decriptions and reflections as a base, Daly tried to dig deeper into the personality structure of the Bengali revolutionaries. In the first part of his article, he presented something like a gallery of Indian, primarily Hindu and Bengali revolutionaries such as Gandhi, Bipin Chandra Pal, Aurobindo and Barinda Kumar Ghose, and Chitta Ranjan Das, symbolically disarming each of them by psychoanalytical stigmatization. For example, Daly drew an analogy between Gandhi's political strategies and the obstreperous rebellions of women and the Irish, considering all these to be childlike reactions. Commenting on the employment of suffering and renunciation as weapons, he wrote: "It is true that this characteristic . . . is predominant in the Hindu, but we may recollect that similar tactics were employed by the Irish people and also English suffragettes. It is, in its essence, an infantile trait." Further, the inflation of something tiny to something almost universal was, according to Daly, an essential part of Hindu culture. This explained, he believed, one element of Gandhi's movement; for it "began from a comparatively small thing, namely a legislative enactment known as the Rowlatt Act, which . . . lost all importance in face of the convulsion which Mr. Gandhi's action produced."[49]

However, Daly had not yet reached the essence of these phenomena. In the second part of the essay, he developed a theory of the revolutionaries' psyche with reference to myths. Speaking of the cell around the paper *Bande Mataram,* published by Aurobindo Ghose, B. C. Pal, and others, Daly found that the secret of these revolutionaries is that they relate their inclinations to an overwhelming love of Mother India. Daly pointed out that deeply hidden incestuous desires are expressed in this fervor for Mother India, and that a pattern of Oedipal fantasies – the little boy fights the brutal father to liberate the wounded mother – is obvious in the appeals with which these Bengalis tried to mobilize fellow-countrymen. Daly further interpreted these revolutionary actions as a form of compensatory behavior. The Hindus, he claimed, "have engraved on their ego an ideal of the mother whose incestual love is denied them, and an insatiable unconscious hate of any power which comes between them and their primitive desires."[50]

This interpretation allowed Daly to suggest an optimistic proposal for British government officials. Since the sources of the Hindus' problems are so deeply anchored, in order to resolve them, the Hindus would have to make an effort to overcome this infantile and feminine tendency and to grow up into a strong and healthy people, free from their present fear of life and of death; while the role of the British Government should be to act like wise parents, who constitute themselves a bridge over which their children may be guided into adult life, and may become gradually fit to face independently the realities and responsibilities of existence.

But, as psychoanalysis teaches, the overcoming of age-old fixations is a matter of generations, not years. For this undertaking Daly offered his service: "It is only by a deep study of the psychology and needs of the Indian peoples, and the application of the knowledge obtained by psychological research, that the British Government can hope to continue to rule them to their best advantage."[51]

Compared to Ronaldshay's, Daly's reflections were the part-time activity of an amateur. There is no indication that he read any publications by the revolutionaries. Thus, he did not realize that there were differences between the political activists he dealt with, nor did he notice that some of them, like A. Ghose and B. C. Pal, had undergone personal changes in the course of their political work. To Daly's lack of political knowledge must be added his lack of insight into Indian religion, philosophy, and culture. Rather, he pasted newly acquired psychoanalytical concepts like labels onto aspects of Indian life where they seemed to fit. It is likely that he could get his work published in the *International Journal of Psychoanalysis* because it reproduced both Western prejudices about non-Western peoples and then-current psychoanalytical concepts. Thus, Daly did his homework for Freud and Ferenczi by applying the insights he had previously gotten from them. He also flattered his military superiors by parroting their contempt for Hindu Indians and providing something like a scientific basis for the prejudice of their inferiority, which could potentially be used as a legitimation for colonial intervention. Daly further boosted the egos of British officials by pointing out their vast responsibilities as educators of the "childlike" Indians, and offered to make himself useful by providing policy solutions based on psychoanalytical insights. He thus tried to please all authorities.

There is no mention of any discussion of this article in the Indian Psychoanalytical Association. But when Daly came back from Europe in 1935, a delegation of that body welcomed him at the pier in Calcutta.[52] Reprints of other articles by him appeared later in the Indian psychoanalytical journal *Samiksa,* which showed not only respect toward him but also the impact of his work, for by then the British had given up this colony, and India had become – at least formally – independent.[53]

CONCLUSION

The differences between Daly and Berkeley-Hill are obvious. Daly was a social and intellectual climber, who became interested in psychoanalysis because it helped him to overcome personal problems. While in India, he had no experience with patients. His knowledge of psychoanalysis was therefore either purely theoretical or related only to his own personal experiences. Berkeley-Hill, on the other hand, was an upper-class renegade who liked to challenge his puritan colleagues with his liberated views and actions. He appears to have been attracted by psychoanalysis for its inclusion of sexual matters and its appeal as a pioneering discipline, and he did not hesitate to apply and propagate psychoanalytical therapies in the army and mental hospitals. His work as a psychiatrist was in many respects avant garde for the 1920s and early 1930s.

Despite these differences, however, their writings on India were strikingly similar. In style and content both were derogatory, and both failed to note any positive aspect of Indian culture. Instead, they compared the behavior of Indians in a negative way with other dependent people, with women, infants, and the Irish, and time and again with European neurotics. To explain group behavior they attributed it to psychopathological defects of individuals, a procedure quite common in the psychoanalytical discussion of their time.

Both Berkeley-Hill and Daly identified themselves fully with British colonialism. For them, self-assertive Indians were a source of threat and thus had to be combatted with all kinds of weapons, psychoanalytical as well as military.

NOTES

1 Berkeley-Hill and Daly were the only psychoanalysts who lived most of their adult lives in India. Other psychoanalysts spent a short time there, including Carl Gustav Jung, Medard Boss, and Erik Erikson. Because they were not part of the British colonial system, their work will not be discussed here.

2 F. Hutchins, *The Illusion of Permanence: British Imperialism in India* (Princeton: Princeton University Press, 1967), 101.

3 A. T. Embree, *India's Search for National Identity* (New York: Alfred A. Knopf, 1972), 75.

4 G. Orwell, *The Road to Wigan Pier* (New York: Harcourt, 1958), 177.

5 O. Berkeley-Hill, *All Too Human: An Unconventional Autobiography* (London: Peter Davies, 1939), 78–79.

6 E. Jones, "Owen Berkeley-Hill 1879–1944," *International Journal of Psychoanalysis* 25 (1944/45):177; G. Bose, "Owen Berkeley-Hill: In Memoriam," *Indian Journal of Psychology* 19 (1944):145–146.

7 S. Freud, "On the History of the Psychoanalytic Movement," *The Standard Edition of the Complete Psychological Works of Sigmund Freud,* ed. J. Strachey, Vol. 14 (London: The Hogarth Press, 1957), 30.

8 "History of the Indian Psychoanalytic Society," *International Journal of Psychoanalysis* 4 (1923):249–252.

9 Berkeley-Hill, "Mental Hygiene," *Indian Journal of Psychology* 2 (1927):1–14; "Indian Association for Mental Hygiene: 'Report'," *Indian Journal of Psychology* 4 (1929):52–55; Berkeley-Hill, "A Note on the Incidence of Neuro-Syphilis among Coloured Races," in *Collected Papers* (Calcutta: The Book Company, 1933), 294–309.

10 Berkeley-Hill, "A Short Analysis of 89 Cases of Epilepsy," *The Indian Medical Gazette* 49 (1914):136–137; "A Report of Two Cases Treated Successfully by Psychotherapy," *The Indian Medical Gazette* 48 (1913):97–99.

11 M. D. Eder, review of Berkeley-Hill, "Two cases . . .," *Internationale Zeitschrift für Psychoanalyse* 1 (1913):586; review of Berkeley-Hill, "Anal-eroticism," *Internationale Zeitschrift für Psychoanalyse* 1 (1913):507; E. Jones, review of "The psychoanalytic method . . .," *Internationale Zeitschrift für Psychoanalyse* 1 (1913):186–187.

12 C. J. Lodge Patch, "A Century of Psychiatry in the Punjab," *The Journal of Mental Science* 85 (1939):386–387.

13 Berkeley-Hill, "The European Mental Hospital," *The Journal of Mental Science* 70 (1924):69–70.

14 Berkeley-Hill, *All Too Human,* 245.

15 Ibid., 243–244.

16 Berkeley-Hill, "A Wassermann Survey of the Inmates of the Ranchi European Lunatic Asylum," *The Indian Medical Gazette* 36, (1921):89–94, here: 91.

17 Ibid., 90–91.

18 Berkeley-Hill, "The European Mental Hospital," 71–76.

19 Berkeley-Hill, "On Habit Formation," *The Journal of Mental Sciences* 75 (1929):298–299.

20 Berkeley-Hill, "A Case of Paranoid Dissociation," *The Psychoanalytic Review* 9 (1922):1–27, here: 22.

21 Ibid., 11.

22 Berkeley-Hill, *All Too Human,* 260–263.

23 Ibid., 265.

24 Bose, "Owen Berkeley-Hill. In Memoriam," 146.

25 Jones, "'Collected Papers' by Lt. Col. Owen Berkeley-Hill," *International Journal of Psychoanalysis* 15 (1934):344.

26 Berkeley-Hill, "The Anal-Erotic Factor in the Religion, Philosophy and Character of the Hindus," *International Journal of Psychoanalysis* 2 (1921):306–338.

27 S. E. Jelliffe, review of "The Anal-erotic factor . . ." *The Psycholanalytic Review* 11 (1924):89–91.

28 Bose, "Owen Berkeley-Hill. In Memoriam," 146; Jones, *Sigmund Freud: Life and Work,* Vol. 3 (London: The Hogarth Press, 1957), 205.

29 Berkeley-Hill, "A Short Study of the Life and Character of Mohammed," *International Journal of Psychoanalysis* 2 (1921):31–53.

30 A. C. Niemeijer, *The Khilafat Movement in India 1919–1924* (The Hague: Martinus Nijhoff, 1972).

31 K. Abraham, "Amonhotep IV (Echnaton). Psychologische Beiträge zum Verständnis seiner Persönlichkeit und des monotheistischen Aton-Kultes," *Imago* 1 (1912):334–360.

32 Berkeley-Hill, "Life and Character of Mohammed," 34, 53.

33 L. Brink, review of 'A Short Study of the Life and Character of Mohammed', *The Psychoanalytic Review* 10 (1923): 226–228, here: 228; C. W. Forsyth, "Epitome of Current Literature. A Short Study of the Life and Character of Mohammed," *The Journal of Mental Science* 69 (1923):114–115, here: 115.

34 M. K. Gandhi, "Hindu-Muslim Unity," in *Collected Works,* Vol. 20 (Ahmedabad: Navajivan Trust, 1968), 89–90.

35 Berkeley-Hill, "Hindu-Muslim Unity," *International Journal of Psychoanalysis* 6 (1925):282–287.

36 Ibid., 285.

37 Ibid., 287.

38 "The Indian Psychoanalytical Society. Annual Report, 1924," *International Journal of Psychoanalysis* 6 (1925):241.

39 Gandhi, "Interview to Indian Psychoanalytical Society," in *Collected Works,* Vol. 28, 109–110.

40 O. Fenichel, review of Berkeley-Hill, "Hindu-Muslim Unity," *Imago* 12 (1926):526.

41 A. Césaire, *Discourse on Colonialism* (New York: Monthly Review Press, 1972).

42 J. Rickman, "Claud Dangar Daly, 1884–1950," *International Journal of Psychoanalysis* 31, (1950):290–291.

43 C. D. Daly, "Hindu-Mythologie und Kastrationskomplex," *Imago* 13 (1927):145–198.

44 "Indian Psychoanalytical Society, Annual Report, 1928," *International Journal of Psychoanalysis* 10 (1929):540.

45 Daly, "The Psychology of Revolutionary Tendencies," *International Journal of Psychoanalysis* 11 (1930):193–210.

46 J. H. Broomfield, *Elite Conflict in a Plural Society: Twentieth Century Bengal* (Berkeley: University of California Press, 1968); "The Social and Institutional Base of Politics in Bengal, 1906–1947," in R. M. van Baumer (ed.), *Aspects of Bengali History and Society* (Honolulu: The University of Press of Hawaii, 1975), 132–145; L. A. Gordon, *Bengal: The Nationalist Movement 1876–1940* (New York: Columbia University Press, 1974), 163–188.

47 Government of India, Home Department, Intelligence Bureau, *Terrorism in India, 1917–1936* (Simla: Government of India Press, 1937); P. C. Bamford, *Histories of the Non-Co-operation and Khilafat Movements* (Delhi: Government of India Press, 1925); P. N. Chopra (ed), *India's Major Non-Violent Movements 1919–1934. British Secret Reports on Indian People's Peaceful Struggle for Political Liberation* (New Dehli: Vision Books, 1979).

48 L. J. L. D. Zetland, Earl of Ronaldshay, *The Heart of Aryavarta, A Study of the Psychology of Indian Unrest* (Boston: Houghton Mifflin, 1925).

49 Daly, "The Psychology of Revolutionary Tendencies," 195–196.

50 Ibid., 197.

51 Ibid.

52 "Indian Psycho-Analytical Society. Annual Report, 1935," *International Journal of Psychoanalysis* 17 (1936):392.

53 Daly, "Hindu Treatise on Kali," *Samiksa* 1 (1947): 191–196; "The Mother Complex in Literature," ibid., 157–190; "The Psychology of Man's Attitude towards Woman," ibid., 231–240.

11

THE IDEOLOGICAL SIGNIFICANCE OF FREUD'S SOCIAL THOUGHT

LOUISE E. HOFFMAN

[T]he conceptual language created by intellectuals in general is therapeutic and ideological as well as cognitive in import.[1]

Examination of the evolution of Freud's social thought validates this central contention of the sociology of knowledge. Freud's development of social psychology during the early decades of the twentieth century was to some extent a logical extension of his existing concepts of individual psychology; but it also manifested, tacitly as well as overtly, the impact of broader social concerns connected with external events and ideologies. Just as Freud explained religion, politics, and other aspects of culture as expressions of unconscious emotional needs and wishes, in works from *Totem and Taboo* to *Civilization and Its Discontents,* so his own psychological system embodied unspoken affective and ideological attitudes – attitudes that were profoundly skeptical of egalitarian social structures.

Today it is hardly novel to assert that, whatever else they may be, scientific theories are mythological systems. That is, their validity is not only objective but also subjective and contextual: They select, classify, and synthesize elements of experience to create (or recreate) order and meaning, using imaginative and symbolic means as well as strictly empirical ones. This statement does not deny the importance of ideas, but affirms that they must be understood in context rather than as freestanding structures with intrinsic or absolute validity.[2]

On occasion, Freud explicitly recognized the fictive character of his central concepts, as in a postscript to his *Group Psychology* where he alluded to "the scientific myth of the father of the primal horde."[3] But the demands of his work – the intellectual task of elaborating his theory, and the political/administrative effort of founding and controlling a movement – often worked to encourage assertions of orthodoxy and exclusivity, so often noted by observers both friendly and hostile.[4] William McGrath argues, also, that Freud's own psychological development carried him in this direction, away from youthful rebellion and toward his "dream of becoming a Moses."[5]

Like many scientists and social scientists, proponents of psychoanalysis have often claimed possession of objective means to universal truths. Thus, Philip Rieff has asserted that, "Offering an analytic that helps men think against all ideologies of the super-ego, Freud is truly revolutionary. He has opened the possibility of suspecting, in a diagnostic way, all symbolics: he has given us a mode of analyzing them," and renounced the creation of his own ideology.[6] So concerned with interpreting myths and symbols, psychoanalysis has until lately been read as fictive mainly by its foes, such as H. J. Eysenck and Karl Popper.[7]

A comprehensive and critical understanding of psychoanalytic social thought, however, requires attention to its historical context and underlying implications. Although critical studies of social psychologists' implicit ideologies are by no means entirely new, only lately have they become common and systematic.[8] This approach permeates Henri Ellenberger's account of the evolution of dynamic psychiatry out of "creative illness" and the conflicting legacies of rationalism and Romanticism, for example.[9] Recent scholars have gone beyond commonplace observations to locate specific sources of Freudian myths in Freud's own life and environment;[10] explore the relevance of psychoanalytic categories to contemporaneous social attitudes and experiences;[11] and identify important aspects of ideological ambivalence in Freud's thought, which was simultaneously critical of established values and an embodiment of them.[12] We are now beginning to see applications of this approach in understanding psychoanalytic social theories.[13]

Freud's environment inescapably influenced his underlying assumptions and concerns, especially in his social thought.[14] As radical new ideologies emerged early in the twentieth century, political and intellectual neutrality became increasingly impossible, even – or perhaps especially – for those who, like Freud and many of his followers, were "outsiders," professionally and ethnically.[15] Despite Freud's reluctance to state political opinions, his social psychology necessarily led him to address, often implicitly and indirectly, the fundamental issues of social and political behavior and goals.

AUTHORITY AND AFFILIATION: FROM MASS PSYCHOLOGY TO GROUP PSYCHOLOGY

Of central importance is Freud's approach to two closely related issues: authority and affiliation. The problem of authority encompasses questions such as the origin, function, and proper sphere of ascendancy and power in collective life, in all kinds of institutions and behaviors, both formal and informal. Associated with it is the problem of affiliation, the ties among members of families and groups of all sizes. Clearly, these two themes – the vertical and the horizontal relationships in society – are inextricably intertwined in consideration of most social questions. Nevertheless, we should identify them separately in an effort to decipher the sometimes ambivalent ideological subtext of Freud's social theory.

It is commonplace to observe that Freud was in many ways a creature of his time, conservative and conventional in his private and social life despite his intellectual innovations and criticisms of the sexual mores of his class. He was, by his own confession, sexually repressed, hard-working, and "inner-directed," disinclined to engage in public controversy outside of professional forums and insistent on the need for rational control in pursuit of individual and social goals. In short, he was a paradigm of nineteenth-century bourgeois individualism.

Like many of his peers confronting mass society, Freud mistrusted collective processes, assuming that the breakdown of hierarchical authority would necessarily lead to chaos and threats to civilization. Even if, as McGrath argues, Freud as a young man expressed liberal sympathies and intense frustration with the retrograde aspects of Austro-Hungarian rule, by 1898 his "counterpolitical" resolution of these conflicts, and his shift from the stance of rebellious son to identification with paternal authority, amounted to an acceptance of the political status quo and a rejection of revolution in arenas other than the intellectual.[16] Within the psychoanalytic movement, Freud admitted no equals, as Jung soon discovered, and exerted a strong will.

Yet however strong his patriarchal authority within the movement, his practice, and his family, in the world at large Freud's position was more tenuous. He was, or at least believed himself to be, professionally, ethnically, and politically marginal. Hannah Decker has demonstrated that Freud was never as isolated as he claimed to be; it is nonetheless important that Freud felt himself to be alienated, and in many ways he was estranged from Viennese society. Although a sense of marginality seems to have reinforced his determination to establish himself as a revolutionary and heroic intellectual innovator, as Frank Sulloway argues, and while he was certainly unhappy with Central European clericalism, militarism, and anti-Semitism, nevertheless the principal alternatives, socialism and mass democracy, struck him as dubious at best.[17]

It is thus not surprising to find that Freud's political attitudes were often ambivalent and, at least implicitly, elitist and anti-democratic in orientation. This attitude was common among Central European academics.[18] But, unlike Thomas Mann, Benedetto Croce, and others who after World War I moved from conservatism to active support of democratic ideals, Freud never substantially altered his position despite his undoubted humane sympathies; rather than inspiring reassessment, the emergence of fascism merely confirmed his pessimism.[19]

In his conservatism Freud resembled contemporary anti-Marxist theorists of social elites such as Gaetano Mosca and Vilfredo Pareto.[20] He was also following the lead of the mass psychologists of the late nineteenth and early twentieth centuries, such as Gustave Le Bon, William McDougall, and Wilfred Trotter. Their theories were the jumping-off point for Freud's own discussion of social psychology in the 1920s.[21] These writers who, like Freud, were often physicians, considered mass behavior actually or potentially pathological. As Robert Nye has recently shown in his perceptive discussion of the French medical profession, nineteenth-century physicians were often eager to establish their discipline as the prime secular authority on social as well as organic disturbances. By attaching the label of pathology to crime, delinquency, and even some kinds of political activity, they enhanced their professional prestige and political role. Quite often their social diagnoses expressed the anxiety of the propertied classes confronting proliferating proletarians at home and growing threats abroad.[22]

In the view of these mass psychologists and diagnosticians of "social degeneration," crowds (or "herds" or "mobs") develop a mass mind that is essentially primitive, irrational, and susceptible to hypnotic suggestion – a breeding ground for psychic epidemics. The mass mind of such a group is dangerous because it has no established structure and recognizes no permanent authority, only the transitory power of demagogues. Small groups and established institutions can foster ties of social affiliation that are potentially rational and positive, these theorists thought; but those operating within large, unstructured groups, particularly ones that challenge established authority, are archaic, regressive, and potentially hysterical.

Le Bon's arguments are typical of this school. In his view, "The substitution of the unconscious action of crowds for the conscious activity of individuals is one of the principal characteristics of the present age"; and he considered that, "Crowds are only powerful for destruction. Their rule is always tantamount to a barbarian phase."[23] The mass psychologists generally perceived movements advocating egalitarian ties and collective action as potential or actual threats to reason, order, and civilization, and justified the need for strict hierarchical control to prevent mass hysteria.[24]

At first, Freud concurred with this assumption of a mass mentality, stating in 1912 that, "I have taken as the basis of my whole position the existence of a collective mind," dominated by irrational and primitive impulses and persisting from generation to generation.[25] One could hardly adopt a more pessimistic approach to the modern era of mass politics. Like the mass psychologists, too, Freud considered leaderless, large, or unstructured groups to be potentially more irrational and regressive than those that are small, organized, or controlled by a strong leader.

The church and the army, Freud's examples of stable, structured groups, are everywhere the most conservative of social institutions, and the most resistant to democratic control. Both, he thought, depend on the illusion of benign patriarchal authority, which engenders ties of affiliation among their members. "The Commander-in-Chief is a father who loves all soldiers equally, and for that reason they are comrades among themselves." Much as Freud disapproved of militarism and Christianity, he nonetheless emphasized the functional usefulness of their provision of substitutes for paternal authority, which he believed essential for the existence of the groups: "The loss of the leader in some sense or other, the birth of misgivings about him, brings on the outbreak of panic . . . the mutual ties between the members of the group disappear, as a rule, at the same time as the tie with their leader." On the dissolution of a religious group, "ruthless and hostile impulses towards other people make their appearance."[26] His own experience of collective political behavior, from observations of radical movements in France in the mid-1880s to his confrontation with Nazi stormtroops in 1938, might well have reinforced his perception of such activities as dangerous.[27]

By 1921, Freud's conceptions had changed, a consequence of both internal evolution and the stimulus of the Great War, which posed both theoretical and personal challenges for him.[28] He retreated from the idea of a distinct mass mentality, deciding instead that groups are governed by forces congruent with those he had found to work in individual psychology.[29] He then criticized the mass psychologists for producing an explanatory shibboleth that failed to analyze precisely how groups are held together. Instead of positing some undifferentiated and utterly primitive mass mind, Freud looked to the forces at work in what he had already identified as the original and most psychologically significant collectivity: the family.[30] Here, he said, is the source and model of all authority relationships (between parents and children) and the first experience of affiliation (among siblings).

The ideology of the horde

Freud's postwar conception of social life, however, was scarcely more democratic in its implications than that of the mass psychologists. Although he attributed social affiliation to particular needs existing within each individual, rather than to some mysterious mass mind, he also retained his predecessors' concept of a persistent primitivism in collective life. His revised version of the "herd instinct" emphasized the ties of authority rather than affiliation within the group. This shift accorded with his anthropological myth of the primal horde, derived from Darwin and elaborated previously in *Totem and Taboo*. His model of the earliest human family was a band dominated by a jealous and violent father who, overcome and killed by his rebellious sons, reappears in the organization of patriarchal family and social life: "in so far as men are habitually under the sway of group formation we must recognize in it the survival of the primal horde."[31] This legend, stressing the power of a single dominant male whose authority precedes (both temporally and psychically) ties among his offspring, implicitly emphasizes society's need for strong leadership and hierarchy. As Freud's social thought developed during the years of crisis and dissolution of the old empires of Central and Eastern Europe, it seems to offer a clear, if perhaps unintended, counterpoint and reaction to the advent of the more egalitarian regimes that replaced them.

The conception of society as horde emerged logically from Freud's Oedipal theory, originally developed and applied in the realm of individual psychology. In *Totem and Taboo,* he extended this notion into a universal social myth, reducing the origins of "religion, morals, society, and art" to the single model of the Oedipus complex. He maintained this fundamental position ever after, arguing in *Moses and Monotheism* that, "in the mass of mankind there is a powerful need for an authority who can be admired, before whom one bows down, by whom one is ruled and perhaps even ill-treated. . . . It is a longing for the father felt by everyone from his childhood onwards."[32] The legend gradually acquired the force of abstract truth.

Affiliation and the patriarchal family

Except perhaps for its polygamy, Freud's primal horde is an exaggerated version of nineteenth-century bourgeois Europe's ideal patriarchal family, which Marxists considered specific to capitalist society.[33] From this universal paternal authority Freud derived the ties of identification or mutual affiliation within the group: Since only the father is free and psychically strong, his offspring are perpetual children, dependent, repressed, and fearful, able to act on their own only in temporary concert. The ties among them are largely unconscious and always ultimately weaker than their need for authority.

In this view, most people never outgrow a profound ambivalence toward authority. They always desire autocratic direction: "The leader of the group is still the dreaded primal father; the group still wishes to be governed by unrestricted force."[34] Such a universal need for paternal love and punishment would explain the repeated failure of genuine democracy and the emergence of demagogues and dictators.

Simultaneously, Freud's father/leader is always the target of resentment. The Oedipal myth, of course, includes parricide: an unwitting act in Greek legend, a deliberate collective effort in Freud's social construct. Because the sons continue to need authority and prove unable to assume mature responsibility themselves, their rebellious conspiracy cannot eradicate their need for him, but only heightens their longing and guilt, which find universal expression in unconscious ties of affiliation among the group's members: Reversing their mutual hostility, they identify with one another psychologically and demand equality among themselves, but specifically not equality with their leader.[35] The horde, therefore, could never be an association of equals, nor can the institutions derived from it.

Freud believed that effective ties of social affiliation actually require the authority of a leader/father, to provide a model for his followers to emulate and admire, and to impose on them the repression that prevents anarchy and generates collective identification among group members. He did recognize that individuals require some means of resisting malign forms of authority. Membership in stable groups that foster hierarchical authority and strong collective identity, such as the church and the military, is one such means. Also, the regressive influence of a single group on its members could be limited if they belong to several groups simultaneously; participating in several different structures of affiliation and authority, Freud believed, would allow individuals to achieve "a scrap of independence" from all of them.[36]

He most feared "rapidly formed and transient . . . noisy ephemeral groups," mob-like, irrational, regressive, and only tenuously civilized:

> Masses are lazy and unintelligent . . . and the individuals composing them support one another in giving free rein to their indiscipline. It is only through the influence of individuals who can set an example and whom masses can recognize as their leaders that they can be induced to perform the work and undergo the renunciations on which the existence of civilization depends.[37]

Just as the Oedipal family structure gave rise to individual conscience and self-imposed repression, Freud thought, so political authority ensured social order and cohesion.

Conscience: from external to internal authority

The ideological significance of this position is evident in Freud's use of metaphors. He observed, for example, that "our mind . . . is no peacefully self-contained unity. It is rather to be compared with a modern State in which a mob, eager for enjoyment and destruction, has to be held down forcibly by a prudent superior class."[38] While oligarchy and institutions of authority could perform such functions in society, within each psyche

Freud found this "prudent" superior force in the third and last of the major personality systems to emerge in his theory: the ego ideal, introduced in 1914 and later elaborated and renamed the superego.[39]

This superego, or conscience, Freud thought, was not present in newborn children, any more than organized government was present in the first prehistoric human groups. Both functions evolved over time, and both derived from the repressions and tensions of the Oedipal constellation.[40] In psychoanalytic theory, each was necessary to the other's development: The Freudian myth of primitive parricide explained social authority as a product of the murderers' guilt and longing for their patriarch, while the epigenetic conception of the personality defined the ego ideal as a displacement of libido enforced by parents and other representatives of social convention to impose adherence to their standards.[41]

Both the internal or mental authority and the external or social authority served as essential means of escaping subjection to the primitive past (individual or collective), transforming instinctual impulses, and attaining rational control, although both were prone to tyranny.[42] Obedience to social authorities, according to Freud, is ensured not only by their use of "unrestricted force," but even more by internalization of their values. Eventually, if this internalization proceeds successfully, even strong instinctual drives will be subdued, as disobedience engenders intolerable anxiety. Thus, authority, once imposed by coercion, becomes an intrinsic psychic function whose operation is necessary to normal life and whose values link individuals with larger groups.

In developing his metapsychology, Freud repeatedly equated political with mental authority: "The primal father is the group ideal, which governs the ego in the place of the ego ideal."[43] Group members, in their quest for reassurance, adopt this same authority, which then becomes a mechanism of affiliation, reinforcing their mutual identification. Thus the political leader substitutes for individuals' consciences and rational processes – potentially a disastrous situation, but usually desirable since, according to Freud, so many individuals lack the strength for full autonomy; their egos are too weak.[44]

The development of Freud's ego psychology, when translated into ideological terms, shows the extent of his cultural conservatism and pessimism. Freud was always skeptical of the ego's potential for conscious, rational control of the personality. Before 1914, he defined the ego largely in terms of narcissistic urges, modified and limited by external reality as internalized in the ego ideal.[45] During the subsequent period, both his own theoretical requirements and the impact of the Great War led him to stress the ego's social and aggressive components.

Soon after the war, Freud described hatred as an ego function that "derives from the narcissistic ego's primordial repudiation of the external world" and ego rather than libidinal instincts as the prime source of sadism: "The ego hates, abhors and pursues with intent to destroy all objects which are a source of unpleasurable feeling for it, without taking into account whether they mean a frustration of sexual satisfaction or of the satisfaction of self-preservative needs."[46] These urges threaten all bonds of authority and affiliation.

The destructiveness of the war, he said, stemmed from the inbuilt human capacity for psychic regression, realized in belligerent states' relaxations of individual ego and superego controls, which permitted and even encouraged "deeds of cruelty, fraud, treachery and barbarity so incompatible with their level of civilization that one would have thought them impossible."[47] The forces of affiliation, he implied, were too weak, or too susceptible to distortion, to compensate for loss of psychic and social authority.

FREUD'S PATRIARCHY AS POLITICAL THEORY

Early in the war, Freud believed that psychic and social equilibrium could be regained with the return of peace.[48] Soon afterward, however, amid endemic political violence and economic deprivation, his optimism faded; he insisted on the regressive character of all instincts and in particular on the aggressive and destructive potential of ego instincts.

Just as repressed libidinal urges are always threats, Freud thought, so "It is quite conceivable that the separation of the ego ideal from the ego cannot be borne for long either, and has to be temporarily undone." Most individuals are subject to such episodes, he maintained, and so, periodically, are entire societies: The orgiastic celebrations of ancient Saturnalia and modern carnivals are relatively innocuous instances of this liberation; but wars, in this view, are also inevitable and also provide "festivals for the ego" of a bloodier sort.[49] Social Darwinists would concur with Freud's implication that war is inevitable, but would deplore his emphasis on the tragedy of this fate.

Having already established the id's passionate primitivism and the superego's tendency to arbitrary tyranny, Freud concluded by describing an ego of most ambivalent nature: part pragmatic and rational, part ruthless and cruel. Individuals can approach psychic maturity only by continuous balancing of these forces, and only a few will succeed at the task. Since the rest are, to some degree or other, subversive of organized society, Freud believed that "civilization has to be defended against the individual" – defended by a psychological elite whose members have achieved internal equilibrium and who possess the force and independence to establish their power. Such leaders, Freud said, "should possess superior insight into the necessities of life and . . . have risen to the height of mastering their own instinctual wishes." Lest they be too responsive to the more primitive urges of their constituents, "it . . . seems necessary that they shall be independent of the mass by having means to power at their disposal."[50] He anticipated that rulers of this quality would prove to be rare, and "regretted the enormous amount of coercion that will inevitably be required before these intentions are carried out," but he saw no alternative if advanced cultures were to survive.[51]

The establishment of social justice, he said, requires stability, organization, and authority; only then will strong emotional ties of affiliation develop to ensure the community's survival.[52] In practice, Freud recognized, the leader might well be little more advanced psychically than his followers; he might succeed more by dominating their weak egos and supplanting their superegos than by any inherent intellectual superiority. A few years later, some of Freud's followers were to offer just such an analysis of Hitler's appeal, which they attributed in part to the excesses of paternalist rule.[53]

Freud, however, deemed this risk unavoidable. Unlike the more liberal of his followers, he could imagine no adequate substitute for strong authority and traditional institutions. Rebellion, whether private or political, he found always tempting and always dangerous if successful. Violence and aggression, when released, carry the force of all repressed aspects of the personality; and whereas libidinal drives are capable of at least temporary fulfillment, the baser ego instincts are not.[54] The Great War had revealed the awful consequences attendant on the breakdown of psychic controls; should authoritarian political structures also decline, he feared, the last bulwark of civilization would be destroyed. However revolution might be rationalized in the name of progress, its triumph would mean collective regression.

Clearly, this myth of collective subjection is incompatible with democratic and socialist ideas, or even with classical social contract theory, which presumes that horizontal ties among group members precede and ultimately override vertical lines of authority, rather than the reverse. Freud's outlook resembles Hobbesian justifications for absolute monarchy, but does provide for some possibility of restraint on authority: An ego ideal formed from several models is not bound to any one. In this respect, Freud's social psychology parallels political concepts of pluralism and balance of powers.

Finally, though, Freud's perspective most resembles Edmund Burke's model of political conservatism, with its emphasis on tradition, hierarchy, and authority as bulwarks against chaos. Burke also considered that society was best ordered when it followed the familial pattern: "we have given to our frame of polity the image of a relation of blood, binding up the constitution of our country with our dearest domestic ties." He, too, believed that civilization depends on a superior authority's repression of irrational drives in the masses: "Society requires . . . that . . . the inclinations of men should frequently be thwarted, their will controlled, and their passions brought into subjection. This can only be done *by a power out of themselves,* and not . . . subject to that will and to those passions which it is its office to bridle and subdue."[55] Like Freud, Burke was alarmed by revolutionary and egalitarian movements that seemed to evoke uncontrollable forces of bloody destruction, threatening civilization.

More than a century after Burke's death, the nineteenth-century liberal belief in progress dissolved in war and revolution. These traumatic events seemed to justify Freud's perception that rational independence is available only to a few and only by means of a gradual, painfully difficult process in which civilization triumphs at great cost to affective life.

FREUD ON COMMUNISM AND NATIONAL SOCIALISM

Events of the postwar period further validated Freud's fears. The democracies between the wars, particularly in Central Europe, did seem moribund, or at least ineffectual. Communism, with its assaults on traditional authority and glorification of rational affiliation, was, Freud suspected, doomed to failure. Although he once reflected that "the [Bolshevik] revolution in Russia – in spite of all its disagreeable details – seems none the less like the message of a better future," such optimism did not accord with his theory and did not last long.[56]

Despite its high ideals, he found Communism psychologically untenable. "Social distinctions," he thought, "were originally distinctions between clans or races," biological entities rather then economic creations; and so efforts to eliminate class differences were bound to fail, and likely to do more harm than good. Founded on an abstract and impossible ideal of egalitarian affiliation, Communism would inevitably yield to psychic reality: the inexorable human needs for authority, hierarchy, and violence. Revolution, Freud predicted, would not eliminate these needs, but all too likely would simply rechannel aggression into new forms, without the restraints of traditional authority. "One wonders, with concern, what the Soviets will do after they have wiped out their bourgeois."[57] The results of such upheaval would be disastrous, psychically and socially.

Much as Freud mistrusted the lower classes, he recognized that, unlike "educated people and brain-workers," "the great mass of the uneducated and oppressed . . . have every reason for being enemies of civilization."[58] He understood that the lower classes might decline to accept traditional authority, once even going so far as to say that, "a civilization which leaves so large a number of its participants unsatisfied and drives them into revolt neither has nor deserves the prospect of a lasting existence."[59]

Precisely because of this radical alienation, though, Freud believed that mass revolutions endanger the bases of civilization and ultimately can only fail.

In assuming that rebels against authority really pursue unconscious libidinal aims, acting out a primitive Oedipal drama, Freud consigned them all to irrationality. They might assault their patriarch, but only in the name of a retrograde and psychologically unattainable collectivity; and they would inevitably relapse into some authoritarian state, perhaps more obnoxious than the one it replaced. He questioned whether Communism did or could genuinely replace the forms of authority it challenged, observing that it "has acquired the energy and self-contained and exclusive character of a *Weltanschauung* . . . an uncanny likeness to what it is fighting against."[60] Earlier he had concluded, reluctantly, that, "It is just as impossible to do without control of the mass by a minority as it is to dispense with coercion in the work of civilization."[61]

No such qualifications appear in Freud's comments on National Socialism, which from the outset he considered a wholly irrational and regressive phenomenon of mass politics. By comparison with Communism, he said, "We feel it as a relief from an oppressive apprehension when we see in the case of the German people that a relapse into almost prehistoric barbarism can occur as well without being attached to any progressive ideas."[62] And, in an elliptical conclusion to *Civilization and Its Discontents,* he hinted that Nazism embodied "the human instinct of aggression and self-destruction" and confronted humanity with a choice between the two "Heavenly Powers," life and death.[63] The outcome of the struggle was uncertain; and so it must have seemed to Freud as he endured the events of his remaining years. It is unclear, from his scattered and oblique references, precisely how Freud would have analyzed Nazism's patterns of authority and affiliation; but it is certain that he saw his worst fears fulfilled in it.

Ultimately, Freud equated the extremist ideologies of left and right, observing that in practice both replaced paternal rule with harsh authorities that demanded total obedience and identification of their subjects:

> We are living in a specially remarkable period. We find to our astonishment that progress has allied itself with barbarism. In Soviet Russia they have set about improving the living conditions of some hundred millions of people who were held firmly in subjection. They have been rash enough to withdraw the "opium" of religion from them and have been wise enough to give them a reasonable amount of sexual liberty; but at the same time they have submitted them to the most cruel coercion and robbed them of any possibility of freedom of thought. With similar violence, the Italian people are being trained up to orderliness and a sense of duty.[64]

This psychological theory of totalitarianism implied that the new forms of authority and affiliation were too exclusive, unrestrained, and exhibited in extreme degree the most dangerous qualities of mass psychology.

CONCLUSION

Ultimately, therefore, Freud found only one reliable source of social cohesion: patriarchal authority.[65] He offered little enough hope even for the psychic and social elite who were capable of rationality and constructive sublimation. Most people, he believed, could never attain true psychic or political independence; among this immature majority, civilization could survive only by the imposition of obedience and conformist affiliation.

Freud's familial conception of social life did not extend to encompass the process of children maturing, but remained static: legitimate, or at least necessary, paternal power forever threatened by fruitless or destructive adolescent rebellion. The ideological tendency of his social thought was thus not toward nineteenth-century liberalism, with its rationalist doctrine of gradual progress in education and political participation; rather, it was more pessimistic, presuming that most change was destructive or illusory. Unlike many other psychoanalysts who espoused liberal or leftist perspectives, Freud in his social psychology adhered to conservative principles.[66]

NOTES

1 F. Weinstein, "On the Social Function of Intellectuals: A Consideration of Erik H. Erikson's Contribution to Psychoanalysis and Psychohistory," in M. Albin (ed.), *New Directions in Psychohistory: The Adelphi Papers in Honor of Erik H. Erikson* (Lexington, MA: D. C. Heath, 1980), 4.

2 The classic statement of this position is K. Mannheim's *Ideology and Utopia: An Introduction to the Sociology of Knowledge,* trans. L. Wirth and E. Shils (New York: Harcourt, Brace, 1936).

3 Freud, *Group Psychology and the Analysis of the Ego* (1921), in *Standard Edition of the Complete Psychological Works of Sigmund Freud,* ed. J. Strachey (London: Hogarth Press and the Institute of Psycho-Analysis, 1953–1974), vol. 18, 135.

4 Ernest Jones discusses these and other conflicts, but often rationalizes them, in *The Life and Work of Sigmund Freud,* Vols. 2 and 3 (New York: Basic Books, 1955 and 1957); Paul Roazen adopts a more critical approach in *Freud and His Followers* (New York: Knopf, 1975).

5 W. J. McGrath, *Freud's Discovery of Psychoanalysis: The Politics of Hysteria* (Ithaca, NY: Cornell University Press, 1986), 313.

6 P. Rieff, "Toward a Theory of Culture: With Special Reference to the Psychoanalytic Case," in T. J. Nossiter, et al. (eds.), *Imagination and Precision in the*

Social Sciences: Essays in Memory of Peter Nettl (London: Faber and Faber, 1972), 107–108. F. Weinstein and G. M. Platt dispute this view in *Psychoanalytic Sociology: An Essay on the Interpretation of Historical Data and the Phenomena of Collective Behavior* (Baltimore: Johns Hopkins University Press, 1973), 2–3.

7 H. J. Eysenck, *Uses and Abuses of Psychology* (Harmondsworth: Penguin, 1953); *Fact and Fiction in Psychology* (Harmondsworth: Penguin, 1965); and, with G. D. Wilson, *The Experimental Study of Freudian Theories* (London: Methuen, 1973), which reject psychoanalysis as fundamentally unscientific. K. Popper concurs in *The Logic of Scientific Discovery* (New York: Basic Books, 1959). More recent and balanced assessments of the scientific validity of psychoanalysis include S. Fisher and R. P. Greenberg, *The Scientific Credibility of Freud's Theories and Therapy* (New York: Basic Books, 1977); A. Grünbaum, *The Foundations of Psychoanalysis: A Philosophical Critique* (Berkeley: University of California Press, 1984); and P. Kline, *Fact and Fantasy in Freudian Theory,* 2nd ed. (London: Methuen, 1981).

8 E.g., C. Wright Mills, "The Professional Ideology of Social Pathologists," *American Journal of Sociology* 43:2 (1943):165–180.

9 H. F. Ellenberger, *The Discovery of the Unconscious: The History and Evolution of Dynamic Psychiatry* (New York: Basic Books, 1970).

10 E.g., M. Balmary, *Psychoanalyzing Psychoanalysis: Freud and the Hidden Fault of the Father,* trans. N. Lukacher (Baltimore: Johns Hopkins University Press, 1979); F. Sulloway, *Freud, Biologist of the Mind: Beyond the Psychoanalytic Legend* (New York: Basic Books, 1979); and C. Schorske, "Politics and Patricide in Freud's *Interpretation of Dreams,*" *American Historical Review* 78 (1973):328–347.

11 E.g., D. Yankelovich and W. Barrett, *Ego and Instinct: The Psychoanalytic View of Human Nature–Revised* (New York: Random House, 1970), Part V; and R. Endleman, *Psyche and Society: Explorations in Psychoanalytic Sociology* (New York: Columbia University Press, 1981).

12 E.g., L. Breger, *Freud's Unfinished Journey: Conventional and Critical Perspectives in Psychoanalytic Theory* (London: Routledge and Kegan Paul, 1981).

13 E.g., J. Schuelein, *Das Gesellschaftsbild der Freudschen Theorie* (Frankfurt a.M.: Campus, 1975); K. Horn, "The Societal Function of Psychoanalysis as Political Psychology," *Sigmund Freud House Bulletin* 3:2 (Winter 1979):49–65; and L. E. Hoffman, "From Instinct to Identity: Implications of Changing Psychoanalytic Concepts of Social Life from Freud to Erikson," *Journal of the History of the Behavioral Sciences* 18 (1982):130–146.

14 P. Roazen, *Freud: Political and Social Thought* (New York: Knopf, 1968).

15 H. S. Hughes, *Consciousness and Society: The Reorientation of European Social Thought, 1890–1930* (New York: Knopf, 1958), discusses the interrelations of social thought with political events and ideologies. On the cultural context of psychoanalytic thought during this period, see F. Weinstein and G. M. Platt, *The Wish To Be Free: Society, Psyche, and Value Change* (Berkeley: University of California Press, 1969); P. Rieff, *Freud: The Mind of the Moralist* (Garden City, NY: Doubleday, 1959); and S. Marcus, *Freud and the Culture of Psychoanalysis* (Boston: George Allen and Unwin, 1984). On "outsiders" in German culture during this era, see P. Gay, *Weimar Culture: The Outsider as Insider* (New York: Harper and Row, 1968). On Freud as an outsider, see S. Rothman and P. Isenberg, "Sigmund Freud and the Politics of Marginality," *Central European History* 7:1 (1974):61–68; P. Loewenberg, "'Sigmund Freud as a Jew:' A Study in Ambivalence and Courage," *Journal of the History of the Behavioral Sciences* 7

(1971):363–369; and M. Robert, *From Oedipus to Moses: Freud's Jewish Identity,* trans. R. Manheim (Garden City, NY: Doubleday, 1976).

16 McGrath, *Freud's Discovery of Psychoanalysis,* Ch. 6, "The Psychic Polity," 230–275.

17 H. Decker, *Freud in Germany: Revolution and Reaction in Science, 1893–1907* (New York: International Universities Press, 1977). Sulloway supports this position in *Freud: Biologist of the Mind,* Chapter 13, although he does concede that Freud was alienated from Viennese society (ibid., 463). On the ambiguities of Viennese culture and politics during Freud's time, see C. Schorske, *Fin-de-Siècle Vienna: Politics and Culture* (New York: Knopf, 1980); and A. Janik and S. Toulmin, *Wittgenstein's Vienna* (New York: Simon and Schuster, 1973).

18 The classic works on German academic conservatism are F. K. Ringer, *The Decline of the German Mandarins: The German Academic Community, 1890–1933* (Cambridge: Harvard University Press, 1969); F. Lilge, *The Abuse of Learning: The Failure of the German University* (New York: Macmillan, 1948); and C. E. McLelland, *State, Society, and University in Germany, 1700–1914* (New York: Cambridge University Press, 1980). Also pertinent is W. Struve's *Elites Against Democracy: Leadership Ideals in Bourgeois Political Thought in Germany, 1890–1933* (Princeton: Princeton University Press, 1972).

19 Hughes discusses Croce's shift from elitism to active anti-Fascism in *Consciousness and Society,* 213–223. Mann's original conservatism is most apparent in his famous work *Betrachtungen eines Unpolitischen* (1918); Fritz Stern has keenly analyzed the ideological implications of this position in "The Political Consequences of the Unpolitical German," *History* 3 (1960):104–134. Essays expressing Mann's subsequent strong pro-democratic opinions are available in *The Thomas Mann Reader,* ed. J. W. Angell (New York: Grosset and Dunlap, 1950).

20 Hughes, *Consciousness and Society,* 78–82, 252–274.

21 G. Le Bon, *La Psychologie des Foules* (Paris: F. Alcan, 1895); W. Trotter, *Instincts of the Herd in Peace and War* (London: T. Fisher Unwin, 1916); W. McDougall, *The Group Mind, A Sketch of the Principles of Collective Psychology* (Cambridge: University Press, 1920). Freud discusses their views in Chapters 2 and 3 of his *Group Psychology.*

22 R. A. Nye, *Crime, Madness, and Politics in Modern France: The Medical Concept of National Decline* (Princeton: Princeton University Press, 1984). Both Trotter and Le Bon were medical doctors. Jaap van Ginneken discusses Freud's debt to the mass psychologists in "Parricide: The Background of Freud's *'Group Psychology and the Analysis of the Ego,'" Psyche* 38 (1984):1124–1148. On the origins and political context of this school, see R. A. Nye, *The Origins of Crowd Psychology: Gustave Le Bon and the Crisis of Mass Democracy in the Third Republic* (Beverly Hills, CA: Sage, 1975).

23 Le Bon, *The Crowd,* 2nd ed. (London: T. Fisher Unwin, 1898), v, xviii.

24 J. Goldstein dissects a case of the politicization of psychiatry in "The Hysteria Diagnosis and the Politics of Anticlericalism in Late Nineteenth-Century France," *Journal of Modern History* 54 (1982):209–239.

25 *Totem and Taboo* (1912–1913), in *Standard Edition,* vol. 13, 157–158.

26 *Group Psychology,* 94, 97–98, and chapters 5, 6, 9 passim.

27 Ginneken, "Parricide"; E. Erikson, *Childhood and Society,* 2nd ed. (New York: Norton, 1963), 281.

28 "Thoughts for the Times on War and Death" (1915), in *Standard Edition*, vol. 14, 275–300. L. E. Hoffman, "War, Revolution, and Psychoanalysis: Freudian Thought Begins to Grapple with Social Reality," *Journal of the History of the Behavioral Sciences* 17 (1981):251–269.

29 *Group Psychology*, 70.

30 Ibid., 73. Hoffman, "From Instinct to Identity," 131.

31 *Totem and Taboo*, 141–143; *Group Psychology*, 123 and chapters 9 and 10.

32 *Totem and Taboo*, 156–157; *Moses and Monotheism* (1937–1938), in *Standard Edition*, vol. 23, 109–110. See also *Group Psychology*, 122. P. Mullahy treats the Oedipus complex as the centerpiece of all psychoanalytic theory: *Oedipus Myth and Complex: A Review of Psychoanalytic Theory* (New York: Hermitage Press, 1948). Hoffman, "From Instinct to Identity," 132–133.

33 F. Engels, *The Origin of the Family, Private Property and the State* (1884; reprint New York: International Publishers, 1972).

34 *Group Psychology*, 127.

35 Ibid., 121, 124.

36 Ibid., chapter 5.

37 Ibid., 129; *The Future of an Illusion* (1927), in *Standard Edition*, vol. 28, 8.

38 "My Contact with Josef Popper-Lynkeus" (1932), in *Standard Edition*, vol. 22, 221.

39 "On Narcissism: An Introduction" (1914), in *Standard Edition*, vol. 14, 67–102. Freud changed the term to super-ego in *The Ego and the Id* (1932), in *Standard Edition*, vol. 19, Chapter 3.

40 "The ego ideal is . . . the heir of the Oedipus complex." Freud, *The Ego and the Id*, 36.

41 "On Narcissism," 100–102.

42 *The Ego and the Id*, 54–55.

43 *Group Psychology*, 127–128.

44 Ibid., 129–130.

45 "On Narcissism," 100.

46 "Instincts and Their Vicissitudes" (1915), in *Standard Edition*, vol. 14, 138–139.

47 "Thoughts for the Times on War and Death," 280–286.

48 Ibid., 286; "On Transience" (1916), in *Standard Edition*, vol. 14, 307.

49 *Beyond the Pleasure Principle* (1920), in *Standard Edition*, vol. 13, 19–20. *The Ego and the Id*, 25. *Group Psychology*, 131.

50 *The Future of an Illusion*, 6.

51 Ibid., 8–9.

52 "Why War?" (1933), in *Standard Edition*, vol. 22, 205.

53 *Group Psychology*, 129–130. L. E. Hoffman, "Psychoanalytic Interpretations of Adolf Hitler and Nazism, 1933–1945: Prelude to Psychohistory," *Psychohistory Review* 11 (1982):68–87.

54 Paul Federn, a pioneering ego psychologist, took a very different position: in *Zur Psychologie der Revolution: Die Vaterlose Gesellschaft* (Leipzig and Vienna:

Anzengruber Verlag/Brüder Suschitzky, 1919), he celebrated the creation of a true society of brothers, liberated from their need for paternal rule by the Austrian revolution of 1918. Cf. Freud, "Instincts and Their Vicissitudes," 138–139.

55 E. Burke, *Reflections on the Revolution in France* (1790; reprint New York: Liberal Arts Press, 1955), 38, 68–69. Roazen, *Freud: Political and Social Thought,* 210.

56 "The Question of a Weltanschauung" (1932), *New Introductory Lectures on Psycho-Analysis,* in *Standard Edition,* vol. 22, 175.

57 Ibid., 177–178, 180. Whereas Communists expected socialization of the economy to eliminate the major motives for social conflict, Freud contended that, "Aggressiveness was not created by property." *Civilization and Its Discontents* (1929–1930), in *Standard Edition,* vol. 21, 113, 115.

58 *The Future of an Illusion,* 39.

59 Ibid., 12.

60 "The Question of a Weltanschauung," 179.

61 *The Future of an Illusion,* 7.

62 *Moses and Monotheism,* 54.

63 *Civilization and Its Discontents,* 145.

64 *Moses and Monotheism,* 54.

65 Hoffman, "From Instinct to Identity," 133.

66 Among early psychoanalysts, Adler, Paul Federn, and others expressed Socialist sympathies; see F. Alexander, S. Eisenstein, and M. Grotjahn (eds.), *Psychoanalytic Pioneers* (New York: Basic Books, 1966). The literature on the "Freudian Left" is too extensive to review here; but see especially the section "From Marx to Freud and Back," in H. S. Hughes, *The Sea Change: The Migration of Social Thought, 1930–1965* (New York: Harper and Row, 1975), and M. Jay, *The Dialectical Imagination: A History of the Frankfurt School and the Institute of Social Research, 1923–1950* (Boston: Little, Brown, 1973).

12

JEAN PIAGET AND THE
LIBERAL PROTESTANT
TRADITION*

FERNANDO VIDAL

INTRODUCTION

After his arrival at the Jean-Jacques Rousseau Institute of Geneva in 1921, 25-year-old Jean Piaget (1896–1980) organized a group to investigate the psychology of religion. According to Piaget, the group was led to consider such methodological questions as

> From which point of view can we say that one religious experience is superior to another? Has this question a psychological meaning? And if it is an exclusively religious question, which criterion will faith have at its disposal to settle the matter, and yet remain sheltered from any questioning from psychology?[1]

For Piaget, these questions did have a psychological meaning. Between 1921 and 1930, he elaborated answers to them, always in close connection with his researches in child development.

One of the major problems Piaget was trying to solve in the 1920s could be formulated as, "How can one believe, and yet remain objective?" To answer this question, Piaget elaborated a science that was consistent with his beliefs. Reciprocally, he formulated his religious beliefs so as to make them fall within the boundary conditions established by an epistemology that prolonged the tradition of evolutionary positivism. For Piaget, psychology could establish "objective" hierarchies of values, by

* Most of the research included in this chapter was done while the author was engaged under subsidy No. 1535.0.82 of the Fonds National Suisse de la Recherche Scientifique. Support was also provided by a Théodore Flournoy Scholarship (University of Geneva, 1985). Thanks to Dr. Paul Ducommun of the Club des Amis de la Nature, Neuchâtel, and to Mme Antoinette Virieux-Reymond for permission to use documents from the Arnold Reymond papers.

determining the "psychological or biological superiority" of certain values. On the basis of empirical findings, he argued, for example, that the immanentist conception of religion was the most evolved and, therefore, superior to the theology of transcendence and revelation strongly revived within Protestantism in the 1920s. These matters are key background elements of Piaget's 1932 book, *The Moral Judgment of the Child.*[2]

In *The Moral Judgment,* Piaget argued that children progress from a morality based on external authority and unilateral respect, to a morality of cooperation based on a sort of social contract among individuals capable (from the cognitive point of view) of adopting other individuals' perspectives. Piaget's pioneer work in moral development can be interpreted as the culmination of his youthful project, "to base morality on science."[3] Such a project was alien to the French-speaking Swiss liberal Protestant tradition. Nevertheless, Piaget's scientific-psychological axiology was aimed at saving the fundamental values of that tradition from the neo-dogmatic tidal wave that followed World War I, which emphasized a transcendentalist conception of religion. Contrary to a still widespread opinion, Piaget's vast intellectual enterprise has not always been exclusively or primarily aimed at solving epistemological problems; it was also directed at answering theological and religious questions on the basis of scientific investigation.

THE PROTESTANT BACKGROUND

The question, "How can one believe, and yet remain objective?" has to be put in the perspective of the history of liberal Protestant theology.[4] Liberal Protestantism is rooted, on the one hand, in the eighteenth-century movement of humanization of Christianity that emphasized inwardness and individualism and rejected external authority. On the other hand, it is also rooted in the efforts made by Protestant theologians to face the increasing secularization of intellectual life by integrating theology and culture. Liberal Protestantism was marked by the thought of Friedrich Schleiermacher (1768–1834) who, at the end of the eighteenth century, tried to reconcile religion and secular culture by postulating the existence of a religious feeling, which was a constitutive part of human psychology, and consisted in a sense of absolute dependency in relation to the universe. Religion was irreducible to rational knowledge or to principles of duty and obligation; religious experience was the object and the condition of theological discourse.

This theology developed into approaches aimed at legitimizing religion by interpreting it as a genuine human experience, *sui generis* but governed by the same historical and psychological laws that govern other human experiences. The psychology of religion, propelled by G. Stanley Hall (1846–1924) and William James (1842–1910) in the United States, and by Théodore Flournoy (1854–1920) in Switzerland, can be seen as one such approach, even though its practitioners would have denied having an apologetic intention. In 1901–1902, James delivered at Edinburgh the lectures that would become *The Varieties of Religious Experience.* Almost at the same time, his friend Flournoy was initiating a vast audience to "religious psychology," his abbreviation for the psychology "of religion" or "religious phenomena." He did so in the context of the chair of Experimental Psychology that the University of Geneva had created for him in 1891 and placed, at his request, in the Sciences Department. This situation – religious psychology in a curriculum of experimental sciences – is emblematic of the liberal Protestant attitude toward religion.

The first things Flournoy did were to fix the limits between psychology and theology, and to define the respective rights of science and faith. The published version of his introductory lecture became the methodological manifesto of religious psychology – an extremely influential text, at least in the French-speaking Swiss liberal Protestant milieu that concerns us here.[5] Flournoy's first methodological principle ("Exclusion of Transcendence") stated that religious psychology did not pronounce itself on the nature (objective or subjective, for example) of the phenomena it studied, and did not discuss such questions as the existence of an invisible or supernatural world. The second principle ("Biological Interpretation") characterized religion as a vital phenomenon that could be investigated with the tools of the different branches of psychology (physiological, genetic, dynamic, comparative, pathological).

Flournoy and other liberal Protestants believed that psychology could not jeopardize religion; for them, the sharp distinction between the realm of science and the realm of faith sufficed to render obsolete the idea of a warfare between religion and science. Their view of science was akin to a conventionalism that preserved the cognitive validity of faith vis-à-vis scientific knowledge. Such an epistemology was strengthened by pragmatism, a philosophy consistent with the liberal respect for variety, the attachment to individual experience, and the rejection of formal dogmas and external authority. Flournoy agreed with James that pragmatism was a "philosophical Protestantism."[6]

The efforts to "detheologize" and "psychologify" religion that Flournoy recommended and carried out were direct descendents of such works as Sabatier's *Outlines of a Philosophy of Religion* (1897).[7] Auguste Sabatier (1839–1901) was the greatest exponent of liberal Protestant theology in the French-speaking world. Like other liberal theologians toward the end of the nineteenth century, he emphasized the psychological side of religious experience, and the historical nature of religious beliefs. Sabatier assumed the premises of Schleiermacher's nonempirical psychology, and argued that religious dogmas were only collective symbols subject to the evolutionary laws presumed to govern human life and thought. For him, the third and last stage of humanity's progress was characterized by the absolute inwardness of revelation, by the belief that God is immanent to the individual and the cosmos, and by a psychological kind of religion. Sabatier thought that in a secularized world dominated by the scientific outlook, this religion would be capable of satisfying the demands of reason, religious consciousness, and faith.

In Sabatier's evolutionist perspective, liberal Protestantism appeared as the most evolved religious attitude, fused with the ideals of scientific knowledge and freedom of thought. Nevertheless, the conception of faith as an essentially individual phenomenon was not evidently consistent with the idea of the Church as a united body of Christians, and with the principle that God transcends both the individual and the Church. The nature of faith (subjective or objective, relative or absolute) therefore became a central object of debate.

Toward the turn of the century, theologians brought up mainly within the liberal tradition started feeling that this tradition had turned religion into a subjective matter dependent on individual conscience alone. It was argued, for example, that liberalism had turned Jesus into a merely human historical character and model of conduct, at the expense of Jesus as redeeming Messiah and eternal spiritual force. According to one critic, Jesus had become "a figure designed by rationalism, endowed with life by liberalism, and clothed by modern theology in an historical garb."[8] For a later theologian, in liberalism "a God without wrath brought men without sin into a kingdom without judgment through the ministrations of a Christ without a cross."[9]

The historical and psychological orientation of liberal theology resulted in a pervasive intellectualistic attitude toward religion. Such an attitude became particularly questionable at the outbreak of World War I.[10] Intellectualism was felt as a betrayal to the nature of faith and the mission of theology, and was deemed largely responsible for the incapacity of the reformed churches to face sociopolitical circumstances effectively. Especially in a spared Switzerland frequently described as the land of democracy, humaneness, and peace, the Great War aroused painful questions about the historical and secular mission of the Church. For example, the declaration of the 77th synod of the Free Church of the canton of Vaud humbly pointed out the church's shared responsibility for the War; with variations, the other churches adhered to this declaration.[11]

Liberalism came under heavy attack after World War I. Critiques originated mainly in a neo-orthodox movement under the leadership of the Swiss theologian Karl Barth (1886–1968). Highlighting the absolute transcendence of God, this movement substituted a sense of sin for the liberal confidence in an indefinite progress conducted by reason, and replaced the immanentism of liberal belief by a doctrine of revelation. What must be emphasized here is that the neo-dogmatic revival was a reaction against the immanentist and subjectivist attitudes of liberal Protestantism, and an effort to restore transcendence as the fundamental ground of the objectivity of religious faith and theological knowledge. Piaget's psychological critique of transcendence, elaborated in the 1920s, related directly to a "neo-liberal" viewpoint that developed parallel to neo-orthodoxy. This relatedness, as well as Piaget's position as a scientific spokesman against the dogmatic revival, can be traced to his intense involvement in a Christian youth movement during World War I.

CHRISTIAN YOUTH

The Swiss Christian Students Association to which Piaget belonged was one of the most active centers of liberal Protestantism in French-speaking Switzerland. Theologians, pastors, writers, scientists, artists, philosophers, and psychologists followed with great interest the religious and intellectual development of youth; this was particularly patent in their participation at the Association's annual fall conference at Sainte-Croix, in the Jura mountains, not far from Piaget's native town of Neuchâtel.[12] The Swiss association was a branch of the World Christian Student Federation, founded in 1895 to oppose the intellectualist and purely theoretical "materialism" that "manifested itself among students as a lack of ideals and feeling for social responsibilities."[13] The motto of the Association, *Faire Christ Roi,* was supposed to represent its members' longing to approach "the person of Christ as a *living personality,* and not as an object of theological argument."[14]

The aspiration of realizing "the ideal of loyalty, moral purity, and renunciation incarnated in Christ" went together with the goal of putting into practice His "law of love," both among students and in society at large.[15] This pervasive approach to the so-called "social question" was close to the late nineteenth-century French doctrine of "solidarism." At the same time, debates about social Christianism and its relation to a possible Christian socialism were very much alive. A minister, for example, preached that only "a synthesis of the ideal of the Church and that of the International" might entail "the kingdom of God in mankind, the advent of God the Father by the advent of human fraternity."[16] Yet, in accordance with a fundamental tenet of Christian theology, materialism was condemned. Since the social body was to be transformed by transforming the human heart, discussions abounded on how the teachings of Christ and the model of His life could inspire in each individual the inner reform that would lead to the renewal of society.[17]

The massive mobilization of young men since the outbreak of World War I slowed down the activity of the movement at large. The Swiss branch of the Federation, however, found itself in the privileged, but difficult position of being able to think peacefully about what was taking place all around neutral Switzerland. "Neutral countries," it would later be recalled, "could only remain silent; confronted with their brothers' suffering, they collect[ed] themselves in mute waiting, and prepare[d] the after-war."[18] Among youth, the main feature of the crisis of liberal Protestantism was a revolt against intellectualism. This phenomenon was very strong in France, but was found throughout Europe, in the United States, and elsewhere.[19] Young people seemed to be less interested in theology than in finding the living reality of God and Christ that, embodied in a religion of action, would help them construct a better postwar world.[20] The exaltation that accompanied the anti-intellectualist trend contributed to nourish the development of a youth-centered, Messianic literature that compensated for the sense of impotence and defeat that pervaded the liberal Protestant milieu during the War. Numerous articles in *The Student World,* the quarterly magazine of the World Student Christian Federation, showed that young intellectuals believed, or at least were told, that a new world would come out of the war, and that they would have a key role in it. Indeed, it was imagined that nobody could understand better than youth the redeeming message of the living Christ.

PIAGET'S WAY TO CHRISTIAN YOUTH

In accordance with the principles of liberalism, an ideal of Christian youth could adopt a variety of forms. In the "student world" described above, becoming an exemplary young man implied two things: adhering to the principles of liberal Protestantism – individualism, immanentism, adjustment of religion to modern thought – and identifying with the prevailing image of youth as idealistic, socially concerned, inspired by Jesus Christ. Like that of his peers, Piaget's adherence to liberal Protestantism meant adopting an ideal image of youth.

Piaget was born into the intellectual bourgeoisie generally oriented toward liberalism. His father, the medievalist Arthur Piaget (1865–1952) was a prominent university figure who had not hesitated to demonstrate and announce the apocryphal nature of a document that legitimized Neuchâtel's aristocracy; for a long time, he remained the foremost local historian. According to Jean's recollections, Arthur Piaget felt that "the current faith and an honest historical criticism were incompatible." Unlike her husband, Rebecca-Suzanne Jackson was "a devout Protestant" who insisted on sending her fifteen-year-old son to the traditional six-week religion course. There, Piaget remembered, he was struck by "the difficulty of reconciling a number of dogmas with biology," and by "the fragility of the 'five proofs of the existence of God'"; this was all the more striking since the pastor "was an intelligent man, who himself dabbled in the natural sciences."[21]

Piaget's narrative follows a traditional conflict model of the relations between religion and science. His autobiography serves scientific triumphalism, and fulfills the legitimizing function of conventional disciplinary history.[22] To do so, however, it omits to explain what "science" and "religion" meant in the specific case of the young Piaget. In 1911, Piaget had had no contact with "biology," but only with a strictly descriptive and classificatory natural history. On the other hand, "current faith" tended to be liberal. Religious instruction was Christ-centered and moralistic, and the literature for catechumens consisted mainly of stories of religious lives, advice to youth, and other writings by liberal Protestant authors.[23]

Surely it is plausible that religious instruction might have included dogmatic and apologetic elements, that Piaget was struck by contradiction, and that he struggled against the education imposed by his mother.[24] Yet it seems possible to qualify the autobiography. Piaget wrote, for example, that about the time of religious instruction, he discovered Sabatier's *Outlines,* whose evolutionistic and symbolic interpretation of dogmas temporarily resolved the conflicts raised by catechesis.[25] It is likely, however, that the *Outlines* itself provided the occasion for one of Piaget's first encounters with the very idea of a conflict between religion and science. Indeed, in the introduction to his widely read book, Sabatier explicitly defined his audience as young men who searched, with all the idealism and sincerity of their age, for a solution to the conflict between science and faith that they were bound to feel. The *Outlines* thus provided a remedy for the disquiet it helped to provoke.

Probably in the summer of 1912, Piaget was initiated to Henri Bergson's philosophy of creative evolution by his godfather, the writer Samuel Cornut (1861–1918). Cornut venerated a heroic figure of Jesus and a romantic image of youth, proclaimed his animosity toward bourgeois hypocrisy and Protestant moralism, preached an ideal of social fraternity, and searched for ways to link personal conscience to the whole living cosmos.[26] Piaget relates that Cornut found him too exclusively absorbed in natural history, and wanted to teach him philosophy. Bergson was the natural choice. Bergsonian philosophy had become youth's battle-cry against intellectualism and rationalism.[27] A Sabatier-inspired young man, duly torn between science and faith and comforted with an evolutionistic panacea, could be easily carried away with *élan vital* and swept by the flow of creative evolution. Already in 1912, Piaget examined some fundamental problems of taxonomy in the light of Bergson's critique of "mechanistic" science;[28] his Bergsonian conclusions then helped to inspire, for example, his stand on natural selection and the theory of mutation.[29]

Piaget's first article outside the field of natural history, published in 1914, was a comparison of Bergson and Sabatier. The religious attitude expressed in that article illustrated what Piaget later called his "Bergson-ian Protestantism."[30] For example, he argued that religious evolution was an aspect of creative evolution, and interpreted moral consciousness, a key concept in Sabatier, as "one of the purest and highest forms of Berg-sonian intuition."[31]

PIAGET, MODEL OF CHRISTIAN YOUTH

The most important expression of Piaget's Bergsonian Protestantism is *The Mission of the Idea* (1915). This prose poem embodied the philo-sophical and religious complex out of which would grow, both as an elab-oration and as a disclaimer, Piaget's project of basing morality on science. At the same time, it was a statement about its author's own identity. The mission of the Idea was that of youth; to work for its accomplishment was, first of all, to become someone who could live up to the task. In June 1915 the Neuchâtel group of the Christian Students Association pictured itself among those who waited "for the sunrise, for the ideal that will come out of the present *mêlée,* and that the future will establish. . . . We have little activity, many aspirations, an ardent need of equilibrium. The most positive moment was the session when Jean Piaget presented his work *'Essay on the Empirical Genesis of Consciousness, and its Reconcil-iation with Religion.'* There were both old and young members. We all felt one thing: that we want to live."[32]

By the time he finished his Gymnasium studies in July 1915, Piaget had become impregnated not only with the values and ideals, but also with the rhetoric and sensitivity of his Christian youth milieu. The key phrase of a letter he wrote to his young naturalists' club in September read: "I do not despise your science, our science (since I am still one of yours); I say that this science results from friendship, and not the other way around."[33] The tone of the phrase and its emphasis on fraternity are representative of the attitudes of a young Swiss Christian intellectual. In November 1915 the Swiss Christian Students Association's bulletin enthusiastically announced a forthcoming double issue containing his alive, inspired, and well-written "hymn or poem as much as 'essay'" enti-tled *The Mission of the Idea* (see Figure 12-1).[34]

Piaget's poetical essay elaborated the emotional and intellectual leit-motifs of Christian youth and of Piaget as Christian young man, in the framework of a metaphysical system with Plotinian overtones. This sys-tem was constructed as a hierarchy of three levels: the Idea, the ideas, and the human formulas of the ideas. Those levels, decreasing in degree of existence, truth, and wholeness, embodied history and progress, that is, the march of the Idea toward an ideal and absolute Humanity. Mys-tical experience was valued as a way of apprehending metaphysical truth, and poetry as a way of expressing it. Conservatism, nationalism, egoism,

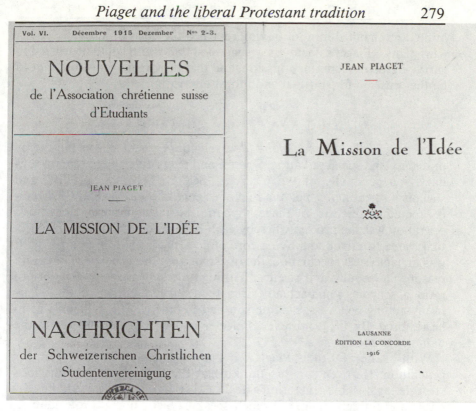

Figure 12-1. Title page for the two editions of *The Mission of the Idea.*

pride, bourgeois inertia, and the churches were violently accused of standing in the way of the Idea. In turn, the mission of the Idea was the rebirth of true Christianity through the realization of the Idea's echoes in human individuals and communities, under the form of justice, equality, women's rights, socialism, the solidarity of science and the people.

In accordance with the belief that Jesus was the archetypal young man, nineteen-year-old Piaget preached that the mission of youth was to become Christlike, and to work for the realization of the Idea on earth. Intellectual young men were the chosen vehicles of the Idea; their intrinsic destiny and inherent duty was to be the Idea's apostles. *The Mission of the Idea* detached divinity from Jesus, replaced theocentricity by idealism, and announced a sort of biological hope by identifying evolution and morality.

Piaget's metaphysical gospel, full of revolt and a sense of sacred indignation, was acclaimed because it proved that Christian youth was still alive, and that a Christian young man was capable of combining intellectual depth and feeling to deliver a message that would stir and orient his peers. Several reviewers praised Piaget's text, celebrated his culture, juvenile ardor, and sincerity, saw in him one of the guides of the new generation, and thanked him for having revealed the heart of idealistic young Christians.[35] Piaget's poem-essay suggested that youth could be trusted to carry out their redemptory mission, and that the Great War would indeed be the occasion for spiritual and moral renovation.

GETTING AWAY FROM "METAPHYSICS"

According to *The Mission of the Idea,* religious orthodoxy was the enemy of science and social salvation. Science and the people had to remain solidary, independently of the Church. "Science becomes socialist, and socialism scientific."[36] Yet, the role of science in the rebirth of Christianity remained unclear. In Piaget's poem, the most important cognitive operation was the process whereby each believer constructed an intellectual frame to surround a living core of personal faith. More narrowly, it was metaphysical speculation, the quest for a synthesis between faith and reason, philosophy and science. Through metaphysics, the diversity of rational schemes could actually strengthen spiritual unity and moral harmony among believers; each person had to practice it if religion was to be restored. By 1917, however, Piaget was decrying metaphysics in the name of science.

With his new attitude, Piaget felt that he distanced himself from his generation. He even saw his thinking at the time as an "unconscious struggle" against his generation's neglect of science.[37] In May 1917 he criticized a prominent figure of French-speaking Swiss liberal Protestantism for disregarding contemporary science and philosophy.[38] A few months later, in a letter to the internationalist and pacifist writer Romain Rolland (1866–1944), he wrote that, for two years, he had been trying to get rid of metaphysics and theology. Faith, he said, is independent of metaphysics, and metaphysics is vain; therefore, the great problem is to base morality on science.[39]

Even if he did not yet know what "science" ought to be, Piaget knew that he wanted to leave metaphysics behind. Such a change of mind related to the dead end to which metaphysics, that is, mainly his enthusiasm for Bergson, had led him in his work in the natural sciences. Between 1912 and 1914, Piaget had been involved in a debate during which he employed Bergsonian ideas to oppose Mendelism.[40] As he became aware of the inadequacy of approaching the problems of modern biology with a mixture of traditional natural history and Bergsonian philosophy, he entered a phase of scientific confusion that still surfaced in 1918.[41] The counterpart of this confusion was a search for a legitimate scientific biology and a nonmetaphysical philosophy.

Such a development was largely dependent on the young Piaget's relationship to the Swiss thinker Arnold Reymond (1874–1958). Reymond illustrated the very significant fact that, in Piaget's world, philosophy was still in the hands of theologians. In Neuchâtel, Reymond taught at both the high school and the university; Piaget followed his courses at both institutions (1913–1915 and 1915–1918), and the teacher became a mentor and a friend.

The sense of his influence on Piaget is illustrated by two lectures delivered in 1913, the first year he taught in Neuchâtel. One lecture was given at the Swiss Christian Students Association, and dealt with the relations between scientific and religious knowledge. Reymond pointed out that both sorts of knowledge were relative and subject to historical change. Yet, he argued, both were objective, even if the problems raised by religious truth could be solved only from within religious life.[42] His viewpoint at the time was consistent with that set forth in a later talk that Piaget would call his own "intellectual and moral catechism."[43] At the 1917 Christian students conference, Reymond argued that the objectivity of even the most apparently subjective Protestant religious attitude was related to the existence of certain permanent functional elements in the history and psychology of religion. These elements, however, were always linked to historically changing beliefs. Thus, the ultimate foundation of religious objectivity was in an ethical and logical core that persisted throughout history.[44]

Piaget's desire to turn to science after *The Mission of the Idea* conformed to his teacher's rationalism. At the public lecture that opened his university course, Reymond set forth a critique of Bergson's philosophy.[45] Like other rationalists, he tended to interpret the intuitionist philosophy of creative evolution as an anti-intellectualism incapable of facing the traditional problems of metaphysics. The young Piaget attended this lecture and, as he recalled, felt closer to Bergson than to his future mentor.[46] Indeed, Reymond challenged the efficacy of applying Bergson's critique of science to such problems as the ontological status of scientific concepts. In so doing, he questioned precisely the ideas that Piaget was elaborating at the time.[47] And in his 1918 book *Recherche,* Piaget would characterize his theoretical solution to the problem of basing morality on science as an "advanced," non-metaphysical Bergsonism, not yet as a scientific endeavor.[48]

THE QUEST FOR SCIENCE

In his autobiography, Piaget emphasized the passage from *Recherche* that announced his more mature thinking on equilibration.[49] But *Recherche* was a vaster project. Its first two parts were a sort of *Bildungsroman* where an impersonal narrator presented, somewhat in the vein of Rolland's enormously popular *Jean-Christophe,* the development of Sebastian, the novel's young hero and only character. Sebastian is absorbed in working out the relations between science, faith, and morality, and in trying to establish the definitive way toward social salvation in a world that is being shattered by war.

Sebastian was Piaget himself, and *Recherche* included a confession on the crises he underwent while looking for a personal equilibrium.[50] In turn, this confession aimed at "explaining" the ideas of an aspiring philosopher by placing them in a psychological and historical context. Finally, the theory set forth after the confession embodied a project for the salvation of society through the rebirth of Christianity and the establishment of a federalist *(à la suisse)* socialism. The theoretical support of this project, which was introduced by a letter to "young socialists," constituted a personal, long-term research program.

This theoretical support for the ideals of Christian youth was no longer based on metaphysics, mysticism, or intuition, all of which were explicitly denigrated, but on certain findings Piaget attributed to contemporary science. On the one hand, he argued, science showed that the ideal regulating "norm" of all organisms, including society, was an equilibrated organization of their component parts. Disequilibrium was illness. European society had been too weakened by the disequilibrium between science and faith to prevent the Great War from taking place. Restore the equilibrium and society would be saved. Politically, federalism was the equilibrium between nationalism and internationalism; socialism, that between bourgeois liberalism and collectivism.

On the other hand, Piaget claimed that science gave knowledge of good and evil, true and false, beautiful and ugly; it therefore provided a basis for morality, even if an act of faith was declared indispensable to give ethical meaning to scientific statements. Science, however, always turned out to be consistent with the choices of faith. The naturalistic ethics proclaimed in *The Mission of the Idea* gained support from the fact that, for Sebastian, "evolutionist moralities have proved that the good is life itself."[51] For Piaget writing on the relation between biology and war, "to struggle against war is . . . to act according to the logic of life against the logic of things, and that is the whole of morality."[52] In other words,

> scientific morality does nothing other than confirm the views adopted by individual conscience . . . and in the same way as we know Aristotle's logic, or how to digest before knowing physiology, we know how to practice the good before learning to know biological equilibria.[53]

Such statements epitomize a major part of Piaget's research program and interpretive framework in the domain of child psychology.

In 1918, Piaget did not yet know how he would turn such a program into a scientific enterprise. Approximately between October 1918 and March 1919 he was in Zurich, getting acquainted with experimental psychology, psychiatry, and especially psychoanalysis.[54] The nascent orientation toward psychology represented a further step away from pure philosophy. This process might have been reinforced by the negative reviews of *Recherche,* which pointed out the insufficiency of biology as a basis for morality, Piaget's ignorance of research on concrete social problems, and the purely verbal nature of such concepts as "equilibrium."[55]

Psychology would enable Piaget to investigate the processes of intellectual and moral equilibrium in and among individuals; philosophy would give him the critical tools to elaborate a global theory. During his Parisian stay (1919–1921), Piaget studied logic, philosophy of science, and different branches of psychology. Recommended by a family friend, Pierre Bovet (1878–1965), he went to see Théodore Simon, collaborator of the late Alfred Binet, who gave him the task of standardizing Burt's tests with children.[56] This was the point of departure of Piaget's psychological career; a few years later, Bovet, director of the Jean-Jacques Rousseau Institute in Geneva, became his employer.

THE PROJECT OF A SCIENTIFIC PSYCHOLOGY OF VALUES

In his autobiography, Piaget wrote that when he arrived at the Rousseau Institute, he organized his research to gain "objectively and inductively knowledge about the elementary structures of intelligence" so that he could later "be in a position to attack the problem of thought in general and to construct a psychological and biological epistemology."[57] The project of developing such an epistemology, however, was only a part of the research program outlined in *Recherche,* inseparable from the project of elaborating a scientific, "psychological and biological" ethics. Contrary to what is usually believed, Piaget thought that psychogenesis could provide positive insights into the validity not only of scientific knowledge, but also of values.

The twenty-five-year-old Piaget's project for a science of values was not alien to the activities of the Rousseau Institute, where the psychology of religion and questions of moral education occupied an important place. While writing in 1925 about the relations between religious feelings and child psychology, Bovet would use Piaget's findings to argue that children's religious attitudes were consistent with their cosmogonies.[58] It must be pointed out that Bovet was a liberal, evangelical, social Christian, as well as a convinced pacifist and internationalist. Formerly an active member of the Swiss Christian Students Association, he remained deeply concerned with the problem of elaborating a Christian moral pedagogy. Moreover, he was among the promoters of the International Bureau of Education (IBE), founded in 1925 to work in favor of international understanding. Piaget became director of the IBE in 1929.

In 1921, the year he arrived at the Rousseau Institute, Piaget organized the group on religious psychology mentioned at the beginning of this chapter. A question asked within the group was, "From which point of view can we say that one religious experience is superior to another?" For Piaget, the answer was: from the viewpoints of genetic psychology and historico-critical philosophy. This answer was first provided, both as a research program and as an act of faith, in a 1921 article, in which Piaget argued that the psychological and philosophical orientations of French-speaking Swiss religious philosophy were convergent, "and that this convergence is indispensable for our intellectual equilibrium."[59]

Piaget affirmed that the dissociation between psychology on the one hand, and faith and religious experience on the other, was a "temporary attitude, aimed at assuring the equilibrium of psychologists themselves as flesh-and-bone persons who want to keep believing while valuing the empirical method." As one such psychologist, Piaget hoped "to associate religious search to the cult of classical logic, simultaneously rationalist and experimental."[60] According to him, the psychological tradition initiated by Flournoy and illustrated by Bovet was characterized by two philosophical features he summed up as "empirical Kantism." One was the conviction that the foundations of "the values of faith" could be discovered empirically in the concrete mechanism of religious phenomena; the other was a systematic skepticism about the possibility of knowing anything beyond scientific data. The logical and philosophical tradition was illustrated by his teacher Arnold Reymond.

Taking up key ideas from Reymond's 1917 talk on the objective features of Protestantism – a talk that had become his own "moral and intellectual catechism" – Piaget argued that the spiritual history of humanity was the process of objectivization, whereby "individual thought subjects itself to a simultaneously logical and moral norm that transcends it, and which is for the logician the true object of religious experience."[61] Piaget sought to continue within psychology his land's theologico-philosophical tradition, with means adapted to the ongoing crisis of that tradition, and through a more satisfying "equilibrium" between faith and science. To do so, he proposed to replace Kant's "faith" in the existence of a transcendental realm by a "rational" faith in "a God that increasingly forms one body with the world, that is, with reason and its structure [*ses cadres*]."[62] All values, including God, thus appeared as immanent to the mind; accordingly, the "norms" of reason were for Piaget simultaneously logical and moral.

Piaget's position was actually less similar to Reymond's than to that of the historico-critical philosopher Léon Brunschvicg (1869–1944), whose courses he had followed in Paris. For Brunschvicg, progress in science and ethics was inherent to those domains, and went in the direction of immanentism. It can be said that in the 1920s Piaget was to a large extent trying to confirm, or at least formulate, Brunschvicg's philosophy empirically. A particularly relevant point is Brunschvicg's belief that religious truth resulted from an epuration of human judgment, from a gradual elimination of egocentrism enabling the human individual subject to become universal. For him, God was universal Reason.[63]

Piaget continued to elaborate his research program in a talk on "Psychology and Religious Values" given at the 1922 meeting of the Swiss Christian Students Association. It was reported that the twenty-six year-old "master in psychoanalysis and general philosophy" was successful among those of the younger generation who seemed "to distrust metaphysics, and have complete confidence in psychology."[64] Explicitly following Flournoy's principles, Piaget postulated a strict separation between science and value judgments. Two conceptions of God would be for science equally true "as individual symbols of a unique ineffable reality."[65] Nevertheless, he argued, even if science cannot say that one value is more legitimate than another, it can establish the "psychological or biological superiority" of one of them. For example, science could arrange the transcendentalist and immanentist religious attitudes in an evolutionary hierarchy, and thus conclude that "from the empirical point of view, and only relatively to individual psychological development, one religious type is more evolved than another, and therefore, superior."[66]

In Piaget's perspective, science did not deal with values themselves, but could help to explain value judgments. A scientific psychology of values would thus investigate – from a developmental viewpoint, and assuming "a parallelism between logic and the theory of values" – the logical links that exist between judgments whose premisses it does not discuss.[67] Once a personal experience has been made, Piaget claimed, psychology could "control" it and verify its logical structure. For example, a militarist socialist would be led to examine whether or not militarism and socialism are logically contradictory, and would then have to make up his mind in the moral and practical domain. The logical and moral experiences were closely linked; contradiction in logic and contradiction in morals were "the two sides of the same phenomenon."[68]

Science could not only control and validate reasoning, but also establish, "from the immanent and biological viewpoint of life and thought," a criterion based on the principle of noncontradiction, interpreted as a "law of psychological equilibrium." From noncontradiction ensued the following criterion: the more a value has the potential to generate other values, the higher it is. Love was therefore the supreme value.[69] After praising "the young psychologist's efforts to establish the means for discovering the internal logic of religious experience and the hierarchy of values that governs it," a rather skeptical YMCA reviewer wrote: "With a vivid and sympathetic interest, we wait for the confirmation that the study of facts will enable him to furnish."[70]

PIAGET'S PSYCHOLOGICAL AXIOLOGY

In 1924, on the basis of his research and of contemporary works in psychology and anthropology, Piaget could assert that the principle of non-contradiction was a psychological and moral necessity, and a function as biological as nutrition.[71] The books on children's mental growth that made him famous had already started appearing in 1923.[72] The clearest example of the connections Piaget established between the development of judgment in morality and in other domains is given by his description of children's causal explanations as evolving from a supernatural, transcendental, and heteronomous physics, where physical law is assimilated to a coercive moral or social law, to a truly mechanistic, implicative, and causal physics, autonomous and immanent to the cosmos.[73]

At the same time that he determined the psychological sequence from transcendence to immanence, Piaget was trying to demonstrate that the disappearance of egocentrism was linked to a "grasp of consciousness" of one's thought processes, and that this "grasp" took place about the age of seven as a result of "contact with others and the practice of discussion."[74] "Cooperation," he claimed, "is the empirical fact [in the domain of moral behavior] whose logical ideal is reciprocity."[75]

Piaget's philosopher colleagues doubted that autism (or egocentrism), social constraint, and cooperation could be neatly organized in successive stages.[76] Nevertheless, his psychogenetic series furnished a clear, empirically testable scheme, as well as good arguments, to the advocates of an active, child-centered pedagogy aimed at forming the builders and citizens of a more democratic, peaceful, and moral world. "Every progress made in the different moral and social domains," Piaget claimed, "results from the fact that we have freed ourselves from egocentrism, and from intellectual and moral coercion."[77]

For those who were familiar with Piaget's religious background and past history, such ideas had significant theological implications. Thus, in March 1928, the Swiss Christian Students Association invited Piaget to talk about immanence and transcendence as religious attitudes. Speaking to an audience described as being deeply influenced by the dogmatic and transcendentalist revival, Piaget claimed that, by approaching values as empirical facts, psychology and sociology had discovered the law of evolution that governed them in the individual and in society. In his opinion, such a law showed the "psychological" superiority of immanentism, thus confirming, for example, the idea that the "gloomy mythology" of the passion of Christ was an eloquent proof of "the inhuman nature of the moral and religious attitude of transcendence," always linked to social coercion.[78]

In accordance with Brunschvicg's critical philosophy, Piaget asserted that the immanentist attitude was by no means subjective, but the most objective possible one. "Immanentism," he wrote, "implies the identification of God, not with the psychological self [which He transcends], but with the [universal and impersonal] norms of thought."[79] For Piaget, religion, morality and science converged in a unique grasp of consciousness of the norms of reason that represented, at the same time, an immanent God, cooperation, and justice, and every free and sincere intellectual search for truth. In sum,

> From the viewpoint of morality, the ego is subjected to norms such as reciprocity or justice. These are the very norms of reason, which apply to action as much as to thought. Morality is a logic of action, as logic is a morality of thought. The activity of reason is one and the same.[80]

Thus, by 1928, what would appear in 1932 as the main conclusion of *The Moral Judgment of the Child* was entirely formulated.

The rather passionate debate that followed Piaget's talk illustrated the disagreements that were tearing Protestantism. Reymond, for example, criticized Piaget for being an extreme subjectivist. The debate culminated in June 1929, when the group of former members of the Swiss Christian Students Association gave Piaget the opportunity to elucidate his position at length. The argument and the style were the same as before. Thus read Piaget's conclusion:

> . . . if, beyond men, one examines the currents of thought that propagate from generation to generation, immanentism appears as the continuation of the impulse of spiritualization that characterizes the history of the notion of divinity. The same progress is accomplished from the transcendental God endowed with supernatural causality to the purely spiritual God of immanent experience, as from the semi-material God of primitive religions to the metaphysical God. Now – and this is the essential point – to this progress in the realm of intelligence corresponds a moral and social progress, that is, ultimately an emancipation of inner life.[81]

Neither Piaget's quite impassioned statements about, for example, Jesus' intellectual and social revolution, nor his arguments about the soul or the divinity found, at least explicitly, any room in *The Moral Judgment of the Child*. The aim of that book was to demonstrate, in terms as objective as possible, the direction in which moral judgment developed, and to reconcile sociology and psychology by presenting development as socialization *and* as an immanent process. As far as the former project was concerned, *The Moral Judgment* described children's development as the progress from heteronomous morality, characterized by obedience to norms seen as eternal and unquestionable, to autonomous morality, characterized by cooperation, reciprocity, and the creation of rules in a system of social contract. The advancement of morality thus paralleled the historical progress from transcendence to immanence in religion. In psychogenesis, morality paralleled the growth from egocentrism and attachment to concrete appearances to the capacity to consider diverse points of view and think abstractly.

Examined *in toto* at the time of *The Moral Judgment,* Piaget's oeuvre manifests a view of mental and historical development that is the same in different domains, including moral judgment, conceptions of physical causality, use of language, reasoning, epistemology, and the history of science. Development in all these realms is a movement from egocentrism, concreteness, heteronomy, authority, and transcendence, to objectivity, abstractness, autonomy, contractual reciprocity, and immanence. This movement is progress: from the child and the primitive to the adult and the modern; from undemocratic to democratic regimes; from dogmatic religions to liberal Protestantism. Piaget's developmental research thus resulted in a scientific axiology that reformulated and realized his youthful project of basing morality on science; it granted scientific and philosophical superiority to menaced liberal Protestant values; and it gave an objective foundation and justification to apparently subjective experiences and beliefs.

IMMANENT LIBERALISM

Demonstrating the deep rootedness of Piaget's thought in religion involves questioning the conflict model that he applied to the description of his own life. This means giving up such nondescript conceptions of "Science" and "Religion" as Piaget employs in his autobiography, and studying their specific forms and relations in particular circumstances. Doing so, however, cannot fail to highlight the function of such a model in Piaget's insertion in the liberal Protestant tradition.

In the process of becoming an exemplary Christian young man, Piaget was largely inspired by an image of youth that postulated the conflict between faith and science as a "must" of young people's inner experience. In the liberal Protestant cognitive framework, such a conflict was in fact the denominator common to the model of youth and the model of the intellectual. Flournoy, for example, admired Galileo, and talked with indignant passion about the astronomer's struggle against the dogmatic Roman authority.[82] For Flournoy's generation, science was objective, and its truth was accessible to everyone who used its methods; religion, in contrast, was subjective, and its truth was rooted in individual experience. For them, the sharp separation between faith and science was not, as for Piaget, a temporary attitude.

Piaget broke with the liberal Protestant tradition. He rejected its pragmatist support, and tried to make religion and science fit each other otherwise than through a dualism so strict that it seemed to harbor conflict. He did so, however, while elaborating an argument against the neo-dogmatic transcendentalist revival aimed directly at liberalism. His scientific axiology was, in part, intended to show that immanentism was the highest and most objective religious attitude, and to justify the identification of God with the universal and impersonal norms of Reason.

Piaget's radical religious immanentism possessed counterparts in other domains; psychology and philosophy have already been examined. But religious attitudes and theological discussions were also closely linked with politics. The founder of the Rousseau Institute, Edouard Claparède (1873–1940), drew close analogies between liberalism, pragmatism, Protestantism, and the scientific method. For him, these analogies did not preclude the total independence of science from extrascientific considerations, and he proposed ways, such as "teleological pedagogy," to bridge the realms of values and science.[83]

Piaget, however, could do without such bridges, even if he did not explicitly overstep the limit between "is" and "ought." If moral progress is immanent, then nationalism and the arms race, for example, are less economic or societal than psychological. They manifest, as Piaget claimed in the early 1930s, a lack of universality of human reason, and they illustrate the fact that, from the international point of view, man is still a primitive or a child.[84] In the perspective of *The Moral Judgment of the Child,* the world could be saved provided that adults placed no obstacles in the way of children's development. As Piaget's thought moved toward immanentism, political discourse waned, and pedagogy lost its significance. Jean Piaget's psychological axiology gave an allegedly objective foundation not to a religious attitude alone, but to a whole complex of "liberal" moral and political positions and expectations, which it thus rendered impervious to the all too numerous refutations of history.

NOTES

1 Piaget, "La psychologie et les valeurs religieuses," in *Sainte-Croix 1922* (Lausanne: La Concorde, 1923), 43. Sainte-Croix is a Swiss town in the Jura mountains where the annual meeting of the Swiss Christian Students Association used to take place. This Association will be designated below as "ACSE," i.e., Association chrétienne suisse d'étudiants.

2 *Le jugement moral chez l'enfant* (Paris: Alcan, 1932); later editions in Presses Universitaires de France. *The Moral Judgment of the Child,* trans. M. Gabain (London: Kegan Paul, Trench, Trubner, 1932); variously reprinted.

3 Piaget, Letter to R. Rolland, 4 August 1917; printed in *Action étudiante* (Geneva), no. 69, 1966, 7.

4 See in particular K. Barth, *Protestant Theology in the Nineteenth Century. Its Background and History* (Valley Forge: Judson Press, 1973); and C. Welch, *Protestant Thought in the Nineteenth Century* (New Haven: Yale University Press, 1972).

5 Flournoy, *Les principes de la psychologie religieuse* (Geneva: Kundig, 1903).

6 Flournoy, *La philosophie de William James* (Saint-Blaise: Foyer Solidariste, 1911), ch. 4. Based on a talk given at the 1910 annual ACSE meeting.

7 A. Sabatier, *Esquisse d'une philosophie de la religion d'après la psychologie et l'histoire* (Paris: Fischbacher, 1897). For Flournoy's terms, see *Principes* (note 5), 5, n. 2.

8 A. Schweitzer, *The Quest of the Historical Jesus* [1906], trans. W. Montgomery (New York: Macmillan, 1968), 398.

9 H. R. Niebuhr, *The Kingdom of God in America* [1937] (New York: Harper, s.d.), 193; quoted in B. M. G. Reardon, *Liberal Protestantism* (London: Adams and Charles Black, 1968), 63.

10 See R. Mehl, *Traité de sociologie du protestantisme* (Neuchâtel: Delachaux et Niestlé, 1965).

11 See *Journal religieux des Eglises Indépendantes de la Suisse romande,* 5 June 1915, 91.

12 See the overview in A. Berchtold, *La Suisse romande au cap du XXe siècle. Portrait littéraire et moral* (Lausanne: Payot, 1963), 122–125.

13 *Aux étudiants des universités suisses,* published by the ACSE (Lausanne: La Concorde, 1920), 5.

14 Ibid., 8.

15 Ibid., 9.

16 M. Neeser, *La théologie des Eglises et de l'Evangile à la lumière des évenements actuels* (Lausanne: La Concorde, 1917), 58.

17 See W. Monod, *Comment on devient chrétien social ou même socialiste chrétien* (Lausanne: La Concorde, 1914); presented at the 1913 annual ACSE meeting. For an overview of the Christian social movement in French-speaking Switzerland, see Berchtold, *La Suisse romande* (note 12), 132–139. For documents, see in particular *Le Christianisme social,* a French monthly whose contributors were often active in the Christian youth movement. For a general overview, see E. G. Léonard, *Histoire générale du protestantisme,* vol. 3 (Paris: P.U.F., 1964), 415–422.

18 *Aux étudiants* (note 13), 11.

19 For critical studies of the image of youth at the time, see P. Bénéton, "La génération de 1912–1914. Image, mythe et réalité," *Revue française de science politique* 21 (1971):981–1009, and R. Wohl, *The Generation of 1914* (Cambridge, MA: Harvard University Press, 1979).

20 See S. de Dietrich, *Cinquante ans d'histoire. La Fédération Universelle des Associations Chrétiennes d'Etudiants (1895–1945)* (Paris: Editions du Semeur, s.d.). As pointed out in a useful overview, the ACSE was a mirror of Protestantism; see A. Reymond, "La pensée philosophique en Suisse romande de 1900 à nos jours," *Revue de théologie et de philosophie* 19 (1931):364–377.

21 Piaget, "Autobiography," in E. G. Boring, et al. (eds.), *A History of Psychology in Autobiography,* vol. 4 (Worcester, MA: Clark University Press, 1952), 237.

22 For a particularly relevant discussion of the conflict model, see M. Rudwick, "Senses of the Natural World and Senses of God: Another Look at the Historical Relation of Science and Religion," in A. R. Peacocke (ed.), *The Sciences and Theology in the Twentieth Century* (Notre Dame, IN: University of Notre Dame Press, 1981). On disciplinary history, see M. G. Ash, "The Self-Presentation of a

Discipline: History of Psychology in the United States Between Pedagogy and Scholarship" and U. Geuter, "The Uses of History for the Shaping of a Field: Observations on German Psychology," in L. Graham, W. Lepenies, and P. Weingart (eds.), *Functions and Uses of Disciplinary Histories* (Dordrecht/Boston: D. Reidel, 1983). For a critical reading of Piaget's autobiography, see F. Vidal and J. Vonèche, "The Role of Autobiography in the Social Sciences. The Case of Jean Piaget," in S. Bem, H. Rappard and W. van Hoorn (eds.), *Studies in the History of Psychology and the Social Sciences,* vol. 1 (Leiden: Psychologisch Instituut van de Rijksuniversiteit Leiden, 1983).

23 See, for example, the editorial "Aux catéchumènes et à leurs parents," *Journal religieux des Eglises Indépendantes de la Suisse romande,* 20 November 1915. The literature for catechumens can be reconstituted from publicity printed in this and other religious journals and magazines.

24 On this last question, see F. Vidal, "Piaget et la psychanalyse: premières rencontres," *Le Bloc-notes de la psychanalyse* 6 (1986): 171–189.

25 Piaget, "Autobiography" (note 21), 240.

26 S. Cornut, "Mors et Vita," in *Essais et confessions* (Lausanne: Payot, 1910), 151. On Cornut, see Berchtold, *La Suisse romande* (note 12), 431–435.

27 W. Cuendet, "Tendances actuelles," in *Sainte-Croix 1916* (Lausanne: La Concorde, 1916); and H. Dartigue, "De l'état d'esprit de la jeunesse intellectuelle avant la guerre," *Revue chrétienne* 63 (1916):278–293, 464–474, 470–588, part I.

28 F. Vidal, "*La vanité de la nomenclature.* Un manuscrit inédit de Jean Piaget," *History and Philosophy of the Life Sciences* 6 (1984):75–106.

29 F. Vidal, M. Buscaglia and J. Vonèche, "Darwinism and Developmental Psychology," *Journal of the History of the Behavioral Sciences* 19 (1983):81–94; and F. Vidal, "*La notion de l'espèce suivant l'école mendelienne.* A 1913 Manuscript by Jean Piaget," ibid. 23 (1987), forthcoming.

30 Piaget, *Recherche* (Lausanne: La Concorde, 1918), 36. See the chapter by chapter summary in H. Gruber and J. Voneche, *The Essential Piaget* (New York: Basic Books, 1977).

31 Piaget, "Bergson et Sabatier," *Revue chrétienne* 61 (1914): 192–200, here: 192–193.

32 *Nouvelles de l'ACSE* 5:8 (June 1915), 234–235.

33 Piaget to the Club des Amis de la Nature, 25 September 1915. Archives of the Club des Amis de la Nature, Neuchâtel. Cf. Piaget, "Les Journées d'Evilard," *Nouvelles de l'ASCE* 5:7 (May 1915):198–200. None of Piaget's ACSE publications has been recorded previously.

34 *Nouvelles de l'ACSE* 6:1 (November 1915), 30. Piaget, *La Mission de l'Idée,* special issue of *Nouvelles de l'ACSE* 6:2–3 (December 1915). Quotations in this chapter refer to the only previously known edition (Lausanne: La Concorde; cover dated 1916, title page dated 1915). See the abbreviated translation in *The Essential Piaget,* (note 30).

35 The reviews found so far are: O. de Dardel, in *La Suisse libérale,* 9 February 1916; G. N[icod], in *Jeunesse* [magazine of the French-speaking Switzerland Young Men's Christian Association] 63:2 (February 1916), 36 (together with a passage from *Mission* reprinted on p. 23 under the title of "Vision"); P. P[ettavel], in *L'Essor social, moral, religieux,* 29 January 1916, 3.

36 Piaget, *Mission* (note 34), 63.

37 Piaget to A. Reymond, undated, but certainly written between 1 November and 15 December 1918. A. Reymond papers, Manuscript department, Bibliothèque cantonale et universitaire (Lausanne/Dorigny).

38 Piaget, review of *Le Christ* by P. Jeannet, *Nouvelles de l'ACSE* 7:4 (May 1917), 123–124.

39 Piaget to R. Rolland (note 3).

40 See note 29.

41 Cf. Piaget's "Avant-propos" to his 1918 dissertation, *Introduction à la malacologie valaisanne* (Sion: F. Aymon, 1921).

42 Reymond, *Vérité scientifique et vérité religieuse* (Lausanne: La Concorde, 1913). Cf. the more accomplished expression of Reymond's thinking, *Philosophie spiritualiste* (Lausanne: Rouge; Paris: Vrin, 1942).

43 Piaget, "L'orientation de la philosophie religieuse en Suisse romande," *La Semaine littéraire,* 1921, 409–412, 412.

44 Reymond, *Le Protestantisme et ses caractères objectifs* (Lausanne: La Concorde, 1918).

45 Reymond, *La philosophie de M. Bergson et le problème de la raison* (Lausanne: La Concorde, 1913).

46 Piaget, "Lettre" [from a collective homage to Reymond], *Revue de théologie et de philosophie* 9, 3e série (1959):44–47.

47 See note 28.

48 Piaget, *Recherche* (note 30), 161.

49 Piaget, "Autobiography" (note 21), 243.

50 I deal with some aspects of the confessional nature of *Recherche* in "Piaget et la psychanalyse" (note 24). It must be pointed out that the relations among the author, the narrator, and the hero of a text cannot be established by simple extrapolation; this caveat applies to the identification of Piaget and Sebastian.

51 Piaget, *Recherche,* 173.

52 Piaget, "La biologie et la guerre," *Feuille centrale de la Société suisse de Zofingue* 58 (1918):374–380, quoted from the English translation in *The Essential Piaget* (note 30), 41.

53 Piaget, *Recherche,* 182.

54 For Piaget's stay in Zurich, see F. Vidal, "Jean Piaget and Psychoanalysis. A Historical and Biographical Note (up to the 1930s)," in S. Bem, et al. (note 22), vol. IV, 1987.

55 A. Reymond, "A propos d'une 'recherche'," *La Semaine littéraire,* 1918, 550–551; and S. Gagnebin, "Recherche," *Revue de théologie et de philosophie,* nouvelle série, n° 7 (1919):131–135.

56 Piaget, "Autobiography" (note 21), 244–245. Piaget wrote that he had been recommended by Bovet in "L'intelligence selon Alfred Binet," *Bulletin de la Société A. Binet et T. Simon* 75 (1975):106–119, here: 107.

57 Piaget, "Autobiography," 246.

58 P. Bovet, *Le sentiment religieux et la psychologie de l'enfant* (Neuchâtel: Delachaux et Niestlé, 1925).

59 Piaget, "L'orientation de la philosophie religieuse" (note 43), 410.

60 Ibid., 412, 410.

61 Ibid., 412.

62 Ibid., 410.

63 See, for example, L. Brunschvicg, *La vie de l'esprit* (Paris: Alcan, 1900). In later works, such as *De la connaissance de soi* (1931) and *Les âges de l'intelligence* (1934), he used, in turn, the results of the research he had inspired. For Piaget's philosophically oriented elaboration of his ideas about the complementarity of genetic psychology and historico-critical epistemology, see his "Etude critique, *L'expérience humaine et la causalité physique* de L. Brunschvicg," *Journal de Psychologie normale et pathologique* 21 (1924):586–607. For his ideas on the parallelism between children's mental growth and the history of science, see "Psychologie et critique de la connaissance," *Archives de Psychologie* 19 (1925):193–210.

64 F. Abauzit, *Du premier Sainte-Croix au dernier Sainte-Croix* (Lausanne: La Concorde, 1922), 9; ACSE meeting report, signed "P.F.," in *Sainte-Croix 1922* (note 1), 12.

65 Piaget, "La psychologie et les valeurs religieuses" (note 1), 49.

66 Ibid.

67 Ibid., 56.

68 Ibid., 69.

69 Ibid., 77–78, 80.

70 Anonymous report of the 1922 ACSE meeting, *Les Cahiers de Jeunesse,* 7:3 (April–May 1923), 185–186. The *Cahiers* were published as a complement to *Jeunesse* (note 35), with the goal of "orienting and stimulating the religious and moral enterprise that is being carried out in youth."

71 See Piaget, "Les traits principaux de la logique de l'enfant," *Journal de Psychologie normale et pathologique* 21(1924):48–101, 89; and "Deux ouvrages récents de psychologie religieuse," *Revue de théologie et de philosophie* 13 (1925):142–147, here:146.

72 *The Language and Thought of the Child* (1923); *Judgment and Reasoning in the Child* (1924); *The Child's Conception of the World* (1926); *The Child's Conception of Physical Causality* (1927).

73 See especially Piaget's 1927 lecture to the Cambridge Education Society, "La causalité chez l'enfant," *British Journal of Psychology* 18 (1928):276–301. For a related discussion on the development of the idea of law, see Piaget in Proceedings of the Société romande de philosophie, *Revue de théologie et de philosophie* 12 (1924):242–243.

74 Piaget, "Le réalisme nominal chez l'enfant, *Revue philosophique de la France et de l'Etranger* 99 (1925):189–234, here: 234. For the complex history of the "grasp of consciousness" idea, see W. R. Woodward, "Young Piaget Revisited: From the Grasp of Consciousness to Décalage," *Genetic Psychology Monographs* 99 (1979):131–161.

75 Piaget, "Logique génétique et sociologie," ibid. 105 (1928):167–205, here 203.

76 See the annual report of the Société romande de philosophie, *Revue de théologie et de philosophie* 15 (1927):315.

77 Piaget, "L'évolution sociale et la pédagogie nouvelle," in T. R. Rawson (ed.), *Sixth World Conference of the New Education Fellowship* [*Ligue internationale pour l'éducation nouvelle*]: *Full Report* (London: N.E.F., s.d.[1932]), 483.

78 Piaget, "Immanence et Transcendance," in Piaget and J. de la Harpe, *Deux types d'attitudes religieuses: Immanence et Transcendance,* publ. by the ACSE (s.l., 1928), 29.

79 Ibid., 36.

80 Ibid., 37.

81 Piaget, *Immanentisme et foi religieuse,* publ. by the Groupe romand des Anciens membres de l'ACSE (Geneva, 1930), 54. For the debate that preceded this publication, see: J.-D. Burger, "Pour la transcendance," *Revue de théologie et de philosophie* 17 (1929):33–40; Piaget's reply: "Pour l'immanence," ibid., 146–152; A. Reymond, "Transcendance et Immanence," *Cahiers Protestants* 13 (1929):161–170; Piaget's reply: "Encore 'immanence et transcendance'," ibid., 325–330 (followed by a short response from Reymond, 331–333).

82 See E. Claparède, *Théodore Flournoy. Sa vie et son oeuvre* (Geneva: Kundig, 1921), 75.

83 See, e.g., Claparède's "Autobiography," in Carl Murchison (ed.), *A History of Psychology in Autobiography,* vol. 1 (Worcester, MA: Clark University Press, 1930), 82; and his *Psychologie de l'Enfant et Pédagogie expérimentale* (Geneva: Kundig, 1920 [8th ed.]), esp. ch. 2.

84 See in particular Piaget's lecture given under the auspices of the Home and School Council in London, "Moral Realities in Child Life," *The New Era in Home and School* 11 (1930):112–114; and "Introduction psychologique à l'éducation internationale," in *Quatrième cours pour le personnel enseignant. Comment faire connaître la Société des Nations et développer l'esprit de coopération internationale* (Geneva: I.B.E., 1931).

PROFESSIONALIZATION, RATIONALITY, AND POLITICAL LINKAGES IN TWENTIETH-CENTURY PSYCHOLOGY*

WILLIAM R. WOODWARD

Reflecting on the chapters that make up this book, we discover that psychology as it was is more fascinating than psychology as it has been reconstructed. Psychology as found in standard "discipline histories" not only has had no place for China or colonial India, but its house historians have consistently neglected to place psychology in relation to contemporary sociopolitical events.[1] They have also tended not to ask the important questions of why psychologists do research at all, and, once they do, of why this research became institutionalized as it has.

The reasons for this mythical situation, in which the proponents of a discipline in its various branches have indulged in self-legitimation through their history writing, need not detain us here.[2] Rather, the purpose of this conclusion will be to relate the individual chapters to some framework issues in the sociology of knowledge and the study of science in culture. Although the chapters largely deal with psychological thought and practice as it became institutionalized and professionalized, many of them also raise rather poignant questions about the readiness of psychologists to accommodate to political circumstance for professional gain.

Since we deal with psychology in its academic and practical settings, rather more than with psychology in popular culture, we have the opportunity to answer the question raised in a previous volume: Did psychology become a profession in the twentieth century?[3] Certainly it did, but at what price? Now the issue is what kind of a profession, and in the

* This project was supported in part by National Science Foundation Grant SES-8319542, National Endowment for the Humanities Grant RH-20620-85, and by the Alexander von Humboldt-Stiftung. I am grateful for a leave of absence from the University of New Hampshire and to Professors Carl-Friedrich Graumann and Heinrich Schipperges at the University of Heidelberg and Professor Karl-Friedrich Wessel at the Humboldt University of Berlin for sponsoring me abroad.

service of what ulterior goals? Fortunately, we have enough material for a preliminary comparative treatment of psychology in various cultural contexts.

PROFESSIONALIZATION AND ITS LIMITS

Social scientists often invoke the following "natural history model" of professionalization, widely shared by historians: (1) a discipline becomes a full-time occupation or "calling" which is (2) "institutionalized" into academic departments, professional journals, and meetings. (3) Such a profession regulates itself through standardized education and training, (4) legitimized by a service orientation toward teaching and (5) protected from the pressure of clients in order to practice "pure research." Do such attributes apply to the actual behavior, as well as to the institutionalizing ideals of psychologists?[4]

Recent secondary literature in the history of psychology has taught us to periodize as historians frequently do, by wars. The years up to World War I, for instance, make up the first generation of professional psychologists, and those up to World War II the second. The chapter by Laurel Furumoto takes previous male historians to task for neglecting the salient fact that the war experience created new contacts, albeit for men, not for women. The occupation of "doing research" and "teaching" took on professional status for some at the expense of others. This is a sobering lesson learned from history, not without relevance to the present.

Furumoto analyzes professions in terms of a model of "professional purity," whereby women occupied the lower echelons in the helping professions and applied psychology, while men filled positions in the higher status branches of academic and industrial psychology. An alternative analytic approach, supplementing Furumoto's status hierarchy model with gender as the operator, is the market model of Magali Safarti Larsen.[5] Kurt Danziger writes that Larsen's account of professional expansion to meet market needs is compatible with his story of an educational psychology pioneering in the use of group statistics, enabling a "new breed of professional educational administrators" to make educational evaluation more "efficient." However, Danziger is well aware that this model cannot be adopted wholesale for the monopolization of psychological knowledge, for he notes that "cognitive schemas and technical practices can be treated as a resource, whereas in the present analysis it is precisely these 'resources' that are regarded as problematic."[6]

This caution alerts us to an uncareful overreliance on professionalization models when the historical data have to do not with occupations but with cognitive contents. Naturally, the cognitive and the social can interact and do. An example is exposed by Ulfried Geuter – the war-related market need for psychologists, the recruitment and selection of officers for the *Wehrmacht,* which began as early as 1927 and expanded after 1935, employing about 450 psychologists by 1942.[7] Here cognitive and social interests are manifest in the tests used to measure character, including expression analysis and psychotechnical measurement of reaction times. Such tests were compatible with a static "characterological" personality model, which persisted in West Germany up to the methodological debates of the late 1950s. By then, as Alexandre Mètraux has shown elsewhere, the so-called Americanization of German psychology brought operational methods such as factor analysis, which changed the nature of personality measurement, not without resistance from those advocating "insight" methods.[8]

Another aspect of professionalization is certification. Nathan Reingold has pointed to a shift from the nineteenth to the twentieth centuries, in which accomplishment gave way to certification "for providing a way of securing a large number of proper practitioners."[9] Later, he maintained, disciplinary groups came to prevail over national and local ones. However, women with the certification of a doctoral degree nevertheless found gender and marriage blocking their entry into academic positions, as Margaret Rossiter has now documented at least up to 1940 in the United States.[10] Presumably, such obstacles continue to exist there and in other countries, though the impact of affirmative action legislation on the professions in the past decade in the United States awaits further research. In Germany in 1941, as Geuter notes, a decree was enacted giving psychology a diploma examination and hence professional status. This appeared at first to be a Pyrrhic victory, thanks in part to the successful opposition of psychiatrists to including examinations about medical subjects in 1942. But psychologists quickly sought and found new fields for their newly certified expertise. One wonders how the certification of the various professional degrees in psychology in the twentieth century affected research and practice in other places.

Sociologists of knowledge have challenged the "natural history" model of professionalization as an ideal. Henrika Kuklick suggests that we need to look beyond researchers' self-serving claims for autonomy.[11] In fact, as seen above, the model must be corrected for sex bias and for contests with the needs of other professions, such as school administration and psychiatry. The last section of this conclusion will show that ideologies of academic, religious, and political sorts have played a directive role in the choice of substantive areas of research and application. Institutional reform and certification requirements also performed changing gatekeeping functions, depending on market needs. In short, a straight "natural history" model of linear development is inadequate to describe the actual growth of the psychological professions.

Professional development also depends directly on patronage – both financial and political – from city and state governments, as well as from foundations and wealthy individuals. During the interwar period, the patrons of educational enterprises treated in this volume were evidently local school boards in the case of Danziger's American educators and the provincial governments in Matthias Petzold's report on republican China. One would like to know more about Chinese and Soviet patronage, for example, which governmental factions supported Kornilov's Soviet Central Institute of Psychology or the Academy of Communist Education in Moscow and the Kharkov institute in the Ukraine where Vygotskii's protégés went in 1930.[12] At the Vienna Psychological Institute between 1922 and 1942, the attempted professionalization of pedagogy and of psychological research dovetailed nicely; each provided status for the other and appealed to a different clientele.[13] A laboratory research program aiming at social control through school reform and welfare measures appealed to the city's liberal social democratic government; but market research attracted the Rockefeller Foundation. This shows that professional ideologies, as Clifford Geertz and Thomas Gieryn have emphasized, need not be compatible. They can provide integration from various role "strains" such as child-centered instruction and evaluation, and they can supply levers to promote social "interests" such as those of institute-building psychologists.[14]

Moreover, various strategies of professional compromise have occurred. In Vienna during Austro-Fascist rule from 1934 to 1938, Karl and Charlotte Bühler created a new department for family research and formed a patrons' group in an effort toward political accommodation. Despite the German takeover, a truly Nazified psychology never appeared in Vienna. In Germany, by contrast, psychologists profited from the need for selection of personnel and won major professional gains by 1942. There, too, strategies varied from professional exploitation to the principled resistance of Wolfgang Köhler.[15] In the People's Republic of China after World War II, psychologists under Soviet influence brought Russian translations and accepted experts, kept to the confines of orthodox Pavlovianism and avoided social problems. But psychologists lost their jobs by 1966, allegedly due to the abstraction of their subject from the social context.

Thus, professional psychologists typically sought to legitimate their discipline in traditional ways by pointing to its social utility and rigorous methodology. However, departures from the "natural history" professionalization model included (1) the shifting demarcation of disciplinary boundaries to meet academic-political and national-political exigencies, (2) the disappearance of utilitarian justification in the pursuit of "pure research" after institutionalization had been achieved, and (3) the reappearance of utilitarian arguments whenever funding was needed. When threatened by Austrian and then German Fascism, for example, psychologists returned to traditional intellectual preserves such as pedagogy, physiological psychology, and characterology. After the demise of the radical Maoist Cultural Revolution in 1976, psychologists could and did take up utilitarian social problems such as delinquency, education, health services, birth control, and labor efficiency.

The natural history model thus does not apply across the board. The market model, the professional purity model, and the status hierarchy ("occupational gender") model all apply partially to some of our cases. However, Talcott Parsons' strain theory might better describe shifting political alliances for purposes of funding, since it posits disequilibria between research programs and public funders' values.[16] Finally, interest models in the Marxist tradition apply insofar as women, American school administrators, German selection personnel, and Austrian social researchers espoused certain political or economic interests, including that of disinterested research.[17] Professionalization models, in short, must be employed with caution, and only careful historical scholarship can trace out the changing context over time.[18] But if academic boundaries are fluid, so are the boundaries between successful and unsuccessful science, a theme to which we now turn.

APPLYING MODELS OF RATIONALITY TO PSYCHOLOGICAL THOUGHT

Here we wish to relate aspects of our chapters with a theoretical or a methodological content to current discussions about the nature of scientific progress. Case studies of working scientists and their "irrational" commitments to paradigms pose problems for traditional theories of scientific "rationality" espoused by Carl Hempel, Karl Popper, and Imre Lakatos.[19] Philosophers of science, troubled by Kuhn's assertion in 1962 that revolutionary shifts in world view intervene between periods of normal science, realized that such shifts represent a different kind of progress from the cumulative testing of theory by experiment.[20] Imre Lakatos softened this dichotomy by suggesting that "research programs" of testable theory and experiment change incrementally during periods of normal science, despite the revolutionary shifts in world view. Larry Laudan erased the dichotomy, taking the instrumentalist position that science simply consists of reducing unsolved problems to solved ones. Instead of confirmation or falsification, rationality entails only "problem solving effectiveness."[21] Here we want to stretch the definition of psychology as profession building in the direction of problem solving, or in post-1962 terms, to shifts in the metaphysical foundations and working methods of psychological science.

Many have questioned the applicability of any theory of progress in natural science to psychology. This is an important issue, yet we will follow the lead of those who find the discussion useful for psychology and the life sciences, quite apart from such demarcation debates.[22] Our concern is with the usefulness of such reconstructions for the historical understanding of psychological thought and research, including the psychological experiment, statistical methods, and theories. We formulate this organization sharply to facilitate discussion and raise possibilities for further research.

Viewing our chapters in the light of recent secondary literature, we encounter at least four identifiable research programs in psychology. We may call them the experimental, the cognitive, the correlational, and the probabilistic traditions. The experimental program, recently christened the Leipzig model, initially involved human subjects of high status who took turns acting as stimulus administrator and as subject.[23] At Cornell University in the United States, E. B. Titchener replaced the Leipzig behavioral measurement of these subjects' responses, followed by a loose introspective report, with a research program of "experimentally based introspection," in which subjects reported sensations under precisely controlled conditions.[14] Moreover, Titchener gave systematic direction to this research, assigning topics to test particular theories of sensation, perception, and thinking. Ryan Tweney's suggestion that this was programmatic research might be usefully compared with Timothy Lenoir's application of Lakatos' model of progress to Kantian biology.[25]

Epistemologically speaking, the acceptance of sensations as the datum of psychology was actually a step toward the acceptance of operationally defined behavior as datum. Study of stimulus and response in human perception gradually turned to stimulus and response in animal subjects. Some researchers justified their method of isolation and control by a physicalist and determinist world view. Thus, Titchener's student, Harvard's Department Chairman E. G. Boring, published on "the physical dimensions of consciousness" in 1932. B. F. Skinner and S. S. Stevens, who both submitted dissertations to Boring in the 1930s, formulated versions of operationalism and behaviorism that justified using quantitative methods to measure human and animal response.[26] Another behavioristic tradition made use of statistical inference. Further research is needed on other behaviorists who adopted R. A. Fisher's analysis of variance methods to generalize the isolation and control to two or a few more variables.[25] Here, as Gerd Gigerenzer argues, a deterministic image of human beings was supported by the use of statistics based on indeterministic assumptions.[27]

An analogous situation occurred in the Soviet Union vis à vis the reigning behaviorist theory of Ivan Pavlov in the 1920s. L. S. Vygotskii's "historical-cultural" approach, muffled as it was from the 1920s to the 1960s, was interpreted as a contribution to the cognitive revolution when it became known in the 1960s. As David Joravsky shows, however, even in Vygotskii's time we can identify conceptual and empirical shifts in

Soviet psychology. In 1924, Vygotskii explicitly criticized physiologists Pavlov and Bekhterev and implicitly the party leaders who took them as gospel of a reductionist psychology. Using Marx's contrast of the bee with a human architect, Vygotskii established on Marxist grounds that intentionality is the distinguishing feature of human consciousness over animal social instinct. His use of a busy house metaphor, based on Sherrington's neurophysiology and Sechenov's model of the "interruption of reflexive activity," artfully brought even physiology to bear against Pavlov's "reflexive psychology" with its telephone switchboard simile.[28]

In the case of reflexology and Russian cognitive psychology, we are presented on the face of it with a revolutionary shift from one research tradition to another. Vygotskii attempted to replace the physiological monism of Pavlovian psychology with an antinomy. Cognition can be treated as expressive signs of physiological movements, hence in functional terms of stimulus and response, and as the understanding of meanings in a cultural world. To grasp this, as Alex Kozulin shows, it is essential to understand Vygotskii's theory of activity. Activity is broadly conceived to include lower and higher mental functions; the key is the Hegelian insight that the physiological is superseded *(aufgehoben)* by the cultural.[29] Did the later "historical-cultural" research program of Vygotskii, Luria, and Leont'ev resolve the anomalies of the tradition of Pavlov and Bechterev? The answer requires us to appreciate the two sources of Vygotskii's work, the European intellectual tradition of Wundt, Janet, and Gestalt theory, which maintained the irreducibility of consciousness to stimulus and response, and Marxist philosophy as a social theory of human activity. Seen in this light, Vygotskii's critical alternative to Pavlovian reductionism and dogmatic Marxist approaches was both continuous and commensurable with the two earlier traditions.

The perceptual theory of Egon Brunswik experienced a fate comparable to that of Vygotskii's ideas, because its European functionalism conflicted not only with Vienna school positivism of the 1920s, but also with American behaviorism. As David Leary deftly shows, Brunswik first had to reconcile the logical positivists' assumption of a one-to-one reference of sense data to their objects with Bühler's basic claim that the subject-object relation is "fundamentally ambiguous."[30] In the late 1920s Brunswik resolved this conflict by adopting the notion that knowledge is probabilistic from Hans Reichenbach and Richard von Mises. In a splendid example of theory and method maturing at different rates, Leary goes on to argue that only in 1939, after using American animal research and statistics, did Brunswik succeed in joining a probabilistic theory with probabilistic methods.

Further research will have to weigh the argument of Gigerenzer and Murray that probabilistic functionalism was not received with sympathy because of the dominance of the experimental and correlational schemas in American psychology. These authors assert that Thurstone's probabilistic ideas in 1927 began without a psychological interpretation when he assumed a normal distribution (instead of a different probability distribution) for stimulus and response. Brunswik dropped the artificial environment of isolated stimulus and response, with its use of statistics as a tool, and replaced it with statistics as a theory that tied together representative variables from a natural environment.[31] This posed an alternative to a determinist conception of humans, in that now the perceiver must guess the structure of the world from ambiguous cues by means of correlational hypotheses.

Another revolution of sorts has occurred within behaviorism. Neobehaviorist learning theory, which Ian Lubek and Erika Apfelbaum call the "dominant paradigm" in American academic psychology, grew in three coherent directions from the 1930s to the 1970s, all of them assuming that reinforcement is the mechanism of behavioral change. John Garcia's anomalous finding of conditioned aversion (distaste for ionized sugar or poisoned bait) became an instance of the replacement of one set of problems by another. This psychologist encountered (1) publication in prestigious American Psychological Association journals during 1955 to 1965, (2) rejection by the same journals as he turned his evidence against the establishment view during 1965 to 1975, and (3) increasing citation in the 1980s, despite a continuing low acceptance rate in mainstream publications.[32] Overcoming neglect in textbooks in the 1970s, and an "asymmetric power relation" in dealing with editors, Garcia insisted on one-trial learning in the absence of reinforcement, and the dominant behavioral paradigm eventually had to be revised. Garcia himself turned from gadfly to hero.

These case studies bear directly on the philosophical claim that apparent anomalies can become instances of a theory.[33] Consistent with Laudan's claim that an aim of science is to minimize unsolved problems, these studies show how theories are modified so that new conceptual structures can handle the anomalous findings. Still questions remain. Once Titchener adopted in part the Leipzig model of psychological experimentation, for example, was his change to a positivistic theory linked to the theoretical preferences of others?[34] Or did his methodological shift to isolation and control of introspective response serve to minimize the anomaly that subjects, even high-status trained ones, give different introspections?

After decades of preoccupation with refined models of rationality whose historical fit is questionable, some philosophers of science presumably feel that the field has drifted too far toward the opposite extremes of anarchism or sociobiological accounts. But do not even they still sell scientific progress short? The neo-behaviorism of mainstream learning theory may well have undergone a "progressive problem shift" through the assimilation of Garcia's findings. However, the defense of established research programs must lead to skirmishes such as this one with considerable regularity. We can predict that philosophers of science will want to give increasing attention to the social production of scientific knowledge in the years to come.

What is the net result of analyzing intellectual history further in terms of "rationality"? The limit of the reconstructionist approach, even in its pragmatic or instrumentalist version, is that it does not usually place ideas in their full historical settings.[35] Conversely, historians occasionally forget that a chief goal of studying science is to understand how its thought develops. One point is clear: philosophers and historians of science who wish to do justice to psychological thought in the twentieth century are adopting a looser terminology of problem solving and degrees of success, and they are attending to details of experimental design, statistical methods, and incommensurate theories hitherto ignored.

POLITICAL LINKAGES OF PSYCHOLOGICAL IDEAS AND INSTITUTIONS

Neither professionalization nor rationality may be taken for granted as models of the growth of psychology in the twentieth century. This we have seen as a consequence of the critiques of sociologists and philosophers from whom some historians of science draw their explanatory frameworks. But might it just be that historians will have to return to more classical methods to find the answers they seek on the nature of progress and innovation?

Intellectual history, as Leonard Krieger notes in a classic essay, has been transformed into sociointellectual history.[35] Two of the most important ideas of our psychological century as it has penetrated general culture and society are the unconscious and the biogenesis of moral and intellectual life. Taking these not as objective constructs but as expressions of a sociopolitical milieu around the time of World War I, we can examine the ramifications for the new intellectual history of the findings about psychoanalysis and genetic epistemology presented here.

Louise Hoffman explores the historical context of Freud's Europe and artfully builds on a trend in Freud scholarship to relativize psychoanalytic theory by turning its own framework back on it.[36] The concepts of authority and affiliation, which Hoffman uses to analyze Freud's political views, are social psychological ones that Freud himself shaped through the Oedipal theory of individual psychology. It has been a theme of the Frankfurt School and the entire reception of ego psychology and psychohistory that psychoanalysis can also serve a therapeutic function for society by exposing unconscious ideologies and to making them conscious.[37] Yet we need to appreciate the embeddedness, too, of psychoanalysis in a social-political climate of "conservative patriarchy" rather different from liberal egalitarian notions of family life and society. Nor was this model of mass behavior and its wise leadership by patriarchal figures, with their repression of anarchic impulses, considered suspect, despite its justification of conventional power relationships.

Perhaps the two practitioners in India described by Christiane Hartnack are extreme cases, with their colonialist disdain for the native Hindus and their scientifically justified prejudice of Indian inferiority.[38] It is indeed remarkable how nicely political and scientific ideologies mapped onto one another – for what else was the assumption of the origin of Islam in an individual neurosis. Both the politicalization of science, in this case psychology, and the "deinstitutionalization" of a scientific doctrine are at work here. Perhaps history in this instance could shed some reflected light on contemporary science transfer.[39]

Looking at psychoanalysis in other contexts, such as the Third Reich, we see a surprisingly similar susceptibility to take sides, either for or against the establishment, resulting in a loss of professional consensus. Consequently, as Peter Weingart puts it, science "runs the risk of losing the chief rationale for being granted this autonomy, namely its claim to providing objective knowledge."[40] Instead of being an institution offering knowledge superior to other kinds of knowledge, psychoanalysis lent the force of its institutional organization, its journals and its practice, to the legitimation of repression.

Was it different in the case of Jean Piaget's genetic epistemology, whose sociocultural origins were in liberal Protestantism? As a teenager writing his first articles in 1914, Piaget was already preoccupied with moral evolution and wrestling with his teacher Arnold Reymond's neo-liberal position on the relationship of epistemology and theology. Fernando Vidal writes that Piaget was seeking "a social salvation in a world that is being shattered by war." In 1918 the 22-year-old Piaget advanced a naturalistic ethics based on equilibrium, namely, "we know how to practice the good before learning to know biological equilibria."[41] What does Vidal's historical insight that an immanentist theology precedes sociobiological thinking in Piaget's life and theory imply for those who accept genetic epistemology as a basis for social or educational thought?

In the next phase of his career Piaget continued to refine his religiously rooted logic of development, concluding in particular that children's moral judgments mature from obedience to transcendent rules toward adherence to the norms of an immanent social contract. He attributed this moral development to a psychological logic, whereby the child learns to resolve contradictory tenets with a higher level noncontradiction. Disturbing, however, are the implications of Piaget's indifference to the separation of objective science from subjective religion advocated by his mentors Theodore Flournoy and Eduard Claparède. If immanentism becomes the identification of God with universal norms of reason, what happens to the watchdog function of "free inquiry"? William James's essay "On the Moral Equivalent of War" suggests that liberalism, pragmatism, and Protestantism were also allied outside of Switzerland as a program for social action. Further study is needed to determine whether Piaget's development represented a positivist slide away from political discourse or a pedagogy that encouraged taking action based on values.[42]

A fascinating link appears here to Chinese society, some of whose future educators were studying pragmatism and functionalism in the United States during the 1920s. Evidently, the intellectual context there was receptive, for the traditional Confucian system had long emphasized action over knowing. Yet Matthias Petzold shows that this claim can also account for Chinese acceptance of multiple external ideologies.[43] The introduction of republican ideas and mass education after the fall of the Qing dynasty in 1911 led to the importation of Western psychologies. The Japanese invasion in 1937 ended this, and following World War II, the government oriented toward the Soviet Union. Marxist theory then replaced functionalist psychology as the official platform for educational reform, bringing a recognition that "psychology should dialectically combine social and natural science methods."

However, with the Cultural Revolution in 1966, psychology was banned, reflecting government recognition of the susceptibility of psychology to politicalization. In the late 1970s in Post-Maoist China, psychology teaching and research were resumed in four universities, and professional associations and journals were founded anew. One wonders whether the ingenuous hopes of Western psychologists for international export of psychological thought will facilitate a genuinely Chinese psychology this time.[44] Conversely, Chinese psychologists have no doubt turned to history in part to consider what institutional forms professional Chinese psychology can take in the future.[45]

CONCLUDING REMARKS

Returning finally to the book as a whole, we are grateful to these authors for leading us to new vistas on psychology in the twentieth century. We have seen in historical epoch after historical epoch that psychologists have taken up research in the service of more complex concerns than are explicitly preserved in their written statements. They have sometimes had the courage to persevere against dominant research traditions. They have even sometimes put professional exigency over moral scruple. Psychologists, like other scientists, are creatures of their political and cultural times and places.

This is in some ways a surprising outcome of the historical research gathered here. One might have expected a primarily emancipatory role from the institutionalization of leading psychological schools of thought. Nevertheless, the *history* of psychology is beginning to have precisely this critical function. As the actual confluences of politics and institutionalization, and of ideas and ideologies, are raised to the level of responsible discourse, psychology's practitioners and consumers can make more conscious and informed choices in the future.[46]

NOTES

1 The best recent discipline histories include E. Hearst (ed.), *The First Century of Experimental Psychology* (Hillsdale, NJ: Erlbaum, 1979); A. R. Gilgen, *American Psychology since World War II: Profile of a Discipline* (Westport, CT: Greenwood Press, 1982); S. Koch and D. Leary (eds.), *A Century of Psychology as Science* (New York: McGraw-Hill, 1985); E. R. Hilgard, *Psychology in America. A Historical Survey* (New York and London: Harcourt Brace Jovanovich, 1987).

2 For critical studies and reviews, see J. O'Donnell, *The Origins of Behaviorism: American Psychology, 1870–1920* (New York: New York University Press, 1985); F. Sulloway, *Freud. Biologist of the Mind: Beyond the Psychoanalytic Legend* (New York: Basic Books, London: Burnett Books/ Andrè Deutsch, 1979); M. G. Ash, "The Self-Presentation of a Discipline: History of Psychology in the United States between Pedagogy and Scholarship," in L. Graham, W. Lepenies, and P. Weingart (eds.), *Functions and Uses of Disciplinary Histories* (Dordrecht: Reidel, 1983), 143–190; U. Geuter, "The Uses of History for the Shaping of a Field: Observations on German Psychology," ibid., 191–228.

3 W. R. Woodward and M. G. Ash (eds.), *The Problematic Science: Psychology in Nineteenth-Century Thought* (New York: Praeger, 1982).

4 For similar questions of other disciplines, see R. Kohler, *From Medical Chemistry to Biochemistry* (Cambridge: Cambridge University Press, 1979); R. Stichweh, *Zur Entstehung des modernen Systems wissenschaftlicher Disziplinen. Physik in Deutschland 1740–1890* (Frankfurt and Main: Suhrkamp, 1984).

5 L. Furumoto, "On the Margins: Women and the Professionalization of Psychology in the United States," this volume. Cf. M. S. Larson, *The Rise of Professionalism: A Sociological Analysis* (Berkeley: University of California Press, 1977).

6 K. Danziger, "Social Context and Investigative Practice in Early Twentieth-Century Psychology," this volume, n. 33.

7 U. Geuter, "German Psychology during the Nazi Period," this volume. For background on the institutionalization of psychology in Germany, see Kurt Danziger, "The Social Origins of Modern Psychology," in A. R. Buss (ed.), *Psychology in Social Context* (New York: Irvington, 1979) and M. G. Ash, "The Emergence of Gestalt Theory: Experimental Psychology in Germany 1890–1920," (PhD dissertation Harvard University, 1982), Part 1.

8 A. Métraux, "Die Methodenstreit und die Amerikanisierung der Psychologie in der Bundesrepublik 1950–1970," in M. G. Ash and U. Geuter (eds.), *Geschichte der deutschen Psychologie im 20. Jahrhundert. Ein Überblick* (Opladen: Westdeutscher Verlag, 1985), 225–251.

9 N. Reingold, "Definitions and Speculations: The Professionalization of Science in America in the Nineteenth Century," in A. Oleson and S. C. Brown (eds.),

The Pursuit of Knowledge in the Early American Republic: American Scientific and Learned Societies from Colonial Times to the Civil War (Baltimore and London: Johns Hopkins University Press, 1976), 54.

10 M. Rossiter, *Women Scientists in America: Struggles and Strategies to 1940* (Baltimore: Johns Hopkins Press, 1982).

11 H. Kuklick, "Boundary Maintenance in American Sociology: Limitations to Academic 'Professionalization'," *Journal of the History of the Behavioral Sciences* 16 (1980):209, also 203, 204. Cf. H. Kuklick, "The Sociology of Knowledge: Retrospect and Prospect," *Annual Review of Sociology* 9 (1983):287–310.

12 See chapters in this volume by D. Joravsky and M. Petzold. Cf. E. Timberlake, "Higher Learning, the State, and the Professions in Russia," in Jarausch (ed.), *The Transformation of Higher Learning, 1860–1930,* note 4, 321–344; J. McClelland, "Diversification in Russian-Soviet Education," ibid., 180–195.

13 M. G. Ash, "Psychology and Politics in Interwar Vienna: The Vienna Psychological Institute, 1922–1942," this volume.

14 C. Geertz, *The Interpretation of Cultures* (New York: Basic Books, 1973). T. F. Gieryn, "Boundary Work and the Demarcation of Science from Non-Science: Strains and Interests in Professional Ideologies of Scientists," *American Sociological Review* 48 (1983):781–795.

15 See Ash and Geuter, note 8, above. Cf. C.-F. Graumann (ed.), *Psychologie im Nationalsozialismus* (New York, Heidelberg, Berlin, Tokyo: Springer, 1985).

16 T. Parsons, *Sociological Theories and Modern Societies* (New York: Free Press, 1967).

17 Cf. V. Wrona (ed.), *Zur Geschichte der marxistischleninistischen Philosophie in der DDR. Von 1945 bis Anfang der sechziger Jahre* (Berlin, GDR: Dietz Verlag, 1979); J. Kuczynski, *Studien zu einer Geschichte der Gesellschaftswissenschaften,* 10 vols. (Berlin, GDR: Akademie Verlag, 1975ff.); H. Ley, *Geschichte der Aufklärung und des Atheismus,* vols. 1, 2, 3, 4/1, 4/2 (Berlin, GDR: VEB Deutscher Verlag der Wissenschaften, 1966ff.). The *locus classicus* is K. Marx and F. Engels, "The German Ideology," in *Karl Marx-Friedrich Engels. Collected Works,* vol. 5 (New York: International Publishers, 1976).

18 A delightful study of the professionalizing *mores* of nine university presidents in the nineteenth century is B. J. Bledstein, *The Culture of Professionalism: The Middle Class and the Development of Higher Education in America* (New York and London: Norton, 1976). Cf. D. W. Light, "The Development of Professional Schools in America," in K. H. Jarausch (ed.), *The Transformation of Higher Learning,* (note 4), 345–365. For the German case, see C. E. McClelland, "Professionalization and Higher Education in Germany," ibid., 306–320. For the growth of the academic profession in France, see G. Weisz, *The Emergence of Modern Universities in France, 1863–1914* (Princeton: Princeton University Press, 1983).

19 T. Nickles, *Scientific Discovery: Case Studies* (Dordrecht: Reidel, 1980).

20 T. Nickles, "Can Scientific Constraints Be Violated Rationally?" in *Scientific Discovery, Logic, and Rationality* (Dordrecht, Holland: Reidel, 1980), 285–316. An older, now classical review is F. Suppe, *The Structure of Scientific Theories,* 2nd ed. (Urbana: University of Illinois Press, 1977). On the "antipositivistic turn" of Kuhn, Toulmin, Feyerabend, Hanson, and Wittgenstein against Carnap, Popper, and other exponents of logical positivism, see K. Bayertz, *Wissenschaft als historischer Prozess. Die antipositivistische Wende in der Wissenschaftstheorie* (Munich: Fink Verlag, 1980).

21 Cf. L. Laudan, *Progress and its Problems: Towards a Theory of Scientific Growth* (Berkeley: University of California Press, 1977), defining anomalies, 28, conceptual problems, 66, anomalies solved, 119.

22 See, e.g., B. Gholson and P. Barker, "Kuhn, Lakatos, and Laudan: Applications in the History of Physics and Psychology," *American Psychologist* 40 (1985):755–769.

23 K. Danziger, "The Origins of the Psychological Experiment as a Social Institution," *American Psychologist* 40 (1985):133–140.

24 R. D. Tweney, "Programmatic Research in Experimental Psychology: E. B. Titchener's Laboratory Investigations, 1891–1927," this volume.

25 T. Lenoir, *The Strategy of Life: Teleology and Mechanics in Nineteenth Century German Biology* (Dordrecht and Boston: Reidel, 1982).

26 Cf. L. D. Smith, *Behaviorism and Logical Positivism: A Reassessment of the Alliance* (Stanford: Stanford University Press, 1986). Cf. W. Woodward, "S. S. Stevens," *Dictionary of Scientific Biography. Supplement* (New York: Scribner's, in press).

27 G. Gigerenzer, "Survival of the Fittest Probabilist: Brunswik, Thurstone, and the Two Disciplines of Psychology," in G. Gigerenzer, L. Krüger, and M. Morgan (eds.), *The Probabilistic Revolution. Vol. II. Ideas in the Sciences* (Cambridge, MA: MIT Press, 1987) [22].

28 D. Joravsky, "L. S. Vygotskii: The Muffled Deity of Soviet Psychology," this volume.

29 A. Kozulin, "The Concept of Activity in Soviet Psychology: Vygotsky, His Disciples and Critics," *American Psychologist* 41 (1986):266.

30 D. E. Leary, "From Act Psychology to Probabilistic Functionalism: The Place of Egon Brunswik in the History of Psychology," this volume.

31 G. Gigerenzer and D. J. Murray, *Cognition as Intuitive Statistics* (Hillsdale, NJ: Erlbaum, 1986). Cf. note 27 above.

32 I. Lubek and E. Apfelbaum, "Neo-Behaviorism and the Garcia Effect: A Social Psychology of Science Approach," this volume.

33 L. Laudan, *Science and Values: The Aims of Science and their Role in Scientific Debate* (Berkeley: University of California Press, 1984). Laudan actually drops Kuhn's term anomaly here, since he is replacing Kuhn's discontinuous theory of progress with a "piecemeal" continuous one. Cf. Laudan, *Progress,* note 25, 119.

34 K. Danziger, "The Positivist Repudiation of Wundt," *Journal of the History of the Behavioral Sciences* 15 (1979):205–230.

35 L. Krieger, "The Autonomy of Intellectual History," in G. G. Iggers and H. T. Parker (eds.), *International Handbook of Historical Studies. Contemporary Research and Theory* (Westport, CT: Greenwood Press, and London: Methuen & Co. Ltd, 1979), 109–126.

36 L. Hoffman, "The Ideological Significance of Freud's Social Thought," this volume.

37 J. Habermas, *Knowledge and Human Interests* (1968) (London: Heinemann Educational Books Ltd, 1972).

38 C. Hartnack, "British Psychoanalysts in Colonial India," this volume.

39 D. Sinha, *Psychology in a Third World Country: The Indian Experience* (Beverley Hills, CA: Sage, 1986). Cf. G. Jahoda, "Psychology and the Developing

Countries," *International Social Science Journal* 15 (1975):461–474; D. Sinha, "The Impact of Psychology on Third World Development," *International Journal of Psychology* 19 (1984).

40 P. Weingart, "The Scientific Power Elite – a Chimera: The Deinstitutionalization and Politicization of Science," in N. Elias, H. Martins, and R. Whitley (eds.), *Scientific Establishments and Hierarchies* (Dordrecht and Boston: Reidel, 1982), 84.

41 F. Vidal, "Jean Piaget and the Liberal Protestant Tradition," this volume. Cf. J. David Arnold, "Psychology of Religion: Placing Paradigms in a Historical and Metatheoretical Perspective," *American Psychologist* 40 (1985):1060–1062.

42 J. C. Gibbs and S. V. Schnell, "Moral Development 'versus' Socialization," *American Psychologist* 40 (1985):1071–1080. Cf. C. Gilligan, *In a Different Voice: Psychological Theory and Women's Development* (Cambridge, MA: Harvard University Press, 1982).

43 M. Petzold, "The Social History of Chinese Psychology," this volume.

44 Cf. S. Kennedy and H. P. David, "Psychology and Policy around the World: Widening Psychology's Sphere of Influence," *American Psychologist,* 41 (1986): 296–297. See also D. Wagner (ed.), *Child Development and International Development: Research-Policy Interfaces* (San Francisco: Jossey-Bass, 1983); D. Wagner, "Child Development Research and the Third World," *American Psychologist* 41 (1986):298–301.

45 C. C. Ching, "Psychology and the Four Modernizations in China," *International Journal of Psychology* 19 (1984):57–64.

46 The call for such a critical function is a recurring theme in the first textbook for the philosophical (including ethical) problems of the natural sciences in East Germany: H. Hörz and K.-F. Wessel (eds.), *Philosophie und Naturwissenschaften* (Berlin, GDR: Deutscher Verlag der Wissenschaften, 1986). Ch. 7 on "the development of natural science, humanism and image of man" cites East and West scholars in urging responsible control of genetic engineering: "it behooves scientists representing the humanistic orientation of scientific and technical progress and the entire progressive and democratic public to be alert, to defend against misuse," 266.

NAME INDEX

311

SUBJECT INDEX